South Africa
in Southern Africa

South Africa
in Southern Africa

Reconfiguring the Region

Edited by
DAVID SIMON

James Currey
Oxford

Ohio University Press
Athens

David Philip
Cape Town

James Currey Ltd
73 Botley Road
Oxford
OX2 0BS

Ohio University Press
Scott Quadrangle
Athens, Ohio 45701, USA

David Philip Publishers (Pty) Ltd
PO Box 23408
Claremont 7735
Cape Town, South Africa

First published 1998

1 2 3 4 5 02 01 00 99 98

British Library Cataloguing in Publication Data
South Africa in Southern Africa : reconfiguring the region
  1. Africa, Southern – Economic integration 2. Africa,
  Southern – Economic conditions
  I.Simon, David, 1957–
  330.9'68'065

ISBN 0852554117

ISBN 0–85255–411–7 Paper (James Currey)
ISBN 0–85255–412–5 Cloth (James Currey)

Library of Congress Cataloging-in-Publication Data is available

ISBN 0–8214– 1263-9 Cloth (Ohio University Press)
ISBN 0–8214– 1264-7 Paper (Ohio University Press)

Typeset in 10/11pt Palatino by Saxon Graphics Ltd, Derby
Printed in Great Britain by Villiers Publications, London N3

Dedication

This book is dedicated to the memory of
Malefane Maema,
*Professor of Rural Social Development
at the University of Natal, Pietermaritzburg,
and an intending contributor to this volume.
He died tragically with his wife in a road accident in October 1996,
while travelling between research and family commitments
in their native Lesotho and Pietermaritzburg.
They leave three young daughters.*

Contents

C. POPULATION AND MOBILITY

CONCLUSION

List of Tables

List of Figures

Preface

The stimulus for this volume was my concern that the substantial literature address-ing the dramatic changes and transitions within present-day southern Africa is focused excessively on the dynamics of individual countries or areas, sectors and communities within them. As a result, many important regional dynamics and pro-cesses which transcend national boundaries have been passing unrecorded and/or unappreciated, both in their own right and in broader comparative and conceptual terms. The fruit of our labours should go a considerable way to redressing this imbalance.

The contributions in this volume have been specifically commissioned and arranged in the format presented here in order to gain the benefits of expertise across a range of issues, countries and academic/professional disciplines, thus broadening the scope and coverage beyond what any one author could offer in a monograph. The contributors represent an impressive array of eminent authorities and able younger scholars with growing reputations in their respective areas of spe-cialisation. In order to maximise the coherence and integration of the volume, the authors were given specific guidelines regarding coverage and the need to develop analytical rather than purely descriptive accounts and to draw on existing empirical and conceptual literatures, in addition to the basic instructions on style and length. They have had to cope with my active editorial role, keeping in regular contact with them and, where appropriate, asking difficult questions and seeking sometimes substantial revisions in order to ensure that coherence and format requirements are met. This persistence was generally borne with good humour and grace, although the revision process did extend the editorial process modestly. Without the techno-logical benefits of email and computer disk transfer, the task would have been infinitely slower.

I would like to thank James Currey and Douglas Johnson at James Currey Publishers, who showed immediate enthusiasm for this project and have secured the co-publication agreements which are so important for ensuring the availability of this book at locally affordable prices, especially in southern Africa itself. An anonymous referee made helpful suggestions. In addition, Justin Jacyno drew or redrew several figures to a high standard, while Liz Young typed my own tables. My family saw somewhat less of me than they would otherwise have done. Several contributors have included their own acknowledgements for source material, infor-mation or other assistance.

David Simon
Englefield Green
Surrey

1 Introduction: Shedding the Past, Shaping the Future

DAVID SIMON

Background and Rationale

Dimensions of Dramatic Change

That momentous day in February 1990, when the world watched in a heady mixture of televisual joy, awe, hope and relief, as Nelson Rolihlahla Mandela strode confidently out of Victor Verster Prison near Paarl, hand in hand with his (now ex-) wife, Winnie, instantly became one of the high water marks of euphoria with which the 1990s began. Six weeks later, Namibia finally achieved sovereignty under Sam Nujoma's South West Africa People's Organisation (SWAPO) after a century-long struggle against German and then South African colonialism. These and other recent dramatic political and economic changes in southern Africa have transformed the region in a few short years from a global flashpoint to one in which peaceful co-operation and development may soon become a reality.[1]

Similar trends in other regions at the beginning of the 1990s led many people to hope that perhaps this final decade of the millennium would, after all, herald a new, more peaceful and less polarised world order, even if not one dominated by the United States in the sense envisioned in President George Bush's triumphalist proclamation. However, events such as the Gulf War, the war and associated atrocities in former Yugoslavia, the Rwandan genocide and many other conflicts burning in the ashes of Cold War certainties, have since served to dampen initial optimism on both counts. Peace remains as elusive as ever, with new battles replacing those which have been, or are in the process of being, settled. Moreover, the actions, inactions and reactions of the major powers still bear many of the hallmarks of Cold War thinking: the shift to newer, less polarised conceptions and interactions among states has not been rapid. This is contributing to the growing disillusionment with 'nation' states and the United Nations system of interstate government on the part of many people around the world. The increased political space for, and legitimacy and roles of, non-state actors and organisations from below, and of international agencies and bodies from above, is certainly ushering in more pluralistic and responsive systems of governance. To some, this situation represents evidence of 'postmodernity', in that the quintessentially modern structures of the so-called 'nation' state and its interstate system are of declining relative importance (Simon 1997a). As we shall see through the chapters of this book, sovereign states are clearly ceding power to suprastate bodies, both intergovernmental and non-governmental, while civil society is playing a more active role in many countries. However, reports of the demise of the state are equally certainly premature.

Southern Africa, more than most regions of the South, has witnessed dramatically changed political and economic circumstances since the late 1980s, augmented by a fund of international goodwill and aid to assist these transformations. South

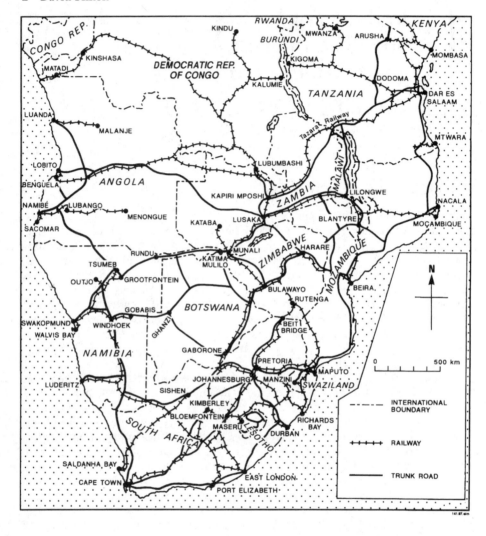

Figure 1.1   *Political boundaries and principal transport routes in southern Africa*

Africa has been a non-racial democracy since May 1994 and is now once again a respected and active member of the international community. Namibia's independence is maturing without external threats or internal instability. The bloody conflict in Mozambique gave way to UN-monitored demobilisation and elections in 1994. Over a million refugees have returned there from neighbouring countries, especially Malawi, Zimbabwe, Zambia, South Africa and Tanzania, and are gradually reintegrating and contributing to postwar reconstruction and recovery. Malawi has finally undergone a transition from decades of despotic rule under Kamuzu Hastings Banda to a more responsive multiparty system under Bakili Muluzi, while an acute political and constitutional crisis in Lesotho appeared to have been overcome following concerted regional intervention by Presidents Mandela, Masire and Mugabe in January 1995, backed by the threat of military action. However, instability increased again during 1997. In Swaziland, King Mswati III has embarked on a modest programme of reform and modernisation to reduce the absolutist nature of monarchic control.

To be sure, there have been setbacks and disasters too, none more costly in human lives than Jonas Savimbi's refusal to accept defeat in Angola's 1992 elections and his decision to resume UNITA's war against the MPLA government of President José Eduardo dos Santos. In 1993/4, around 1,000 Angolans per day were dying as a direct and indirect consequence of this war. After many false starts, by mid-1997 the latest agreement to demobilise combatants, establish a unified army and share power under a government of national unity formula, appeared to be being implemented. However, the situation remains far from stable and is ultimately contingent, at least in part, on resolution of the crisis in the neighbouring Democratic Republic of Congo (formerly Zaire). Prospects for such a resolution have increased markedly since May 1997, when Laurent Kabila's forces and their backers in neighbouring states finally succeeded in evicting the former dictator, Mobuto Sese Seko, a long-standing supporter of UNITA in Angola. However, UNITA still appears to be hedging its bets, failing to commit many of its soldiers and weapons to demobilisation and even apparently acquiring new war materials. The meaning of such a move is all too clear. In Zambia, the government of President Chiluba's Movement for Multiparty Democracy is thoroughly discredited amid widespread evidence of corruption and incompetence; its 1996 election victory was hotly disputed, and 'development' appears to be as elusive as ever. In Zimbabwe, the adverse impacts of the Economic Structural Adjustment Programme (ESAP), coupled with President Robert Mugabe's increasingly quixotic rule, are resulting in growing hardship and disillusionment, to which the paltry one-third turnout in the 1996 election bears eloquent testimony.

Thinking About Regional Futures
Much has been written about these events and processes within the individual countries of southern Africa, and it is not my purpose to add to that literature here. By contrast, remarkably little attention has been devoted to specifically regional dynamics in post-apartheid southern Africa, despite the profound challenges and opportunities presented by the political and economic transitions. The only exception to this relative silence applies to the formal regional institutions, especially the Southern African Customs Union (SACU) and the erstwhile Southern African Development Co-ordination Conference (SADCC), which was restyled the Southern African Development Community (SADC) in 1992. However, even this literature is replete with repetitive and synoptic overviews at the expense of detailed studies.

Now that the dust of the momentous political metamorphoses in the region has settled, it is opportune to evaluate the situation and the ongoing processes of (re)negotiation and transition, both for the inherent interest of what is happening within southern Africa and in order to distil more conceptual and theoretical insights which may be of wider and comparative value – hence the plural 'futures' in the title of this sub-section. Given the dramatic pace and extent of change in such a polarised, unequal and hitherto conflict-ridden region, there are likely to be valuable lessons for other regions in the South (and potentially also the North).

Accordingly, the first and most basic objective of this book is to highlight some of the principal and often very interesting and exciting dimensions of contemporary transfrontier interaction and co-operation in post-apartheid southern Africa. Following from this is the second objective, namely, to analyse the extent to which these phenomena and processes represent continuities or new dynamics which are distinct from those of the apartheid era, when relations between an increasingly internationally isolated South Africa and its neighbours were often fraught or hostile. As such and thirdly, the book provides an important case study of regional dynamics and the role of rapid geopolitical transitions in changing the nature of interaction and the prospects for regional integration and trading bloc formation against the backdrop of the evolving global trade regime under the auspices of the newly formed World Trade Organization. Although a few contributors make comparative references to other regions, the principal concern is with southern Africa. Finally, and more conceptually, this volume contributes to a rethinking of the nature, importance and role of regional geopolitics and political economy, both in the sense of a relative decline in real state sovereignty as discussed above and also in relation to alternative analytical frameworks.

All too commonly, especially within the realist school of international relations and political science, geopolitical regions in the South are regarded as comprising little more than the sum of their constituent countries. This perspective has at least three major shortcomings. First, it focuses attention disproportionately on the most powerful players and tends to discount the impact of the often significant influence of smaller countries. Second, it assumes that there is little interaction among the countries of a region which holds significance for external constituencies. Finally, and following from the previous points, it implies an approach to interstate relations which still relies heavily on Cold War perceptions, categories and procedures. All of these will be challenged both explicitly and implicitly in this book.

Crucial to an understanding of regional dynamics in southern Africa, and, indeed, the nature of current reappraisals and repositionings, is the enormous asymmetry between South Africa, which constitutes the demographic, economic and political core of the region, and the other states, which are themselves remarkably heterogeneous. Recent history in the region has been characterised by efforts on the part of the 'Frontline' and other neighbouring states to co-operate against apartheid South Africa, not only on account of apartheid and the associated destabilisation programme launched by Pretoria against its neighbours during the 1980s but also because of its sheer economic dominance.

Throughout the 1990s, and especially since the ANC-controlled Government of National Unity took office in 1994, relations between South Africa and its neighbours have improved markedly, to the point of full 'normalisation'. President Mandela and his cabinet ministers are acutely aware of the need for peaceful co-operation *for mutual benefit* if the region's future is to be secure. This implies that relations will have to be pursued on a very different basis from in the past, with unilateral chauvinism in the name of nationalism replaced by multilateral consultation, accommodation and collaboration. Conversely, the smaller countries, in particular, are anxious for a 'peace dividend' and investment and technical assistance from

South Africa to help redress the legacy of destabilisation, to repay support for the ANC in exile and to promote economic development and trade. The difficulty, even at the level of intergovernmental relations, is how to ensure mutual benefit through enhanced interaction without suffering the strong polarisation of investment and migration which undermined earlier efforts at formal regional co-operation else-where in Africa and beyond. Equally, however, this book documents and analyses some of the major interactions and dynamics which are occurring beyond, and per-haps in spite of, the efforts at control by official state institutions.

Conceptual Orientations

This last point provokes the fundamental question of what the future is likely to hold for southern Africa. Will it be 'business as usual' in a situation where little other than the faces and flags of government have changed and where existing dispari-ties and contradictions so deeply rooted in local and regional histories of disposses-sion and inequality persist? Worse still, will unfulfilled expectations, dashed hopes and continuing high levels of unemployment contribute to growing disorder and disintegration where neither person nor property is secure? Alternatively can the euphoria and expectations of epochal change which successively accompanied Namibian independence, peace in Mozambique, the establishment of the 'new' non-racial South Africa and the political demise of Banda's despotism in Malawi be translated into action towards more equitable and sustainable futures? Will the regional order continue to be dominated by states willing to co-operate loosely but still jealously guarding their own territories and sovereign powers, or is it possible to envisage a process leading to a more politically and institutionally integrated order in which the exclusive/inclusive rigidity of national borders might be de-emphasised (see e.g. Nugent and Asiwaju 1996)?

A central issue in this regard will be the ability and willingness of South Africa's political, economic and scholarly elites to shed their traditional inward-looking pref-erences, which were greatly exacerbated by apartheid isolation. Accordingly, the rel-evance and importance of countries north of the Limpopo River were commonly denied or ignored until very recently because of the claimed uniqueness of apartheid or on account of a supposedly uniformly disastrous postcolonial eco-nomic and political record in black Africa. Consequently, and in a manner redolent of neocolonialism, the major Western powers and increasingly also Japan and Taiwan were seen as the main reference points in terms of seeking political legiti-macy, trade relations and social comparison. As I argued at greater length a few years ago (Simon 1994), there is an urgent need for academics and practitioners to refocus on South Africa as a key part *of* southern Africa and indeed the rest of the continent, rather than merely having a physical location *in* Africa. How quickly and to what extent such attitudes are changing beyond the superficial platitudes already heard in the wake of the 1994 elections, remains to be seen. The evidence to date appears mixed.

Many black South Africans have long looked north for inspiration, in recognition of their Africanness, as a source of solidarity in the face of apartheid oppression and as inspiration for possible liberation. However, as Sally Peberdy indicates in Chapter 11, gratitude among many black South Africans for past support from neighbouring and other African states has rapidly given way to anger and frustration at the new wave of African migrants to South Africa who, it is claimed, are depriving the vic-tims of apartheid of jobs. This xenophobia is rising. As mentioned above, however, political leaders have gone to some lengths to assure South Africa's neighbours that the government is committed to conducting its future relations with them on a very different basis from that before 1994. President Mandela has been particularly prominent in this regard. The degree of progress in this sphere is analysed in several chapters. Business leaders – at least from the major companies – have certainly moved quickly to position themselves in neighbouring markets through acquisitions, joint ventures, partial shareholdings or the reacquisition of firms which had previously been nationalised or which they had been forced to sell when relations with South Africa were cut on account of apartheid. While new investment and technical upgrading are generally being welcomed, concerns at renewed/enhanced South African economic dominance in the region are also growing in local business circles.

One other important change has been in South African media attitudes to, and coverage of, the rest of Africa. This is now far more dispassionate and extensive than previously, and is certain to assist in changing popular prejudices. Some politicians and academics are also becoming increasingly aware of policy lessons to be learnt from experiences elsewhere with mass infrastructure and housing provision schemes. Colin Stoneman examines this issue in relation to Zimbabwe in Chapter 6.

Following from the foregoing discussion, we must ask whether it is even appropriate to envision the future in singular terms (i.e. 'the future'), as this implies a coherence or uniformity of approach and dynamic, as, for example, in terms of progressive regional integration along the lines of the European Union, the institution so commonly but not entirely appropriately held up as a model. In keeping with these postmodern – and now finally also substantively postcolonial – times throughout southern Africa, does it not behove us to consider more diverse, pluralistic development processes which permit divergent as well as convergent futures? Rather than sketch scenarios, I will offer some more conceptual thoughts.

Many authors have interpreted postmodernism and postcolonialism in terms either of discrete periods (i.e. after the modern and colonial respectively) or of forms of expression and aesthetics. However, as I have recently argued (Simon 1997a), it is far more helpful to conceive of them as different modes of enquiry and practice (ways of seeing and doing). This is particularly so in relation to regions of the South, where the experience of modernity has been uneven and incomplete at best and where it is exceedingly difficult to discern any clear break between what might be termed the modern and postmodern periods respectively. Thus conceived, postmodernism refers to a decentring of single hegemonic official ideologies and discourses (of modernity, modernisation and/or 'the truth') and an acceptance of the validity of alternative, pluralistic explanations and practices. As such, it offers the prospect of less conflictual, directed and 'linear' orthodoxies and social processes, in that greater local autonomy and diversity can more readily be accommodated. This is also categorically not the totally relativistic, self-indulgent, leisured and playful approach advocated by many in the North, and which precludes any consensus or meaningful social action. Similarly, while southern Africa is now unambiguously postcolonial in an epochal or chronological sense, it is more helpful to think of postcolonialism being concerned with the cultural politics of identity, especially as practised by previously oppressed and marginalised groups. In many respects, this resonates with the ethos of postmodernism, in that different identities and cultural politics need to be accommodated and legitimised.

With particular respect to South Africa, authors including Mabin (1995) and Thornton (1996) have argued that 'the apartheid project' represented a particularly bizarre but determined form of modernism, and that the current post-apartheid transition therefore constitutes a postmodern beginning, where different discourses, agendas and practices vie with one another in a period of remarkable openness and optimism. Somewhat surprisingly, therefore, Thornton regards apartheid South Africa rather than the post-apartheid state as postcolonial:

> I shall argue that the current moment in South Africa is indeed postmodern in a number of respects, but it is not postcolonial. In a nutshell, I shall argue that Apartheid was a form of rampant modernism and that post-Apartheid is therefore postmodern. It is also after the 'colonial' of course, but I would reserve the label 'postcolonial' for Apartheid itself (Thornton 1996:136).

> In comparison with the rest of Africa, the issue of postcolonialism is obscured by the fact that the institutions that might once have been characterised as 'colonial' have long been rendered indigenous. For the bureaucracy, and for the vast majority of educated South African people, there is no 'overseas educated' elite speaking a foreign language (although they all speak a great many local languages) (ibid:139–140).

This position evidently reflects a certain tension between an appreciation of the postmodern which blends periodisation with a 'problematic' (i.e. mode of analysis), and a view of the postcolonial as a problematic in the very specific sense of a rupture from the administered colonial polity and an indigenisation of the modern state bureaucracy and its modernising project. This latter seems contradictory, in that Thornton simultaneously argues (correctly) that the apartheid state sought to impose a single, hegemonic and discriminatory world view under the guise of conflict avoidance. This certainly has little to do with my sense of postcoloniality as outlined above. At present, South Africa is characterised by all manner of contradictory and divergent discourses and cultural politics, often incomplete and simplistic, as the perpetrators of apartheid seek to reinvent themselves in goodness and many former victims explore, recover or articulate their histories and identities. At the same time, virtually everyone claims to subscribe to the foundational myth or 'imagined community' of the New South Africa, namely the 'rainbow nation' as coined by Archbishop Desmond Tutu. Such a situation of dynamic flux, openness and accepted contradiction would seem both postmodern and postcolonial in essence.

Patrick Chabal (1996:37) offers another perspective on postcolonialism, which recognises it as a problematic but situates it primarily in and in relation to 'Western' discourse:

> In the sense in which it is used in current cultural and ideological parlance, it refers to the implications of the postcolonial or postimperial condition for the definition of our own identity in the West today. It is, therefore, more a concern about ourselves than about those who do live in actual postcolonial societies.

This also therefore excludes the self-conscious and deliberate cultural politics of identity and historical recovery by different voices within constitutionally postcolonial societies.

With such different conceptualisations in current debate, some observers might despair and seek recourse to more familiar 'realist' interpretations. However, that approach relies heavily on Cold War terms, categories and modes of analysis, which are not sufficiently open to many of the most interesting and exciting reformulations of identity, 'development' goals and politics which are undoubtedly occurring (to different extents and in response to diverse mixtures of global and local influences) in different parts of southern Africa today. This is in many senses, both material and ideological, a region in transition, and transitions are almost invariably periods of exceptional excitement, openness, flux, experimentation, uncertainty and even tension and contradiction. Different paths and policies are tried, some then abandoned or surrendered, others adopted and still others formulated in complex blends of continuity and change, of hybridisation and pastiche.

In terms of 'development' too, the current transitions ought to provide space for a variety of official and unofficial discourses and agendas, especially as the interventionist role of the state is supposedly declining. This would accord well with the postmodern spirit outlined above (see Simon 1997b for detailed analysis). In reality, as will emerge below, the evidence suggests that only a few governments actively encourage such diversity. The norm is for them still to advocate a particular official orthodoxy – like the Reconstruction and Development Programme (RDP) and the Growth, Employment and Redistribution strategy (GEAR) in South Africa – which remains heavily modernist in thrust, and at best to tolerate other discourses over which they have no control. Moreover, many non-official development discourses and practices are also still strongly modernist, as evidenced in this book.

Under the circumstances, no attempt has been made to impose a particular theoretical or analytical toolkit on the contributors to this book. Although we all consider ourselves progressive, clear differences of both conceptual framework and specific view will be evident. The objective has been to gather a group of high calibre authors to report, analyse and – where appropriate – speculate on the basis of first-hand research into some of the major dimensions of contemporary change and policy reformulation across the region. Put differently, we explore various direct and indirect aspects of the so-called 'peace dividend' or 'post-apartheid dividend' on the regional scale.

How Real Is the 'Peace Dividend'?

In this section, I offer some analysis of the nature and extent of this concept, namely, the 'returns' to southern Africa's investment in peace and the ending of apartheid and other sources of conflict. These are discussed under headings which reflect principal categories of potential direct and indirect dividends, all of which are subsequently taken up in later chapters.

Military Expenditure
The most direct approach is to examine recent military expenditure patterns of southern African states. In a very real sense, this represents the baseline, showing the extent to which the cessation of hostilities and the new spirit of co-operation have been translated by governments into a shift of resources away from the military sphere and into potentially productive investment and social expenditure. *A priori*, one would expect significant reductions in the sizes of the armed forces and in new weapons purchases. There was certainly much talk of such trends, both in South Africa itself as apartheid's 'total strategy' was abandoned and the new government took office, and in other countries which were under pressure to reduce total state expenditure under stringent structural adjustment programmes. In South Africa, conscription for national service was abolished and retrenchments were made from the South African Defence Force (SADF), even as significant numbers of members of the former liberation movements' armed wings, the ANC's Mkhonto we Sizwe (MK) and the PAC's Azanian People's Liberation Army (APLA) were being integrated into the new South African National Defence Force (SANDF). However, proposals inherited from the apartheid regime to modernise the navy by purchasing corvettes and submarines to replace ageing vessels were embraced by the new ANC Minister and Deputy Minister of Defence, Joe Modise and Ronnie Kasrils. This proved immensely controversial, provoking a storm of protest from diverse political constituencies demanding that the great expense be spared, espe-

cially now that South Africa faced no conceivable maritime threat, and that the resources be reallocated towards implementation of the government's flagship Reconstruction and Development Programme (RDP). It has certainly been deeply ironic to hear Modise and Kasrils, themselves former MK commanders, defending the proposed purchases in terms indistinguishable from those used by their apartheid predecessors. This irony, and its implications in terms of the persistence of vested institutional interests and the limits of supposedly radical reform promised by the incoming ANC government, have not been lost on many South Africans. Debate has raged on ever since, and at the time of writing (mid-1997), the government still seems committed to making the naval purchases.

Table 1.1 shows a clear trend of declining aggregate military expenditure in the region from a peak in 1993. Most remarkable has been the reduction by the two largest spenders in 1993, namely South Africa and Angola. South Africa has cut its expenditure by US$1,100 million (28.2 per cent) in three years, and Angola by US$875 mn (an astonishing 79.5 per cent). The Angolan data are, however, somewhat distorted by the fact that expenditure in 1993, following UNITA's resumption of the civil war, had risen by almost 60 per cent above the 1992 level. The importance of South Africa's cutback is both domestic – in terms of the alternative uses to which the resources are being put – and regional, in terms of pruning the overall volume of armaments and number of military personnel along its borders and hence reducing tensions. It is worth noting that South Africa accounted for over 68 per cent of total regional military expenditure in 1993 but that, notwithstanding its substantial cutbacks, the percentage had actually risen to 72.9 per cent by 1996. Hence aggregate expenditure by the other states had fallen even faster than South Africa's.

In addition, it is clear that the trend towards reduced overall expenditure has masked significant increases by Botswana, Namibia and Zimbabwe, as detailed in Chapter 2. Namibia's new purchases reflect an alarmed reaction to Botswana's own acquisitions, fearing that the border dispute between the two countries over the seasonally inundated island of Kasikili/Sedudu in the Chobe River might be used as grounds for Botswanan aggression against it. Botswana's response was – and remains – that it is merely enhancing its capability in the event of an external threat and in order to enable it to participate more effectively in UN or African peacekeeping missions, and that it has no aggressive intentions towards Namibia. Nevertheless, Namibia has felt the need to respond by acquiring additional armour and other hardware, mainly from Russia. Namibian representations, including to

Table 1.1 *Southern African regional military expenditure trends (US$mn at constant 1993 prices)*

Country	1992	1993	1994	1995	1996
Angola	648	1,100	515	300	225
Botswana	100	140	222	226	226
Lesotho	38	31	31	33	38
Malawi	19	20	21	21	24
Mozambique	101	118	105	58	65
Namibia	67	57	56	65	81
South Africa	3,300	3,900	3,400	2,900	2,800
Tanzania	107	90	88	87	88
Zambia	62	58	59	62	42
Zimbabwe	225	209	196	233	251
TOTAL	4,667	5,723	4,693	3,976	3,840

Source: Willett, 1997

SADC's newly established Organ on Politics, Defence and Security, failed to generate sympathetic condemnation of Botswana. Indeed, the South African Minister of Defence issued a statement effectively supporting Botswana's right to make such purchases and arguing that these would help defend the region in the event of any (unspecified) external threat. This is yet another example of logic and rhetoric which appear to have more in common with apartheidspeak than with current government policy. Such developments highlight how easily a competitive arms build-up, with important direct and indirect implications for peace and envisaged development expenditures, can resume even in a generally peaceful and co-operative regional atmosphere.

Other data on military personnel reveal that military force sizes have remained constant or have fallen in every country, nowhere more dramatically than in Mozambique following the end of armed conflict there (Chapter 2). As elsewhere, the extent to which such troop reductions translate into reduced expenditure and tension, on the one hand, and enhanced economic production and welfare, on the other, depends on how successfully the retrenchees have managed to reintegrate into civilian life. High levels of long-term unemployment among former combatants, as in Namibia since 1990, can easily generate political tensions for the new governments and, if there is recourse to hidden or stolen arms, also crime and instability. In this context, Alex Vines examines one widely neglected aspect of the military legacy of apartheid and other regional conflicts, namely, the proliferation of small arms (Chapter 3).

Notwithstanding counter-tendencies in a few countries, there has been a substantial overall reduction in the size of armed forces and of military budgets across the region since 1993, reflecting and simultaneously reinforcing the new circumstances. This represents the most direct and measurable 'peace dividend'. However, it remains unclear to what extent the reductions in expenditure have been converted into peaceful and productive uses. In South Africa, there is evidence of substantially increased state expenditure on health, education and housing, without a commensurate increase in overall government budgets. In Zimbabwe and several other countries, however, social expenditures have been some of the first and principal victims of government cuts imposed under structural adjustment and economic recovery programmes in order to reduce public expenditure and public debt as percentages of national GDP. Under such circumstances, the benefits are far smaller, principally the reduced military expenditure, without any multipliers through redirected spending, and have to be offset against the social costs of higher unemployment and its consequences. For such countries, the peace dividend may therefore be very small indeed.

Military Training and Peacekeeping
Another important dimension of post-conflict military change is the reorientation and (re)training of soldiers to fulfil different future roles in the 'new southern Africa'. In the immediate aftermath of the Zimbabwean, Namibian and Mozambican peace agreements and elections, the profound challenge of integrating previously warring combatants coming from very different military traditions (conventional army and guerrillas using different weapons systems and trained in or by diverse countries) had to be tackled quickly. In all these countries, British Military Advisory and Training Teams (BMATTs) have played a leading role which is generally agreed to have been successful. Other donor countries have undertaken military assistance programmes, although unfortunately with some rivalry and little co-ordination. Since 1994, South Africa has itself been undertaking the difficult inte-

gration and rationalisation process, largely using its own resources and staff but assisted by a small BMATT team (Chapter 2).

The role of extra-regional peacekeepers, under the United Nations banner, has declined in southern Africa following the completion of the Namibian and Mozambican transition supervision processes. Although nearing the end of its current mandate, the latest UN observer force in Angola, UNAVEM III, is by far the largest involvement within southern Africa. Set up to oversee the 1994 ceasefire, demobilisation of fighters and integration of the new national army, it has a broader mandate and somewhat better resourcing than its failed predecessor during the 1991–92 ceasefire and election process, UNAVEM II (see Chapter 2).

Privatised Security and Military Operations

One new development in the wake of conflict diminution and large-scale demobilisation in the region has been the growth of privatised security services and specialist armed units. At least two distinct forms of operation can be distinguished. The earlier and more widespread trend since approximately 1989–90 has been for the recruitment of former combatants, but especially those previously deployed as irregular special forces by South Africa and its allies, to work as armed private security guards in urban areas. The number and size of such companies have grown dramatically in response to a perceived surge in crime against property in many countries.

At one level this provided relevant employment – for which little if any retraining was required or provided (no matter how desirable) – for people who would adjust with difficulty to civilian life and who, in many cases, were disoriented and likely to be socially outcast on account of their previous activities. Perhaps the most overt connection is hinted at by the name of one such company established in Namibia shortly before independence, namely Coin Security: coin is a contraction of counter-insurgency, and a long-standing jargon term in the South African military and its associates. This firm was set up specifically to recruit former operatives from Koevoet ('Crowbar'), South Africa's notorious counter-insurgency commando in northern Namibia and southern Angola. Faced with high unemployment among former SWAPO guerrillas following Namibian independence, a co-operative security firm was subsequently established from among their ranks. At another level, however, at least initially, this trend was often regarded with concern, in that discipline among former irregular forces and guerrilla fighters, still able to assert authority with a gun in their holster, could not be taken for granted. Many people regarded such guards with great suspicion, especially if they had fought for an opposing unit.

The second, far more specialised and limited type of operation has been the establishment of mercenary or related armed intervention units. The most widely known and active is Executive Outcomes, a firm founded by former South African security force and foreign affairs/military intelligence staff specifically to recruit retrenched or resigning SADF personnel (and selected former allies) and to deploy their accumulated skills for private gain. Ironically, their first significant assignment was in Angola at the behest of President Dos Santos, to assist with security around sensitive installations and the diamond mines, and with military training of the Angolan army against UNITA prior to the 1994 ceasefire and demobilisation. Previously, of course, Executive Outcome's personnel would have been working with and training UNITA forces on South Africa's behalf. Subsequently, the company has grown in size and has undertaken similar operations in several African countries, including Sierra Leone and the former Zaire (Ashworth 1996).

This is a highly efficient and effective force, which claims to be engaged solely in peacekeeping, security and training activities but is widely thought to have been engaged in active fighting. Executive Outcomes has been condemned as a mercenary force by many governments, the UN and international human rights agencies, all of which have sought the intervention of the South African government to restrict its activities. To date, however, no specific measures have been taken beyond the issuing of statements of concern and a request that foreign governments refrain from signing contracts with Executive Outcomes and from granting visas to its personnel. In early 1997, the recruitment (apparently against domestic, Australian and British advice) of Executive Outcomes and an allied UK-based firm, Sandlines International, to assist the Papua New Guinean government put down a long-standing rebellion on Bougaineville Island, precipitated an army mutiny which forced the revocation of the contract and ultimately led to the downfall of President Julius Chan.

This most recent intervention, the first outside Africa, has heightened concern at the potential global reach of this and similar firms. In official and popular minds, they are regarded as mercenaries but clearly there are many beleaguered political leaders and groups willing to employ them regardless of their previous pedigrees or current international opprobrium. Strategically, the central questions are whether such privatised peacekeeping and military activities are likely to grow in scale and influence, and whether this might have substantial geopolitical implications for stability and emerging post-Cold War orders. The former is difficult to answer at this stage, but senior government and international agency officials regularly express concern that the lack of official status and accountability of Executive Outcomes and their ilk, especially on account of their previous records in fighting apartheid's wars, does pose a definite danger. Intergovernmental or multilateral agreements and procedures could be disregarded or deliberately circumvented, xenophobia against such foreign agents and their perceived backers could increase, and they could just as easily prove destabilising as stability-enhancing. Such concerns are certainly justified, although at another level it is pertinent to question why there has been such a furore when the same governments and multilateral organisations are steadily implementing their own privatisation programmes to reduce the active role of the state and the size of official payrolls. The answer seems to be twofold. First, this phenomenon represents a spontaneous 'privatisation', which bypasses or circumvents official channels. In other words, such firms are not tendering for and carrying out duties on behalf of their home governments or international agencies. Second, defence and national/regional security are universally regarded as 'core' responsibilities of states, which it is inappropriate to privatise. Hence firms like Executive Outcomes are perceived as usurping the role of states and intergovernmental organisations like the UN or the Organisation of African Unity (OAU), which claim to play by agreed club rules and which see peacekeeping as their own exclusive prerogative. It will indeed be important to monitor future developments, as this trend – which could easily prove attractive to former soldiers and specialist operatives demobilised from armies and guerrilla forces around the world – may well turn out to have significant implications for the existing international order and methods for maintaining and enhancing it. So far southern Africa has the rather unwanted distinction of being a 'market leader' in activities which may serve to reduce as much as enhance the peace dividend.

Rationalising Formal Regional Institutions

Southern Africa has inherited a surfeit of regional institutions with different histories, memberships and initial objectives, but which have experienced a substantial degree of convergence to the point of overlap since the turn of the decade as they have sought to adapt to changing circumstances and secure a future role. This situation is widely recognised as being both unnecessary and unsustainable. The most important bodies are the Southern African Customs Union (SACU), dating from the establishment of the Union of South Africa in 1910, the Southern Africa Development Community (SADC) and the Common Market for Eastern and Southern Africa (COMESA). The predecessors of the latter two were established at the beginning of the 1980s. Talks and negotiations are continuing but have generally made little substantive progress to date beyond internal change within each organisation. Despite overlapping or even entirely common memberships and objectives, the constituent countries and existing secretariats have been unable to agree on any form of merger, dissolution or, conversely, a new division of labour among them. Focusing on SADC, the organisation which has arguably confronted the issues most directly, not least because of South Africa's membership since 1994, this process warrants critical evaluation. The task is undertaken in a comparative context by James Sidaway and Richard Gibb in Chapter 10.

If more streamlined and sustainable institutional arrangements could be introduced, this would represent another direct saving of financial and personnel resources, thereby contributing to the peace dividend. Meanwhile, another related recent development might in time contribute to the maintenance of peace and cordial interstate relations within the region. In 1996, SADC established its Organ for Politics, Defence and Security. Designed to expand and replace the former forum of national leaders of the Frontline States faced with South African destabilisation in the late 1970s and early 1980s, it will function at arm's length from its parent body. Many people in the region and beyond are already pinning substantial hopes on its potential role as arbiter, peacemaker and even peacekeeper, but the OPDS (under the unfortunate unofficial abbreviated title of 'the Organ') has as yet barely come into formal being and lacks resources and a clear *modus operandi* beyond holding heads of state summits separate from the main SADC summits.

Indirect Peace Dividends and New Forms of Development
Indirect dividends include those activities or programmes now able to be undertaken by virtue of the reallocation of resources away from military and security uses, and those taking place outside formal state structures but for which the transformation of prevailing conditions has been crucial. Many of these aim to promote 'development'. The focus here is on the many concrete cross-border developments involving two or more countries which are occurring. Most have far-reaching implications for the people, states and institutions concerned, and for our comprehensions of regional change. Those covered in this book include multilateral initiatives to establish a regional electricity grid (Tore Horvei), cross-border National Parks or other conservation zones linked to environmental objectives and the promotion of tourism (Eddie Koch), and structural change and co-operation in export-oriented commercial agriculture using the example of sugar (Steve Atkins and Alan Terry).

Other issues, such as the currently contested nature of trade relations and other forms of interaction between South Africa and Zimbabwe, highlight the ambivalences and uncertainties regarding competition versus co-operation. Zimbabwe was the leading light and most economically sophisticated country within SADC until South Africa joined in 1994; now President Mugabe in particular and Zimbabweans in general are having to adjust to playing second fiddle (Colin Stoneman). For other countries in the region as well, South Africa's re-established legitimacy and the normalisation of relations hold both opportunities and challenges, which are exemplified in several of the contributions to this book. They will provide a variety of perspectives, including contextualised case studies and the historically contingent experiences of individual migrants, to give due attention to 'views from below' (Kavita Datta). Such developments have potentially great importance in themselves but also point to some of the limitations of, and challenges facing, governments and regional institutions because these activities are not being undertaken under their auspices.

Finally, the book addresses sensitive but crucial region-wide processes occurring outside of formal organisations or agreements. These include the spread of HIV/AIDS and the inadequacy of efforts to tackle the pandemic (Douglas Webb); the increasing flow of both legal and illegal migrants to South Africa from the region and beyond – a flow currently giving rise to xenophobic tendencies within South Africa (Sally Peberdy); and the intensifying competition for transit freight traffic between the region's various transport corridors now that immediate economic considerations rather than political or strategic factors dominate consignors' decision-making. This is discussed in relation to the reintegration of Walvis Bay into Namibia, itself a very tangible peace dividend for that newly independent state (David Simon).

Inevitably, any publication of this sort has to be selective. However, two other themes were originally intended for inclusion but the contributions ultimately failed to materialise. The first was a Mozambican perspective on that country's relations with South Africa, especially in relation to the newly formalised Mosagrius scheme to settle white South African commercial farmers in Niassa and Cabo Delgado provinces, and the planned development corridor linking Maputo with Gauteng. The second theme was the increasingly critical water shortage in the region, especially in South Africa's interior. Malefane Maema was to contribute this chapter, focusing particularly on the Lesotho Highlands Water Project, a major bilateral initiative (with multilateral funding) to channel bulk supplies to South Africa's economic heartland of Gauteng. However, he and his wife died tragically in a motor accident on Van Reenen's Pass in KwaZulu-Natal before he was able to complete the task. As indicated on the frontispiece, this book is dedicated to his memory. Fortunately, recent publications by Larry Swatuk (1996) and Hussein Solomon (1996) offer assessments of regional power and water resources and initiatives, therefore going some way to filling the void.

Structure of the Book

The book is divided into three main sections, corresponding to broad subject areas and themes evident in the analysis of contemporary southern Africa, and in order to maximise the internal coherence of the material. The first of these, 'Transcending the Past: the Politics of Dis- and Re-engagement', opens with a chapter by Susan Willett, examining recent trends towards reduced military expenditure and efforts to reorient military priorities in southern Africa. Her analysis expands and broadens some of the themes addressed above in relation to the peace dividend. Thereafter, Alex Vines documents the extent of small arms proliferation across the region and considers the implications of this worrying trend and ways in which it might be tackled. Next, Eddie Koch explores the controversial proposals, plans and developments in respect of transboundary conservation zones in southern Africa, with particular reference to the nexus centred on the borders between South Africa, Mozambique and Zimbabwe. Finally, Greg Mills analyses the continuities and processes of reformulation within South African foreign policy in general and in relation to neighbouring countries and Africa in particular.

The second section is concerned with 'Changing Geographies of Production and Economic Integration'. Colin Stoneman offers a critical assessment of Zimbabwe's economic record before and after the implementation of structural adjustment policies, the role of South African interests in an unbalanced relationship, and the lessons which post-apartheid South Africa would do well to learn. In the following chapter, David Simon details the complex negotiations over the reintegration of Walvis Bay harbour into Namibia from South African control, and evaluates Namibian ambitions to establish a regional transport corridor and industrial hub centred on the port, including an export processing zone. Steve Atkins and Alan Terry then examine the changing political and social economy of sugar production, such as a rapid shift in location and towards the use of outgrower schemes, and their implications for economic development, against the backdrop of the World Trade Organization's agenda for trade liberalisation. Next, we are offered an insider's perspective by Tore Horvei on the rapid pace of progress towards the establishment of a regional electricity grid stretching as far north as the Democratic Republic of Congo and Tanzania, and symbolised by the recent formalisation of the Southern African Power Pool. South Africa lies at the heart of this network, and its parastatal, Eskom, is the lead agency. Finally, James Sidaway and Richard Gibb examine the three principal regional institutions and offer comparative insights into SACU and SADC and progress towards renegotiated treaties more appropriate to post-apartheid circumstances in the region. This seems a more fruitful way to explore key similarities and differences between the organisations than by means of the separate chapters originally proposed by the authors.

The third section, 'Population and Mobility', contains three chapters. Sally Peberdy considers contemporary patterns of regional migration – both legal and illegal – to South Africa, highlighting the legislative basis for successive policies up to the present. Kavita Datta provides a detailed and sensitive study of gender dimensions of labour markets and recent migration by women within Botswana and from that country to South Africa. Finally, Douglas Webb offers a sobering assessment of the rapid spread of HIV/AIDS throughout southern Africa, and its implications for the sexual and economic politics of regional reintegration. In a brief concluding chapter, the editor then draws together some of the major themes and issues covered and reflects upon the process of insiders and outsiders writing about this region in the throes of potentially far-reaching political, economic and social change.

Note

1. In this book, southern Africa (Figure 1.1) refers to the ten adjacent countries of Angola, Botswana, Lesotho, Malawi, Mozambique, Namibia, South Africa, Swaziland, Zambia and Zimbabwe, unless specific circumstances demand otherwise. For example, Tanzania and the Democratic Republic of Congo (formerly Zaire) are included within the newly formed Southern African Power Pool discussed in Chapter 9, while Tanzania and now also Mauritius are members, along with the other ten states, of the Southern African Development Community (SADC), which is examined in Chapter 10. The DRC and Seychelles also joined SADC in 1997.

References

Ashworth, M. (1996) 'Privatising war, by "The Executives", and Africa's new enforcers', *The Independent*, 16 September. London.

Chabal, P. (1996) 'The African Crisis: Context and Interpretation', in Werbner, R. and Ranger, T. (eds) *Postcolonial Identities in Africa*. Zed, London.

Mabin, A. (1995) 'On the Problems and Prospects of Overcoming Segregation and Fragmentation in Southern Africa's Cities in the Postmodern Era', in Watson, S. and Gibson, K. (eds) *Postmodern Cities and Spaces*. Blackwell, Oxford.

Nugent, P. and Asiwaju, A.I. (eds) (1996) *African Boundaries: Barriers, Conduits and Opportunities*. Pinter, London.

Rifkind, M. (1996) 'Africa – Time to Take Another Look'. Speech by the Foreign Secretary, Malcolm Rifkind, to the Royal Institute of International Affairs, Chatham House, London, 28 November.

Simon, D. (1994) 'Putting South Africa(n) Geography Back into Africa', *Area* 26(3): 296–300.

Simon, D. (1997a) *Rethinking (Post)Modernism, Postcolonialism and Post-Traditionalism: South-North Perspectives*. Research Paper 22, Centre for Developing Areas Research, Dept. of Geography, Royal Holloway, University of London. A revised version appeared in 1998 in *Environment and Planning D: Society and Space* 16 (2): 219–45..

Simon, D. (1997b) 'Development Reconsidered: New Directions in Development Thinking', *Geografiska Annaler* 79B(4): 183–201.

Solomon, H. (ed.) (1996) *Sink or Swim? Water, Resource Security and State Co-operation*. IDP Monograph Series 6. Institute for Defence Policy, Halfway House, South Africa.

Swatuk, L. (1996) *Power and Water: the Coming Order in Southern Africa*. Southern African Perspectives 58, Centre for Southern African Studies, University of the Western Cape, Bellville.

Thornton, R. (1996) 'The Potentials of Boundaries in South Africa: Steps Towards a Theory of the Social Edge's, in Werbner, R. and Ranger, T. (eds) *Postcolonial Identities in Africa*. Zed, London.

Willett, S. (1997) 'Defence Forces in the Southern African Region'. Paper presented to the conference on 'Conflict Management and Security Co-operation in southern Africa', Foreign and Commonwealth Office, London, 28 April.

A.
Transcending the Past: the Politics of Dis- and Re-engagement

2 In the Wake of War: Military Transitions in Southern Africa

SUSAN WILLETT

Introduction

To many observers Africa appears to be a continent beset with crisis and violent confrontation. It is a region where the concepts of intrastate conflict, collapsing states and failed states find numerous and facile applications (Von Hipple 1997). Zartman (1995) defines a collapsed state as 'a situation where the structure, authority (legitimate power), law, and political order have fallen apart'. During the 1980s and early 1990s, the southern African region was exemplary of Zartman's description. It was fraught with violent inter- and intrastate conflict, collapsing states (Angola and Mozambique), the deterioration of central authority, the disintegration of social cohesion, widespread corruption, ethnic strife, humanitarian disasters, refugee flows and over-expenditure on defence. Between 1980 and 1988 an estimated 1.9 million people were killed or died from war-induced famine in Angola and Mozambique alone (Ohlson and Stedman 1994). When the civil war in Angola resumed in 1992, the death toll reached one thousand per day. Although technically not at war, South Africa witnessed over 3,500 deaths that same year from internal violence.

Since the collapse of apartheid and the end of the Cold War, however, there has been a remarkable improvement in the regional security environment. Negotiated settlements in Namibia, South Africa and Mozambique have successfully drawn to a close years of armed conflict. Only the fate of peace in Angola remains uncertain, despite the persistent and determined efforts of the UN missions, UNAVEM III and MONUA. Otherwise the inter- and intrastate violence that once seemed so prevalent in the region is gradually being replaced by new national and regional mechanisms which, despite their embryonic form, are beginning to manage conflict, restructure societies and instigate reconciliation (Chapter 10). The transition from conflict to peace is also encapsulated in the new emphasis on sustainable development, macroeconomic prudence, multiparty democracy and reconciliation within the region. In this respect the trends in southern Africa provide some cause for optimism on the African continent, providing a testing ground for post-conflict political resolution.

The task of ensuring the durability of peace and democracy in the region is, however, formidable. Understanding and tackling the causes of past and potential future violence are essential for identifying the opportunities for building long-term peace and reconciliation. Theories of how and why violent conflicts occur generally distinguish between structural factors, on the one hand, and accelerating or triggering factors, on the other (Peck 1996; Azar 1990). Structural factors, which must be viewed as long-term, include interrelated political, social and economic factors such as the failure to meet basic human needs, linked to population pressures, the level and distribution of wealth, natural resource distribution, environmental degradation and the ethnic content and distribution of power in society. Accelerating or triggering factors operate in the context of the above adverse structural factors but involve specific events and the attitudes or decisions of dominant actors, which provoke or encourage violence. Triggering factors include the unequal distribution of power, the abuse of military power, the proliferation of small arms, ideological conflict and struggles related to natural resources. How these triggers activate violence depends heavily upon the specific context. In southern Africa the adverse structural problems of systemic poverty, environmental degradation, authoritarianism and ethnic tensions were compounded by the triggers of violence embodied in the apartheid system's policy of regional destabilisation and superpower interventions which encouraged a high degree of militarisation reflected in the proliferation of small arms (Chapter 3), high regional military expenditures amounting to an estimated US$5.72bn (International Institute of Strategic Studies 1994) in 1993 and the arming of over half a million people (Table 2.1).

The postwar consolidation phase will remain fragile and unstable while the legacy of militarism continues. Thus measures to deal with the consequences of war, such as reconstruction programmes, have initially focused on demilitarisation measures, including the implementation of disarmament and demobilisation programmes, reform of the armed forces, the reintegration of ex-combatants into civil society, and reconciliation between former adversaries including the creation of regional mechanisms for conflict resolution (OECD 1996). The transformation of southern African security forces represents a formidable task, involving the domestic transformation of norms, structures and functions, while simultaneously redefining their external relationships with regional and international actors. Despite this challenge, demilitarisation is already palpable in the regional decline in military expenditure, in the demobilisation of combatants and in the assertion of civil authority and the rule of law.

This chapter examines the adjustment procedures that the security forces of the major actors in the region are undergoing, starting with the changing patterns of military expenditure; the reductions in force levels and the creation of new armies through the integration of former adversaries; demobilisation and the reintegration of combatants into civil society; and finally emerging forms of military co-operation in the region, including peacekeeping.

Table 2.1 *Size of armed forces in Southern Africa, 1993*

Country	Personnel Numbers (statutory and non-statutory forces)
Angola	177,000
Botswana	7,500
Lesotho	2,000
Malawi	10,400
Mozambique	93,000 (undergoing demobilisation)
Namibia	8,100
South Africa	100,000
Tanzania	49,600
Zambia	24,000
Zimbabwe	46,900
Total	520,900

Source: IISS (1995) *Military Balance 1994–95*, plus interview data.

Note: These figures should be taken as very rough estimates, and not as definitive, since defence statistics within the region are notoriously unreliable. They are nevertheless useful in indicating the general trends taking place in the region.

Military Adjustment Problems

Security planners in the region face the challenge of finding a balance between their primary military function of defending national territory and the sovereignty of the state and the increasingly demanding task of producing collective solutions to issues such as border patrols, demining, international crime, disaster relief, economic reconstruction and environmental monitoring, particularly of the maritime environment. At the same time, the internal role of military forces in support of police functions is still widespread within the region. In South Africa, for instance, the South African National Defence Force (SANDF) is deployed in KwaZulu-Natal in an internal peacekeeping capacity. This role is highly unpopular with military personnel who are eager to shed their counter-insurgency image and rise above domestic politics by transforming themselves into a modern, professional force serving the interests of the state. Despite its unpopularity, this secondary security role is likely to endure while national police forces remain weak, corrupt and ineffectual and violence and crime proliferate.

Patterns of Military Expenditure

In a region that has been characterised by conflict and authoritarianism, and where the military is used to being able to access the lion's share of government expenditure, the current climate of defence budgetary constraints is exceedingly difficult to adjust to. Regional military expenditure has fallen by 30 per cent since 1993. The totals presented in Table 1.1 capture the general downward trend in recent defence expenditures. Table 2.2 provides details of defence expenditure as a percentage of GDP. Given multilateral and bilateral pressure from donors to reduce defence expenditure and reallocate resources for development goals, it is likely that regional defence spending will continue to decline in the foreseeable future. The discussion below elaborates on David Simon's broad overview in Chapter 1 by means of more detailed analysis of individual countries and the issues raised by current trends.

South Africa: The country's first all-inclusive democratic election held on 27 April 1994 marked a defining moment in its turbulent history. The forty-six-year-old system of apartheid was consigned to the annals of history. Militarism, a central feature

Table 2.2 *Southern African military expenditure as a percentage of GDP*

Country	1993	1994	1995
Angola	20.0	8.4	4.7
Botswana	3.8	6.8	6.8
Lesotho	4.9	5.6	5.5
Malawi	9.5	13.0	1.6
Mozambique	9.0	7.0	3.6
Namibia	2.3	2.3	2.6
South Africa	3.2	2.7	2.2
Tanzania	3.2	2.9	2.9
Zambia	1.5	1.8	1.9
Zimbabwe	3.8	3.5	4.2
Regional Average	**6.1**	**5.4**	**3.6**

Source: Calculated from IISS (1995) *Military Balance 1994/95*, and (1997) *Military Balance 1996/97*.

Note: These percentages may differ from those in the text which have been calculated from other sources.

of the apartheid system, was reflected in relatively high levels of military expenditure, the central role of senior military personnel in decision making by the executive, the excessive use of force against civil society and a total lack of accountability and transparency in civil and military affairs.[1] In contrast, the newly elected Government of National Unity has brought with it a strong commitment to transparency, accountability, the rule of law, the empowerment of civil society, freedom of speech and civil control of the military. It has also laid emphasis on the socio-economic uplifting of the black majority in order to redress the economic legacies of apartheid. An emphasis on demilitarisation and the assertion of civil authority is reflected in the reallocation of government expenditures to meet the goals of the Reconstruction and Development Programme, the restructuring of the South African security forces and a downsizing of the defence industrial base.

Military expenditure has declined substantially since 1989. In real terms the military budget has decreased by over 50 per cent, from a high of 4 per cent of GDP in 1989 to just under 2 per cent in 1996 (Batchelor and Willett 1998; EIU 1995b, 1996d, 1996e). As a percentage of government expenditure, it declined from 19.6 per cent in 1989 to just over 10 per cent in 1995. The bulk of the defence cuts have been achieved by disbanding and scaling down various units of the defence force, closing military bases, ending conscription, reducing personnel in the procurement agency (ARMSCOR), selling off obsolete equipment and cancelling certain equipment projects.

Zimbabwe: Following the winding down of South Africa's destabilisation programme from 1989 onwards, Zimbabwe has haltingly introduced defence cuts. In the aftermath of the Mozambique Peace Accord and elections in October 1994, the costs associated with its operations in Mozambique virtually disappeared. Nominal military expenditure declined from about 6.1 per cent of GDP in 1990 to about 3.7 per cent in 1994, but subsequently increased to about 5 per cent in 1995/96. Yet as a percentage of government expenditures the 1994/95 defence budget allocations increased (EIU 1996f). There are two major reasons for this. First, there are short-run costs associated with the further demobilisation of troops, and secondly, it would appear that, despite agreeing to cut force levels over recent years in terms of the Economic Structural Adjustment Programme (ESAP), President Mugabe plans to re-equip and modernise the ZDF in line with the contemporary military trend for smaller, more professional and well equipped forces. However, under pressure from the World Bank and the IMF, overall defence expenditure has been targeted for a 40 per cent reduction in an attempt to reduce the public expenditure deficit (EIU 1996f). The military have been attempting to resist IMF-imposed cuts, but there is considerable pressure from the Zimbabwean public for the military to share more of the burden of public expenditure cuts (Baynham 1995).

Official figures on the distribution of resources within the defence budget suggest that wages and salaries account for a large proportion (about 70 per cent), with the procurement budget accounting for only 5 per cent of the total defence budget (Willett 1997). In 1996, official figures claimed that only Z$15 million was allocated to the procurement budget, a paltry sum by anyone's calculation. Press reports concerning shady procurement deals would suggest, however, that very little of the procurement budget is, in fact, transparent.[2] Under considerable pressure, the Ministry of Defence has been attempting to reorganise the military to make efficiency savings. Military camps have been closed and a brigade has been disbanded.[3] This reorganisation programme is running concurrently with the retrenchment exercise to reduce troop levels.

Mozambique: Mozambique's military expenditure is incorporated in the national defence and security budget, which includes spending on the police and intelligence services. The figures are not disaggregated so it is difficult to assess how much is being spent on the military. Moreover, official statistics on military expenditure must be treated with healthy scepticism as the Mozambican government lacks a tradition of transparency and accountability in this sensitive area. International sources indicate that defence expenditure remained at a high level in the early 1990s despite the cessation of hostilities in 1992. This was partly because the cost of demobilisation kept the defence and security budget high as a proportion of government expenditure until completion of that process in 1995. Since then, donors have applied considerable pressure on the government to reduce the country's defence burden. The US and UK governments, supported by the World Bank, have been the driving force behind this pressure. Initially the US pushed for a cut of some two-thirds, but following negotiations with the government, agreement was secured for a 30 per cent reduction.

Initially reluctant to impose cuts on military expenditure, the government now appears to accept the necessity of changing national priorities and reallocating resources to health and educational expenditures.[4] Defence expenditure is thought to have accounted for 4 per cent of GDP in 1996, which was coming into line with the regional average of 3–4 per cent of GDP.[5] Recurrent military expenditures were planned to fall by 36.7 per cent in real terms in 1995/96.[6]

Senior military personnel within the Ministry of Defence claim that the scale of the cuts has undermined the ability of the newly created army, the *Forcas Armadas de Defensa de Mocambique* (FADM), to transform itself into a professional army, as it lacks the resources to conduct training, equip troops, maintain bases, purchase fuel and even clothe and feed soldiers.[7] External observers confirm the point that, while a basic military structure is in place, it is not being maintained because of lack of resources.[8] The fact that the military maintained very large forces prior to demobilisation suggests that there should be more resources to spend per soldier despite existing cuts, but this assumes that soldiers were being paid during the civil war – something which was rarely the case. They survived by means of plunder, organised banditry and the support of peasants (Hanlon 1991). The present lack of resources can partly be explained by the fact that a larger proportion of the security budget is being allocated to the police force which is currently confronting a huge crime wave.[9] Not all observers are convinced, however, that the poor state of the military is due to the lack of resource allocation. They point to the widespread existence of corruption amongst senior officers and politicians who have been siphoning off resources for personal gain. This situation is likely to continue while Mozambique's defence budgetary process lacks transparency and accountability.

Botswana, Lesotho and Namibia: In the region there are three notable exceptions to the general trend of decline in military expenditures, namely, Botswana, Lesotho and Namibia, which have all recently reversed earlier cuts. Most of these increases are accounted for by outlays on new equipment. For instance, in 1995 and 1996 Botswana embarked on an ambitious programme of arms acquisitions, including the placing of orders for 36 Scorpion light tanks from Britain and F-5 combat aircraft from Canada (Rakabane 1997). An earlier attempt to buy 50 second-hand Leopard tanks and 200 army trucks from the Netherlands was blocked by Germany which found itself under intense lobbying pressure from Namibia (Brummer 1996). In addition to these purchases, Botswana plans to increase its troop levels from 7,500 to more than 10,000 soldiers and is building a hi-tech airbase in the southwest of the country with support from the United States. These trends have raised alarm among neighbouring countries, particularly Namibia which has a territorial dispute with Botswana (see Chapter 1). In response to these trends, Namibia has increased its defence budget in the last few years in order to purchase Russian equipment.

In justifying the growth in Botswana's military capabilities, military leaders argue that they need to be ready for any eventuality and that the current peaceful situation in southern Africa may not endure. Perhaps more convincingly, the Botswanan army needs to equip itself for peacekeeping operations. To date, it has been involved in peacekeeping in both Mozambique and Somalia. Peacekeeping needs a considerable amount of equipment for logistical support, but it is questionable whether tanks and aircraft are required for this task. A more likely explanation for the military build-up lies in the fact that dynamic economic growth has enabled Botswana's leaders to purchase the prestige symbols of an emerging sovereign state.

While Namibia may have genuine cause for concern over the implications of Botswana's enhanced military capability, South Africa's reaction has been somewhat alarmist (Brummer 1996). South Africa's military expenditure may be below 2 per cent of GDP, but it represents almost twice the combined military expenditures of all its neighbours put together, enabling it to retain an overwhelming military balance of power in the region (Table 2.3). Moreover, the scale of Botswana's military acquisitions pales into insignificance besides South Africa's planned purchases of corvettes, combat aircraft and submarines. Given this fact and South Africa's role in regional destabilisation in the not too distant past, the onus is on the new South African government to build confidence and trust about its intentions within the region and to overcome the residual fears that still exist about its hegemonic intentions.

Force Levels and Integration

In the immediate aftermath of a conflict there is an urgent need to restructure the military and paramilitary police forces. The creation of a professional and accountable military is a prerequisite for political stabilisation. It is also crucial for the process of reconciliation in deeply divided societies. The new military force should be representative of the population as a whole and contain a well balanced mixture of previous adversaries. Creating such a force is a delicate process, and as the cases of Zimbabwe and South Africa show (see below), there can be a benefit from the presence and mediation of politically neutral and professional advisers such as the British Military Advisory Training Team (BMATT).

Table 2.3   *Military balance: southern Africa*

Country	Milex *	Armed Forces	MB T	AP C	AIF V	ART Y	Cbt.Air	HEL	Ships
Angola	n/a	82,000	200	100	50	300	109	40	10
Botswana	229	7,500	36	30	none	16	21	none	n/a
Lesotho	26	2,000	none	none	none	2	none	none	n/a
Malawi	13	8,000	none	none	none	9	none	1	n/a
Mozambique	104	12,000	80	250	40	100	43	4	10
Namibia	56	8,100	none	20	none	none	none	none	none
South Africa	2,899	100,000	250	3,000	1500	390	243	14	1
Tanzania	69	34,600	75	100	none	300	24	none	22
Zambia	39	21,600	30	13	none	100	59	12	n/a
Zimbabwe	188	45,000	40	100	none	20	52	none	n/a

Source: *The Military Balance, 1995/96*, IISS, London; US Arms Control and Disarmament Agency (1996) *World Military Expenditures and Arms Transfers, 1995.*

Note: *Military Expenditure (1994 US$ m)

The BMATT not only trains soldiers and helps restructure the forces, but also assists in the setting up of efficient decision-making structures and inculcates a sense of professionalism and new values concomitant with the role of the military in a democratic society. The British are almost unique in providing such support and much more of this type of activity could be undertaken by the donor community.

South Africa's transition to legitimate non-racial rule prompted a major refocusing of Britain's military training assistance programme in the region and beyond. In consultation with the countries concerned, the emphasis has shifted to providing military training as a tool for preventative diplomacy and peacekeeping. In practice, this means the building of capacity so that African states can undertake peackeeping duties internationally, an issue being promoted by the UN and some foreign donors but hotly debated within Africa. Such roles clearly require a rather different orientation and training from conventional military activities. Accordingly, and also to maximise the effectiveness of such training, BMATTs were reorganised on a regional basis in 1994. Apart from the South African involvement, which is due to end in 1997/8, there are now two modest regional BMATTs, one for West Africa based in Accra, and another for southern Africa, based in Harare. According to informed sources, the latter comprises eight officers under the command of a brigadier. The principal focus is on armies, with naval or air force training provided if necessary. The BMATTs are funded by the Foreign and Commonwealth Office and the Department for International Development (until 1 May 1997 the Overseas Development Administration) in pursuance of three linked goals: strengthening links between the UN and regional organisations; helping to train African troops; and building up logistical capacities (Rifkind 1996). The actual training is undertaken in different countries of the region, involving both soldiers from individual countries and joint groups. For example, in April 1997, a joint peacekeeping training exercise involved some 200 soldiers from nine SADC countries, including – for the first time – South Africa. This was naturally therefore very significant politically, symbolising collective hopes for regional peace and co-operation[10].

Zimbabwe: At the end of Zimbabwe's civil war in 1980 there were roughly 130,000 combatants, of whom 97,000 were in the Rhodesian Security Forces, 20,000 were Zimbabwe African National Liberation Army (ZANLA) guerrillas and some 10–12,000 were Zimbabwe Independent People's Revolutionary Army (ZIPRA) forces.[11] Following independence and the election in 1980, elements of these three armies were merged to form a new national army, the Zimbabwean Defence Force (ZDF) of some 51,000 people. After some major problems in the early stages of integration, the BMATT team was invited in. Initially 58 strong, but quickly expanded to 150, it was instrumental in ensuring the success of Zimbabwe's integration programme and in creating what is now perceived to be one of Africa's most professional armies (Rupiyah 1995).

South Africa: Inspired by the Zimbabwean experience, the Government of National Unity invited BMATT to oversee the process of integration in South Africa in 1994. Total personnel, including civilians, of the integrated forces in the newly created South African National Defence Force (SANDF) has been put at 130,000, representing a 30 per cent increase over pre-integration levels.[12] The integrated forces consist of the former South African Defence Force (SADF), together with the defence forces of the former 'independent' homelands, Transkei, Bophuthatswana, Venda and Ciskei (TBVC) and the opposition forces of the ANC, namely, Umkonto we Sizwe and the Azanian People's Liberation Army (APLA) of the Pan African Congress. Integration was expected to be completed by the end of 1997.[13] The basic structure of the SANDF differs little from its predecessor, the SADF, in that it is composed of four services, namely, the army, navy, air force and medical service and supporting staff departments. Conscription has, however, been ended and a greater emphasis is being placed on the development of professional and technologically advanced military forces. The new military doctrine emphasises the maintenance of a peacetime core fighting force of some 37,000 whose numbers can rapidly be built up to around 300,000 in times of tension with the use of reserves from the Citizen Force (trained civilian reserve force).

In post-apartheid South Africa the integration of forces is seen as an important political process designed to facilitate reconciliation in the course of building a multi-ethnic force representative of the nation as a whole. Despite the often claimed success of integration within the SANDF, it has not been without its problems. For instance, the ethnic composition of the SANDF, which has undoubtedly improved with integration, may deteriorate with the start of demobilisation during 1997. Fears are being voiced that a large percentage of demobilised soldiers come from the non-statutory forces which, almost by definition, are black. Moreover, there is considerable controversy within the armed forces about the continued domination of whites within the military hierarchy. In the near future more than half the handful of senior black officers above the rank of colonel will be retiring. Simultaneously, attempts to 'fast track' black officers through the ranks create huge resentment amongst white career officers who are more experienced. Resentment towards positive discrimination has led many white officers to take severance pay and leave the force.

Another problem created by integration is budgetary. The total costs of integration are estimated at R2.2bn, placing upward pressure on the staff budget and operating costs at the expense of the capital expenditure budget.[14] This makes it very difficult for the SANDF to find the resources to meet its current equipment requirements.

Mozambique: Mozambique's experience with integration has been far more problematic than the difficulties experienced in South Africa. Under the 1992 Rome Peace Accord it was agreed to create a new national army, the FADM, by integrating 30,000 Frelimo and Renamo combatants. The idea was to draw 15,000 soldiers from each force. In the event, only about 8,000 to 11,000 troops have volunteered,[15] a large proportion of them officers rather than other ranks, thus making the armed forces very top heavy. It is thought that low pay and the demobilisation package offered to ex-combatants by the UNDP, combined with combat fatigue, have created strong disincentives for combatants to volunteer for the armed services. From a national security perspective this is highly embarrassing for the Mozambique government.

As military spokesmen from the FADM point out, under existing budgetary allocations they can barely feed and barrack the existing number of soldiers, let alone the full complement of 30,000. Moreover, there are no resources for training or equipment to turn the FADM into a professional army. Certain foreign diplomatic missions in Mozambique, such as the British, Portuguese and US, recognise these problems as genuine and have recently decided to contribute some resources for the training and restructuring of the FADM.

Angola: Angola's attempt at creating an integrated army has been beset with insurmountable difficulties. It was planned to incorporate 26,000 UNITA soldiers into the newly created national army, the *Forcas Armadas de Angola* (FAA), which is finally to number 90,000. However, as of 18 February 1997, only 6,053 UNITA soldiers had been formally integrated into the FAA (*Angola Peace Monitor* 1997a). The exercise has been proceeding very slowly because of the interference by UNITA commanders in the selection and incorporation procedures, and poor planning and logistical difficulties experienced by the FAA. In addition, many UNITA soldiers have deserted the assembly camps. In his report to the UN Security Council in March 1997, the UN Secretary General, Kofi Annan, declared that there had been 26,407 desertions by 4 March.

The process of integration has been hampered by the deep mistrust and hostility of the opposing forces in Angola. The UNAVEM III mission overseeing the process of integration withdrew in August 1997 on the expiry of its mandate. However, as the integration and demobilisation had not been completed on schedule, a new observer mission, MONUA, was established for a limited period, which expires shortly after the current demobilisation target date of 28 February 1998. There are still a number of flashpoints in the southern part of the country between government troops and UNITA (although these may be deserters), and there are a growing number of reports that UNITA has been stockpiling new weapons (*Angola Peace Monitor* 1996a, 1996c, 1997c). Moreover, it is almost certain that UNITA's elite troops were not sent to UN quartering areas.

Demobilisation and Reintegration

The successful demobilisation and reintegration of former combatants into civilian life is a crucial condition for political stability and the rebuilding of war-torn societies. In post-conflict situations, it is generally a matter of priority for governments, which often call for international assistance with various aspects of their demobilisation programmes.

The demobilisation and reintegration of former combatants are closely linked stages of a complex process. Demobilisation is the procedure of converting combatants, whether belonging to an official army or to guerrilla forces, into civilians. As a general rule, this process begins with the assembly of former combatants in special areas or camps (cantonments), where they surrender their weapons and uniforms and await final discharge. Demobilisation is completed when combatants have received their discharge papers and formally left the military command structure. Reintegration, which only happens over time, implies both that former combatants are accepted as full members of their community and that they attain full self-sufficiency through productive employment.

In a region such as southern Africa, where systemic poverty and unemployment have been exacerbated by the devastating effects of war, demobilisation and reintegration have been found to be much more demanding than governments, NGOs and multilateral organisations initially expected. There is always the risk, confirmed in practice, that where demobilisation has been poorly conducted, unpaid or undisciplined troops have turned into renegade bandits preying on villagers and road traffic, or have even remobilised to form insurgencies challenging the established regime. Apart from its effect on political stability, this kind of insecurity can have a devastating effect on economic activity. The challenge is to develop cost-effective demobilisation programmes which are deemed satisfactory to the former combatants themselves.

South Africa: The South African government planned to start the demobilisation of around 30,000 soldiers before the end of 1997. The process is due to be phased over a three-year period, with completion at the end of 1999. The cost of demobilisation is to be borne by the defence budget, a factor which will ensure that the personnel budget will remain relatively high in the short to medium term. In contrast to many other countries in the region, demobilisation will be paid for by the South African taxpayer with little or no external financing. Demobilised troops will be given skills training to prepare them for civilian life. There has been some concern about the ability of ex-combatants to be fully reintegrated into civilian life as unemployment is very high in South Africa, particularly within the black community where it is reported to be as high as 50 per cent (Handley and Mills 1996). In the absence of employment opportunities, the potential for ex-combatants to fall into crime is great. There is also the possibility of ex-combatants becoming involved in localised conflict. Following the absenteeism of a considerable number of ex-guerrillas from the Walmenstal assembly camp in October 1994, there were reports of ex-combatants becoming involved in the violence in KwaZulu-Natal.

In addition to demobilisation it is expected that there will be a significant number of retrenchments as long-serving military personnel take advantage of the voluntary severance packages being offered to all public sector workers in the government's attempt to reduce the number of public sector employees. Force levels are expected to stabilise at around 75,000 once demobilisation has been completed by the end of the century.

Zimbabwe: Under considerable donor and domestic pressure, the Zimbabwean government is officially committed to reducing force numbers from 51,000 in 1992 to 40,000 by the end of the century.[16] It appears that President Mugabe is keen to retain relatively high numbers in the military, partly because of the debt he owes to those who fought for independence, but also because he has aspirations for power in the region, particularly through the role of peacekeeping, which requires relatively high personnel levels. At the time of writing (May 1997), Zimbabwe has 1,000 soldiers deployed as peacekeepers in Angola. However, according to one analyst, the only way that Zimbabwe can maintain a professional and well equipped military force within the context of the present budgetary constraints is by cutting military personnel by at least 20,000 to bring troop levels down to 25,000.[17] This is likely to be achieved by a combination of demobilisation, natural wastage and a freeze on recruitment.

The demobilisation of troops is to be phased over a period of time to prevent problems of criminality arising within civil society from the presence of large numbers of disbanded soldiers. Having learnt the hard way from its previous demobilisation programme in the early 1980s, when many soldiers ended up destitute, the government has gone to some lengths to develop training programmes for its recent round of demobilisation, incorporating carpentry, metal work and agricultural skills training as well as business training for the more educated soldiers. This programme has only been made possible, however, through a significant aid contribution from the European Union.

Mozambique: In Mozambique demobilisation has been orchestrated by the UN peacekeeping missions. Some 93,000 soldiers have been demobilised since the end of the war in 1992. Until May 1996 the ex-combatants were receiving demobilisation pay from the UNDP, but this has run out and it is unclear how the vast majority of demobilised soldiers will now sustain themselves economically. Without any hope of income generation, certain groups have returned to the sort of banditry which occurred regularly in the lead-up to the election. This tends to be geographically concentrated in urban areas. Anecdotal evidence suggests that the rise in crime in Maputo and Beira is linked to the large presence of demobilised soldiers, although some observers point to the fact that few of the criminals who are caught are in fact ex-soldiers. This difference of opinion reflects a broader disagreement about the success or failure of demobilisation in Mozambique. While there has certainly not been the level of expected banditry that some had predicted, it would be naive to assume that adjustment to civilian life has been unproblematic (e.g. Government of Mozambique 1995). AMODEG, the association for demobilised soldiers, has reported that many ex-combatants feel that their interests have been overlooked in the postwar settlement. Demonstrations and roadblocks set up by ex-combatants are a regular feature along major roads and are becoming increasingly sinister. AMODEG has encouraged peaceful protests, but in Zambezia and Sofala provinces there have been violent riots and mutinies. The weakness of the newly created army and the poor discipline of the police force suggest that it will be difficult to contain such a situation if it continues unabated.

Angola: In Angola, the 1994 Lusaka Protocol demanded that government troops be disengaged and that over 62,000 UNITA soldiers be confined to assembly areas and disarmed. Not all of these were due to be demobilised: some 40,000 UNITA troops are to be deployed in the unarmed 'fourth arm' of the FAA, which is designed to utilise demobilised soldiers to carry out rebuilding and reconstruction work. A further 5,000 UNITA members are to be incorporated into the national police force and the *Policia de Intervenção Rapida* (PIR), or Rapid Intervention Police. With the disbanded MPLA troops, a total of about 100,000 combatants are planned to be demobilised (Saferworld 1996).

UNAVEM III has experienced enormous problems with the demobilisation process, largely due to the lack of co-operation, particularly from UNITA, which consistently slowed down the process by resisting the confinement of its combatants. Under threat of sanctions by the UN, however, UNITA completed the quartering of 63,000 troops by 20 November 1996 (*Angola Peace Monitor* 1996c). About 7,000 of those registered were found to be under the age of 18. The *Angolan Peace Monitor* (1996b) reported that over 70 per cent of those quartered were not combat forces. Many observers believe that Savimbi has retained his best soldiers in the strategically vital regions of the Lunda provinces and Cabinda. Meanwhile, because of the delays, soldiers in the cantonment camps grew restless and desertions became commonplace. By November 1996, some 12,543 UNITA soldiers had deserted, leaving 55,013 in the camps (EIU 1995a, 1996a).[18]

The general state of economic collapse in Angola has become a direct threat to the reintegration process as the economy is currently unable to absorb such large numbers of demobilised soldiers. Resources for their retraining have not been forthcoming from the international community. Consequently it is unlikely that the ex-combatants will be able to reintegrate into civilian life. With Savimibi able to generate resources from illegal diamond mining in Lunda Province, he always has the option to carry on the war and pay his elite soldiers. Under these circumstances, the chances of success with the demobilisation of UNITA troops seem remote. There has been an uncomfortable feeling in Angola that history may be about to repeat itself. It may be, however, that the overthrow of President Mobuto Sese Seko in Zaire in May 1997 will have a positive effect in Angola, as Savimbi's lifeline for arms is cut off and the conduit for his illegal diamond business dissolves, thus forcing UNITA to comply and co-operate with the peace process (*Angola Peace Monitor* 1997b).

Demobilisation and reintegration are prerequisites for internal stability and development in post-conflict societies. Yet the experiences of Angola, Mozambique, South Africa and Zimbabwe suggest the need to avoid expeditious mass demobilisation, so as to reduce the risks of creating a large pool of disaffected ex-combatants, which would be conducive to the spread of crime and banditry and in extreme cases, such as Angola, may precipitate a return to war.

Slowing down the pace of demobilisation will inevitably limit the scope for reducing military expenditures in the short run and therefore for improving budget deficits. Donors who are pressurising countries in the region to make deeper cuts in their defence budgets need to balance long-term stability gains against short-term economic stabilisation objectives in what can only be described as a highly sensitive transition process. This is because, in the short to medium term, the general acquiescence of soldiers to disarm and demobilise depends chiefly on the extent to which the security environment and the viability of the continuing political processes are seen to be taking shape (Berdal 1996). In the long term, however, social and economic progress reflected in enhanced employment opportunities, food security and welfare provision are the definitive factors which will ensure effective demobilisation and reintegration into civilian life.

Regional Security Co-operation

Peace and democracy are by no means guaranteed while a wide range of structural problems continue to dominate the region. These include the mass migration of political and economic refugees (Chapter 11), environmental degradation, the exhaustion of natural resources, the proliferation of small arms (Chapter 3), and international crime syndicates dealing in drugs and stolen cars, all of which transcend national borders and require co-operative solutions if further conflict is to be avoided at some future date. Ensuring long-term peace and stability in the region requires a commitment to resolve these continuing sources of conflict.

At a regional level, attempts to tackle these structural problems are taking place through the Southern African Development Community (SADC) (Chapter 10). Areas of common interest identified as a catalyst for bringing the states of southern Africa closer together include the mutual development of water resources, conservation of soil and water, improved communications and the planning of a southern African electricity power grid (Chapter 9), the promotion of regional trade and the eradication of cross-border crime. At its 1992 inaugural meeting, SADC also committed itself to regional co-operation on political, military and security issues. Moves towards regional security co-operation were influenced, in part, by the formation of the Conference on Security, Stability, Development and Co-operation in Africa (CSSDCA) in 1991, which in turn was modelled on the Conference on Security and Co-operation in Europe (CSCE) (Nathan 1992). The CSSDCA stressed the critical relationship between peace and development on the African continent, as well as emphasising that the security and stability of each African country are inescapably connected to the security of all African states. The CSSDCA adopted an integrated approach to security, grouping policy proposals in four 'calabashes' — security, stability, development and co-operation (African Leadership Forum 1991). The founding document of the SADC provided the following motivations for its mandate on political, military and security issues:

> War and insecurity are the enemy of economic progress and social welfare. Good and strengthened political relations among countries of the region, and peace and mutual security, are critical components of the total environment for regional co-operation and integration. The region needs, therefore, to establish a framework and mechanisms to strengthen regional solidarity and provide for mutual peace and security (SADC 1992).

SADC has proposed a similar framework to guide the Regional Security Council (RSC), on which all governments are to be represented. It is designed to act as a forum for joint consultation on a wide range of conflict prevention and peacekeeping issues. The long-term objective of the regional security regime is to engage the region in active security dialogue and prevent conflicts from breaking out, or, should this fail, to contain conflicts and end them. The range of issues embraced by the SADC's interpretation of security has liberated the concept from its preoccupation with state-centred perspectives that focus almost entirely on threats to the regime and its interests, namely regime security, to one that is more inclusive and covers political, developmental and economic threats to society. These determinants are interlinked and it is now widely recognised that emphasising one above the others can have detrimental effects on national security. It follows that security does not rest on force alone, or even upon the threat of force.

The formalisation of SADC's security aspirations took place in January 1996, when SADC Ministers for Defence and Foreign Affairs met in Gaborone, Botswana, to agree the terms of reference for the setting up of a SADC Organ on Politics, Defence and Security.[19] Progress towards achieving SADC's security goals is, however, constrained by the lack of established procedures and mechanisms and of the relevant skills and techniques required for conflict resolution and mediation. To date mediation efforts, such as in the Lesotho crisis, have tended to be *ad hoc*, reactive and somewhat heavy-handed, although more recent attempts by South Africa to mediate regional problems, as in the case of the Zairean crisis prior to Mobutu's overthrow, suggest a maturing of methods.

So far it is in military forms of co-operation that most progress has been made. This may be explained partly by the fact that the military have at their disposal more resources than other parts of the SADC machinery. The role of the SANDF is particularly important in this respect. Following requests from neighbouring states, it has developed programmes to enhance their defence capabilities through military assistance and training, logistical support and disaster relief. In an attempt to improve the SANDF's capacity to conduct combined operations in the region, the South Africans have offered the resources and experience of ARMSCOR as a regional arms procurement agency. Exchanges of personnel and observers, combined exercises, and the opening up of SANDF training establishments are some of the practical measures taken recently in order to improve regional confidence and security.

Moreover, there is strong support within certain quarters of the South African establishment for selling South African armaments to regional neighbours, ostensibly to assist allies and friends, while simultaneously facilitating combined military operations as and when required (Cilliers 1995). The South African arms lobby has argued that dependence on the major Western military suppliers can compromise national security policies. However, such altruism is hardly the reason for promoting arms sales within the region; the primary motivation derives from commercial and political advantages for South Africa. The policy would enhance scale economies for the South African defence industry at a time when domestic arms requirements are declining, and create long-term regional customers for spares, repairs and replacements.

Ultimately, the potential for realising SADC's broader security goals depends upon establishing a genuine collective identity at the regional level, something likely to prove difficult in practice. It is questionable whether a collective sense of purpose can bind the countries of the region in the way that opposition to apartheid did among the former Frontline states; a loose alliance based on geographical contiguity may be the most likely outcome. With South Africa now a key actor in the evolution of any future regional security arrangement, the issue of convergence of interests and complementarity with its neighbours is central to the prospects for regional integration and a collective agenda (Solomon and Cilliers 1996). Thus although the security debate highlights regional integration, there is growing concern among South Africa's neighbours that the evolution of SADC may weaken national sovereignty and individual national interests. Residual fears about South Africa's hegemonic intentions and rivalry for regional influence are contributing to an underlying unease within SADC. In particular, President Mugabe of Zimbabwe, who was the leader of the Frontline states, is believed to resent being usurped from his position as a regional leader by South Africa's dominance in regional security issues. Partly as a result of these fears, common security efforts are currently confined to *ad hoc* co-operative measures rather than the establishment of a formal security alliance. Even in those areas with the greatest potential for deeper future interaction, such as conflict resolution and peacekeeping (see below), policies are evolving in a somewhat haphazard manner, with little support among members for a formalised decision-making institutional framework.

One important area for regional confidence and security building through military co-operation has been the development of a regional peacekeeping force with South Africa's participation. Given the role of South Africa's troops within the region less than a decade ago, this has enormous import (Shaw and Cilliers 1995; Solomon and Cilliers 1996). As noted earlier, in April 1997, soldiers from nine southern African countries took part in peacekeeping training in Nyanga in north-eastern Zimbabwe under the expert guidance of BMATT. Funding for the programme was provided by the British Foreign and Commonwealth Office, which contributed £300,000, a sum matched by the Zimbabwean government (Meldrum 1997). Major Cobus Valentine of the SANDF is reported to have said of this process, 'This is the first time we are part of a regional peacekeeping force. We are building a foundation of understanding and co-operation for the future. This will only get stronger.' (*ibid*). Although the primary purpose of building a regional peacekeeping force is for Africans to take more responsibility for security on the African continent, it also acts as a regional confidence and security building measure by bringing former adversaries together to work towards the common cause of peace (Solomon and Cilliers 1996).

The participation of southern African forces in international peacekeeping is, however, constrained by the lack of adequate resources, particularly at a time when governments are under considerable external pressure to keep military expenditure down. Logistical problems are particularly acute owing to the lack of procurement resources. The international community appears oblivious to this contradiction in its policy approach. If it wants southern African countries to take on more responsibility for the continent, then certain concessions need to be made. Apart from providing financial resources, donors could do much more in providing support for training and preparing peacekeeping units, particularly in the use of specialised and heavy equipment, transport systems and complex logistical support systems, which is the backbone of most peace support operations.

Conclusions

In southern Africa, tangible steps have been taken towards demilitarisation and disarmament in an attempt to secure long-term peace and security in the region. Both are prerequisites for the more profound task of tackling the underlying structural causes of insecurity which have been at the heart of this region's violent past. Despite concerted attempts at demilitarisation, significant problems have been encountered with the demobilisation and reintegration of troops. This suggests that far greater long-term support needs to be provided by external agencies to encourage the full reintegration of ex-combatants into civilian life. At the root of this problem lies the need to create greater economic security for all, particularly in a post-conflict situation where the existing structural problems have been compounded by the carnage and destruction of war. The challenge of fully reintegrating ex-combatants into civil society is linked to the task of post-conflict economic reconstruction, which is all too often neglected by those international agencies concerned with peace-building and post-conflict resolution.

Much needs to be done to address the particular needs of post-conflict economies, and to recognise the exceptionality of their situation, the fragility of their stability and their propensity for collapse, before embarking upon standard economic recovery packages. Here it is important to recognise the role of international agencies, not just as neutral agents but as active accelerators of either peace or conflict. To an extent, international agencies are becoming more proactive in their attempts to facilitate post-conflict recovery, as witnessed by donor insistence that governments cut military expenditures. But this in itself provides no guarantee that the most vulnerable in society will benefit from any subsequent peace dividend.

At a regional level, donors could play an important role in supporting capacity building within the SADC, to strengthen its institutions and provide training and support for its role in mediation. But perhaps more importantly, donors should target development programmes which will help to enhance the moves towards regional economic co-operation. Economic insecurity remains the single largest threat to the region's long-term stability. Donor support to enhance sustainable development and strengthen civil society is thus vital to the durability of peace and democracy within the region (Stewart and Wilson 1994). The desirability of such goals meets with universal acceptance, yet the difficulties of their attainment, challenging at the best of times, are compounded by the economic dislocation and destruction of war and by the legacy of protracted militarism and political repression. Countering this negative legacy, the progress towards demilitarisation and democracy within the region gives some cause for optimism, particularly in view of the possibility of using defence savings to stimulate socio-economic gains – the so-called peace dividend discussed in Chapter 1.

Notes

1. For an account of the militarisation of South African society in the 1980s, see Cock and Nathan (1989).
2. 'Ministry of Defence pledges to improve accountability', *Herald,* 25 September 1996.
3. '4 camps closed as army streamlines its resources' *Herald,* 5 February 1996.
4. Improvements are sought in both the coverage and the quality of the health and education services. A coherent national health strategy is now being developed and is supported by a consortium of donors including the UK's DFID (formerly the ODA). The programme is designed to increase basic health coverage from 40 to 60 per cent of the population by 2000, with a particular emphasis on improvements in child and maternal health care services.
5. Interview with Mike McKinley, Chargé d'Affaires, US Embassy, Maputo, 20 November 1996.
6. Although no reliable figures exist, some informed observers estimate that the defence and security budget was around US $71mn in 1996, equivalent to about 4.2 per cent of GDP (see also EIU 1996b, 1996c).
7. This problem was raised by Colonel Bange from the Mozambique MoD and confirmed in interviews with Mike McKinley from the US Embassy, Maputo,(20 November 1996) and Jeff Livesey from the UK High Commission.
8. This assertion is based on the eye-witness account of Jeff Livesey, the Deputy British High Commissioner, who has travelled extensively around the country visiting army bases. Such accounts were confirmed by US embassy officials.
9. The police are now thought to receive a greater share of the defence budget than the military, which is appropriate given the rising rate of crime and the lack of any immediate external threat to Mozambique's territorial sovereignty.
10. I am grateful to David Simon for these details.
11. These figures are based on estimates presented in Rupiyah (1995).

12. This is an official figure, but in reality personnel numbers are thought to be lower as a result of desertions and failures of non-statutory forces to register at assembly points.
13. Briefing on the Defence Budget to Portfolio Committee on Defence, Cape Town, 4 April 1995.
14. *ibid.*; see also EIU 1995b, 1996d.
15. No precise figures exist; these estimates are based on those of the external assessments by the British and US missions in Mozambique.
16. Interview with Brigadier Ruwodo, Director of Finance, Ministry of Defence, Harare, 26 November 1996.
17. Interview with Martin Rupiyah, University of Zimbabwe, Harare, 25 November 1996.
18. UNITA has blamed the desertions on poor living conditions and bad food in the camps (See EIU 1996a: 10).
19. SADC statement *The SADC Organ on Politics, Defence and Security* issued by the Meeting of SADC Ministers Responsible for Foreign Affairs, Defence and SADC Affairs, Gaborone, Botswana, 18 January 1996.

References

African Leadership Forum (1991) *The Kampala Document: Towards a Conference on Security, Stability, Development and Co-operation*, ALF, Lagos.
Angola Peace Monitor (1996a), Vol III(2), October, London.
Angola Peace Monitor (1996b) Vol III(3), November, London.
Angola Peace Monitor (1996c) Vol III(4), December, London.
Angola Peace Monitor (1997a) Vol III(8), April, London.
Angola Peace Monitor (1997b) Vol III(9), May, London.
Angola Peace Monitor (1997c) Vol IV(4) December, London.
Azar, E. (1990) *The Management of Protracted Social Conflict: Theory and Cases*. Dartmouth, Aldershot, UK.
Batchelor, P. and Willett, S. (1998) *Disarmament and Defence Industrial Adjustment in South Africa*. Oxford University Press, Oxford for SIPRI.
Baynham, S. (1995) 'Zimbabwe: Pax Africana', *African Security Review*, 4(3): 50–52.
Berdal, M. (1996) *Disarmament and Demobilisation after Civil Wars: Arms, Soldiers and the Termination of Armed Conflict*. Adelphi Paper, No 303. Oxford University Press, Oxford for the International Institute of Strategic Studies.
Borges Coelho, J. and Vines, A. (1995) *Demobilisation and Re-integration of Ex-combatants in Mozambique*, Refugees Studies Programme, University of Oxford.
Brummer, S. (1996) 'Botswana Splashes Out on Arms', *Weekly Mail and Guardian*, 4 April, Johannesburg.
Cilliers, J. (1995) 'Towards a South African Conventional Arms Trade Policy', *African Security Review*, 4(4): 3–20.
Cock, J. and Nathan, L.(eds) (1989) *War and Society: The Militarisation of South Africa*. David Philip, Cape Town.
Economist Intelligence Unit (1995a) *Country Profile, Angola 1995–96*. EIU, London.
Economist Intelligence Unit (1995b) *Country Profile, South Africa 1994–95*. EIU, London.
Economist Intelligence Unit (1996a) *Country Report, Angola, 3rd quarter 1996*. EIU, London.
Economist Intelligence Unit (1996b) *Country Report, Mozambique, Malawi 3rd quarter 1996*. EIU, London.
Economist Intelligence Unit (1996c) *Country Profile, Mozambique 1995–96*. EIU, London.
Economist Intelligence Unit (1996d) *Country Report, South Africa; 2nd quarter 1996*. EIU, London.
Economist Intelligence Unit (1996e) *Country Report, South Africa: 3rd quarter 1996*. EIU, London.
Economist Intelligence Unit (1996f) *Country Profile, Zimbabwe 1995–96*. EIU, London.
Government of Mozambique, (1995) *Establishing the Basis for Economic and Social Development: Key Policies*. Report Prepared by the Government of Mozambique for the Meeting of the Consultative Group Meeting for Mozambique, Paris, March.
George, P. (1996) 'The Impact of South Africa's Arms Sales Policy on Regional Military Expenditure, Development and Security', in *Sakerhet och utveckling i AFRICA*. Utrikesdepartement, Ds 1995, Norstedts Tryckeri Ab, Stockholm.
Handley, A. and Mills, G. (1996)(eds) *From Isolation to Integration: The South African Economy in the 1990s*, South African Institute of International Affairs, Johannesburg.
Hanlon, J. (1991) *Mozambique: Who Calls the Shots?* James Currey, London.
International Institute of Strategic Studies (Various) *The Military Balance*. Brassey's, London for the IISS.
Meldrum, A. (1997) 'Africans Practise Art of Regional Peacekeeping', *The Guardian*, London, 14 April.

Nathan, L. (1992) 'Beyond Arms and Armed forces: a New Approach to Security', *South African Defence Review* 15: 12–21.

OECD (1996) 'Draft DAC Policy Orientations for Development Co-operation in Conflict Prevention and Post-Conflict Recovery', DCD/DAC(96)31. Paris.

Ohlson, T. and Stedman, J.S. with Davies, R. (1994) *The New is Not Yet Born: Conflict Resolution in Southern Africa*. The Brookings Institution, Washington, DC.

Peck, C. (1996) 'Organisations and Co-operation in Preventive Diplomacy: Strategic Management and Co-ordination', paper presented at workshop on 'An Agenda for Preventive Diplomacy: Theory and Practice', Skopje, Macedonia, 16–19 October.

Rakabane, M. (1997) 'Bizarre Arms Race', *New African*, London, January.

Rifkind, M. (1996) 'Africa – Time to Take Another Look?' Speech by the Foreign Secretary, Malcolm Rifkind, to the Royal Institute of International Affairs, Chatham House, London. 28 November.

Rupiyah, M. (1995) 'Demobilization and Integration: "Operation Merger" and the Zimbabwe National Defence Forces, 1980–1987, in Cilliers, J. (ed.) *Dismissed: Demobilisation and Reintegration of Former Combatants in Africa*. Institute for Defence Policy, Halfway House, South Africa.

Rupiyah, M. (1996) 'Post War Restructuring in Southern Africa: The Region's Defence Structures', Department of History, University of Zimbabwe, Harare (mimeo).

Saferworld (1996) *Angola: Conflict Resolution and Peace-building*. Saferworld Report, London, September.

Shaw, M. and Cilliers, J. (eds)(1995) *South Africa and Peacekeeping in Africa*, Vol. 1. Institute for Defence Policy, Midrand, South Africa.

Solomon, H. and Cilliers, J. (1996) 'People, Poverty and Peace: Human Security in Southern Africa', *IDP Monograph Series*, No. 4, May.

South African Ministry of Defence, (1996) *Defence in a Democracy: White Paper on Defence, 1996*, Pretoria, May.

Southern African Development Community (1992) *Towards the Southern African Development Community: A Declaration by the Heads of State or Governments of Southern African States*. SADC, Windhoek.

Southern African Development Community (1993) *Southern Africa: A Framework and Strategy for Building the Community*. SADC, Harare, January.

Southern African Development Community (1996) *The SADC Organ on Politics, Defence and Security*, Statement issued by the meeting of SADC Ministers responsible for Foreign Affairs, Defence and SADC Affairs, Gaborone, Botswana, 18 January.

Stewart, F. and Wilson, K. (1994) 'Conflict and Development: What Kinds of Policies Can Reduce the Damaging Impact of War?' in Tansey, J. *et al.* (eds) *A World Divided: Militarism and Development After the Cold War*. Earthscan, London.

US Arms Control and Disarmament Agency *(1996) World Military Expenditures and Arms Transfers 1995*. US Government Printing Office, Washington, DC.

Von Hipple, K. (1997) 'The Proliferation of Collapsed States in the Post-Cold War World' in CDS (ed.), *Brassey's Defence Yearbook 1997*. Brassey's, London.

Willett, S. (1997) *Military Expenditure Trends and development Co-operation in Southern Africa: South Africa, Angola, Zimbabwe and Mozambique*. Report prepared for the Development Co-operation Directorate, OECD, Paris, January.

World Bank (1995) *Memorandum of the President of the International Development Association to the Executive Directors on a Country Assistance Strategy of the World Bank Group for the Republic of Mozambique*. Report No 15067-MOZ, Southern African Department, World Bank, Washington, DC, 7 November.

Zartman, W. (ed.) (1995) *Collapsed States: The Disintegration and Restoration of Legitimate Authority*. Lynne Rienner, Boulder, CO and London.

3 Small Arms Proliferation: A Major Challenge for Post-apartheid South and Southern Africa

ALEX VINES

Introduction

Small arms have long been viewed as an insignificant fringe of the conventional arms trade. But the end of the Cold War has changed that: while sales of major weapons have declined, the trade in light weapons, including small arms, has increased significantly and has become uncontrolled, with separatist groups, criminal syndicates and beleaguered governments all purchasing significant amounts of weaponry. The manufacture and international trade of these weapons remain highly decentralised, with ever cheaper products. Nearly 300 companies in more than 50 countries are involved in the industry. The collapse of the Soviet Union in 1991 and the absence of any effective export controls have also added to the flood of weapons on to the market, exacerbated further by large quantities of surplus weapons from past conflicts making their way to new conflict zones through a growing network of semi-official and secret arms pipelines (Berdal 1996: 18–20).

One of the most important defining characteristics of a light weapon is that it does not require any form of infrastructural support to facilitate its use. Unlike weapon systems, a light weapon can be used with minimal training and expertise. Light weapons also benefit from a low rate of obsolescence, which means that they remain useful over a long period. Small arms appeal to smugglers because they combine high value with low density, as do drugs. Profit margins can be large. The social and economic impact of light weapons should also not be underestimated, as was seen in March 1997 in the collapse of state control in Albania. Individuals and communities which oppose the state can easily acquire light weapons and directly confront not only national security forces but, in some instances, the international community.

Southern Africa is suffering from increasing armed crime fuelled by easy access to cheap and plentiful supplies of small arms. At present most armed activity is socially and economically driven, but there are signs that easy access to weapons is also encouraging militant political groups to consider armed, rather than democratic, opposition. This chapter examines the two main sources of small arms in southern Africa, Angola and Mozambique, and their impact on the region, especially on South Africa. The urgency of dealing with the flood of small arms on to the open market in the 1990s is one of the greatest challenges that post-apartheid southern African governments face. It has implications not only for post-conflict reconstruc-

The author would like to thank the British American Security Information Council (BASIC) for supporting this research.

tion but also for regional economic growth and the strengthening of civil liberties and civil society.

Angola

Angola returned to civil war within one month of its first nationwide elections, held in September 1992. The war ended in an uneasy peace in November 1994 with the Lusaka Protocol. The human cost since fighting resumed is impossible to determine with precision, but the United Nations reported that as many as 1,000 people were dying daily from conflict, starvation and disease in mid-1993 – more than in any other conflict in the world at that time (cited in Human Rights Watch 1994: 8–22).

The renewed conflict, and the concomitant human rights abuses and violations of the laws of war, were fuelled by new flows of light and heavy arms into the country. The government imported arms in 1991 and 1992 in violation of the Bicesse Accords, notably from Russia and Brazil. When war resumed in Angola, it went on an international shopping spree, spending an estimated US$2.5 billion on weapons in 1993 and 1994. Up to 1996, Angola had become Africa's number one arms purchaser. Weapons were bought from numerous sources. Russia inherited from the former Soviet Union the distinction of being the largest arms supplier to Angola, which represented its primary market in Africa during this period. Other nations apparently involved in arming the government include Brazil, Bulgaria, the Czech Republic, Israel, Portugal, Poland, Spain, the Slovak Republic, Ukraine, Uzbekistan and North Korea.

During the war, the rebel *Uniao Nacional para a Independencia Total de Angola* (UNITA) engaged in significant illegal imports of weapons in contravention of UN-imposed sanctions. Initially most of UNITA's weapons came via South Africa, but as the war progressed and South Africa changed, UNITA shifted the main part of its sanctions-busting operations to the former Zaire and Congo (Human Rights Watch 1996: 15–17).

Arms Embargoes
The May 1991 Bicesse Accords prohibited both the government and UNITA from acquiring new weaponry (the so-called 'Triple Zero' clause). Following Angola's return to full-fledged war in January 1993, the government unilaterally declared the Triple Zero clause obsolete on 23 April. In mid-1993, all three members of the Observing Troika (the United States, Russia, and Portugal), as well as other nations such as the UK, announced a lifting of their national bans on military supplies to the government. The UN Security Council then imposed an international arms embargo on UNITA in September 1993.

Despite the signing of the Lusaka Protocol in November 1994, both the government and UNITA continued to acquire additional weapons. UN officials reported that there had been little they could do but watch. Requests to investigate suspected new weapons imports required forty-eight hours' notice, which afforded the government time to remove any offending material before inspection. Although the government had informed the UN and Joint Commission, monitoring and overseeing the process, of some shipments prior to delivery, this was more the exception than normal practice and was often deliberately confusing, such as giving the wrong dates or ports of arrival.

Since the Lusaka Protocol, UNITA appears to have obtained much of its weaponry from private sources rather than foreign governments, although there is some evidence that Zaire has become its most important source of support. UNITA continues to use the former Zaire as a transit area and conduit for weapons transfers, and maintains a number of small bases there. Much of the weaponry is brought in by private charter firms. Some arms are transported across the Angolan border by land; they arrive not only by vehicle, but in rough terrain are transported by human caravans, mostly by women (Human Rights Watch 1996: 16). UN personnel have shown little interest in monitoring new weapons flows into Angola. Despite international pressure in 1996 on the UN Angola Verification Mission (UNAVEM III) to make this a priority, little initiative has taken place on the ground. Indeed, the UN failed to demand that UNITA soldiers who were quartered brought their weapons along. Airports are not closely monitored and UNAVEM's intelligence networks appear weak. With the UN having downgraded its forces in 1997, UNAVEM's record on disarmament and that of its successor, MONUA, are poor.

Disarmament
During the interim period after Bicesse in May 1991 and before the September 1992 elections, UNAVEM II lacked the resources (or the mandate) to try to implement effective arms control measures and thereby reduce the number of weapons available in the country. The weapons collected at the assembly areas were poorly guarded and stored in unsecured locations in the camps. Moreover, these weapons were of poor quality and limited quantity, indicating that both the MPLA and UNITA were retaining their best (Vines 1993).

This pattern seems to have been repeated in 1996. Although UNITA had quartered some 69,093 soldiers, its record on weapons handed in was much poorer. The November 1996 figure of 29,698 personal weapons and 4,521 crew-served systems was mostly of old and obsolete light weapons, while ammunition figures were also low.[1] Reports from across the country suggested a hoarding of better quality weapons and large arsenals, particularly in northern Angola.

The government was not very co-operative either. The UN Humanitarian Co-ordination Unit in Luanda asked both sides to provide it with details of their arsenals, including the types of small arms in their possession. The Unit has also tried to make inventories of the types of weapons systems found in Angola. Its data base remains preliminary, blocked by lack of political will to help by either side. The government was more helpful than UNITA in providing some details about types and locations of where landmines are laid.[2]

The lack of interest in disarming came at a time when 70,000 people were to be demobilised and when banditry was on the increase. Assessments made of soldiers from both UNITA and the government in 1996 indicated that the majority of them did not wish to return to agricultural production.

Although the Angolan Police General Command issued a decree on 20 March 1995, forbidding the importation and trade of arms and ammunition throughout the country, this had little impact.[3] Attempts to disarm civilians have been unsuccessful. By 1 February 1997 only 102 crew-served weapons and 2,642 different types of firearms had been retrieved by the police.[4] Light weapons remained readily available throughout Angola and a growing trade in them developed. They could be bought from soldiers for as little as a second-hand shirt. Both government and UNITA soldiers were active in selling their weapons. Zambian police report that dealers exchange trucks of mielie (maize) meal for shipments of guns, and along the Namibian border such exchanges have been for second-hand clothing and drugs.[5]

The easy availability of guns made armed crime commonplace, especially by police and military personnel. Between 500,000 and 700,000 AK-47s were distributed to civilian groups around Luanda in 1992.[6] The *Associação Angolana dos Direitos Humanos* (Angolan Human Rights Association) found in 1993 that in one Luanda prison there were some 720 government soldiers and police awaiting conviction, almost all charged with homicide by firearms in the Luanda area.[7]

The government preferred to turn a blind eye to such indiscipline, sometimes allowing soldiers to loot and intimidate with guns in compensation for little or no pay. In 1996 there was a rotation of troops deployed in Luanda, permitting those stationed there to engage in crime in lieu of payment. Many of the police in Luanda use extortion and crime in order to augment their income. Many Angolan citizens have little respect for the police, who are blamed for much of the urban violence. The result has been a mushrooming of private security firms; numbering just six in 1995, they had increased to 77 registered companies in 1996.

Ordinary crime was often violent. Gunshot wounds in Luanda had increased by 70 per cent since the Lusaka Protocol, according to the medical director of Luanda's Josina Machel hospital interviewed in June 1995. Angola is in every respect a country rife with guns, many of them available on the market for domestic use or export. Shipments of weapons can be arranged through the police or military officials. In November 1995 the Angolan authorities were tipped off about a network smuggling Pioneer hi-fi speakers filled with guns and flown to Brazil. In January 1997 government officials, UNITA and freelance traders alike were shipping weapons into Zaire (now the DRC) as the market there expanded with the growing hostilities. Shipments out of Luanda are also trucked down to Namibia. One truck driver interviewed in Luanda, in March 1995[8] said:

> I'm given guns frequently to deliver in Namibia. These are then put onto smaller vehicles and taken to the clients. I believe these come directly from military stores. All my papers are organised by military officials here in Luanda. They must be making lots of money.

Mozambique

As Angola was tilting back to war in October 1992, a ceasefire for Mozambique was finally agreed in Rome on 4 October, ending a 16-year civil war which had cost some 100,000 civilian lives and ruined much of the economy. The ceasefire signalled the start of a UN- supervised peace process, which culminated in Mozambique's first ever multiparty elections on 27–29 October 1994. The UN's Operation in Mozambique (ONUMOZ) had applied lessons learnt from the flawed Angolan peace process, in particular that elections should not be held before both sides had been demobilised and that peacekeeping operations should not be conducted on the cheap (Vines 1995).

Light weapons were the arms most commonly used in the Mozambique conflict. Russia supplied the majority of them, although China also provided some. In early 1992, Russia provided a Swiss-funded project with details of what it had shipped to Mozambique as part of the planning process for demobilisation. These details remain confidential. INTERPOL reported in 1995 that some 1.5 million AK-47s were distributed to the civilian population during the course of the war in Mozambique. Renamo received weapons from Rhodesia and later from South Africa. Kenya also provided ammunition in the late 1980s, while some weapons were supplied by Portuguese, German, American and Gulf sources. Much of Renamo's weaponry consisted of recirculated Chinese and Russian light weapons. Renamo also relied heavily in the last years of the war on weapons captured from the government forces. The government distributed tens of thousands of AK-47s to civilian militia units in 1982. Very few of these were ever returned (Vines 1996).

Disarmament

Disarmament was implicit in ONUMOZ's mandate as part of demobilisation. The term 'demobilised soldier' was defined as an individual who 'Subsequent to E-Day was demobilised at the decision of the relevant command, and handed over the weapons, ammunition, equipment, uniform and documentation in his possession.'[9]

Weapons brought into the Assembly Areas (AAs) were temporarily stored there. The only deterrent was two padlocks that secured the structure, for which the Camp Commander held one key and the UN's military officer at the AA the other. In practice this worked because the quality of weaponry was poor and the soldiers had hidden better weapons elsewhere. João Baptista, a Frelimo soldier from Massingir AA, explained:[10]

> We knew that guns make good business. So we kept the best for ourselves. I have sold some to dealers from Joni and I keep others for the future. The secret is to keep them in good condition. Frelimo was never going to pay us for the years we were made to fight. We have to look after ourselves.

Eduardo Adao, a Renamo soldier from Changanine AA, gave a similar account:[11]

> Guns can mean food. We do not want to be hungry. Before the elections we saw that we were being betrayed by the politicians. Why give up the guns to weaken us further? We handed in the bad ones. Business is good with a gun.

The situation was complicated by the fact that both parties deliberately ordered that weapons be hidden. Consequently not every soldier arrived in an AA with a weapon as expected. The number of weapons collected from paramilitary troops was also low and the munitions submitted were of poor quality for similar reasons.

Even though the General Peace Accord stipulated that '...all collective and individual weapons...should be stored in warehouses under the United Nations' control,' both sides initially refused. A spin-off of the growing unrest in the AAs in 1994 on the part of combatants waiting to be demobilised was the reluctant agreement of both sides that ONUMOZ could transport military equipment in excess of 200 arms from each AA for safe-keeping in one of three Regional Arms Depots (RADs), in Nampula, Chimoio and Matola (Table 3.1). The first such transfer took place on 15 March 1994, and they continued until the end of 1994, with ONUMOZ infantry overseeing the process (Breman 1996: 73).

The circumspect nature of ONUMOZ's mandate largely prevented the peacekeeping forces from tackling arms caches outside the Assembly Areas. However, the Ceasefire Commission (CCF) approved a mechanism to ascertain the existence of undeclared depots and caches. This 'verification process' was to take place after demobilisation and before the October 1994 elections. But because of delays in

Table 3.1   Weapons registered during ONUMOZ's verification phase

* Various arms	46,193
* Various types of ammunition	2,703,733
* Various types of mines	19,047
* Kilograms of explosives	5,687
* Individual grenades	4,997
* Intact boxes	220

Other military equipment registered

Unilaterally Demobilised Government troops – 12,736
Armed, Paramilitary, Private & Irregular troops – 43,491

Source: ONUMOZ

demobilising, it did not start until 30 August and made little progress because both sides showed little interest. The teams did visit 744 sites of arms caches before the mandate expired, but many others were not visited because of the short time-frame for the operation and failure to gain access to some sites.

Very little of the arms and ammunition recovered and registered was destroyed. This mainly comprised a small amount of unstable munitions. Weapons and equipment placed in the RADs were categorised as: operational, repairable and beyond repair. Only material deemed to be 'beyond repair' was destroyed. Although the UN assessed various options for destroying additional weapons in metal foundries, this was deemed too expensive and did not take place. An ONUMOZ request in 1993 for an additional US$52.5 million to ensure more comprehensive disarmament throughout Mozambique was turned down in New York.

Only after the elections and following international pressure, including from the US, was the issue of arms caches made a priority. In October, the US had already presented the Mozambican government with a hard-hitting 'non-paper' threatening to 're-evaluate our future development assistance program in Mozambique' unless the government co-operated in five key areas, including access to regional arms depots (Human Rights Watch 1995). In September 1994, ONUMOZ officials had also tried to push on several occasions for access to large weapons caches, especially in the final build-up to the elections. This included attempted access to a large arsenal maintained in the Interior Ministry in central Maputo. Such violations of the terms of the Accords were never exposed publicly and usually resulted in compromise. In the case of the Interior Ministry, Aldo Ajello, the UN Special Representative, negotiated for the cache to be declared and it remained under government control. These actions were also politically motivated to build up Renamo's confidence prior to the elections.

With a successful conclusion to the elections on 27–29 October, ONUMOZ, encouraged by international pressure, engaged more actively in clearing and destroying weapons caches. Eric Lubin, aide to the UN Special Representative, admitted:[12]

> Ajello was a politician. He knew that neither side wanted to hand in their guns. He had seen the fight over mine-clearance and had decided that pushing this issue would only delay the peace process further. The priority was the elections. Once they had passed successfully, disarmament could be safely pursued in the closing months of the mandate.

Stung by criticism that he had not acted against arms caches earlier, Ajello embarked upon a high profile trip in search of caches in November 1994.[13] Amongst many of ONUMOZ's Civpol and infantry units there was also little will to confront this issue. One peacekeeper from Urubat, the Uruguayan unit patrolling National Highway 1, said:[14]

> Active disarming is dangerous. That is not why we are here. We are here to watch and if they give us their weapons then fine. ONUMOZ's mandate is not to send back bodybags to Montevideo.

A Zambian military official from Zambat was equally philosophical:[15]

> We see wandering groups with guns frequently. We record this but can't do much. The quartering areas are closed and nobody wants to know about this stuff. Same with arms caches. We get reports of where these are. Some are in no-go zones. They know and we know that these are out of bounds. The ones we get to are the old weapons, the ones that they no longer want. In that sense we offer a free clearance service.

In November 1994, just after the elections, the South African edition of *Cosmopolitan* magazine carried a feature about a former Renamo combatant, João Jorge, who had become involved in light weapons trafficking from Mozambique into South Africa. The account illustrated how Renamo had been hiding its weapons throughout 1995 and how former combatants were engaged in selling significant quantities of these to South Africans. João Jorge was described as,

> one of three or four people who knew the location of dozens of weapons caches dotted from Machado to Massingir. He had been a confidant of his brigade commander and had himself seen the burial of most of the weapons. Thousands of Chinese and Russian rifles, handguns and rounds of ammunition lay under shallow crusts of earth, waiting to be retrieved. João Jorge would use the men of Giraffe Platoon [an ex- Renamo unit] as his diggers and carriers.

> The plan was that the platoon members would denude every weapons cache that they could safely locate in southern Mozambique. They would enter and leave South Africa through Red Cross camps and barren stretches of the Kruger National Park, operating in teams of five or six, at staggered times, and bring back to South Africa small shipments every few days. The weapons would then be reburied in Kruger National Park, to be retrieved when needed. João Jorge would create a distribution network inside South Africa. He would bribe long-haul truckers who ferried goods between the northern Transvaal [now Northern Province] and the PWV [now Gauteng] to take a few extra packages on each trip. He would warehouse in Johannesburg's flatlands. He would buy several vehicles to move the arms into the townships, welded into door frames, roofs and petrol tanks. He would sell his wares to anyone who wanted them and could pay.[16]

Reintegration of Former Combatants

Unlike demobilisation which ended in late August 1994, the social and economic reintegration of demobilised combatants is an open-ended process which will last for several years. A Refugee Studies Programme (RSP) pilot study focused on the experiences of ex-combatants in Zambezia province (Borges Coelto and Vines 1995). Based on a sample of 2,700 combatants, it found that the average age of conscription was twenty and that most individuals had spent an average of ten years in military service. It also highlighted the poor training received in the army which has made the ex-soldiers a very poorly skilled group.

A major obstacle to the social and economic reintegration of the ex-combatants is the weak economy. Only a few jobs are offered in formal employment in Zambezia province, mostly by economic agents who are themselves undercapitalised and who have reservations about investing in a community which is not yet stabilised, particularly in terms of security. Compounding this problem is the fact that employers, including the government and its local departments, tend to regard ex-combatants as potentially violent people who would be likely to disrupt the workplace.

A misconception amongst international donors was that small-scale agriculture could facilitate the reintegration of ex-combatants in Mozambique. For several decades, small-scale agriculture on its own has not had the capacity to guarantee the subsistence of the rural family. The RSP study found that the average number of dependants of demobilised ex-combatants in Zambezia was 7.5, thus forming an average family of eight to nine persons.

Income has had to be complemented by various types of wage labour. The result was that ex-combatants were not dispersed through small-scale agriculture. Instead, they were leaving their families in the fields and looking for income-earning alternatives, particularly in informal trade in the cities. In addition, the weakness of small-scale agriculture as an alternative is exacerbated by problems such as lack of roads and rural shops, land shortages and the prevalence of landmines.

A second study by the Refugee Studies Programme has shown that there is little evidence to link former soldiers with armed crime in Maputo (Borges Coelho 1997). Some ex-combatants were possibly involved in petty crime, such as in the informal market (*dumba nengue*) of Estrela Vermelha, where many of the products on offer have been stolen, or in local drug dealing such as in Bairro Militar (sometimes nick-named Colombia). However, many of the threats made by ex-soldiers about their links with serious crime were bluff designed to extract government concessions. Overall, ex-soldiers are reintegrating quickly, and it is already difficult in Maputo to distinguish them from other groups, or to suggest that they are any more prone to engage in crime.

Armed Crime and the Police

Reports such as that of 20 December 1996, when unidentified gunmen ambushed and wounded a South African tourist, are not rare and Mozambican police figures show a yearly increase from 19,630 in 1993/4 to 22,602 in 1994/5 and 24,300 in 1995/6. The proliferation of small arms is recognised by the government as a problem. The then Home Affairs Minister, Manuel Antonio, announced in April 1995 that a master plan had been drawn up to deal with the large quantity of illegal weapons circulating in the country. This included stepping up patrols along the main roads, re-establishing police district commands and increasing co-operation between the Mozambican police and police forces in neighbouring countries.

In the first three months of 1995, the police smashed 30 armed gangs and discovered 69 arms caches. Between January and July 1995, they reported seizing over 6,000 guns and 24,000 rounds of ammunition. A total of 1,070 arms came from Sofala, followed by Zambezia province with 1,047. The government claimed that between November 1995 and November 1996, the police discovered 50 arms caches, collecting more than 1,000 guns and hundreds of mines and grenades. They also report that, in the same period, they neutralised 214 bands of robbers and recovered 105 cows and 337 cars.[17] Reports of new arms caches being found are a weekly occurrence in the national press.

However, popular confidence in the police is low and these figures papered over a crisis in poor policing in much of Mozambique. 102 police were expelled in 1995 for activities against police ethics. Policemen have regularly disregarded the law and the constitution and a constant stream of reports of police maltreatment of detainees, especially outside Maputo, reach groups like Human Rights Watch.

Police and military officials are often the main sources of gun running, making action against them more difficult. Arthur Canana, the governor of Manica province, admitted that weapons fuelling an illegal arms trade have been sold out of police stations. 'There is nothing we can do about indiscipline of certain officers, which is making the problem worse.'[18] In November 1996, Attorney-General Sinai Nhatitima, in his report on crime to parliament, made devastating accusations against the police. He claimed that many of the guns used by criminals came from the police. 'Guns are stolen or "disappear" from the arsenals and are lent out, rented or sold to be used in criminal activities.'

Neutralising arms caches became the first issue on the agenda at a meeting between President Chissano and the Renamo leader, Afonso Dhlakama, on 5 February 1996 and again on 21 December 1996. Both men were concerned about the dangers of bands of men carrying weapons outside their control. They decided to set up a working group, with members appointed by the government and Renamo, to deal with the dismantling of arms caches. This fell short of an earlier demand by Renamo to set up a tripartite commission from the South African and Mozambican police forces and former Renamo military officers. The issue subsequently become one of political contention, with Renamo wanting a higher profile for itself through a Commission and the government arguing for a working group, a label designed to stamp its authority over Renamo.

The problem cannot be underestimated. Lionel von Dyke, director of the Zimbabwean-based Mine-Tech security firm, pointed out that arms caches are a much bigger threat than landmines:[19]

> We are finding arms caches all the time. Even in the middle of towns. I am amazed that the UN didn't have these shown to it or hadn't destroyed them if they did. The weapons and ammunition around here are a time bomb. Not necessarily for renewed war, but there are plenty of guns and thousands of rounds of ammunition to keep criminals and poachers in business for decades.

Mine-Tech had found that, in central Mozambique, where it is clearing mines as part of the Cahora Bassa power line rehabilitation scheme, the numbers of armed groups seen by its men were increasing during 1996. The same is true of incidents of the relaying of landmines and attacks on the roads. Some of these actions were targeted at halting renewed government administration because the local people were involved in drug production and contraband trading, reasons for wishing to keep such areas closed. Mine-Tech personnel have increasingly found that weapons, especially small arms and mines, have been removed by unknown individuals before arms caches can be destroyed.

In response to banditry along main roads, the Mozambican authorities formed special police units. 'Lightning Battalion' is one such unit, which was deployed on 2 June 1995 along highway 215 (Maputo-South Africa) after the killing of South African tourist Chris Joubert by men armed with AK-47s and the injuring on the following day of another South African. Four gangs, consisting of sixteen criminals operating along the road, were arrested in the following weeks. Thirteen AK-47s, four pistols and three other semi-automatic weapons were captured in the operation. There have also been reports that 'Lightning Battalion' has beaten up suspects.

'Lightning Battalion' was created because the regular armed forces, FADM, refused to take on internal policing responsibilities. The Rapid Intervention police had also argued that their role was predominantly urban-based policing. One reason for the reluctance of regular units to involve themselves in such activities is that a significant proportion of armed banditry is carried out by current or former soldiers, who are often known to serving officials. One FADM soldier, who did not want to be named, claimed:[20]

> We make money by selling guns from the arsenals. Some of our people also engage in banditry to get extras. It's a way to survive. I don't agree with it; it's a continuation of bad habits from FAM [the old government army].

Lazero Mathe, director of FADM's equipment unit, admitted that the situation was chaotic, saying: 'We have more weapons of war than military personnel. The only problem is that we don't know how many or where most of these weapons are.'[21] He also admitted that weapons identified for destruction that had been put into three regional warehouses by UNOMOZ, were 'not accounted for.'

One potential highwayman, from Gaza province, Alfredo, is nineteen. He explained why he got involved in crime.[22]

> There is no work for me. I have few skills except using a gun and it's easy money. The occasional action makes money. I used to be Frelimo, then joined Renamo, then joined Frelimo. I have played war for both. Now I work for myself and my group. As long as we move around, we get few problems. We can pay for information about police activity. Prices have gone up since those South Africans got involved. Our secret is to be careful. We try not to kill people, but accidents can happen during confusion.

Another young man involved in armed crime, who paid his way out of jail in 1995, explained that for the young it was one of the few ways to make ends meet. João, who is thirty one, explained:[23]

What is there for people like me to do? A gun gives me a job! My family struggle on the land and they can't feed me. I need to help them. The police use guns all the time to make money. So can I! Everything around here is about money. Eh, without it you have nothing. So I make money with a gun.

Most Mozambicans appear to regard armed crime as an occupational hazard, and still remember the war years. It is urban crime, especially in Maputo, that has risen sharply, although the police figures for armed crime in 1996 suggest that it may now have peaked. The police recorded 2,370 crimes against property, of which 658 were robbery, 135 of these armed, a slight reduction from 1995.[24] Violent crime declined dramatically immediately following the appointment of Almerino Manhenje as the new Home Affairs and Police Minister in 1996. He had quickly ordered police action against known crime gangs, and a new unarmed and better trained police unit was also mobilised. However, travelling on some main roads outside cities at night remains a calculated risk. There are waves of armed crime and although the situation around Maputo had greatly improved in early 1997, in other districts, such as along the Zimbabwean border, there continued to be serious problems. That country also experienced a spill-over effect. Armed robberies in the last quarter of 1995 increased by 30 per cent in Zimbabwe's eastern Manicaland province along the Mozambican border.[25]

Foreigners and the Mozambican elite have invested in private security systems and guards. In a recent study on the reintegration of Maputo ex-combatants, 24 per cent of the 476 interviewed had found employment as security guards.[26] They were provided with training, together with weapons, vehicles, radio communications and several types of weapons.

Guns for Hoes and Food
Mozambique's Christian Council (CCM), the umbrella body of the main Protestant churches, is trying to reduce violent crime by collecting anonymously guns that are in illegal hands. The 'Guns into hoes' programme was conceived during the peace process in 1991 but, after lengthy delays, finally got off the ground on 20 October 1995. By January 1997, it had collected 874 firearms, 79 other weapons (knives, etc.) and over 20,000 armaments ranging from bullets to bazooka shells.[27] In the first five months of the programme, an average of 115 weapons per month were handed in to the CCM. This has now declined to between 15 and 20 per month. Some of these weapons were destroyed and made into anti-militaristic sculptures for display at Maputo's International Trade Fair (FACIM) in August 1996.[28] The programme was planned to last two years and had an initial budget of US$1.2 million from Germany and Japan. Most of the money was to provide incentives for people to come forward and hand in their weapons: bicycles, sewing machines and agricultural hand-tools were offered in return. Anyone providing information leading to the discovery of a significant cache might acquire a tractor.

However, the programme is short of money and people have been complaining that they have not been rewarded for handing in weapons. The programme has also operated only in the far south, around Maputo city. There are additional complications, such as the recent case of Delphina Armando Cossa in Maputo, who received a sewing machine in exchange for her brother's pistol. The CCM discovered several bicycles already given out by the Council for other weapons. Using more than one family member, the brother has been slowly turning in a store of weapons without attracting attention to himself.[29]

The *Associação dos Desmobilizados de Guerra* (AMODEG) had contacted the CCM in mid-May 1995 to assist it with providing good quality beans and flour in exchange for guns from demobilised soldiers. The presumption was that ex-soldiers had access to a number of guns and ammunition and that offering food in this way might encourage them to exchange some of their weapons in times of food short-age rather than using them to commit crime in order to survive.[30]

Co-operation with South Africa

In March 1995, during a visit to South Africa by President Chissano, a formal secu-rity agreement between the two countries was signed. Under this agreement the South African Firearms Investigation Unit and the Mozambican police force would operate jointly in southern Mozambique against arms traffickers and others. The agreement also provided for a regular exchange of information and access to detainees for interrogation in either country.

In 1995 these joint Mozambican-South African police operations resulted in the destruction of 45 arms caches in southern Mozambique. In July of that year, Mozambican and South African police officers jointly destroyed over 270 firearms and a large quantity of ammunition in front of the press. Much of this weaponry had been hidden around Maputo province. The second phase of the joint operation, Operation Rachel II, seized a further 273 firearms, 148 of them AK-47s. Most of these were destroyed either in situ or in front of television cameras near Maputo, on 6 September 1995.[31] The third phase, Operation Rachel III, between 21 July and 11 August, proved very successful in Gaza, Inhambane and Sofala provinces. More than 5,500 machine/sub-machine guns (including 1,177 rifles) were captured, along with 78 pis-tols, 518 anti-personnel mines and 3 million rounds of ammunition of various calibres.

Security co-operation between South Africa and Mozambique could expand fur-ther. The Mozambican Defence Minister, Aguiar Mazula, and his South African opposite number, Joe Modise, signed a Letter of Intent on 4 February 1996, autho-rising the SANDF to enter Mozambican territory 'in zones of difficult access for Mozambican police and security forces' and also on 'hot pursuit' operations against armed groups already engaged in South Africa. A joint commission of the defence ministries on frontier problems has been extended to include joint exercises.[32]

The Regional Light Weapons Trade to South Africa

The destination of many of the firearms leaving Angola and Mozambique is South Africa. The influx of illegal firearms is stimulated by political conflict, growing crime and a sustained, perceived need for self-protection (Cock 1995). Criminal gangs have armed themselves to intimidate and control certain areas and are increasingly using light weapons in criminal activities linked to financial gain.[33] Crime is esti-mated to have cost the South African economy R31.3 billion, or 5.6 per cent of GDP, in 1995. From 1989 to 1995 South African murders increased by 61 per cent, armed robberies by 119 per cent and rapes by 80 per cent (Oosthuysen 1996: 10).

The two main external sources from which illegal firearms are smuggled are Mozambique, via Swaziland or Durban port, and Angola, via Namibia, Zambia or Botswana. But South Africa itself is the main source for the illegal small arms mar-ket. In mid-1996, there were 3,503,573 licensed firearms in South Africa, owned by 1,933,222 citizens, representing an increase of over 60 per cent from the 1986 total of 2,492,633 licensed firearms (Besdziek 1996: 18). In 1996 the demand for firearms licences averaged 20,000 new requests per month, a clear response to increasing lev-els of violent crime.

The rate of theft is equally dramatic. From 1 April 1990 to 12 September 1995, the South African Police suffered the loss of 7,621 firearms. Furthermore, a recent stock-taking exercise in the Eastern Cape revealed that the Transkei Police (now integrated into the South African Police Service) could not account for 2,120 (38 per cent) of the 5,634 firearms issued to them. Between 1 April 1993 and 30 June 1995, only 69,736 firearms were seized by the South African police, but a reported 169,783 firearms entered the illegal weapons market as a result of thefts and losses over the same period. Thefts from army base arsenals such as Youngsfield in the Western Cape where 103 7.7mm rifles, 7 R-1 rifles, 5 5.56mm assault rifles and a 9mm pistol were reported missing in 1996, also represent a serious problem.[34]

The availability of firearms was worsened by the fact that, prior to majority rule, thousands of firearms were legally issued to individuals in the former TBVC states and self-governing territories for self-defence purposes. The same thing happened in townships with the ANC's Self-Defence Units (SDUs) which were established in response to the violence of the apartheid state. The authorisation for civilians issued with these firearms was withdrawn in 1995 and after 31 October 1995 people retaining such weapons could face prosecution. However, in Kwazulu-Natal this had little impact: by the deadline only 48 firearms had been handed in.

The inter-relatedness of criminal activities is increasingly evident: the illegal arms trade is linked to vehicle theft or robbery, and illegal firearms to drug trafficking (from Zambia and Namibia). Crime networks have become well established so that the same networks are often used for smuggling firearms, drugs, vehicles, ivory, rhino horn, gem stones and precious metals. Mandrax, much of it originating in Pakistan, is imported through Mozambique and Zambia and traded on to South Africa and to a lesser extent to Mexico and Holland. When arresting four members of a suspected million dollar Bulgarian car-theft syndicate in March 1997, police were astonished to find papers stating that 10,000 AK-47 assault rifles would be delivered with 'the grenade-chargers missing'.[35]

There are gangs which specialise in providing firearms and assist in their distribution. Some groups are comprehensive, being involved in the trafficking of whatever is in demand. The South African Police Service reported that, in 1995, seven organised crime syndicates, primarily participating in drug trafficking, stock-theft, housebreaking or diamond and gold-related offences, were also involved in the illegal firearms trade. In early 1996 the Firearms Investigation Unit was monitoring the activities of more than 2,800 suspects known to be involved in the trade. The Minister of Safety and Security, Sydney Mufamadi, told Parliament in June 1996 that there were 481 known crime syndicates operating in South Africa, 112 of which were involved in vehicle and weapons smuggling.[36]

There is little doubt that the availability of firearms has increased violent crime. However, the number of illegal weapons circulating in South Africa is not known; figures given range from 400,000 to 8 million. The number of weapons seized by the police is low. They estimate that they seize 10 per cent, at most, of the weapons entering the country illegally. During 1993 the South African Police seized 11,660 firearms, compared with 14,460 firearms in 1994 and over 15,000 in 1995. The South African media frequently report that AK-47s are used in armed crime, playing on images of communist onslaught encouraged during the apartheid years (Cock 1995: 110). In fact, pistols and revolvers are the popular tools of armed crime in South Africa, including in the taxi wars (see below). Tables 3.2 and 3.3, based on South African Police Service statistics, show that in the majority of crimes, such as armed robbery, housebreaking and car theft, a pistol is preferred to an assault rifle, the simple reason being that pistols and revolvers are much easier to conceal. Attacks on security companies, which attract gang type attacks, many of them armed with AK-47s and using armour-piercing bullets, represent an exception not shown in the tables.

Table 3.2 *Weapons seized in South Africa, 1993-b*

Weapon & Type	1993	1994	1995	1996
RIFLES				
AK-47	1,403	1,589	1,392	1,169
Other	1,170	1,297	1,512	1,476
Shotguns	593	691	632	599
Total	3,166	3,577	2,916	3,244
PISTOLS				
Stechkin machine pistols	20	10	4	2
Scorpion machine pistols	11	16	32	3
Makarov	174	164	172	221
Tokarev	77	56	58	263
Other	4,327	5,150	6,934	8,803
Total	4,609	5,396	7,200	9,292
REVOLVERS	1,894	2,364	2,842	2,812
HOME-MADE WEAPONS	1,991	3,123	2,713	2,806
GRAND TOTAL	11,660	14,460	16,291	18,094
Ammunition Seized: 1993–5				
	1993	1994	1995	1996
7.62mm	119,610	103,424	40,717	48,299
Other	1,194,826	203,367	108,259	105,439
TOTAL	1,314,436	306,791	148,976	154,838

Source: South African Police Service

In March 1997, an illegal arms dealer in central Johannesburg offered a selection of small arms, including AK-47s, R-4s and Stechkin, Scorpion, Makarov and Tokarev pistols. He complained that:[37]

> When I started this business, I bought up a whole lot of AKs from suppliers in Mozambique. But there is little demand for them. I have good stocks, and can offer you a good price, R200 each. I need to move stock, otherwise I'll be out of business. I need cash to buy pistols. That's what people want and I'm always short on stocks.

A total of 8,407 murders were reported by the South African Police Service in the first six months of 1995, of which 3,346 (39.8 per cent) were committed with firearms; 80.13 per cent of these were in KwaZulu-Natal and Gauteng. In the same

Table 3.3   *South Africa: calibre of weapons used in murders*

	1994		1995	
Weapons Used	Deaths	% Weapons Used	Deaths	% Weapons Used
Assault Rifle	458	5.9	408	5.7
Pistol/Revolver	5,872	75.3	5,377	75
Rifle/Shotgun	753	9.7	763	10.6
Homemade/Unknown	720	9.2	621	8.7
Total	**7,803**	**100**	**7,169**	**100**

Source: South African Police Service

period the police recorded 26,563 robberies under aggravating circumstances using firearms (Table 3.4); 83.2 per cent of these were also committed in Natal and Gauteng. Firearms have also been used frequently in so-called taxi wars. From January 1994 to April 1996, a total of 505 people were killed and 901 injured in 1,306 incidents of taxi-related violence. Although much of this has been intended to eliminate competitors overtrading and operating on lucrative routes, taxi drivers have been diversifying their operations, moving into the profitable market of transporting and trading in firearms, which are often bartered for drugs such as cannabis and in exchange for ferrying illegal migrants from border areas to Gauteng.

Although automatic weapons are not used extensively in armed crime, there does appear to be a market for them in South Africa. In his recent study of small arms proliferation in southern Africa, Glenn Oosthuysen warned that such weapons may be being stockpiled by political groups, especially in KwaZulu-Natal, pending an upswing of violence (Oosthuysen 1996: 14). Dealers also appear to be stockpiling, while former Renamo bases in southern Mozambique and secret locations in the Kruger National Park are also being used as depots for the arms trade from where the guns are then transported to the Ngwavuma area in KwaZulu-Natal.[38]

The Pan Africanist Congress (PAC), the former Azanian People's Liberation Army (APLA), members of the Revolutionary Watchdogs (RW) and a dissident APLA group called The People's Concern (TPC) are also known to maintain weapons stockpiles. Three large arms caches uncovered by the Lesotho Police on 6 May 1995 provided documentation indicating that APLA members committed murders, attacks and robberies. Ultra right-wing groups and security force dissidents have also been responsible for planting arms caches. Few of these have been recovered and even operations to uncover ANC caches have been unsuccessful. In October 1994, the SANDF conducted Operation Rollerball, designed to recover ANC caches in South Africa and neighbouring states. It recovered only 70 AK-47s, 935 handguns, 53 pistols and 316 limpet mines. Many cache sites could not be found and others were already empty (Oosthuysen 1996: 7). The truly international nature of the arms trade to South Africa was demonstrated in October 1994. Police recovered 277 rifles and pistols and about 47,000 rounds of ammunition from a large container from the United States; the American dealer was trying to market the shipment in South Africa.

The limited or non-existent customs and security control over cargo being transported into South Africa is conducive to arms smuggling. Compared with Zimbabwe, which has 7 border crossing points, South Africa has 52, including 36 airports classified as 'international', although many of these lack air traffic control, regular policing, customs, or immigration checks (Mills 1996: 15). However, in 1997 the

Table 3.4   *South Africa: use of firearms in violent crime*

Year	Murder	Attempted Murder	Robbery
1991	3,803	Not Available	17,821
1992	6,122	13,276	26,665
1993	7,764	16,024	33,198
1994	7,803	17,744	43,279
1995	7,169	18,202	45,216

Source: National Crime Investigation Service, SAPS

Note: These figures will not be comprehensive because black South Africans in the townships tend still to opt for unlicensed weapons, whereas whites usually seek licences.

South African authorities reduced the number of entry points for bulk commercial traffic to 34; the number of 'international' airports has been reduced to 8.The theft in 1997 from the container depots in Durban harbour of a freight container of weapons exported by ARMSCOR is also an indication of future potential problems. Eight weapons are still missing, showing the uncontrolled and unprotected manner in which firearms-related transactions can be carried out.

Operation JUMBO II, a joint operation between the South African Police Service and the SANDF in 1995, resulted in 1,244 firearms being recovered in KwaZulu-Natal, the Eastern Cape and Gauteng. However, during these sweeps, criminals tended to hide or relocate temporarily. In 1996, the South African Police launched a series of search and seizure operations, such as Sword and Shield, Operation Anvil and Operation Rooivalk, in which 3,568 firearms were seized.

As elsewhere in southern Africa, there has also been a significant growth in the private security industry in South Africa (Chapter 1). In January 1995, there were 2,707 security companies and 78,390 security officers, 40,000 of them armed, registered with the Security Officers' Board. However, many companies are not registered with the organisation and it is estimated that there may be as many as 200,000 private security personnel in South Africa, some of them being fronts for paramilitary training and right-wing groups.

Co-operation Agreements

In addition to an agreement with Mozambique, an agreement with Swaziland was signed on 10 August 1995. Swaziland is seeing a rapid increase in the domestic use of firearms, in growing violence linked to the struggle for political reforms in the Kingdom. Police report an increased trade in guns from Mozambique to Swaziland. In the past, Swaziland was mainly a transit point for guns to KwaZulu-Natal province in South Africa.

One impact of the joint Mozambican South African police operations in southern Mozambique is that the trafficking routes have changed. Fewer guns cross the land borders now; they have increasingly been diverted to the sea route into Durban port, where only between 1 and 10 per cent of containers are ever checked. Alternatively, more weapons are procured via Angola, where a greater variety of weapons in better condition is coming on to the market. This is having a knock-on effect, as both Zambia and Namibia are also seeing an increase in local demand as weapons pass through them. Arms traffickers, mainly Xhosa women, are moving to the Angolan border to trade clothing and drugs (cannibis and mandrax) in exchange for guns from impoverished UNITA soldiers. They expect to make some US$300 profit in Gauteng on each gun they bring back (Smith 1995: 27). The average shipment is between 10 and 17 weapons. One gun dealer, calling himself only David, trades out of northern Namibia. In April 1996 he admitted:[39]

> Business is great, demand is booming in South Africa but also in new places, such as Swaziland, Tanzania and Zambia. The prices are also going down for me in Angola. I can get anything. I have orders from Europe also. Whatever you need, I can get.

In early 1997, arms flowed into Zaire from Angola due to the latter's support for the anti-Mobutu rebels. With the change of government following Mobutu's overthrow, weapons traders are again using Zambia, the Democratic Republic of Congo and the Great Lakes region as an arms pipeline to South Africa. The regional and international nature of the business is clearly evident.

Within SADC there has been much debate on new regional security arrangements following the democratisation of South Africa in 1994. The focus has been on setting up a body for regional security co-operation, either as a sector or as an organ. At a meeting in Gaborone on 28 June 1996, SADC established the Organ on Politics Defence and Security (OPDS). This institution operates differently from other SADC bodies: it reports directly to the SADC summit of heads of state, rather than to the SADC secretariat, and is chaired by a troika, with one member of the troika exchanged annually. This organ also replaces the old Frontline states club (Cilliers 1996).

Escalating crime in southern Africa has also contributed to countries in the region forming what have become in effect sub-committees to the OPDS: the Southern Africa Regional Police Chiefs Co-operation Organisation (SARPCCO) and the Inter-State Defence and Security Committee. SARPCCO was launched in 1995 and is mandated to work with INTERPOL, preparing and disseminating information on criminal activities which would benefit member countries. This was followed in 1996 by a meeting of senior police officers in Midrand, South Africa, to map out joint strategies to combat crime. At this meeting, it was agreed to establish a Central Data Base on cross-border crime intelligence at the INTERPOL sub-office in Harare.[40] The police chiefs identified many obstacles to crime prevention in the region such as inadequate information, lack of communication networks, corruption amongst law enforcement agencies, shortage of resources and a lack of common legislation. There is no doubt that regional initiatives such as SARPCCO are important and it is only through regional co-operation that crime, such as the proliferation of small arms, can be combated. But in early 1997 SARPCCO lacked resources and remained little more than an e-mail link between police chiefs.

Conclusions

The increasing failure to control the flow of illegal weapons in southern Africa may yet have significant implications for democracy and civil liberties (Smith 1996: 55). Amnesty and incentive schemes in South Africa do not appear to have been successful to date. Very few weapons have been recovered in this manner. If the situation continues to deteriorate, the government's response may become more draconian. Freedom of movement and police powers for searching individuals and their property are both areas in which human rights groups need to be vigilant. It is also important to try to prevent arms transfers to governments or organisations grossly violating internationally recognised human rights and the laws of war, and to promote freedom of information regarding arms transfers worldwide. Rather than just being prescriptive, exposing significant arms transfers and pushing for international transparency can act as an early warning system of future potential conflict.

The southern African states should also be willing to provide details about their weapons transfers and other military assistance to other countries. As a rule, if a country believes that it is in its national interest to make a particular arms sale, it should be willing to divulge the details of the sale and provide its justification. This is particularly necessary in the case of arms transfers to human rights violators, when the possibility of weaponry misuse is high.

Recognition of the need for disclosure, or 'transparency' as it is called by the international security community, led to the establishment of the United Nations Conventional Arms Register in December 1991. The register was created to promote 'transparency so as to encourage prudent restraint by states in their arms export and arms import policies and to reduce the risks of misunderstanding, suspicion or tension resulting from a lack of information'. Nations are asked voluntarily to submit data on their arms imports and exports, but only for seven categories of major weapons systems: tanks, armoured vehicles, large calibre artillery systems, combat aircraft, attack helicopters, warships, and missiles and missile launchers. Small arms and light weapons are currently not part of the Register. Clearly the UN Register should be expanded to include these categories. The Southern African Development Community should set up its own register which would include small arms. This should fall under the remit of the Defence and Security Organ launched by SADC in 1996.

Small arms often caused the greatest devastation to civilians during southern Africa's wars. In the post-apartheid era of reconstructing and reconfiguring the region, controlling them must form an essential part of rebuilding a peaceful and secure southern Africa.

Notes

1. UN Security Council S/1996/1000, 2 December 1996.
2. Interview with Peter Simkin, Director of UCAH, May 1996.
3. *Radio Nacional de Angola*, Luanda, in Portuguese 1900 GMT, 20 March 1995.
4. UN Security Council S/1997/115, 7 February 1997.
5. Interviews with Zambian Police, Lusaka, April 1996 and Namibian police, May 1996.
6. Figure provided by Minister of Social Assistance, Albino Malungo, Luanda, March 1995.
7. AADH, 'Relatorio Sobre As Visitas Efectuadas Pela AADH As Cadeias de Luanda,' January 1994, pp.1–6.
8. Interview with Jose Mano, Luanda, March 1995.
9. 'General Peace Accord for Mozambique,' reproduced in UN Department of Public Information, *The United Nations and Mozambique 1992–1995*. New York: United Nations Department of Public Information, 1995, p.116.
10. Interview, Maputo, March 1995
11. Interview, Maputo, April 1995.
12. Interview in Paris, February 1995.
13. Barnaby Phillips, 'Renamo's 'phantoms' of the bush worry UN,' *Daily Telegraph*, 18 November 1994.
14. Interview, Xai Xai, September 1994.
15. Interview, Xai Xai, September 1994.
16. Malcolm Fried, 'The Gun,' *Cosmopolitan*, November 1994.
17. *The New York Times* (New York), 2 March 1997.
18. Christopher Bishop, 'Arms for Africa. Deadly trade poses threat to stability,' *The Sunday Times* (RSA), 27 August 1995.
19. Interview, Harare, April 1996.
20. Interview, Maputo, March 1995.
21. *South African Press Association*, 24 July 1996.
22. Interview, Maputo, March 1995.
23. Interview, Maputo, March 1995.
24. *Noticias* (Maputo) 4 March, 1997.
25 Zimbabwean police source, Harare, April 1996.
26. At least seven companies were mentioned, namely Delta, Proteg, Alfa, Sosep, Securitas, Tivonele and Bassopa.
27. Interview with Boaventura Zita, CCM, Maputo, 4 March 1997.
28. *ELO Ecumenico* (Maputo), No.32, August 1996.
29. *The New York Times* (New York), 2 March 1997.
30. *Noticias* (Maputo) 26 May 1995.
31. The total captured was 685 AK-47 rifles, 154 sub-machine guns, 255 rifles, 47 mortar tubes, 29 RPG-7s, 2 anti-aircraft heavy machine guns, 170 mortar bombs, 84 anti-personnel mines, 5 pistols and 23,415 rounds of ammunition.
32. *Domingo* (Maputo) 11 February 1996.
33. This section is compiled from interviews with the South African Police in Pretoria in April 1996 and March 1997.
34. *The Weekly Mail & Guardian* (Johannesburg) 7–13 March 1997.
35. *The Star & SA Times International* (London) 12 March 1997.

36. *The Sowetan* (Johannesburg), 20 June 1996.
37. Interview, Johannesburg, 7 March 1997.
38. The production of 'Zip-guns' or homemade firearms is also a problem in KwaZulu-Natal. The number seized by the Security Force members in the province outstrips the combined number of homemade weapons seized in the other provinces of South Africa eight fold.
39. Interview, Windhoek, April 1996.
40. Caiphas Chimhete, 'Region Adopts Holistic Stance Against Crime,' *Southern Africa News Features* (Harare), 11 September 1996.

References

Berdal, M. (1996) *Disarmament and Demobilisation after Civil Wars. Arms, Soldiers and the Termination of Armed Conflicts.* Adelphi Paper No. 303, Oxford University Press, Oxford for the International Institute of Strategic Studies.

Besdziek, D. (1996) 'Into the Breach: Reversing the Proliferation of Firearms in South Africa,' *African Security Review*, 4(6): 17–32.

Borges Coelho, J.P. and Vines, A. (1995) *Pilot Study on Demobilization and Re-integration of Ex-combatants in Mozambique.* Refugee Studies Programme, University of Oxford.

Borges Coelho, J.P. (1997) *Re-integration of Ex-combatants in Maputo,* Refugee Studies Programme, University of Oxford.

Breman, E. (1996) *Managing Arms in Peace Processes: Mozambique.* UNIDIR, Geneva.

Cilliers, J. (1996) 'The Evolving Security Architecture in Southern Africa,' *Africa Insight*, 26(1): 13-23.

Cock, J. (1995) 'A Sociological Account of Light Weapons Proliferation in Southern Africa,' in Singh, J. (ed) *Light Weapons and International Security.* Indian Pugwash Society and BASIC, Delhi.

Human Rights Watch (1994) *Angola. Arms Trade and Violations of the Laws of War since the 1992 Elections.* Human Rights Watch, New York.

Human Rights Watch (1995) 'Mozambique', *Human Rights Watch World Report 1995*, Human Rights Watch, New York.

Human Rights Watch (1996) 'Angola. Between War and Peace. Arms Trade and Human Rights Abuses since the Lusaka Protocol,' *Human Rights Watch Short Report*, 8(1)(A), Human Rights Watch, New York.

Mills, G. (1996) *War and Peace in Southern Africa: Crime, Drugs, Armies and Trade.* World Peace Foundation Reports No. 13.

Oosthuysen, G. (1996) *Small Arms Proliferation and Control in Southern Africa.* The South African Institute of International Affairs, Johannesburg, with the assistance of the US Institute of Peace.

Smith, C. (1995) 'The International Trade in Small Arms,' *Jane's Intelligence Review* 7(9), September.

Smith, C. (1996) 'Light Weapons and International Trade,' in UNIDIR (ed.) *Small Arms Management and Peacekeeping in Southern Africa.* UNIDIR, Geneva.

Vines, A. (1993) *One Hand Tied: Angola and the U.N.* Catholic Institute for International Relations Briefing Paper. London, June.

Vines, A. (1995) *Angola and Mozambique. The Aftermath of Conflict.* Conflict Studies 280, Research Institute for the Study of Conflict and Terrorism, May/June.

Vines, A. (1996) *Renamo. From Terrorism to Democracy in Mozambique?* Centre for Southern African Studies, University of York; Eduardo Mondlane Foundation, Amsterdam; James Currey, Oxford.

4 'Nature has the Power to Heal old Wounds': War, Peace & Changing Patterns of Conservation in Southern Africa

EDDIE KOCH

In one of those human interest stories that newspapers use to fill their pages during the quiet season, a local South African paper reported that a group of 'illegals' (people who flee across the border between South Africa and Mozambique are no longer considered refugees) had been caught and devoured by a pride of lions. The event was apparently not an isolated one. Lions in the Kruger National Park seem to have developed such a taste for human flesh during the 1980s, when refugees flooded through the reserve to escape the civil war in Mozambique, that some conservationists estimate that one in every three of the big cats is now a 'maneater', and game parks in other parts of the country refuse to stock their land with 'surplus' lions caught in the park for this reason. The grisly report signifies the terror with which thousands of people living on the border of the Kruger National Park experience South Africa's premier wildlife and leisure resort.

Since the demise of apartheid in South Africa, however, a new concept has emerged around the nature reserves that exist along the borders between that country and its neighbours: Peace Parks. This involves the notion that it is possible to link the relatively unspoilt African habitat that exists in many of the frontier areas between South Africa and the former Frontline States, and the wildlife it hosts, into a continuous, almost contiguous, chain of national parks, game reserves and other forms of wildlife estate. The creation of this super zone of wild plants and animals has two principal objectives. First, in line with current conservation thinking – which favours a move away from the creation of protected islands of biodiversity – the idea is to establish, wherever possible, large intact ecosystems where plant and animal species are able to interact with one other in conditions as natural as possible (e.g. Hales 1989; Wells and Brandon 1992). To this end, the World Conservation Union (IUCN) and the World Wide Fund for Nature (WWF) have recently been pursuing the possibility of establishing large protected zones of biodiversity across political boundaries (Thorsell 1990; Thorsell and Harrison 1990). Southern Africa is one of the prime locations for these global initiatives. Second, it is expected that the area could become the nucleus of a major tourism industry that will generate jobs and revenues in regions that were most devastated by the wars of the immediate past.

Numerous projects have been proposed as a way of giving effect to the idea in the near future. In late 1996, the Mozambican government approved, in principle, the idea that a large chunk of its territory in Gaza province should be linked to the Kruger Park in South Africa so that the area can be jointly administered as one of the world's largest protected ecosystems. The KwaZulu-Natal conservation authorities and Mozambique's forestry and wildlife department are in the advanced stages of a plan to link the Tembe Elephant Park in northern KwaZulu-Natal with the Maputo Elephant Reserve in southern Mozambique. The South African tobacco magnate, Anton Rupert, who has long had an interest in such schemes, established the Peace Park Foundation at the end of 1996 to pursue similar projects in other parts of southern and central Africa. The popular travel magazine, *Getaway*, published an article at about the same time, which illustrated how extensively the economy and shape of the region could be transformed early in the new millennium if these ideas are implemented: 'If these plans came about, areas would be created in which humans, plants and wildlife would share the greatest and potentially most profitable conservation system on earth', it was suggested (Pinnock 1996: 88–97).

In some cross-border park scenarios, there is an emphasis on community ownership of the wildlife estate, tourism lodges and the benefits these are intended to bring. Many of the proposals stress the need for intergovernmental co-operation, in order for these superparks to materialise. In the more optimistic accounts, there is talk about the ability of nature to heal old wounds. In all of them, there is a common call for the zones that once signified terror to be converted into places of peace.

This chapter examines the impact that the wars of destabilisation have had on the wildlife and conservation estate of southern Africa. It then looks more closely at the concept of peace parks and the way it is being applied in southern Africa. The final section evaluates the prospects for cross-border game reserves, one manifestation of the peace dividend that is now being paid to the region, to achieve the kind of economic reconstruction and regional reconciliation that has been ascribed to them.

'When Two Elephants Fight it is the Grass that Suffers': War and Wildlife in the 1980s

Since 1960, there have been violent struggles against colonial rule in Mozambique, Angola, Namibia and what was then white-ruled Rhodesia. In the post-colonial period, mainly from the late 1960s onwards, civil war has afflicted Mozambique and Angola as well as South Africa. Lesotho, Zimbabwe and Botswana were exposed to aggression and covert military operations launched from South Africa (Steiner 1993). The financial cost of South African-sponsored wars of destabilisation in Angola, Malawi, Mozambique, Namibia, Zambia and Zimbabwe has been estimated at between US$45 billion and US$60 billion since 1980 (Steiner 1993; Rob Davies, pers. comm.). The figures compiled by the Southern Africa Research and Documentation Centre, UNICEF and the United Nations Economic Commission for Africa take into account direct damage to infrastructure and disrupted trade operations as well as lost opportunities for growth. The statistics may be inflated because they are based on an assumption that economic growth would have taken place had the wars not occurred, and include estimations of what this growth would have been, which are not necessarily valid (Rob Davies, pers. comm.). However, they do provide a rough indicator of the massive cost that warfare has brought to the region.

Westing (1992) has noted that militarisation, in the form of either armed conflict or extensive expenditure on armed forces, can have a range of negative impacts on wildlife conservation and protected areas. Direct damage can take the form of site destruction, through the use of explosive and chemical devices, or it can be directed at specific components of the flora and fauna through activities such as illegal logging and hunting of wildlife. Damage to the infrastructure of a protected area as well as the personnel responsible for administering the park can also take place.

Indirect damage can result from disruption of tourism and the revenues it brings to park authorities. Wartime privation can cause armies as well as civilians to undertake excessive exploitation of the natural resources inside a protected area. Even where there is no actual armed conflict, the presence of military operations in and near parks can be disruptive. This can exacerbate hostility on the part of local people, and training activities inside parks can damage forests and other vegetation (Westing 1992). Each of these effects can be identified in different parts of the southern African region during the period of warfare over the last 30 years. They are discussed here on a country-by-country basis.

Angola

The London-based Environmental Investigation Agency (EIA) reported spectacular claims that up to 100,000 elephant were killed during the 1980s by the rebel movement, UNITA, in Angola. The allegations were based on evidence presented to a US congressional committee by an American animal rights group which stated that illicit ivory from these hunts was taken from Angola in trucks of the South African Defence Force, whose troops were at that stage providing covert support for UNITA, and then tranported across Namibia to South Africa, from where it was consigned to Hong Kong or Taiwan by air or sea. The proceeds were used to pay for war materiel provided to UNITA by the South African military (EIA 1989).

Subsequent investigation has found these claims to be grossly exaggerated, but UNITA has confirmed that it did use poached ivory to pay for some of its arms supplies. Rebel leader, Jonas Savimbi, revealed this to a French reporter for the magazine, *Paris Match*, in 1988, while another UNITA commander told an American reporter that his movement had earned US$1 million from ivory sales. Colonel Jan Breytenbach, commander of South Africa's notorious 32 Battalion, has described how elephant were slaughtered in parts of Angola where he operated. He told reporters that he had first-hand information that UNITA soldiers were conducting a 'massive extermination campaign' against Angola's elephants which had turned southern parts of Angola into a 'sterile lifeless green desert' (pers. comm.; see also Potgieter 1996).

Officers in the Cuban army, which supported government forces during Angola's civil war, were also involved in the illicit ivory trade. The head of the Cuban expeditionary forces in Angola, General Arnaldo Ochoa Sanchez, also trafficked in ivory. Shortly after he returned to Cuba in 1989, the general was convicted of corruption, including ivory smuggling, and executed (EIA 1989; Ellis 1994). In 1992 a South African army major, Marius Meiring, was extradited to the United States after his accomplices had been caught selling rhino horn in that country to federal agents posing as purchasers. Evidence which emerged during the court hearings showed that Meiring obtained the rhino horn from a South African colonel, who in turn dealt with an Angolan hunter. Officials from the US Fish and Wildlife Service believe this was just part of a wider illicit wildlife trafficking ring involving military officers from various forces involved in the Angolan conflict (*The Nation*, 15 February 1993).

Anstey notes, however, that subsistence hunting during the war kept many rural Angolans from starving. Crude assessments show that wildlife represents more than 70 per cent of available red meat protein in a country the formal economy of which has been rendered derelict by war (Anstey, no date). This is probably the main reason why the status of large mammals in protected areas has declined by up to 90 per cent since the 1970s – especially rare and endangered species like the black rhino and giant sable.

Mozambique

Mozambique is among the poorest countries in the world, not least because civil war, waged by the right-wing rebel movement with support from South Africa in the 1980s, forced the government to spend some 45 per cent of total revenue on military activities. The effects on wildlife reveal a similar pattern to that in Angola. Information about the wildlife populations in Mozambique is scarce because of the war but indications are that some species – especially elephant, lion, crocodile and leopard – have been slaughtered by heavy illicit poaching. Mozambique's country report for the United Nations Conference on Environment and Development (UNCED) in 1992 lists another four species in a 'desperate situation' (roan antelope, tsessebe, black rhino and sitatunga) while another four are categorised as 'endangered' (ostrich, giraffe, cheetah and the marine dugong). The survival of various species of marine turtles that breed on beaches along the coast is mentioned as cause for concern (Republic of Mozambique 1991).

In 1974, at the start of the war, Mozambique's elephant herds probably numbered between 50,000 and 65,000. In 1992 the population was estimated at 13,350 and still declining. Small herds that have survived the ravages of war inhabit remote regions in the northern provinces of Tete, Niassa and Cabo Delgado. A small number, probably less than 50, survive in the Maputo Elephant Park in southern Maputo province. Another small herd has retreated into the relatively inaccessible swamps of the Marromeu Delta, where the Zambezi River fans into the Indian Ocean north of Beira. Abdul Adamo, former director of the Department of Forestry and Wildlife, stated in an interview in April 1992:

> Five years ago, when the army overran Renamo [the right-wing rebel movement] bases, they confiscated 19,000 tusks from various rebel camps. Information from my staff in the field and from a number of rebel defectors confirms that Renamo poaches elephants and exchanges the ivory for guns and ammunition.

Ellis (1994) notes that Mozambican ivory may have triggered the initial military involvement in the illicit smuggling of ivory throughout the southern Africa region. During the Rhodesian war of independence, officers from the white-dominated army's special forces operating in remote border areas between Mozambique and Zimbabwe in the 1970s sometimes stumbled across dead elephants which had strayed into minefields. They would salvage the ivory from these corpses and then pass it on to contacts they had in the South African special forces, who were providing covert support to the Rhodesians at the time. Over time, the South African Defence Force's Directorate of Military Intelligence came to accept ivory as part payment for support given to the Rhodesian counter-insurgency units.

In 1986, Elija Chamba, head of the Department of Forestry and Wildlife in Maputo, stated that 'substantial' quantities of ivory had been discovered at Renamo's headquarters located in the Gorongosa Game Reserve – the biggest and best-known in Mozambique before independence – when it was overrun by government troops. In 1986 'hundreds' of elephants were found in the same park with their heads split open so that the tusks could be removed. 'As a result of the war waged against Mozambique by Renamo, wildlife personnel had lost their lives and infrastructures in conservation areas had been destroyed,' he added (Mozambique Information Agency 1986).

In 1991, government troops captured hundreds of documents when they routed rebel guerrillas from a base at Nhamagoda in Sofala province. One written by Renamo chief, Afonso Dhlakama, requests the 'price of every missile (and)...the price of every kilogram of ivory'. It adds that 'Renamo can arrange the ivory. Renamo can arrange the landing strip for the plane' (*Weekly Mail*, Johannesburg, April 1992).

In 1993, a defector from the rebels' former logistical headquarters for Gaza province, situated at Ngungue close to the boundary of the Kruger National Park, told researchers that a group of South African soldiers had arranged for the delivery of supplies to the camp in exchange for elephant tusks (US Defence Intelligence Agency, no date). Early that year, the South African police arrested a senior rebel officer in the Kruger Park after they caught him in a sting operation trying to sell ivory (Piet Lategan, pers. comm.).

But Mozambique's war zones provided a battleground for many different armies and each of them took part in illicit looting of the country's natural resources. Zimbabwean troops stationed along corridors between Beira and the border appear to have been involved in the illicit ivory trade and shipped large consignments of tusks back home. This was highlighted in 1989 when Captain Edwin Bhundani Ndleya, an officer in the Zimbabwean army, was murdered after he had threatened to expose rhino horn smuggling by Zimbabwean officers serving on the side of government forces in Mozambique (*Parade*, July 1989).

There is also evidence that high-ranking members of the Mozambican army were implicated in illicit poaching of elephant and other mammals. A team of conservationists surveying the wildlife populations of the Marromeu Delta in October 1990 saw teams of government soldiers hunting buffalo and hippo with automatic rifles. They operated an organised industry in which meat from the animals was stripped, laid out on racks to dry and then exported in helicopter gunships for sale in the markets of Beira.

> Buffalo (the herds of which have made the Marromeu legendary among professional safari hunters), waterbuck, reedbuck and hippo have all declined by between 80 and 90 per cent over the last 13 years...In view of the scale and intensity of the hunting, it is likely that the bulk of the operations is for commercial game rather than subsistence (Anderson *et al.* 1990: 14–16).

The war affected the Forestry and Wildlife Department severely. Most conservation areas are located in remote and undeveloped zones which were used as launching bases for guerrilla activity. Of the 38 conservation areas in the country, less than 10 per cent were kept staffed for a significant period after the civil war engulfed all regions in the mid-1980s. Most had their equipment and physical infrastructures severely damaged or totally destroyed. A number of officials were killed (Costa *et al.* 1993; Dutton 1994).

Zimbabwe

Zimbabwean territory was subjected to some attempts at armed incursions during the early 1980s period of 'total strategy', but the country did not suffer the kind of destabilisation experienced by Mozambique and Angola. However, the government was forced to increase its defence budget in order to station troops in Mozambique, where they were deployed mainly to keep the vital rail link between Harare and the port of Beira open. Border areas along the Mozambican frontier were also subjected to raids by Renamo rebels, conducted in retribution for the government's support to Mozambican troops.

The volatile security situation – during the period of liberation struggle and also during the civil war in Mozambique – forced Zimbabwe's wildlife authorities to shut down the Gonarezhou National Park. Located in the southeast of the country on the Mozambican border, this is the second largest park in Zimbabwe. During the Mozambican war, it experienced serious management problems and a breakdown in infrastructure (*Daily Gazette*, 3 May 1994).

The Environmental Investigation Agency claims that Zimbabwean troops were involved in the killing of some 1,000 of the park's total population of 4,500 elephants

(EIA 1989). This figure is also probably exaggerated. It is true that the carcasses of 1,000 to 1,500 elephants were found in the park, but many of these fatalities came about because of drought (*Daily Gazette*, 3 May 1954).

Sources in Zimbabwe's Wildlife Department acknowledge that illicit poaching did affect the elephant population of Gonarezhou during the war, but say that this was carried out by individuals within the police force and the national army as well as members of the national parks authority (Mike Murphree, pers. comm.). In 1989 Rowan Martin, head of the Wildlife Department, stated that 'in the past two years the escalation of illegal hunting for ivory within Zimbabwe is very noticeable. As elephant populations decline in countries to the north, the pressure on elephants is expected to intensify' (EIA 1989: 21).

Researchers note that wars in southern Africa had a major impact on the illicit ivory trade in the 1980s. One study notes that South Africa, because of its links with armed forces in Mozambique and Angola and also the involvement of its military in the ivory trade, ensured that it became a focal point in the flow of ivory – and rhino horn – from Africa to the Far East, accounting for half of all ivory imports in the southern Africa region (Ellis 1994: 63):

> The involvement of just about every army in southern Africa in ivory trafficking and other smuggling could be interpreted as evidence of the triumph of material interests or market forces over ideology, or as a rather bleak commentary on the nature of armies and wars (*ibid.* 58).

South Africa

The effects of militarisation on wildlife conservation in South Africa are of a different kind. The De Hoop nature reserve near Arniston in the Western Cape is still a military zone. In the 1980s it was used to test long-range ballistic missiles capable of carrying nuclear warheads developed by ARMSCOR in collaboration with Israeli scientists. At least two reserves in South Africa have been used by the South African Defence Force as missile testing sites. There was also evidence of extensive military activity in game reserves near the border between northern Natal and Mozambique. An investigation by the Johannesburg newspaper, *The Weekly Mail*, conducted in 1991, discovered that the KwaZulu conservation authorities operated a 'secret services' division. Its job was to spy on ivory and rhino horn smugglers – a duty performed by most conservation agencies in southern Africa. But many officers running the unit were highly trained soldiers who fought in Rhodesia's elite counter-insurgency brigades during that country's war of independence. They engaged in paramilitary exercises in and around the game reserves of northern Natal and this helped fuel the antagonisms that existed between the local residents and rangers (*The Weekly Mail*, 15–21 November 1991). Local residents complained, for example, that white officials dressed in the uniforms of the conservation authority took part in roadblocks set up by the military (Clive Poultney, pers. comm.).

There is now an accumulation of evidence to show that the SADF used the Kruger National Park to provide support for Renamo bases across the border in the 1980s. A SADF unit based in the park, known as the Kruger Commando, had its headquarters in Skukuza and was used to track down illegal refugees fleeing from Mozambique to refugee bases located on the western border of the park, in the former homelands of Gazankulu and KaNgwane. The commanding officer of this unit, Colonel Gert Otto, personally supervised support operations for Renamo and moved around extensively inside Mozambique from jumping off points in the Kruger Park. Otto was removed from his post after being suspected of involvement in smuggling rebel-poached ivory out of Mozambique through the park (Senior officer in SA security forces, confidential communication; Ellis 1994).

Colonel Otto was, in fact, also responsible for the first attempt to promote a cross-border park between the Kruger Park and Mozambique. He hoped to make use of his contacts with Renamo officers active in the area to secure support for the scheme. The colonel set up a corporation called Mozaic, the objectives of which included 'stabilising the area next to the Kruger National Park, generating profits that would help reduce expenditure by the South African Defence Force', and to 'provide intelligence to the security forces' (Mozaic Mission Statement, no date; *Guardian*, 11 November 1991).

The Kruger Park was also used during the era of apartheid's 'total strategy' to entertain secret cabinet meetings and to host official visitors who were breaching the embargo on diplomatic contacts with the apartheid state. In the 1980s the National Intelligence Service built a secret camp called Jakkalsbessie in the park without approval from the National Parks Board for hosting such clandestine meetings. Alarmed at the prospect that this would reinforce perceptions that the conservation authority was co-operating with the apartheid state, the Board's director insisted that the secret camp be taken away from the NIS and handed back to the park authorities (Robbie Robinson, pers. comm., 2 May 1994).

Protected areas and wildlife in southern Africa have thus suffered considerable damage because of social conflicts stemming from past colonial styles of conservation management as well as from the negative impacts of warfare and militarisation that affected most of the region in the post-colonial period.

While other countries in Africa, most notably Kenya, developed a thriving tourism trade based on their wildlife assets, armed conflict in the 1980s denied most countries in southern Africa this opportunity. In Mozambique, for example, the Gorongosa National Park was the centre of a fairly brisk tourism traffic in the early 1970s. Plans to upgrade facilities there were under consideration when the country won its independence from Portugal in 1975. However, attacks by Frelimo fighters during the war caused the reserve to shut down. It reopened after independence but closed again almost immediately as it was occupied by Renamo insurgents (Catterson *et al.* 1991).

The Peace Dividend: Relying on Nature to Heal Old Wounds

It is surprising that, despite the devastating effects of war described above, southern Africa still ranks among the leading wildlife regions in the world. Botswana and Namibia, for example, each have more than 12 per cent of the territory for protected wildlife (Steiner 1993). Zimbabwe has allocated 12 per cent of its surface area for protected area conservation. Large amounts of communally-owned land in the rural areas are used for wildlife programmes. South Africa has less than 6 per cent of its surface area dedicated to protected wildlife estate and a relatively small amount of community-owned land is allocated to conservation programmes. But both countries have reputations for maintaining some of the best managed conservation estates in the world (Makombe 1994).

The region has some of the world's largest wildlife zones for large mammals. Animal populations include the largest herds of elephants anywhere in Africa. Reserves and national parks in the subcontinent currently provide the only safe refuge for black and white rhino, which verge on being poached to extinction in the rest of Africa:

One of the largest contiguous elephant and wildlife ranges left in Africa (with a population in excess of 150,000 elephants) is centred on Victoria Falls and includes areas of Angola, Namibia,

Zambia, Botswana, Zimbabwe and Mozambique. Wildlife populations in the region include the largest herds of elephant found anywhere in Africa (Zimbabwe ca 75,000; Botswana ca 45,000) as well as rhinos. The latter, however, have been subject to massive poaching in recent years (Steiner 1993: 11).

Westing (1992) also notes that war can have some unintended positive impacts on wildlife conservation. The major wartime benefit is reduced exploitation of natural resources in a given area because of the dangers associated with entering the zone. For example, during the Zimbabwean struggle for independence, the population of elephants in the Hwange National Park increased beyond the local carrying capacity, mainly because the situation had become too dangerous for poachers to operate there.

In Angola and Mozambique, war has had contradictory effects on the biological richness of the land. 'The paradox is that from the environmental perspective, Angola is a land with enormous positive potential; it lacks the array of environmental crises that face the rest of the continent' (Anstey no date: 1). Angola's various biomes sustain a rich combination of species. The floral diversity is the second highest in Africa with 1,260 endemic species. Fauna include 4 species of marine turtle, 3 types of crocodile and 275 mammals. The avifauna include 872 species, with the Gabela escarpment area being a centre of endemicism and among the top 10 most important bird conservation sites in Africa (ibid.).

Extreme environmental degradation has been largely restricted to coastal zones and the larger urban centres. One example is on the Angola-Namibia border, where the Angolan side has a relatively pristine habitat while the Namibian side has experienced severe degradation owing to extensive settlement and cattle grazing. This borderline shows up clearly on satellite images (Anstey no date; Marsh and Seely 1992: 4).

Similar patterns have been identified in Mozambique. The low overall population density and the forced abandonment of large areas because of the war have resulted in the regeneration of the vegetation and soil in large parts of the countryside. In the densely populated areas around the cities, along the transport corridors and near the coast, the opposite has happened. Here difficulty of access to land and other resources for most of the population and the use of agricultural techniques that are not suited to local conditions have made the problem of degeneration of resources acute (Moyo et al. 1993).

Even before the end of armed hostilities, other countries in the region were instrumental in carrying out a range of conservation reforms designed to make peace between parks and the neighbouring people. The most famous example is the CAMPFIRE programme in Zimbabwe, implemented in many parts of the country in the late 1980s. This is designed to enable rural people in communal areas to derive real benefits from wildlife through controlled and sustainable use. Although CAMPFIRE has met with varying success rates, it has demonstrated that innovative strategies can reduce tensions betwee human needs and the preservation of wildlife (Makombe 1994).

The Concept of Peace Parks

International, transnational and border parks and similar protected landscapes have an unrealized potential for reducing international tensions and for creating conditions which make peace more likely. Besides their direct influence on the enhancement of peace, these parks can also result in improved management of natural resources and the protection of indigenous minority people...Various conditions of sovereignty, ownership, control, tension and dispute, and degree and broadness of interest produce a number of different situations in which parks can improve or aid in the creation of peaceful conditions. The creation and management of protected areas need not wait for peaceful conditions nor for agreeable partners on both sides of a border. The position taken here is that these parks can precede, lead to, and result in, as well as help to maintain, peace among nations and communities (McNeil 1990: 25).

The World Conservation Union (IUCN) estimates there are currently at least 70 cross-border parks involving 65 countries in Europe, North America, Asia, Africa, South America and Central America. A study produced by the organisation in 1990 notes that a surprisingly large number of protected areas have been established in frontier regions, especially where populations are low and borders tend to follow the crest line of mountain ranges or river contours where scenic values are high (Thorsell and Harrison 1990).

Countries and regions within countries tend to develop outwards from a central seaport or fairly central capital city. This often results in the last wilderness zones being located in frontier regions. Frequently these wildlife zones are too small to support viable populations of species. This problem can be solved by linking the area to a larger zone that may exist on the other side of the border (Brown 1990; Allen 1995).

Peace Parks in Southern Africa
The idea of peace parks has taken hold in southern Africa. The most advanced transfrontier plan in the region is a scheme to link the Kruger National Park in South Africa, the Gonarezhou National Park in Zimbabwe and several conservation areas across their border with Mozambique – including a hunting concession area that straddles Kruger, known as Coutada 16, the Zinave National Park and the Banhine National Park (Tinley and Van der Riet 1991).

Associated with this scheme, and in some studies an integral part of it, is a plan to extend this envisaged cross-border megapark southwards so that it joins a transfrontier conservation zone linking Swaziland with Mozambique across the Lebombo Mountain range that forms a border between the two countries. A chain of game reserves in South Africa's KwaZulu-Natal province – currently being consolidated into the Greater St Lucia Wetland Park – could also link with a conservation area surrounding the Maputo Elephant Park in southern Mozambique (Figure 4.1).

On the western side of the subcontinent, a cross-border reserve comprising the Kalahari Gemsbok Park in the Northern Cape province of South Africa and a similar conservation area in the Botswana Gemsbok National Park has been in *de facto* existence for several years. Plans to establish a joint management system are now being mooted and the Namibian authorities are considering joining a slice of the Kalahari desert in their territory to this park (*Star*, Johannesburg 31 October 1990; Chris Brown, pers. comm.).

The Caprivi region of Namibia contains a number of small to large conservation areas that could be consolidated and linked to derelict game reserves in southern Angola (Brown 1990). The Kaokoland Natural Resource Conservation area has been linked to the Skeleton Coast Park in Namibia and these will be adjacent to the Iona Park in southwest Angola. A link between the Hwange National Park in Zimbabwe and the Nxai Pans National Park as well as the Makgadikgadi Pans Game Reserve in Botswana has also been suggested (*ibid.*).

Namibia's wildlife department has plans to link the Kaudom National Park in Namibia to a natural resource area in the eastern Bushmanland region. These areas, in turn, may be linked to a conservation area in the Okavango Delta in Botswana. Conservation officials in Namibia have suggested that the entire region be developed as a Bushman World Heritage Area (Brown 1990). The Huns Mountains and Fish River Canyon in Namibia could be linked together and then with Richtersveld National Park in South Africa (Chris Brown, pers. comm.).

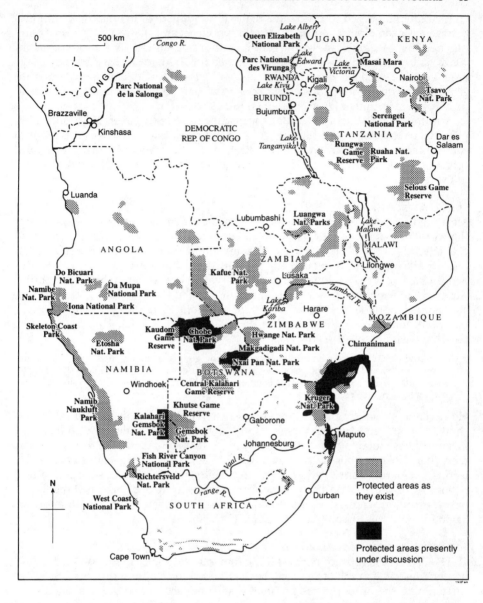

Figure 4.1 *Principal existing national parks and superpark expansion plans*

A community-based resource area that will straddle the Rovuma River running between Mozambique's northern Niassa province and Tanzania, is also being planned by Mozambican conservation authorities and their counterparts in Tanzania in conjunction with the IUCN branch for southern Africa (Simon Anstey, pers. comm.). A small cross-border park will link the Chimanimani Forest in Zimbabwe with a moist forest area across the border in Mozambique's Manica province (Environment Development Group 1994).

A number of distinct conceptual approaches have been generated around the potential of building peace parks in this part of the continent. It is worth exploring some of these, as they have serious implications for the ability of transfrontier conservation initiatives to achieve the objective of economic and social reconstruction in the region.

The Romantic Vision
Most media reports describe cross-border conservation initiatives as being among the world's most exciting experiments in protecting biodiversity. This is especially characteristic of the plans that place Mozambique at the centre of southern Africa's peace park initiative. Several scenarios, especially those reported in the South African media, depict a huge swathe of conservation territory stretching from South Africa in the west across Mozambican territory to the Indian Ocean islands in the east. Some reports suggest that a 'mirror image' of the Kruger Park should be created in Mozambique (*Star* 9 September 1991, 26 September 1992). This cross-border park has been described as follows:

> The world's greatest ecotourism treat – incorporating big game country with exciting marine environment-would be the one place on earth where one can see the world's largest mammals (whales), the world's largest mammals (elephants) and the vast numbers of other animals and birds (*Star*, 26 Septemer 1992).

However, it is unlikely these grandiose visions (Figure 4.2) will be realised in the short term, and most conservationists are now aware that unless the complex of social realities, not depicted on the glossy maps that accompany the rosy scenarios for a chain of superparks in southern Africa, is addressed there is little chance for using cross-border conservation as an effective tool for rural reconstruction in the region. Nevertheless, the Peace Parks Foundation, headed by Anton Rupert, the business tycoon who also chairs WWF-SA, was established in 1997 in an effort to begin realising this dream (*African Wildlife* 1997: 40).

The Social Development Approach
The IUCN report on peace parks and the romantic version of these potential cross-border conservation initiatives have been criticised for ignoring the social realities surrounding the proposed programmes – and the fact that land demarcated and protected as conservation estate frequently deprives resident people of resources they rely on for survival.

The wartime demographics of Mozambique, for example, were once regarded as a positive factor for conservation. Large tracts of land were abandoned as the population either fled the country or moved to the coastal cities and internal transport corridors. With the advent of peace and the spontaneous repatriation of people to their home villages, it would appear that this opportunity has now been lost. Booth and Lopes have recorded a large and unregulated influx of people into the Chicualacuala district and estimate that there are already some 160,000 people living in and alongside the Coutada 16, which lies at the heart of the planned peace park in Mozambique. In addition, large communities are said to be resident in the

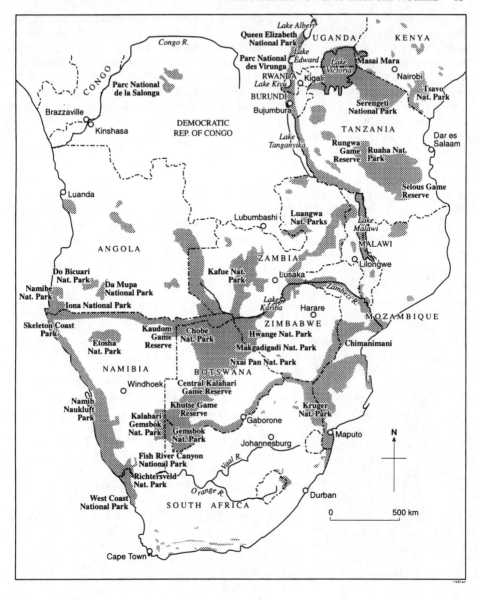

Figure 4.2 *The limits of the envisaged transboundary superpark network*

Banhine and Zinave National Parks, also key elements in the greater peace park vision (Booth and Lopes 1994). Grossman and Laforte (1994) note a similar settlement of about 3,000 people inside the Maputo Elephant Park.

Removing people, who are trying to rebuild their homes and to recover from the trauma of a bitter civil war, to make way for protected wildlife zones would be an exercise in extreme cynicism. Spontaneous and rapid resettlement, along with an almost complete lack of land-use planning on the part of the Mozambican authorities concerned, is listed by Booth and Lopes (1994) as the greatest threat to the long-term viability of the peace park concept.

In South Africa, we have seen that there is extensive congestion and social complexity in the villages bordering the Kruger National Park. Some commentators estimate that the park has up to 6 million neighbours (Chris Marais, pers. comm.). Some of the 'villages' are in fact rural townships with high population densities. Internal relations between the various social strata are frequently complex and conflictual. In addition, there is a variety of overlapping and competing claims for land – both in areas where people have been resettled after being forcibly removed as well as in original ancestral land, some of which is located inside the Kruger Park.

Efforts to establish a clear relationship of custodianship between the park and its original inhabitants are fraught with difficulties. To draw the boundary between people who are park 'neighbours' and those who do not have any traditional link with the land is close to impossible. In Zimbabwe, one of the critical success factors for CAMPFIRE (the Communal Areas Management Programme for Indigenous Resources and the Environment) is that projects are located in shared and defensible space in the sense that the small relatively cohesive communities have well demarcated political boundaries and a fairly coherent understanding of who their members are (CAMPFIRE Association 1990; Child and Petersen 1991). These boundaries have been shattered in South Africa and Mozambique, although, in the latter, the small size of settlements holds out some opportunities for a fairly rapid reconstruction of village integrity.

Closely related to demographic dislocation and flux is the absence of stable local government. This constraint takes different forms in most of the countries concerned. The post-independence system of rural administration in Zimbabwe has made it possible for communities to own their wild resources and exploit these effectively. However, there are conflicts between district and village levels over the allocation of resources, and increasing pressures for district governments to use wildlife revenue to finance their own operations rather than development projects for the villages most affected by wildlife. In addition, there is a tendency to ignore traditional leadership and social networks. This limits the extent to which all strata within the settlements participate fully in the operations for CAMPFIRE programmes (Murombedzi 1993).

In South Africa the opposite applies. Traditional institutions of local government – chiefs and their tribal authorities – were propped up by Pretoria in the period of apartheid. The internal consensus-building procedures that marked these institutions in the pre-colonial period were frequently but not always disrupted. The result is a series of bitter and intractable conflicts in the South African countryside between the tribal authorities and civic organisations that emerged as the organs of popular mobilisation during the struggle against apartheid. Frequently a situation of dual power exists in the rural village; often neither institution has a stable presence in the area. This makes it extremely difficult, as conservationists who work in these areas confirm, to establish stable partnerships (Levin and Mkhabela 1994).

Local government in Mozambique is frequently absent or exists only in embryonic form. Several writers have commented on the clash between the post-independence administration created by the Frelimo-led government and the traditional institutions of chiefs and headmen that operated during Portuguese colonial rule. Indeed efforts by Frelimo to declare that 'the tribe is dead' and to stamp out all associated institutions are often cited as the main factor that fuelled the civil war. Tribal chiefs and headmen stripped of their power became the main support base for the Renamo rebels. In some parts of Mozambique, there are in fact three different parties that have implemented their own rudimentary forms of local government in the wake of the war: traditional chiefs, government administrators, and Renamo's regional leadership (Finnegan 1989, 1992; Booth and Lopes 1994; Grossman and Laforte 1994; Vines 1996).

Existing district and village structures in Zimbabwe sometimes discriminate against women, who play a vital role in the management of family diets and use of natural resources. Some councils in Zimbabwe, for example, have excluded single women from the definition of household heads able to qualify for revenues generated by CAMPFIRE programmes, while allowing single men to be included (Kiss 1990). The Purros project in northwestern Namibia resolved this problem by creating a new institution to manage the wildlife-based tourism project operating there. Women play an important role here in decisions about the allocation of revenues (Jacobsohn 1992). Kiss (1990) notes that conservation authorities frequently face a dilemma when it comes to dealing with local authorities. The existing structure may not be reaching all strata of the settlement but to create an alternative structure from scratch is time-consuming and could generate conflict with the existing power blocs.

A legal framework for communal wildlife utilisation is lacking in Mozambique. As things currently stand, the state owns all wildlife. Drastic revisions are required for the kind of enabling environment that exists under Zimbabwean legislation to come into being in Mozambique. In addition, the law regarding land tenure in Mozambique has been described as verging on anarchy. Three or more parties frequently claim some form of tenure or lease over the same piece of land and many of these contested claims occur in areas marked for the development of a peace park. A massive political effort on the part of the government is required for any form of development, including wildlife-based programmes, to succeed (Environment Development Group 1994).

The effects of war on Mozambique's wildlife department have already been noted. All the feasibility studies for the proposed peace park stress that institutional weaknesses represent a major obstacle to wildlife rehabilitation programmes. Conflict in Zimbabwe's conservation agencies has also debilitated plans to reconstruct the Gonarezhou National Park. There is also a considerable degree of flux in South Africa's conservation establishment. After the 'freedom elections' in 1994, 9 relatively autonomous provinces replaced the 4 'white' provinces and 10 'ethnic' homelands that existed previously, requiring the amalgamation and reorganisation of different conservation agencies in the new regions. The various conservation agencies are still debating the exact relationship between the national conservation authority and the provincial ones. Some agencies believe that parks management should be devolved to provincial level, especially as this would allow revenues to be used for local development.

However, the region covered by the planned peace park between South Africa, Mozambique and Zimbabwe is especially well-endowed with projects that are already trying to link social development with wildlife protection. Some of Zimbabwe's most successful CAMPFIRE programmes are located in the Beit Bridge district across the Limpopo River from the Kruger National Park. On the other hand, the prospect of mining in some of South Africa's last wilderness areas is a highly emotive subject. Heated controversies have also arisen in the Kruger National Park, while the Wildlife Society of Southern Africa (now the Wildlife and Environment Society of South Africa) waged a long and ultimately successful campaign to prevent a local mining company from opening coal deposits in the reserve during the apartheid era. The same Society is currently spearheading resistance to plans by an Australian multinational company to prospect for alluvial diamonds in the environmentally sensitive Madimbo Corridor along the Limpopo River boundary between South Africa and Zimbabwe (Allen 1995).

There is now no alternative but for the interested parties and stakeholders in these regions to negotiate various forms of community-based conservation arrangements. For this reason the Environment Development Group, in its feasibility study for the Mozambican government, has emphasised the need to move away from strictly protected wildlife areas towards an emphasis on multiple resource use by the residents of rural settlements. This could combine with other forms of land use such as plantation forestry, agriculture and livestock, depending on the ability of the relevant Mozambican authorities to implement a coherent regional development plan.

The study stresses that a peace park of the type outlined in the 'grand vision' scenarios has to remain a long-term possibility. The emphasis in the short term should be on the internal rehabilitation of protected areas, with a simultaneous stress on the creation of community-based programmes that involve conservation and also other forms of land use. These individual and national components of a peace park would justify existence in their own right. There is no need for a national park in one country to be matched by a similar protected area in the adjacent state (Environment Development Group 1994). A menu of different and self-standing projects on each side of national borders could ultimately be incorporated into a wider transfrontier zone resembling a patchwork quilt of wildlife conservation areas.

Nevertheless, events are moving apace. The WWF-SA has recently been instrumental in setting up a new organisation, called the Peace Park Foundation. Headed by former WWF-SA chief executive, John Hanks, it is dedicated to supporting peace parks all over Africa. One of its first objectives is to establish transfrontier conservation areas between South Africa and Mozambique – on the borders between the Kruger National Park and Mozambique's Gaza Province and on the KwaZulu-Natal border with Maputo Province.

In addition, an American billionaire, James Ulysses Blanchard III, was given the green light by the Mozambique government in early 1997 to develop a massive theme park – comprising resort hotels, game lodges, a revitalised Big Five game reserve, and a steam train – in a broad swathe of coastal land the size of Israel, located between Maputo and the KwaZulu-Natal border (*Africa Confidential* 1997: 8; *Economist* 1997; Mozambique News Agency 1997: 3). In the process, an earlier commitment to permit a major South African pulp and paper company to establish a large plantation in the area was abrogated, ostensibly on the grounds of its negative environmental impacts (Holt-Biddle 1996). The contract with the Mozambican government for this highly controversial project states that it will reintroduce large mammals to southern Mozambique and reopen a historic elephant migration route between the Tembe Game Reserve in northern KwaZulu-Natal and the Maputo Elephant Park, which falls within Blanchard's concession area. One of Blanchard's senior consultants, Eugene Gouws, has recently stated that the American will cooperate with and facilitate efforts to create an integrated conservation zone across the political boundaries in the area (pers. comm., April 1997).

A number of economic factors favour the peace park process in the region. Most of the communal land in all three countries that will be included in the proposed transfrontier park is located on semi-arid savanna. Several studies indicate that consumptive (hunting) and non-consumptive (tourism) uses of wildlife in this kind of habitat have comparative advantages over cattle and maize farming. On semi-arid rangelands wildlife lends itself to multiple use – including tourism, safari hunting, cropping and the sale of venison. At the same time, these forms of development maintain the natural resource base, unlike the other forms of land use that are available to residents and landowners in these areas (Child 1990).

A recent study on the economic uses of the Kruger National Park notes that the reserve generates substantially more social and economic benefits than would other forms of agricultural use. The park is budgeted to yield a gross income of R90 million (about US$25 million). It employs about 3,000 people and pays a wage bill of R50 million per annum. The study estimates that the spin-off effects of foreign and domestic tourism have created an extra 13,000 jobs and contributed some R429 million (US$119 million) to the country's GDP. Of the 700,000 visitors each year, some 300,000 stay in hotels and lodges surrounding the park. At present, 33 hotels, 12 private game parks and a substantial number of guest houses are located on the outskirts of the park. There is thus no doubt that the park has contributed to the development of the regional economy, especially on its southern borders where tourist traffic is at its highest (Engelbrecht and Van der Walt 1993).

A small tourist lodge in Maputaland has been able to generate 300 permanent jobs from a small investment of some R80 million (about US$26 million), which is greater than the employment opportunities generated in nearby mines and industries which require a much higher capital investment. The peace park movement in southern Africa could help to galvanise similar success stories as part of the opportunities that peace has brought to many other parts of the continent, but not if conservationists try to impose their ideas about wildlife preservation and conservation on to the indigenous realities of these regions.

References

Africa Confidential (1997) 'Blanchard's Beach', 38(6), 14 March. London.

African Wildlife (1997) 'Peace Parks Initiative'. 51(3): 40.

Allen, A. (1995) 'Golden Horseshoe' Wilderness; a Lucky Break or a Kick in the Teeth for Conservation? (with several responses by other parties), *African Wildlife* 49(6): 6-11. (see also *African Wildlife* (1996) 50(4): 23).

Anderson, J.L., Dutton, P., Goodman, P. and Souto, B. (1990) 'Evaluation of the Wildlife Resource in Marromeu Province with Recommendations for its Use,' unpublished survey commissioned by Lomaco, October.

Anstey, S. (no date) 'Conflict and Conservation; Striking a Balance', *NCS Bulletin*.

Booth and Lopes (1994) 'The Feasibility of TFCA Development in Southern Maputo Province', in Environment Development Group.

Brown, C. (1990) 'Existing and Potential Trans-border Conservation Areas in the Southern Africa Region', Republic of Namibia, Ministry of Wildlife, Conservation and Tourism, Windhoek, September (mimeo).

Campfire Association, The (1990) *People, Wildlife and Natural Resources – The Campfire Approach to Rural Development in Zimbabwe*. Harare, July.

Catterson, T., Kir, A., Rossi, M. and Dutton, P. (1991) *A Provisional Programme for the Forestry/Wildlands Sector*. Ministry of Agriculture, Maputo.

Child, B. (1990) 'Assessment of Wildlife Utilization as a Land Use Option in the Semi-arid Rangelands of Southern Africa', in Kiss.

Child, B. and Petersen, J.H. (1991) *Campfire in Rural Development: The Beit Bridge Experience*. Department of National Parks and Wildlife Management, Harare.

Costa, F., Anstey, S. and Chande, B.A. (1993) *Mozambique: Demobilisation of Soldiers/Staff Training for Forest and Wildlife Management*. IUCN: Gland.

Dutton, P. (1994) 'A Dream Becomes a Nightmare: Mozambique's ferocious 15-year bush war has devastated a once rich and abundant wildlife', *African Wildlife* 48(6): 6–14.

Economist, The (1997) 'Theme-park Tourism', 3 May. London.

Ellis, S. (1994) 'Of Elephants and Men: Politics and Nature Conservation in South Africa', *Journal of Southern African Studies*, 20(1): 53–69.

Engelbrecht, W.G. and Van der Walt, P.T. (1993) 'Notes on the Economic Uses of the Kruger National Park', *Koedoe*, 36(2):

Environment Development Group (1994) *GEF Transfrontier Conservation Areas and Institution Strengthening Project: Preparation Studies*. Draft Final Report, Environment and Development Group, March.

Environmental Investigation Agency (1989) *A System of Extinction: The African Elephant Disaster*. EIA, London.

Finnegan, W. (1989) 'A Reporter at Large', *The New Yorker*, 22 May. New York.

Finnegan, W. (1992) *A Complicated War; the Harrowing of Mozambique*. University of California Press, Berkeley and Los Angeles.

Grossman, D. and Laforte, A. (1994) 'The Feasibility of TFCA Development in Southern Maputo Province', in Environment Development Group.

Guardian, The (1991) 11 November. London.

Hales, D. (1989) 'Changing Concepts of National Parks', in Western, D. and Pearl, M. (eds) *Conservation for the Twenty-First Century*. Oxford University Press, Oxford.

Holt-Biddle, D. (1996) 'A New Conflict Rages; Different Development Options for Southern Mozambique Spark a Fierce Debate', *African Wildlife* 50(2): 15–18.

Jacobsohn, M. (1992) 'The Crucial Link: Conservation and Development', in Cock, J. and Koch,E. (eds) *Going Green: People, Politics and the Environment in South Africa*. Oxford University Press, Cape Town.

Kiss, A. (ed.) (1990) *Living with Wildlife: Wildlife Resource Management with Local Participation in Africa*. World Bank Technical Paper 130, Washington, DC.

Levin, R. and Mkhabela, S. (1994) *The Chieftancy, Land Allocation and Democracy in the Eastern Transvaal Central Lowveld*, Working Paper 10, Conference on Community Perspectives on Land Reform, Johannesburg, March.

Levin, R. and Solomon, I. (1994) *Forced Removals and Land Claims in the Eastern Transvaal*, Working Paper 12, Conference on Community Perspectives on Land Reform, Johannesburg, March.

Makombe, K. (ed.) (1994) *Sharing the Land: Wildlife, People and Development in Africa*. IUCN/Regional Office for Southern Africa and IUCN Sustainable Use of Wildlife Programme, Harare.

Marsh, A. and Seely, M. (eds) (1992) *Oshanas; Sustaining People, Environment and Development in Central Owambo, Namibia*. Desert Research Foundation of Namibia and Swedish International Development Authority, Windhoek.

McNeil, R.J. (1990) 'International Parks for Peace', in Thorsell.

Moyo, S., O'Keefe, P. and Sill, M. (1993) *The Southern African Environment; Profiles of SADC Countries*, Earthscan, London.

Mozaic (undated) Mission Statement. Unpublished memo.

Mozambique Information Agency (1986) *MozambiqueFile*, November. Maputo.

Mozambique News Agency (1997) *AIM Report* 101, 8 January. London.

Murombedzi, J. (1993) 'State versus Local Control of Natural Resources: the Case of the Campfire Programme in Zimbabwe, Centre for Applied Social Sciences, University of Zimbabwe, Harare, December, unpublished paper.

Pinnock, D. (1996) 'Superparks: a Dream Impossible', *Getaway Magazine*, November: 88–97.

Potgieter, S. C. de Wet (1996) *Contraband: South Africa and the International Trade in Rhino Horn and Ivory*. Queillerie, Strand (South Africa).

Republic of Mozambique (1991) *Country Report for UNCED 1992*. Maputo.

Steiner, A.M. (1993) 'The peace dividend in southern Africa: prospects and potentials for redirecting military resources towards natural resource management'. Paper at UNDP Conference on Military and the Environment, 'Past Mistakes and Futures Options', New York, February.

Thorsell, J. (ed)(1990) *Parks on the Borderline: Experience in Transfrontier Conservation*. IUCN, Gland.

Thorsell, J. and Harrison, J. (1990) 'Parks that Promote Peace: a Global Inventory of Transfrontier Nature Reserves', in Thorsell.

Tinley, K.L. and Van der Riet, W.F. (1991) 'Conceptual Proposals for Kruger-Banhine: a Trans-frontier National Resource Area', Southern Africa Nature Foundation, Stellenbosch (unpublished).

US Defence Intelligence Agency (no date) Classified Document 14D. Washington, DC.

Vines, A. (1996) *Renamo; From Terrorism to Democracy in Mozambique* (2nd edn). James Currey, Oxford.

Wells, M. and Brandon, K. (1992) *People and Parks: Linking Protected Area Management with Local Communities*. World Bank WWF and USAID, Washington, DC.

Westing, A.H. (1992) 'Protected Areas and the Military', *Environmental Conservation* 19(4): 343–88.

5 South Africa's Foreign Policy: from Isolation to Respectability?

GREG MILLS

Introduction

The 'old' South Africa's foreign policy was characterised, at the level of official government-to-government relations, by increasing international isolation and opprobrium. In terms of 'unofficial', non-governmental relations, the African National Congress (ANC)'s campaign to exacerbate this isolation through international sanctions was a key pillar of its anti-apartheid strategy. As a result, it was expected that, with the end of apartheid, the 'new' South Africa would be able to play a dramatically improved, more positive, international role.[1] However, the record of the new South Africa's foreign policy since the elections of April 1994 has been one of sharp contrast.

On the one hand, high-profile and controversial dealings with Libya, Iran and Syria during 1996–7 thrust Pretoria's foreign policy under the international spotlight. For what purpose and to what extent, it was asked, was the ruling ANC willing to endanger its international trade and investment links by encouraging close ties with so-called pariah states, even if they were its old allies and friends? The sudden about-turn in President Mandela's stance on the issue of diplomatic relations with Taiwan and the People's Republic of China (PRC), which was resolved in favour of Beijing in October 1996, finally put to rest one on-going policy conundrum, albeit in somewhat dramatic fashion. But the seemingly haphazard manner in which such decisions were made and articulated also gave rise to concern about the nature of the policy process and the role of the Minister as well as the Department of Foreign Affairs (DFA). In this regard, concern has been expressed about the nature of the President's foreign schedule, for example: while he has visited Asia several times as President, he has yet to travel to Latin America, an omission which has not gone unnoticed by a region of increasing importance as a trade and investment partner. Also, in another area, the reason for the drawn-out nature of the trade negotiations over a Free Trade Agreement (FTA) with the European Union (EU), was presented to the South African public as the result of a principled stance taken by the South African government over its preference for partial membership of the Lomé Convention. However, what was not made clear was the fact that the South African negotiators in these complex talks were attempting to negotiate without having undertaken a thoroughly calculated modelling of the costs and benefits of the FTA to South Africa.

I am grateful to James Barber and Alan Begg for their helpful comments in the preparation of this paper. All faults remain mine alone, however. An earlier and abridged version of this chapter was published in the 1997 *South African Yearbook of International Affairs*.

On the other hand, there have been a number of successes. First, on the organisational side, the DFA has displayed an increasing willingness to interact openly with civil society in the formulation of policy. The publication of the *South African Foreign Policy Discussion Document* in June 1996 and the subsequent holding of a Foreign Policy Workshop in Johannesburg in September, were illustrative of this new approach. In the same vein, the Department has also staged a number of consultative workshops and seminars open to participants from the academic community, the media and elsewhere.[2]

Secondly, prompted by the Zaire-Rwanda refugee crisis late in 1996, South Africa appears to have at last shed some of its sensitivity about adopting a less apologetic and more assertive regional/continental role. President Mandela's assumption of the Chairmanship of the Southern African Development Community (SADC) at the Annual Conference held in Maseru in August 1996, has also thrown the responsibility of redefining the Community's purpose and functions on to its largest regional actor. Pretoria's efforts in attempting to facilitate a peaceful conclusion to the civil war in Zaire, now the Democratic Republic of Congo (DRC), which peaked with the staging of talks on board the South African Navy vessel, *SAS Outeniqua*, in May 1997, also thrust South Africa into the international diplomatic limelight.

While there may still be some regional sensitivities (particularly from Zimbabwe) about the Republic's new-found authority in these areas, it has clearly dawned on South Africa's leaders that if their country is to assume the status of an African power and address some of the continent's problems, they will have to engage with those problems. This responsibility, even if unsolicited, is undoubtedly the destiny of the continent's major economic and diplomatic power. This diplomacy has set a new standard for the continent, for Mandela's government has been under pressure since its inception to play a more active role in pushing Africa towards democracy, stability and prosperity. But a number of interventions by the President himself in African crises during 1997, culminating in the very high-profile effort to broker a settlement in the former Zaire, raised, in turn, considerable doubts about Pretoria's ability to influence events on the African continent. They also raised doubts about the formulation and conduct of South Africa's Africa policy.

The President's attempts to effect democracy in Nigeria and reconciliation in Angola; to persuade Zambian President Frederick Chiluba to allow his predecessor, Kenneth Kaunda, to participate in his country's 1997 elections; and to nudge Swazi King Mswati III to introduce democratic reforms speedily, must all be counted more as failures than successes. Moreover, it would appear that Pretoria and South African business were clearly out of step over events in the former Zaire, with the government exhibiting little knowledge of the extent of actual or potential South African business involvement there, and not caring to involve businessmen in discussions during the negotiation process. This sort of behaviour is far from the reality of today's global economy.

Certainly Laurent-Desiré Kabila's revolution against the Zairean dictator, Mobutu Sese Seko, presented the biggest test of South Africa's foreign policy efficacy in Africa. Deputy President, Thabo Mbeki, has since hailed the overthrow of Mobutu as the signal event in what he has described as an 'African Renaissance', an epithet that caught the imagination of the world. Mbeki first used the phrase in the United States in a landmark speech delivered to the US Corporate Council on Africa in April 1997, in which he said that the time had come for Africans to take responsibility for bringing the continent out of its dark ages of tyranny and poverty into a renaissance of democracy and prosperity (*Sunday Times*, Johannesburg, 27 April).

As South Africa's Deputy Foreign Minister, Aziz Pahad, has also argued: ·

> The African renaissance is about how to achieve the objectives of turning things around in Africa. It is a multifaceted approach to turn Africa around from a continent with vast potential which is currently underutilised. This is linked to multiparty democracy, good governance, a move away from state-controlled economies, a better relationship between unions, government and business, and the building of civil society institutions.[3]

He noted that at the heart of the notion lay the poser, 'How do we deal with African conditions to create sustainable development?'

However, the extent of South Africa's influence remains unclear, and it is this lack of influence that lies at the heart of questions about the future direction of its African foreign policy. In this, Africa's mixed fortunes are clearly a priority issue for South African foreign and regional policy as it seeks to make Africa the centrepiece of its foreign relations. The growing importance of commercial issues in foreign relations also has implications for South African foreign policy.

Interpreting South Africa's Foreign Policy

South Africa has clearly had a vast amount on its diplomatic plate since the resumption of normal international relations in 1994, in terms of the expansion of bilateral and multilateral ties, the integration or 'combination' of personnel within the DFA, and also with respect to the number of policy issues which have arisen from the end of political isolation. In the continuously shifting scene of international relations, foreign policy does not rely so much on direction as on orientation or 'leaning'. In South Africa's case, its foreign relations could be said to lack the necessary broad orientation and strategic purpose.[4] There is a danger of South Africa developing a self-image as a benign foreign policy godmother. For it has perceived itself to have a long list of guiding principles including: as a symbol of democracy and human rights; as an even-handed friend of all, as epitomised by the underlying spirit of 'universality'; and as an international go-between and mediator. Unless South Africa is to end up with an insolvent foreign policy, it will have to define and prioritise its objectives and take cognisance both of its own limitations and of the nature of the world outside. The wide-ranging variety of self-appointed roles is one of the key problems in identifying South Africa's foreign policy orientation.

The ANC spent decades appealing to the world's conscience to work to end the morally repugnant system of apartheid. Now in power, as the friendlier ties between South Africa and so-called pariah states illustrate, they appear to be incapable of making any moral judgements about who they should deal with and who they should not, instead preferring to treat all comers equally. From their background, it would be expected that discriminating against countries that support terrorism is a pretty easy call, and terrorist groups an even easier one. Although morality is a contested principle of foreign relations, South Africa – and President Mandela in particular – has overtly attempted to seize the moral high ground, and it is this facet beyond all else which gives the country such international stature.

Critics have argued that South Africa has essentially a *'twin-track'* foreign policy. On the one hand, it pursues the national interest above all else, including human rights,[5] hence the opening of relations with Beijing in preference to Taiwan and the close ties with Indonesia, Cuba and Libya. Yet, on the other hand, perhaps mindful of the success of its own recent transition, Pretoria displays outward concern over human rights and democratisation elsewhere. As President Mandela noted before assuming power in 1993, 'Human rights will be the light that guides our foreign policy' (Mandela, 1993: 88). Since the 1994 elections, this approach has notably manifested itself in stricter control over the export of South African manufactured arms (especially through the operation of the National Conventional Arms Control Committee – NCACC), but not an end to arms sales.

Many countries would, of course, agree with this stance (if they cared about democracy), though – as with President Mandela's blast at Nigeria at the 1995 Commonwealth Heads of Government Meeting (CHOGM) in Millbrook – few would express such sentiments. The difficulty in trying to follow a foreign policy dictated by human rights considerations is becoming increasingly apparent to the government. As deputy minister Aziz Pahad put it in September 1996,

> We start from the premise that South Africa is committed to human rights. The problem we face in this regard is the issue of possibilities and limitations on South Africa in the real world. How do we get human rights enforced and implemented in the international environment? There must be a possible [sic] contradiction between South-South co-operation and the values which we may want to project. There has to be interaction between theory and practice.[6]

To confuse the issue even further, a *third* foreign policy track is evident in all of this: since 1994 Pretoria would appear to have attempted to redress the foreign policy imbalances of the apartheid era (and the National Party) by a shift towards the opposite direction without going all the way. Hence its policy stance towards the Middle East which could be said to have shifted from being pro-Israeli to being pro-Arab; or changes in its policy towards the United States and Cuba. The public furore that erupted in January 1997 over proposed South African arms sales to Syria[7] once more raised fundamental questions about the coherence of and responsibility for Pretoria's foreign policy, which this review seeks to address, notably:

- What is the overriding objective of South Africa's foreign policy?
- What strategies could be adopted to achieve this objective?
- What tactics could be utilised to ensure that correct strategies are adopted and followed?
- What other factors will shape South Africa's pursuit of its foreign policy?

Setting Foreign Policy Priorities

The DFA has attempted to redress a perceived lack of policy consistency and co-ordination through the formulation of the aforementioned *South African Foreign Policy Discussion Document,* a sort of draft White Paper. Once comments on this paper have been absorbed, a foreign policy framework will be formulated based, in the words of Foreign Minister Alfred Nzo, 'on national consensus'.[8]

The opening up of South Africa's policy process was a unique, probably unprecedented exercise. Undoubtedly, too, it is desirable for South Africa's foreign policy experts to establish a general understanding of the values on which decisions and standpoints are premised. It is also important to establish a clear chain of command, throughout which there would be an acceptance of South Africa's role in the international community and of the evolving nature of that community.

The *Discussion Document* does not provide this lead, however. Its stated design is to assist the government in the task of 'shaping, directing and executing South Africa's foreign policy'. Put frankly, the *Document* can best be described as an ambitious but misguided foreign policy wish-list which understates the importance of the international operating environment, and South Africa's abilities and resources to work within that context – in other words, its capacity to act, which always has limitations. This is of critical importance. Foreign policy, by its nature, often has to be reactive – responding to unanticipated and often unwanted developments in the international setting. The government's aim should be to develop a systematic response in the biological rather than the mechanical sense – that it responds and reshapes according to the environment.

The *Discussion Document* identifies an all-inclusive list – variously described – of pillars, cornerstones, principles and priorities for South Africa's foreign policy covering virtually everything from 'responsible global citizenry' to 'the advancement of human rights and the promotion of democracy' to support for 'the work of the UNHCR (United Nations High Commissioner for Refugees)', and to 'secure worldwide peace, promote disarmament, prevent genocide, restrict proliferation of nuclear arms of mass destruction and achieve a new world security regime'. Ironically, the *Document* states that 'South Africa's policy initiatives should be modest and not overly ambitious'. Though few would take exception to these noble goals, it is doubtful, given South Africa's limited resources and size, that all of these can realistically be achieved.

A Prioritisation of Goals

Clearly the necessary move from South Africa's current foreign profile to a nuanced foreign policy requires the prioritisation of goals and the creation of an orderly and systematic manner of achieving these, mindful, of course, of domestic personnel and resource limitations. In this regard, democratic South Africa's foreign policy and diplomacy need to be based on an understanding of its self-interest in the global village. The *national interest* may be said to be underpinned by the general values enshrined in the Constitution, and encompasses the security of the state and its citizens and the promotion of their social and economic well-being, as well as the encouragement of global peace and regional stability and development. Put simply, this is achieved by a focus primarily on two strategic areas:

- encouraging stability and development in southern Africa;
- securing incremental improvements in investment and trade links worldwide.

Achieving Goals

The aforementioned strategic 'pillars' of foreign policy could, in South Africa's case, involve tactically, in turn:

- keeping South Africa's established trading and investment partners on-side;
- encouraging new links with emerging markets in the Asia-Pacific region and elsewhere;
- representing the interests of southern Africa in international fora, and
- extending assistance to the region where necessary in the interests of stability and development.

In this, South Africa's policies and the manner in which it interacts with the outside world will thus be shaped by a number of factors, including:

- **The role of personalities**: This is a crucial factor. President Mandela's stature in the international domain has meant that South Africa's image (and its foreign policy) tends largely to be equated with the President's profile. As a result, policy has often followed his public statements, rather than the other way round. His successor(s) will have to co-ordinate responsibility, and learn to rely on those involved in the process of policy formulation to make the right decisions, which s/he will then articulate to a greater extent than at present. Of course, given the nature of modern diplomacy, a head of state cannot be expected to be a mere microphone and will from time to time take a prominent foreign policy role. As the Syrian arms episode illustrated, the role of spokespeople needs to be carefully circumscribed: in that instance, it was perhaps less a case of dealing with rogue states than with rogue spokespeople.

- **South Africa's external political relations**: As noted above, it is critical here for South Africa to identify what the key objectives in its foreign policy are – notably the economic and physical well-being of South Africans. Only with this in mind (and with an appreciation of its own strengths and weaknesses, as well as the nature of the world outside) will it be able to establish and maintain a foreign policy orientation – to 'lean' in the direction arguably of securing incremental improvements in its trade and investment ties, and towards closer relations with the neighbouring states.

- **Familial ties**: These obviously will help to define relations with Europe; especially with the United Kingdom, given the preponderance of UK passport holders (1.1 million) in South Africa as well as the Commonwealth ties, with Portugal (600,000 passport holders), and through southern Africa's diaspora in South Africa.

- **The success of the South African 'experiment'**: The success of South Africa's transition to democracy, and the extent of external involvement in the country over the long term, hinges on the success of its economy and the existence of economic opportunities, and on its stabilising role in southern Africa. This is related, in turn, *inter alia*, to the role of leadership, the implementation of the Growth, Employment and Redistribution macro-economic strategy (GEAR), levels of interaction with the global economy, regional stability, socio-political stability (including crime), as well as its image as a responsible, reliable international partner.

- **The world around**: Southern Africa's and, further afield, Africa's transition to economic, political and security normalcy will have a profound effect on South Africa's image and fortunes, especially given its increased business interaction with the subcontinent. South Africa could also stand to profit in a role as a bridgehead for international trade with the region.

- **Resources**: These relate to the availability of personnel (leadership especially), natural and financial resources, and also South Africa's technical attributes and skills. The allocation of diplomatic resources and the focus of external business activity will in the future be determined by a number of criteria, including:
  - levels of trade and investment (both ways), and rates of growth;
  - sustainability of growth, which relates to: the size of the population (market); population growth and demography; population wealth; and GDP/manufacturing ratios;
  - and, obviously, the availability of South African resources, diplomatic or otherwise, including personnel and finances.

It is thus desirable for South Africa's foreign policy experts to establish a general understanding of the values on which decisions and standpoints are premised. It is also important to establish a clear chain of command (which was notably absent in the Syrian affair), throughout which there would be an acceptance of South Africa's role in the international community, and of the evolving nature of that community.

South African Foreign Policy Making in an Ideal World

Ideally, as with all other spheres of government policy, the President and the Cabinet should have the responsibility for the definition and execution of foreign policy. This should be subject to the scrutiny of Parliament acting as the representatives of the people of South Africa. In this, the media, professional associations, academics, and a variety of interest groups and concerned citizens will be encouraged to make inputs into the formulation of policy, and to comment on its execution (see Mills 1996a).

In this, too, the Minister of Foreign Affairs should be charged by the Cabinet to ensure and co-ordinate the execution of South Africa's foreign policy, and to act as the government's channel of communication with other governments and international institutions. The DFA is, in all of this, the Minister's primary instrument for discharging his/her responsibilities. Its primary function should be to promote the interests of South Africa internationally by establishing and maintaining diplomatic relations; by seeking acceptable solutions to international problems affecting South Africa's interests; and by participating in international initiatives and organisations.

The Reality

The realities of government and personalities have, however, impacted – sometimes negatively – on the machinery of foreign policy making. In this regard, it is necessary to recall from where South Africa has come in the foreign domain. In 1990, the government was extremely isolated, with only 30 overseas representations, and at that time the ANC's 28 diplomatic offices and efforts abroad were focused on increasing that isolation. Today, South Africa has relations with all but 22 (including North Korea, Iraq, Somalia, Liberia, Haiti and Sierra Leone) of the 170 or so countries and institutions holding diplomatic status; it has 108 residential diplomatic accreditations (75 embassies/high commissions) abroad (as opposed to 167 in South Africa, of which 96 are embassies/consulates) and 44 non-residential accreditations. To give a comparison with similar sized powers, Argentina has 80 embassies, 52 consulates and 5 multilateral missions and Chile, 66 embassies and 8 multilateral missions.[9]

The development of new diplomatic and international relations has thus involved bringing in different parties with markedly opposing styles and contrasting ideological baggage. As a result, Pretoria has, not surprisingly, hitherto followed a foreign policy underscored by the principle of 'universality' – essentially the opening of diplomatic doors to any state interested in doing so. Foreign policy has thus become a highly personalised affair, with President Mandela's international superstar status overshadowing all else. His deputy and heir-apparent, Thabo Mbeki, also takes a keen interest, echoing his earlier, and pre-government, role as head of the ANC's department of international relations. His active participation is facilitated by the comparative absence of high-profile leadership in the foreign ministry. The minister, Alfred Nzo, is interpreted as being 'Mandela's man' in the Cabinet, with his capable deputy, Aziz Pahad, a close ally of the deputy president.

Like other government departments, the Department of Foreign Affairs has inevitably been embroiled in a process of transition – of the integration (or combination) of personnel from the National Party (NP) government, the homelands and extra-parliamentary groups. The 'old' DFA comprised 1,917 staff. Following the election in 1994, 139 'overseas trained officials' (including ANC cadres) as well as 415 former TBVC (Transkei, Bophuthatswana, Venda and Ciskei) homeland diplomats joined. (There were originally 695 TBVC officials slated for the DFA, though 147 were transferred to other departments and 133 accepted early retirement packages.)

In order not to exceed the 2,166 posts prescribed by the Public Service Commission (PSC), prior to 30 April 1996 259 redundancy packages were approved. From July 1996 to January 1997, 112 applications for severance packages were received. Of the 80 ambassadors abroad in January 1997, 20 were political appointees, 42 were from 'previously disadvantaged' communities, and 10 were women. Such an inevitably turbulent process cannot have been helped by the temporary nature of leadership in the DFA. The appointment of its Director-General, Rusty Evans, was due to expire at the end of September 1997, and rumours abounded, too, as to who might replace him. This has not been, perhaps, the most healthy environment in which to set foreign policy priorities.[10]

Finally, the role of the Parliamentary Portfolio Committee on Foreign Affairs is, *inter alia*, to 'monitor, investigate, enquire into and make recommendations relating to any aspect of the legislative programme, budget rationalisation, restructuring, functioning, organisation, structure, personnel, policy formulation or any other matter it may consider relevant, of the government department or departments falling within the category of affairs assigned to the committee'. However, the relationship between the legislature and the executive is still in a process of 'evolution', as the then Chairperson of that committee, Raymond Suttner, has pointed out (see Suttner 1996). Although parliament is no longer operating in the rubber-stamping role that was the case in the past, the committee is at times not given an opportunity, as Suttner has admitted, to make an input and where it is (as over the two Chinas issue), its voice does not appear to be heard. The committee is, in a more positive vein, in a better position to hold the ministry accountable, while parliamentary approval of the ratification of treaties is now required.

Budget Shrinkages and the DFA/DTI Interface
In terms of resource allocation, budget shrinkages have meant that the DFA will in future have to disperse its resources in a creative manner which best represents South Africa's national interests. The department was allocated R1.146 bn in the 1996–7 Annual Budget, only a 0.7 per cent increase on the previous year. Already far below the domestic inflation rate of around 9 per cent, this cut has been exacerbated by the 20 per cent fall in the value of the Rand in 1996, consequently increasing the cost of upkeep of foreign missions. The 1997–98 budget has increased by 12.4 per cent in nominal terms. In this, the Cabinet has sliced R130 million off a request for capital projects for improvements to South Africa's foreign missions originally costed at R152 million. This will make an expansion in the number of missions more difficult, and the books will probably have to be balanced by 'downsizing' in some countries, in the form of staff cuts, the closure of whole consulates or even embassies, and the possible use of 'sleeping diplomats'. The sharing of missions with other SADC member states has also reportedly been mooted (see *Business Day*, 10 January and 16 April 1997).

The issue of representation abroad is complicated by the experience and qualifications of such representatives and their skills, and raises, in turn, the question of the value of having separate Departments of Foreign Affairs as well as Trade and Industry (DTI). It has been asked whether South Africa should not do what, for example, the Australians have managed successfully, and simply merge the two, but maintaining two separate ministers. This would certainly facilitate policy homogeneity (which was notably absent over the issue of the Indian Ocean Rim initiative in 1995) and would stimulate DFA expertise in foreign trade and multilateral economic issues which it does not possess at present (at least not at the level of the DTI). The setting up of special units dedicated to expanding trade – along the lines of the French *Poste D'Expansion* – is another possibility. Alternatively, the DFA should play a greater role in co-ordinating the various departments concerned with foreign relations: DTI, Defence, Culture, Sport, Tourism, Transport, and so on.

The Importance of Foreign Economic Relations

In an age when much about foreign relations is, in essence, foreign *economic* relations, it is inevitable, given the need to address social inequalities through economic growth, that South Africa's foreign policy will be geared to this end. As Nelson Mandela put it in 1993:

> The primary motivation of the ANC's foreign economic policies as a whole will be to place South Africa on the path of rapid economic development with a view to addressing three key problem areas: slow growth, severe poverty, and extreme inequalities in living standards (Mandela 1993: 93)

It is impossible to buck geography. There will therefore inevitably be an African focus, though care will have to be taken to balance this against other demands and priorities. Trade with Africa amounted to 8.3 per cent of the overall total in 1995; with the European Union (EU), 33 per cent; with the North American Free Trade Area (NAFTA – Mexico, US, Canada), 9 per cent; with the states of Latin America's Mercosur grouping, 1.7 per cent; with Asia and the Middle East, 26 per cent; and with the surrounding states of the Southern African Customs Union (Botswana, Namibia, Lesotho and Swaziland), 8.5 per cent (see Mills 1996 for these and other trade figures; also Table 5.1).

South and southern Africa are, however, minor players in the global economy. In 1993, SADC's total share of global economic output was just 0.58 per cent, or 0.13 per cent without South Africa (Herbst 1996). South Africa itself is a dwarf in the global context, with a GDP just one-third of that of the Netherlands and only 6 per cent of Germany's. However, its comparative dominance in the subcontinent does give it an international voice, particularly in an era when African powers are expected to take greater responsibility for continental affairs.

The Regional Dimension

South Africa is clearly the regional giant, and what happens to its domestic circumstances will inevitably affect its regional environment and *vice versa* - hence southern Africa's oft-stated priority in Pretoria's foreign policy calculations. As President Mandela noted to the UN General Assembly in October 1994 (see Department of Foreign Affairs, 1996: 18):

> We are a part of the region of Southern Africa and of the continent of Africa. As members of the Southern African Development Community [SADC] and the OAU [Organisation of African

Table 5.1   *South Africa's top ten trading partners, 1995 (R mn)*

Country	Position 1994	1995	Total	Imports	SA Exports
Germany	2	1	20583.6	16029.9	4553.7
UK	3	2	19042.3	10755.4	8286.9
USA	1	3	16337.0	11511.5	4825.5
Japan	4	4	14990.5	9880.1	5110.4
China/Hong Kong	6	5	6478.8	3472.5	3006.3
Italy	7	6	6415.6	4005.9	2409.7
Switzerland	5	7	6040.9	2382.1	3658.8
Taiwan	8	8	5774.0	3220.2	2545.8
Zimbabwe	–	9	5507.0	964.1	4542.9
Belgium	9	10	5365.4	2129.0	3236.4

Note: The grand total for South African trade in 1995 was (1994 figures in brackets): imports, R97,285 bn (R75,601); exports, R102,323 bn (R90,133).

Unity], and an equal partner with other member states, we will play our role in the struggle of these organisations to build a continent and a region that will help to create for themselves and all humanity a common world of peace and prosperity.

To complicate the balancing act between Africa and other diplomatic commitments, South Africa will also have to juggle the need for domestic development and its leadership of southern Africa, especially given the regional political sensitivities concerning its dominance and past role. For the South African economy is nearly four times as big as the other 11 members of the SADC combined, or nearly twenty times the size of the next largest (Table 5.2).

However, South Africa faces many 'complexities' in managing the nature of its co-operation (let alone integration) with the southern African region, most immediately over Pretoria's discussions with the European Union on the proposed Free Trade Agreement. These relate, firstly, to the restructuring of the Southern African Customs Union agreement, which is already being fundamentally altered by trade liberalisation under the prescriptions of the World Trade Organization.[11] Secondly, in dealing with SADC, there are problems concerning the process of integration, as SADC moves from 'development co-ordination' to development and trade integration.

Pretoria's negotiations with Europe over the FTA are probably the single most important short-term foreign economic policy issue facing South Africa (and a graphic example of the need for a consistent foreign policy orientation), not only given the value of bilateral trade and investments and their potential expansion, but also because of the effects of the agreement on South Africa's image as a trading partner to reckon with. In 1996, the EU accepted 25 per cent of South Africa's exports and supplied 42 per cent of its imports. In June 1994, South Africa was offered a FTA by the EU's Council of Ministers. In spite of support from SADC and the African, Caribbean and Pacific (ACP) countries that South Africa be accorded full Lomé status instead, the Council also decided to exclude South Africa from the trade preferences enjoyed by the ACP nations and to grant it only qualified accession to the Lomé Agreement. This partial membership was formally agreed in April 1997.

The EU's negotiating mandate for the FTA was released in March 1996, to which Pretoria responded finally in December the same year with its own negotiating terms. Much of this delay resulted from a debate within South Africa over the effects and theoretical desirability of a FTA, especially since the EU mandate excluded some 39 per cent of South African agricultural products (or 4 per cent of total South African exports to the EU) from the proposed agreement. Presuming that South Africa can produce an exact policy mandate (and this is debatable in the absence of a thorough cost-benefit economic model), negotiations were expected to be con-

Table 5.2 *Southern African regional perspective (1993)*

	Area (sqkm)	Population (mn)	GDP (US$m)	GDP/head
Botswana	600,400	1.2	3,740	2,670
Lesotho	30,400	1.7	510	408
Swaziland	17,400	0.7	950	1,174
Namibia	823,100	1.3	2,508	1,716
Zimbabwe	390,600	9.6	4,514	420
Zambia	752,600	7.9	3,995	352
Mozambique	801,600	14.0	1,467	97
Angola	1,25m	8.9	6,179	601
Malawi	118,500	8.9	2,019	192
South Africa ('94)	1,22m	42.3	117,200	2,771

Source: The Standard Bank, *South Africa in Figures, 1996.*

cluded before the end of 1997, though the implications of the envisaged FTA will be debated for some time to come. It will mean, for example, that EU Member States could potentially have more preferential access to the South African market than to those of its SADC neighbours. At this stage it is thus not clear how South Africa's bilateral trade relations might, in short, impact on the potential route for South African-SADC integration. The objectives of the SADC free trade protocol are to:[12]

- further liberalise intra-regional trade in goods and services on the basis of fair, mutually equitable and beneficial trade arrangements;
- ensure efficient production within SADC reflecting the current and dynamic comparative advantage of its members;
- contribute towards the improvement of the climate for domestic, cross-border and foreign investment;
- enhance the economic development, diversification and industrialisation of the Region;
- establish a Free Trade Area in the SADC Region.

Importantly, the SADC free trade protocol binds South Africa to SADC in its negotiations, whether with the EU or, potentially, with the US over a free trade agreement. The SADC protocol explicitly states (p. 16): 'Nothing in this Protocol shall prevent a Member State from granting or maintaining preferential trade arrangements with third countries, provided such trade arrangements do not impede or frustrate the objectives of this Protocol' and 'any advantage, concession, privilege or power granted to a third country under such arrangements is extended to other Member States'.

Finding its African Roots

President Mandela has argued that 'South Africa cannot escape its African destiny. If we do not devote our energies to this continent, we too could fall victim to the forces that have brought ruin to its various parts' (Mandela 1993: 89). Aside from improvements in relations in the more obvious areas of political and security interaction, there has also been a tremendous growth in South Africa's trade and investment ties with the African continent. In terms of foreign investment, in 1994 South Africa's foreign assets in Africa, in direct investment, stood at R3.752 billion, with total African assets at R6.143 billion. This may perhaps be low by comparison with the total of South African foreign direct investment (FDI) abroad of R74 billion (1994), but the figure is increasing all the time with an estimated additional South African-African investment of around R9 billion since the election in 1994.[13]

The trade relationship (excluding SACU) shifted up some 30 per cent for 1993–94 from a total of R8.457 billion (exports, R6.827 billion; imports R1.629 billion) to R10.986 billion (exports, R8.632 billion; imports, R2.354 billion), and again leapt some 52.6 per cent between 1994 and 1995 to R16.771 billion (exports, R13.916 billion; imports, R2.855 billion). This amounts to roughly 8 per cent of South Africa's total trade flows.

It is important, however, to view these increases not only as a part of South Africa's total trade (which is significant though not excessively so), and trade as a part of a pattern of general relations with the continent (which is important), but also in terms of the potential for the future (which could be the most significant). In this, trade could be said to be led by South Africa's other interests, whereas with the EU, for example, trade is the lead in the relationship.

These changes in its African relations are also illustrated by the increase in the number of South African-based companies operating in the subcontinent: For example:

- The Standard Bank now operates in 14 African countries, with a total of 103 African branches. South Africa's top eight banks represent US$6 billion of the total US$8 billion capital of African banks.[14]
- South African mining investments and interests are becoming increasingly diversified throughout the continent.
- South African Breweries now operates in Zambia, Mozambique and Tanzania, in addition to Botswana, Lesotho and Swaziland. In mid-1997 it also bought into a brewery in Angola which it had operated before that country's independence.
- Shoprite-Checkers have opened retail supermarket stores in Zambia, while Pick 'n Pay plans to expand into Namibia, Botswana, Kenya and Zimbabwe.

This expansion has been made possible by political and economic change throughout the continent, and has been largely facilitated through privatisation campaigns. In this, South Africans possess the competitive advantage of geographic location coupled with knowledge of African working conditions, sensitivities and opportunities. And when one considers that South Africa, according to the DTI, currently supplies just 15 per cent of sub-Saharan Africa's imports and just under 30 per cent of SADC's imports, Africa *must* be an attractive growth market, given South Africa's inherent advantages.

In this regard, it is also important to note that, although the SADC was set up to provide for region-wide development-type project assistance, the success of regional development is to a great extent going to be dependent in the future on increased levels of private investment in projects which are attractive for sound commercial reasons, which, in turn, are dependent on relative stability and growth potential. These projects include (see Mistry 1996):

- The Maputo Corridor project with Mozambique, potentially one of the most positive and ambitious cross-border development projects in southern Africa. The first phase of the project entails the construction of a highway (starting in early 1998) – a toll road from Witbank in South Africa to Maputo in Mozambique – estimated to cost over R600 million. Only 10 per cent of the costs will be covered by public funds, and the rest is expected to be raised by a consortium of private investors. This represents the first BOT (Build, Operate and Transfer) road in the region and one of very few cross-border toll roads in the world (Mozambique New Agency 1997: 2). The next stage involves the rebuilding of the adjacent railway line as well as the modernisation of Maputo Harbour at a cost of R150 million. Maputo is the nearest port to South Africa's industrial heartland, and before Mozambique's independence used to carry 40 per cent of the old Transvaal Province's foreign trade. This figure is only at 5 per cent today, which gives an estimation of the potential for this scheme.
- A second area, particularly in Mozambique, Namibia and Angola, concerns the exciting possibilities for the opening up of new gas and oil fields (Chapter 9).
- Power generation and transmission. In June 1996, power executives from South Africa, Zimbabwe, Botswana, Zambia and Zaire gathered in Kinshasa to discuss plans to build export links across the region from the Inga River hydroelectric scheme on the Congo River. With a potential to generate 44,000 MW (compared to Cahora Bassa's installed capacity of 2,000MW), the Inga Dam so far has a capacity of 17,775MW. Currently it produces only about 650-700MW, just enough for local demand. Sub-Saharan Africa's current generating capacity is 48,646MW, 82 per cent of which is supplied by South Africa. Studies by the African Development Bank have estimated that a regional approach to power system development could result in generating savings of some US$3 billion between

1995 and 2010, could save some US$400 million annually in operating costs, and provide US$800 million annually in export income (Chapter 9).

Of course, the success of regional programmes is dependent on the pace of privatisation and deregulation within southern Africa, and on the path of political development and the creation of conditions of socio-political stability.

Conclusion

To continue to punch beyond its weight in the international arena and capitalise on the virtual global hero-worship of its current President, Pretoria will have to ensure that its foreign policy has a significant economic underpinning, thereby providing a product for its Department of Foreign Affairs and the country's other representatives abroad to sell. At the same time, to stretch the analogy, even if a nation is able to punch beyond its weight, it gains little if it is only a flyweight taking on the heavyweights. There is a need for South Africa to learn discretion, and not to lean all over the place in the international arena.

To maintain a flexible foreign policy capable of coping with global change, there will always be a need to understand and monitor the continuously shifting international milieu. In this, South Africa will require carefully defined foreign policy goals and priorities and not the ambitious wish-list articulated at present. Looking to the future, a state that wishes to pursue a human rights agenda internationally will have to be 'pure' at home. This encompasses styles of domestic governance, as well as issues concerning crime, policing and arms sales.

Given the need to attract investment funds and the primary concern of potential foreign investors about rates of return, a cogent economic policy is critical for a successful foreign policy overall. With Africa standing in the middle of many of the currents of change in today's global economy, there are a number of ways in which South Africa should focus its foreign policy, particularly towards Africa.

First, South African foreign policy requires a co-ordinated strategy and should not comprise solely short-term reflexes to domestic, regional, continental and worldwide problems. In today's global economy it is no longer appropriate to attempt to maintain a highly compartmentalised approach which in practice seems to differentiate between aspects of policy (trade, political, military), government departments and business.

Second, South Africa's foreign policy has to be geared to allow the greatest possible manoeuvrability in the global economy, in an ever more competitive search for niche markets and products. In this, there is a need to drop the distinction between domestic and foreign policy, which has occurred by default through globalisation anyway. The Growth, Employment and Redistribution economic strategy, in this sense, is South Africa's foreign policy, given that the country's future prosperity hinges on domestic economic well-being.

Third, related to this, there is a need to juxtapose South African commercial and foreign policy. In the search for greater markets and investment against fierce competition, the South African government will need to maintain close co-ordination with business in its foreign interactions, particularly in Africa.

Fourth, the global economy militates against turning inward. The aforementioned juxtaposition thus demands: the co-option and/or recruitment of more experienced (mid-career) diplomats with experience in business and from a variety of cultural and language backgrounds; the calibration of the scale of diplomatic representation according to the scale of perceived benefit; the establishment of bilateral commercial commissions and special commercial centres with key states for the purpose of creating and widening networks and important personal interactions (just as military-military contacts are used as an important foreign policy vehicle); the broadening of participation in trade missions, and the targeting of companies for involvement where they might have interests; and the assigning of a greater number of commercial officers to foreign missions, improving their ratio with respect to political-military officers. A survey of South African missions in 1997 shows this ratio to be around 6:1 (609 to 103) political-military officials to those accredited to handle economic issues. There is also a need for government to create expertise where there is none available in the private sector, expertise capable of implementing and sustaining and not just articulating aggressive commercial diplomacy.

Fifth, South Africa's foreign policy must have proportion and balance between Africa and traditional and big emerging markets. The foreign playing fields and policy horizons are no longer what they were. South Africa cannot focus on Africa alone and should not fall into that temptation in its foreign policy: dealing with its established trading partners in the (broadly-defined) West and creating new links with the big emerging markets is the key to economic well-being and South Africa's security. This requires fresh foreign policy strategies, not only for Africa, but for other previously unexplored markets, such as those termed the 'Big Ten' emerging markets – Argentina, Brazil, China, India, Indonesia, Mexico, Poland, South Korea and Turkey, and including South Africa itself.[16] In this way, too, there is a need for South Africa to prioritise its partnerships in Africa, to look at those states with large populations, large resource bases and large markets which could play an important role.

Sixth, despite South Africa's growing business links with Africa, its continental foreign policy cannot afford to be focused exclusively on export promotion. With the most advanced, productive and balanced economy in Africa, with a vibrant democracy and with a potent military force, South Africa has to take a broader view of its African role. This role will have to link in with efforts to improve human rights, safeguard the environment and deal with criminal and other policy issues, but nonetheless it should not be founded on high-flown principles but rather on the day-to-day realities and needs of the continent. Here the need to improve conditions, systems and institutions of governance and assist leadership is paramount. This assistance has to take on practical forms: such as, for example, the provision of frameworks for tax regimes, intellectual property rights, stock market operation and regulation, anti-corruption measures, corporate governance skills, an independent judiciary, and so on. Improvements in these areas can only encourage greater investment in the continent. In another area, South Africa should take care to offset Africa's negative trade deficit with the Republic through the encouragement of outward (continental) flows of investment.

Seventh and finally, related to this, there is a need for South Africa to continue to encourage African economic and democratic reform. Without a continued reduction of trade barriers and deregulation, trade (and economic growth) will slow down. To do this, there is a requirement for a realistic view about the way Africa works and its challenges.

Notes

1. For an exposition of apartheid South Africa's foreign relations, see Geldenhuys (1984). On the years of transition, see Mills (1994) and Carlsnaes and Muller (1997). For a detailed discussion of South Africa's foreign economic relations, see Mills et al. (1995) and Handley and Mills (1996).

2. These were focussed on: Asia (19 November 1996); on the Southern African Development Community (SADC) (20–21 January 1997); Central and Eastern Europe (18 April 1997); and the Middle East (21 April 1997).
3. Interview, Pretoria, 22 July 1997.
4. I am grateful to James Barber for this point.
5. I am grateful to Chris Landsberg for this characterisation.
6. Summary of concluding remarks at DFA Foreign Policy Workshop, Randburg, 9-10 September 1996, pp.8-9. For an excellent summary of the problem in addressing the issue of human rights and foreign policy, see Foreign and Commonwealth Office, *Human Rights and Foreign Policy*. London: Foreign Policy Document No 268. This document provides a summary of action which might be taken in both the bilateral and multilateral context with regard to human rights violations.
7. For a detailed explanation of the cause and effect of the Syrian arms sales issue see Mills et al. 1997.
8. Foreign Minister Alfred Nzo, DFA Foreign Policy Workshop, Randburg, 9-10 September 1996.
9. See *Business Day*, 10 and 13 January 1997. South Africa currently has 75 embassies or high commissions in foreign countries, while there are 96 embassies or high commissions in South Africa. South Africa also has consulates in 18 countries, and 57 countries have consulates in South Africa. South Africa has accredited a nearby embassy to cover 44 countries, while 7 countries have non-residential accreditation in South Africa. Interestingly, the Republic's 1996-97 foreign affairs budget amounted to US$250 million, while Chile and Argentina's were US$130 million and US$456 million (1995-96) respectively, though each had a similar number of foreign missions to South Africa. In the Argentine case, the budget includes the cost of trade representatives.
10. This information was supplied in correspondence with the Department of Foreign Affairs, dated 15 January 1997.
11. The importance of SACU receipts for the BLSN states is critical in their negotiating position on the EU free trade agreement. Currently, income from SACU accounts for 46 per cent of Swaziland's government budget, 15 per cent of Namibia's, over 50 per cent of Lesotho's and 16 per cent of Botswana's (*Business Day*, 9 September 1996; see also Chapter 10).
12. Protocol on Trade in the Southern African Development Community Region, 9 September 1996, pp. 7-8.
13. See *South African Reserve Bank Quarterly Bulletin*, September 1996; and for data on South Africa's increased African investments, see *Business Day*, 4 October 1996.
14. *Financial Mail*, 5 January 1996; Ryan, C. 'Standard's African Adventure', *Millennium* October-November 1996, pp. 96-102.
15. Interview with DTI official, November 1996.
16. For an excellent overview of the challenges of the global economy and the opportunities offered by these emerging markets, see Garten, (1997).

References

Carlsnaes, Walter and Muller, Marie (1997) *Change and South African External Relations*. Thomson, Johannesburg.
Department of Foreign Affairs (1996) *South African Foreign Policy Discussion Document*, Pretoria.
Garten, J. (1997) *The Big Ten*. Basic Books, New York.
Geldenhuys, Deon (1984) *The Diplomacy of Isolation*. Macmillan and the South African Institute of International Affairs, Johannesburg.
Handley, Antoinette and Mills, Greg (eds) (1996) *From Isolation to Integration: the South African Economy in the mid-1990s*. SAIIA, Johannesburg.
Herbst, J. (1996) 'Africa and the International Economy', in Handley and Mills.
Mandela, N. (1993) 'South African Foreign Policy', *Foreign Affairs*, November/December.
Mills, Greg (1994) *From Pariah to Participant: South Africa's Evolving Foreign Relations, 1990-1994*. SAAIA, Johannesburg.
Mills, G. (ed.) (1996b) *The South African Yearbook of International Affairs 1996*. SAIIA, Johannesburg.
Mills, Greg et al. (eds) (1995) *South Africa in the Global Economy*. SAIIA, Johannesburg.
Mills, G., Callahan, T., Geldenhuys, D. and Fabricius, P. (1997) 'US-South Africa Relations and the "Pariah" States', *SAIIA Reports*, No. 2.
Mistry, P. (1996) 'Building Infrastructure in Southern Africa and the New South Africa', *South African Journal of International Affairs* 4 (1): 56-71.
Suttner, R. (1996) 'Parliament and the Foreign Policy Process' in Mills (1996b).

B.
Changing Geographies of Production and Economic Integration

6 Lessons Unlearned: South Africa's One-way Relationship with Zimbabwe

COLIN STONEMAN

Introduction

On independence in 1980 the new government of Zimbabwe proclaimed a commitment to socialism involving priority for the interests of workers and peasants, raising the minimum wage and extending its application to farm-workers and others. The ruling ZANU-PF (Zimbabwe African National Union – Patriotic Front) party under Robert Mugabe asserted that it was not going to make the mistakes of older independent countries; Zimbabwe was not going to be 'another Kenya' (Zambia was not even mentioned). Unfortunately this did not mean that it intended to learn from their mistakes, rather it seemed to mean little more than that Zimbabweans felt superior to the 'basket cases' that many of its neighbours had become. Even in relation to Mozambique and Tanzania, where the leaders and ruling parties had a similar rhetorical commitment to socialism, the solidarity at a political level rarely extended into the economic sphere. Only in the case of the convenient advice against conducting ill-thought-out radical experiments was Mozambique's Samora Machel listened to (Stoneman and Cliffe 1989: 15), but the class consequences of such inaction were not similarly pursued.

The result was that Zimbabwe repeated most of the mistakes and few of the achievements of its neighbours. Nearly two decades later, South Africa too feels that its superiority in many respects makes experience to the north of little relevance. In both cases this attitude was based on a high degree of ignorance of both the scale of the successes and the causes of the failures of the other countries. In both cases, pursuit of 'the national interest' (usually meaning the interests of capital), and using the recent economically disruptive independence struggle as excuse, has damaged weaker neighbouring countries unnecessarily. Similarly, failure to learn lessons eventually weakened both labour and national capital in the case of Zimbabwe, and may well do so in the case of South Africa as well. Thus Zimbabwe failed to give adequate commitment to the Southern African Development Co-ordination Conference (SADCC) region, and partly as a result it was eventually steam-rollered by the World Bank into abandoning any pretence of even a national development policy, let alone socialism. South Africa seems to be taking the same route, in weakening its best allies in the fight against globalisation and in neglecting valuable regional lessons on the dangers of gradualism.

Explanations for this failure in the case of Zimbabwe must include a range of factors, from the constraints imposed by the Lancaster House Constitution and the geopolitical circumstances of the 1980s with South Africa still under apartheid, through to recognition of the embryonic level of class development in Zimbabwe and the consequent ease with which an opportunistic party could appear to represent the interests of peasants, workers, and 'the national interest' all at the same time (Stoneman and Cliffe 1989: 37–40). Even amongst the élite who saw themselves as socialists or even Marxists, an ability to analyse adequately the nature and power of the forces massed against their rhetorical programmes was largely absent, as even was any habit of conducting analyses in class terms. Thus we read in the *Transitional National Development Plan* (Republic of Zimbabwe 1982: para 5.38) that:

> to attract domestic and foreign investment, it is essential to create and maintain a favourable investment climate [which] should be consistent with the aspiration of creating an egalitarian socialist and democratic society.

South Africa is clearly in a much stronger position to resist pressures, given the presence of the South African Communist Party and COSATU (Congress of South African Trade Unions). But already the tripartite alliance seems to exist mainly on paper, with the ANC government effectively abandoning the Reconstruction and Development Programme (RDP) out of supposed 'realism' in the face of pressure from international capital. Thereby, as in the case of Zimbabwe, both 'the national interest' (the interests of national capital) and workers' interests are casualties to a programme of incorporation of the South African élite into a niche being designed for it in the world market in order to pre-empt any attempt at a newly industrialising country ('NIC') type strategy.

As I shall argue, all national classes, bourgeoisie, labour and peasantry, stand to lose, with only small fractions of the first, mostly rural, mining or comprador, benefiting. One irony is that this 'solution' is in fact being sold as a 'NIC' type strategy, although it is manifest that not only are almost all components of the strategy the precise opposite of those employed in the NICs, but so are the main beneficiaries (in particular as regards fractions of capital). A striking illustration of the ideological blindness generated by the current orthodoxy was presented to me at a recent (1995) investment conference in southern Africa where I was invited to speak on 'Can southern Africa be a NIC?' In my talk I enumerated some key aspects of the NICs' strategies, including such familiar characteristics as the interventionist nature of their governments and their hostility to foreign capital. I was both preceded and followed by speakers and discussants from the platform and the floor, none of whom even referred to my contribution in the course of advocating blanket incentives to foreign investment, privatisation and deregulation – so that South Africa (or Zimbabwe) could become a 'new NIC'. Ideologies can become so self-evident to those in whose interests they are (or are thought to be) that any facts which do not fit in *must* be deemed to be false or else wrenched out of context.

Lessons from Zimbabwe

Why Zimbabwe is relevant to South Africa

In this section I advance two arguments. First, I argue that the experience of Zimbabwe in its first decade of independence provides more lessons of relevance to the future South Africa – and the future southern African region as a whole – than can be gleaned from the fashionable comparisons with Latin America or the newly industrialising countries (NICs) of Asia. Second, I argue that Zimbabwe's record was very much better than the popular (but ideologically inspired) mythology allows. This means that many of the lessons are positive, although of course some are negative.

Zimbabwe and South Africa have shared much common experience over the last century, having both been granted effective independence from Britain under white minority rule, South Africa in 1910 and Zimbabwe (as Southern Rhodesia) in 1923.[1] Both countries have experienced wars in response to black nationalist liberation movements, and international sanctions designed to lever whites out of political power. In both cases the international pressure has stopped well short of full support for the liberation movements, indeed it was both so delayed and of such low intensity as to raise suspicions that it was little more than nominal. This is surely related to the fact that both economies are to a significant extent dominated by diversified transnational corporations with bases in Europe and North America, and in the case of Zimbabwe the further fact that many South African companies made their first foreign investments there, and soon came to control about a quarter of economic activity (Lines 1988). When the whites indicated willingness to surrender their monopoly of power – from 1979 in Zimbabwe and from 1990 in South Africa – most international pressure seems to have been immediately redirected to ensuring that blacks did not gain a monopoly of power, and that white economic interests should survive the loss of political power largely intact.

Herein lies the relevance of Zimbabwe's experience, because the survival of white economic power meant the dashing of the hopes of the black majority, and the imposition of a range of constraints against redistribution, causing disillusion with the new government and making it ever more repressive (see also Dashwood 1996). This effect may be intensified in South Africa, where the ratio of whites to blacks is about 1 to 7 compared with the 1 to 50 ratio in Zimbabwe at independence.

The achievements

Political democracy and multiracialism. Zimbabwe has remained a multiparty multiracial democracy from the time of independence under majority rule in 1980, and has to date held four general elections that have generally been regarded as being relatively free, if not altogether fair because of some intimidation of opposition parties (EIU 1995/3: 7).

The 1991 US State Department report on human rights (EIU 1992/2: 10) gave a mixed judgement on Zimbabwe. On the positive side, it said, were the ending in 1990 of the state of emergency, a generally independent judiciary and no evidence for the existence of political detainees. It was less happy with some of the activities of the Central Intelligence Organisation and the police which had, it said, banned political meetings, interfered with local government elections, and violated freedom of assembly. In a similar manner the freedom of the press has survived despite intemperate attacks on the opposition press, mainly by the government-controlled press and Zimbabwe Broadcasting Corporation (EIU 1996/3: 8). In summary, the political record of Zimbabwe, whilst far from being unblemished, is in fact rather good by Third World standards, and especially so in African terms.

Social development. It is widely recognised that Zimbabwe's main achievements since independence have been in the field of social welfare, especially education and health, with primary education becoming effectively free and universal almost immediately after independence, while secondary education enrolments had risen eight-fold by 1987, by which time about three-quarters of all children were getting some secondary education.

The health of the population improved in the 1980s, with free health care being made available to the families of all those earning less than Z$150 a month. Access to the services was improved with a rapid expansion of primary health care through the opening of rural health clinics. In 1991 Zimbabwe was praised in a World Bank report for having the most advanced birth control facilities in Africa, with 36 per cent of the population using modern methods. And in 1992 the World Bank published a report, *Investing in Health*, which praised Zimbabwe's health care system, presenting it as a model for other countries to follow, but neglecting to mention, as the health minister, Dr Timothy Stamps, angrily pointed out, that it was currently being dismantled by the consequences of the structural adjustment programme (EIU 1994/2: 13). A more general reversal of social gains in the 1990s is charted in Gibbon (1995).

Economic development. Between 1979 and 1989 Zimbabwe's GDP grew at a compound annual rate of just over 4 per cent, or about 1 per cent in per capita terms. The average African growth rate in the 1980s was about 1.5 per cent, very close to the growth of South Africa, and therefore representing an annual 1.5 per cent decline in per capita income.[2] In what follows I use figures from 1990 (although more recent ones are available) as they show the outcome of the first decade before policy was seriously affected by the World Bank/IMF 'reforms'.

The economy is better balanced than that of South Africa, being much less dependent on mining, which in 1990 contributed 8.2 per cent to GDP, with agriculture contributing 12.9 per cent and manufacturing industry 26.4 per cent, and other industrial activities (construction, electricity and water, transport and communications) contributing a further 13.0 per cent.

By 1990 exports constituted 32 per cent of GDP, up from 27 per cent in 1979 and a low of 21 per cent in 1982–83. This may be compared with South Africa where exports were 23.7 per cent of GDP in 1995. Calculations of the GINI-Hirschman index for export diversification (Ncube 1992) confirm the better balanced nature of Zimbabwe's exports. The indices were 0.9 for South Africa and Zambia, 0.8 for Botswana, 0.6 for Malawi, 0.5 for Mozambique, 0.4 for Swaziland and 0.36 for Zimbabwe.

Finally it should be remarked that Zimbabwe has good infrastructure, including a sophisticated financial sector and stock exchange. In these respects it is among the best in Africa, although not achieving the scope and sophistication of South Africa. However, and again as in South Africa, the disparities between provision in urban areas and the communal farming areas are extreme.

The constraints

Constitutional. Although the Lancaster House agreement erected a hurdle that required ZANU-PF to win 63 per cent of the vote to gain power, this was in fact achieved (Stoneman and Cliffe 1989: 32). However, there was a second line of defence, innocuously concealed in a provision to protect property rights. Most significant was the prevention of significant land reform of the type that has been an essential ingredient of nearly all successful development experiences. Much good, well-watered land remains underutilised, while government has poured significant resources into improving the return from poor, dry and degraded land.

With whites owning an almost complete monopoly of industry and business (bus companies were the only significant exception), black entrepreneurs had few legitimate means of breaking into profitable enterprise. Even 18 years after independence whites still dominate the ownership of the economy; in the early 1990s the list of 'top executives' in the *Buyers' Guide* of the Confederation of Zimbabwe Industries (CZI) listed 1,030 people, of whom just over 1,000 had European names and about 20 were apparently of Asian origin, leaving under 10 who were black. The only inroads that have been made have had to come about through corruption or nationalisation, both generally associated with economic inefficiency. In practice there was little outright nationalisation because of the financial constraint. To encourage and facilitate local ownership the Indigenous Business Development

Centre (IBDC) was created in 1991, but has not to date been very successful. Despite its access to President Mugabe and the ZANU-PF Politburo, it has little economic clout, possibly, according to the President, because of the way white business and finance have closed ranks to protect their position. This was a major election issue in 1995.

Social and political. The Lancaster House Constitution helped to freeze the income distribution as well as the wealth distribution in Zimbabwe. Economically this meant that the domestic market remained tiny, and industry had little incentive to invest to meet the needs of the majority, because they still had incomes too low to make these needs felt; what new investment there was mainly went into the rapidly rising export trade. Very few new jobs were therefore created, and in 1990 employment at 1.19 million was only 12.7 per cent of the population of about 9.4 million, down from 13.7 per cent in 1980 (when the total population was 7.4 million) and 16.7 per cent in 1975 (when the total population was 6.3 million).

Despite much rhetoric about the need for jobs and more labour-intensive investment, especially in the National Plans, the government introduced few policies, instruments or subsectoral plans to bring this about, as these would have represented a real challenge to the autonomy of capital and a short-term threat to profitability; private investors naturally responded to the actual situation presented to them, which favoured capital intensity (Stoneman 1988: 51).

The low level as well as the character of investment was thus responsible for the stagnant labour market. Co-operatives, which the government sponsored as an income-generating concept, generally failed because of the failure to introduce an appropriate legal structure and through lack of financial and managerial support.

Destabilisation. Attacks by South Africa destroyed military supplies and much of Zimbabwe's air force in 1981–2, and several smaller acts of sabotage followed. The major consequences, however, were indirect, as South Africa ensured that Zimbabwe was unable to use its natural transport routes through Mozambique. Before 1975 three-quarters of Zimbabwe's external trade went through Beira or Maputo, but from 1975 until 1985 hardly any. Instead, both export and import costs were sharply raised by the need to haul goods about three times as far overland to and from the South African ports. From the early 1980s Zimbabwe began using its own troops to protect the Beira Corridor, consisting of a road, railway and oil pipeline (EIU 1986/3: 27 and later). Other destabilisation threats, including the fomenting of the conflict in Matabeleland, meant that the Zimbabwe National Army and other armed forces totalled about 50,000 and cost about 10 per cent of the government budget (usually more than the budget deficit), thereby squeezing the state's ability to continue adequate funding for health and education expenditure.

Threats were made at different times to hold up the passage of trade in order to reinforce pressure to moderate Zimbabwe's policy of support for Frelimo and the ANC (Zimbabwe was never able to offer the ANC bases as Mozambique, Tanzania and Zambia did). More generally, it can be stated that South Africa had a large interest in *not* seeing a successful multiracial experiment on its doorstep.

International financial institutions. None of the major aid providers, whether bilateral like the UK and the US or multilateral like the World Bank, had an interest in funding a genuine social or economic experiment in Zimbabwe (Stoneman 1992: 104). British financial support for land resettlement was token (£50 million), capable of affecting less than a tenth of the families in need, although the government of

Zimbabwe did not succeed in providing the matching funds even for this small amount. Much of the 'aid' promised under the 'Zimcord' agreement in 1981 turned out to be loans on commercial or barely concessionary terms. Despite the depth of the problems created by the preceding apartheid-like policies, interventions to solve them were generally frowned on and market solutions favoured. The impression given was that the judgement was not whether policies were working, but whether according to market dogma they *should* have been working. Thus although a World Bank loan disbursed in 1981 to set up an export revolving fund for manufacturing industry had proved hugely successful, because it had been operating in the context of Zimbabwe's controlled foreign exchange allocation system, the Bank reversed its own plans to increase and extend the fund. This followed apparently unproblematic negotiations, and after an unexplained delay in signing, the Bank announced that the funds would not be forthcoming until the trade regime was liberalised (Stoneman 1992: 103).

The outcome of this international sabotage was that in the second half of the 1980s debt repayments became larger than new aid inflows so that the net outflows exceeded 5 per cent of GDP; despite this the country managed an average growth rate of over 4 per cent. A few countries like Ghana that were deemed to be success stories did appear[3] to grow slightly faster at 5 per cent – but on the basis of net *inflows* of 5 per cent of GDP.

The failures

Response to political constraints. ZANU-PF's perceived desire to monopolise power and patronage and its heavy-handed attempts to impose the party on Matabeleland in fact created a monster of tribalism where none existed. The result was an invitation to the South Africans to exploit the divisions – an invitation which they accepted cleverly (Hanlon 1986). The initial coalition government fell apart, and there ensued a bloody war of oppression of much of the population in Matabeleland which has left a legacy of bitterness to this day.

The government ensured that it got the worst of both worlds by professing a radical socialism whilst doing nothing effective about it because of internal and external opposition, apparently hoping meanwhile that the pilloried capitalist structures would deliver the growth that would finance their own expropriation. Pragmatic caution thus meant that it avoided necessary radical measures at home for fear of losing the aid promised for honouring the Lancaster House Constitution, while high-principled rhetoric on foreign policy issues meanwhile alienated most donors. For example, Zimbabwe opposed both the Soviet takeover of Afghanistan and the US invasion of Grenada in the United Nations.

It may thus not be too severe a judgement to say that a set of impeccable egalitarian principles ended up as little more than a cover for the expansion of a buccaneering capitalism to a small black élite, with the eager connivance of a white élite which was sharp enough (unlike the world at large) to see through the rhetoric to the opportunity offered for its own survival.

Response to economic constraints. One of the most obvious and admitted failures in Zimbabwe was in job creation. The number of school leavers, a majority of them with O-level or better qualifications, rose from under 50,000 in 1980 to over 200,000 ten years later. Meanwhile the number of jobs created rose by less than 200,000 over the whole decade.

What was needed to complement the battery of constraints on capital was a battery of incentives to push it in the direction of job creation and longer-run foreign exchange saving and earning capacity. The actual criteria were invariably too short-term, with many proposals being rejected simply because they would have harmed the balance of payments in the current financial year (Stoneman 1988: 51).

A parallel failure occurred in the area of land reform. Only about 50,000 families had been resettled in the 17 years since independence – less than a third of those that were planned to be resettled in the first three years (Palmer 1990). Instead the government devoted most resources to aiding farmers in existing, often environmentally degraded communal areas. At first this seemed to be successful. The communal areas' share of the marketed production of both maize and cotton rose from below 10 per cent before independence to well over 50 per cent in typical years from the mid-1980s (Weiner 1988: 68–9). This overwhelming demonstration of the falsity of the widely accepted claim by commercial farmers that commercial farms were essential for either food security or export earnings (cotton was then rising to challenge tobacco as a major export earner) resulted in a new argument – *that land redistribution was not necessary*! Now, however, following a World Bank report which belatedly confirmed independent researchers' conclusions that commercial farmers were underutilising at least half of their arable land (EIU 1991/2: 10–11), both economics and fairness are agreed in pointing towards the need for the major land reform that was so successfully opposed in the 1980s. Unfortunately, constraints on government expenditure and a more conservative political climate are now ensuring that land redistribution is still extremely slow and the main beneficiaries are likely to be small commercial farmers rather than the peasants (Dashwood 1996; Cousins *et al.* 1992).

The lesson from the dramatic production increases of the 1980s is clear: the peasants will be efficient producers when given a fair share of resources – but these resources must include fertile, reliably watered land. Equity and economic efficiency are *not* in conflict, as was implicitly assumed in the Lancaster House Constitution's determination to prevent significant land redistribution; rather they go together. In March 1992, to loud trumpet fanfares, the long promised Land Acquisition Act was passed unanimously by parliament, but by early 1997 only 16 farms had been taken over (albeit with compensation at the market rate as was possible before the Act). The main consequence so far has been bad publicity for the government, as most of the farms have, officially as an interim measure pending mobilisation of funds, been leased to senior civil servants and politicians. The UK government meanwhile has offered to fund a second phase of land reform which, like the first phase in the early 1980s, would be conditional on free-market acquisition of the needed land and would require the government to find an equivalent sum in counterpart funds. In 1997 President Mugabe again threatened to take about half the remaining white farmland – circa 5 million hectares – restricting compensation to improvements and buildings, but was effectively prevented by the World Bank and the IMF and bilateral donors. However, the threat prompted the Commercial Farmers' Union to offer to make available about 500,000 hectares and to aid in both developing the land for resettlement and raising international funds to purchase and meet resettlement costs. It remains to be seen whether this offer will lead to a fruitful compromise. A revealing assessment by ordinary Zimbabweans of the first decade of independence is given by Nyanguru and Peil (1991).

Structural adjustment. In October 1990 the government introduced a programme of trade liberalisation, which eventually developed into a full World Bank-type economic structural adjustment programme (ESAP as it is called locally). The need for this was said, both by politicians and business, to be because of the failure of earlier policies (Stoneman 1990).

Whatever the causes or desirability of ESAP, it was in practice very poorly implemented. Another factor in the early failure of the programme may·have resulted from a conscious decision on the part of the World Bank to prevent Zimbabwe backsliding on the reforms by delaying disbursement of the promised funds for over a year during which the relaxation of import controls forced high borrowing, a crisis devaluation, and an unintended approach to the IMF for a new programme (EIU 1992/1: 6–7). Some of the proposed changes parallelled reforms that were needed and often recommended in any case under the old system, such as removal of the 'cost-plus' formula in the price control system or introduction of higher tariffs in order to transfer the windfall gains made by importers from the licence holders to the Exchequer (Riddell 1992). Other reforms might have been beneficial given adequate safeguards, such as monitoring to ensure that infant industries were protected even if ailing adults were allowed to disappear.

The key expected benefit of the programme – rising exports – failed to materialise, at least until 1994. In 1992 the Minister of Finance, Dr Bernard Chidzero, admitted that exports, far from rising from 29 per cent to 34 per cent of GDP as forecast, had fallen to 28 per cent in 1991, and 1992 and 1993 showed no improvement. In just two years, therefore, Zimbabwe shifted from a situation in which it was running a balance of payments surplus with falling international debts, to one in which its accounts were deep in the red with international indebtedness rising steeply. The consequences to the country had all been negative, but for the World Bank and the IMF an embarrassing counter-success story had been defused. However, a dramatic increase in trade in 1994 following huge tobacco, maize and sugar exports raised the export ratio to 38.6 per cent, but the trend was not sustained in 1995 and it remains too early to be sure that commodity-export-led growth is now succeeding. Certainly the basis for manufactured exports has been seriously undermined, with manufacturing value added 21 per cent lower in 1995 than in 1991, and about one-third below what it would have been had the trend in growth of the 1980s continued.

While the World Bank and the Zimbabwe government continue to be optimistic about the longer-term benefits of ESAP, there is no doubt about who is paying the short-term costs. Official statistics show that real wages have fallen by over 30 per cent since 1990 and there are many indicators of declining education and health care standards. The ability of many poor people, especially in urban areas, to meet their basic needs has also declined (Tevera 1995; Gibbon 1995).

The lessons for South Africa – and the region
No one, of course, has the blueprint for South Africa's ideal future strategy in predictable or unpredictable circumstances, and it would be ridiculous to pretend that the lessons from Zimbabwe's experience can be passed through a machine that adapts for South Africa's different circumstances and constraints to yield infallible advice. Such a mistake has led to failure too often in the past. But even commoner has been the arrogant mistake of seeing one's own country and situation as unique and refusing to learn from others' mistakes.

Democracy. In Zimbabwe it was manifest from the start that all political patronage was going to flow through ZANU-PF, and there was therefore an immediate inflow into its ranks from its erstwhile enemies, including white farmers and businessmen. These made common cause with elements already inside who had reservations about Mugabe's socialist and egalitarian aspirations. Because there were few mechanisms for legitimate redistribution, the combination of whites with economic power and blacks with political power provided both fertile ground for corruption and paralysis on many contentious policy issues. The ANC is now in a similarly dominant political situation in South Africa, and is similarly paralysed in many respects.

Education and employment. The case for a large rise in educational expenditure is irresistible on grounds of morality and justice; a good economic case can also be advanced in that few if any countries have been able to develop with an unhealthy, illiterate workforce, so although the economic return may be some time coming, it is nevertheless a necessary investment. The problem is, as the Zimbabwean case shows, that it is far from a *sufficient* investment, and if the only outcome is hundreds of thousands of unemployed school leavers, many with Ordinary-level and Advanced-level school certificates and even university degrees, even the human gain is slight (some might say negative).

If education is protected for political and social reasons the cuts will have to come disproportionately from somewhere else (the World Bank will now support some protection of education and health), and that will probably be in some area of expenditure that seems less essential or of less immediate political importance, such as investment, support for training, industrial support services, subsidised site-and-service stands, and various job creation measures. One of the main victims in the cost-cutting 1995/96 budget was investment, which was cut from 11.4 to 6.1 per cent of total spending, while the 1996/97 budget only partially restored the level with capital spending budgeted at 9.2 per cent of the total.

Planning and protection. South Africa faces very similar problems to Zimbabwe. Less than 10 per cent of school-leavers have been finding employment in the late 1980s and early 1990s (Zimbabwe's record at 20 per cent was marginally better, at least up to 1990) and unemployment amounts to 30–50 per cent of the work-force, while foreign capital will only bring capital-intensive investment.

Therefore the development of infant industries, house-building, infrastructural improvement and job creation need to be brought together in a domestic programme that will require planning rather than reliance on world market forces. In the medium term, government subsidies to labour-intensive production of basic needs, especially housing and water and electricity services, will serve both to create employment and to raise domestic demand. But production of tradeable basic needs will need protection against imports from established producers, and infrastructural improvements will need careful planning to ensure that the extra government expenditure 'crowds in' rather than 'crowds out' private investment. More orthodox analysts (see, for example, Jenkins 1997) place more emphasis on macroeconomic balance, arguing that the 'crowding out' effect is dominant. Although large deficits, whether internal or external, are ultimately unsustainable, smaller deficits may be the price of any growth, and 'successful' conservative policies may mean acceptance of continuing poverty.

In addition to expansionist but prudent internal planning, another leg of policy inevitably has to confront world market conditions and to expand and diversify exports, for the southern Africa market is far too small to permit a successful attempt to emulate the semi-autarchic policies of India or China. A key element in exporting must be the relationship with Europe, and the most favourable outcome would be if South Africa were to gain Lomé-type non-reciprocal duty-free access to the EU market. This would potentially benefit other countries in the region as well, for many of their exports are excluded from Europe at present as having too much content imported from South Africa; this 'rules-of-origin' problem falls away where the imports are from fellow ACP (African, Caribbean and Pacific) countries. Unfortunately the EU has ruled out more than partial access to Lomé for South Africa and has tied even this to a counter-proposal that South Africa and Europe should form a free trade area. South Africa rejected this in early 1997 and in February Spain blocked Lomé membership for South Africa until conditions, including access to South African waters for European fishing vessels, were granted. At the time of writing (mid-1997), the signs are not propitious for an agreement between the two regions that would benefit the Southern African Development Community (successor to SADCC) during the remaining lifetime of the Lomé agreement. Further uncertainty concerns what is to replace the agreement after 2000. The EU's present position is that the aspects of Lomé which were beneficial to ACP partners and which needed to be granted exemptions by GATT on account of their non-reciprocity, can no longer be maintained as they are contrary to World Trade Organization rules.

The World Bank. Despite the above criticisms, the Zimbabwean experience of the World Bank has been very positive at the project level. The problem for Zimbabwe, and potentially for South Africa, has been with the Bank's increasing conditionality at the macro level.

The World Bank is a fact of life and the relationship with it does not have to be conflictual. It is not a monolithic institution, and neither is it the fount of all wisdom. It has the resources to know more about most small countries than they do themselves, so its advice may often be the best technically. But it is not disinterested, and the key item on its agenda is development of the world market as a whole, with individual countries merely forming desired pieces in the jig-saw, even if, as in the case of Zimbabwe, they were doing better outside.

How Zimbabwe Neglected SADC Countries

Another lesson that South Africa could learn from Zimbabwe's mistakes lies in the abuse of relative economic power by a stronger partner in what is supposed to be regional organisation for mutual benefit. Although the SADCC survived as an organisation despite all that the apartheid state could throw at it (Kisanga 1991: 128–85), a number of its members were ruined economically by destabilisation, so that membership was of little economic significance, and Zimbabwe lost markets.

It is not just with hindsight that we can see that it need not have been like this. As early as 1981 Zimbabwe was criticised by analysts for its refusal to budge on what it perceived to be the national interest – 'perceived', for some of the advice conditioning the perception was ideologically inspired by the World Bank. A prime example was the decision in 1981 to expand the Hwange thermal power station along the lines originally drawn up under the minority Smith regime, and promoted by the Anglo-American Corporation of South Africa (AAC) which owned the neighbouring Wankie colliery. The World Bank, heavily influenced by the United States' 'constructive engagement' policy towards South Africa, was prepared to fund what amounted to a consolidation of links with the apartheid-ruled state, but not to fund the construction of a link to the Cahora Bassa dam in Mozambique, where there was over-capacity and great further potential (Thompson 1988: 248–9). Zimbabwe was warned that no country should risk importing more than 15 per cent of its energy from a neighbouring country (despite the long period of unprob-lematic imports from Zambia during the UDI period). Zambia, of course, was anoth-er country to suffer from the World Bank's favoured option, for Zimbabwe phased out its purchases from Zambia as Hwange came on stream between 1985 and 1987. Freed of such ideological constraints, fruitful co-operation with Mozambique began in the 1990s, too late of course to play a role in resisting destabilisation.

Although there is little point in developing detailed counterfactual scenarios, some have argued that the benefits to Mozambique, from increased revenue and economic development in the area of the dam and power link, could have been part of a programme of economic co-operation which would have greatly inhibited the rise of the South African-funded Renamo terrorist movement. Zimbabwe itself would have benefited, not only from obtaining a cheap source of power, but also through increased trade and possibly through avoiding the later huge costs of deploying around 10,000 troops in Mozambique to keep open its trade routes through the Beira Corridor. These were estimated at half of total defence costs which consumed 10 per cent of GDP. The importance of the corridor to Zimbabwe may be illustrated by the fact that in 1987 over 200 companies (including a few from Botswana and Zambia) subscribed Z$5,000 each (then US$3,000) to set up the Beira Corridor Group (BCG) to support economic, logistical and marketing support to the newly secured route.

But short-sighted policies also influenced Zimbabwe's relationship with Botswana, Malawi and Zambia. In all three cases political tensions may have con-tributed to less than friendly economic relations which ultimately harmed all par-ties and lost the opportunity for greater gains from co-operation. After the Matabeleland 'troubles' in the mid-1980s, Botswana found itself harbouring Zimbabwean refugees from the fighting, many of whom Zimbabwe was inclined to see as 'dissidents' paid by South Africa to destabilise it. Similar sensitivities were involved in relation to Zambia, where Kenneth Kaunda had supported Joshua Nkomo's ZAPU, and had imprisoned ZANU fighters during the 1970s. Malawi, although a member of both SADCC and the Preferential Trade Area, was generally seen to be sympathetic to both South Africa and Renamo.

How South Africa Has Harmed Zimbabwe and the Region

It is unrealistic to expect nations – like people – to behave altruistically. Nevertheless, altruistic, or at least co-operative, pretensions are often proclaimed, and there is no reason why attempts should not be made to bring reality closer to the advertisement. This is especially desirable when there are conflicts of interest – between immediate and longer-term aims, and between narrow lobbies and the wider interest. We have seen how, in Zimbabwe, short-term, sometimes sectional interests harmed both the interests of neighbouring countries and Zimbabwe's longer-term interests through weakening the region of which Zimbabwe was an inextricable part. It is depressing, though not surprising, to find history repeating itself with South Africa.

A good example concerns the renegotiation of the South Africa – Zimbabwe trade agreement. The two countries have had bilateral agreements going back to 1929, which have been renewed and modified a number of times, although the most recent major changes were made in 1964. The agreements have included a mixture of tariff preferences and quotas, often seen to be in Zimbabwe's favour as the weak-er, less developed partner, allowed to protect its infant industries to a greater extent;

however, the quotas rarely let Zimbabwean exporters take more than about 5–10 per cent of the South African market, so the threat to South African business interests was hardly significant. A formal renewal or renegotiation was required in 1992, and this need not have caused serious problems from the South African end, following its survival through the 1980s despite the generally hostile relations, including South Africa's attacks on Zimbabwe's natural trade routes and an abortive attempt on the part of Zimbabwe to lead a trade boycott of South Africa. An interim renewal of the 1964 agreement pending renegotiation of a new one would thus surely have been possible. Instead, in the dying days of the apartheid regime Zimbabwe was punished for its continuing hostility, and when in May 1992 South Africa imposed tariffs ranging between 40 and 90 per cent on a range of clothing and textiles to protect itself from a surge of imports from Asia, Zimbabwe was not excluded, despite the fact that its small manufacturers were unlikely ever to win more than about 10 per cent of the market. After protests, a temporary waiver was agreed until the end of the year pending the signing of a new trade agreement, but despite promises to renew the waiver in early 1993, this was not done, and the wider trade negotiations ground to a halt.

In June 1994 after the ANC formed the Government of National Unity in South Africa, the Zimbabwean trade minister, Herbert Murerwa, and Trevor Manuel, his South African counterpart, agreed to talks, but progress was extremely slow. In March 1995 a 'joint economic co-operation agreement' was signed, which led in August to agreement in principle for rebates on textiles and clothing tariffs for Zimbabwean exporters equivalent to the situation which had obtained in 1992 before tariffs were raised. Protests from South African industrialists that Zimbabwe would be used as a backdoor by Asian exporters postponed its implementation until February 1996, and the following month South Africa invoked the World Trade Organization protocols as disallowing such trade preferences to Zimbabwe. In June 1996, after Zimbabwean industrialists had called for a 'trade war' against South Africa (*Mail & Guardian*, 7 June 1996), the new trade ministers, Nathan Shamuyarira of Zimbabwe and Alec Erwin of South Africa, set up three joint committees. These produced a compromise formula in which tariffs of 15 to 30 per cent were to be paid on imports from Zimbabwe (compared with up to 85 per cent for other imports, but still a high barrier compared with the 0 to 17.5 per cent range before 1992) but only for a quota of 3.2 million items (5.5 million had been expected)(EIU 1996: 24). Although this package of concessions is now formally in place, some Zimbabwean exporters claimed that it was still not functional in early 1997. As far as a wider bilateral agreement is concerned, Mr Shamuyarira was reported in early March as saying that he would only believe in an agreement when it was implemented (EIU 1997).

Sarnia – A Regional NIC?

Nevertheless South Africa has not turned its back on the region, but it may still need reminding that the interests of the region are not just a matter of altruism. Its own long-term interests are more assured in a wealthy region than an impoverished one.

Immediate problems for South Africa include completing the stalled renegotiation of the bilateral trade agreement with Zimbabwe, revising the SACU agreement (see Chapter10) and making its policy consistent with the new SADC trade programme. The need to develop a coherent regional policy has been used as a reason to explain the delays in settling the first two problems over the past six years, and it is certainly true that care needs to be taken that bilateral agreements do not hamper the implementation of a regional agreement, as all the countries concerned are members of SADC. But trade relations are only a part of what is needed in the region, and indeed not necessarily the most important part, as is recognised frequently by SADC, for example in the words of the former executive secretary: 'How can tariffs inhibit trade when there is nothing to trade? . . . the greatest single barrier to trade is lack of production. Hence our motto: Let production push trade rather than trade pull production' (SADCC 1988: 30).

If then we can imagine a future dynamic, growing 'Sarnia' (or Southern African Newly Industrialising Area), what characteristics would it have beyond freer trade? It would certainly be South Africa- (or Gauteng-) led, but in an enlightened way that allowed expression of the interests of other countries and regions. This would imply a raised level of government competence and democratic accountability, combined with an ability to apply sanctions to countries (such as Malawi under Hastings Banda) or regions (such as the present KwaZulu-Natal) which violated such standards. It would have an industrial strategy, and macroeconomic stability (in particular an average government budget deficit below the economic growth rate) would be a target but not an obsession, with planned interventions and high investment taking precedence over short-run inflation, money supply or deficit targets. Sarnia would also have a policy for food security developed from the present SADC policy, and regional policies for energy, water and communications. It would also have common policies for foreign investors, especially in mining, so as both to promote region-wide prospecting and also to prevent international mining companies from forcing countries into zero-sum games of undercutting each other in offering favourable terms.

Notes

1 In the case of Zimbabwe, Britain retained reserved powers, that it scarcely exercised until the 1960s, when its refusal to grant full independence without majority rule precipitated the famous Unilateral Declaration of Independence (UDI) by the white minority regime in 1965.
2 Of course some countries did dramatically better, but this is invariably explicable in terms of dramatic advantages over Zimbabwe, for example Botswana's enormous diamond revenue, Gabon's oil, etc.
3 Although, as Simon (1995) has pointed out, there is evidence that much of the improvement may have been in *recording*, rather than *raising*, the level of economic activity.

References

Cousins, B., Weiner, D. and Amin, N. (1992) 'Social Differentiation in the Communal Lands of Zimbabwe', *Review of African Political Economy*, 53: 5–24.
Dashwood, H. (1996) 'The Relevance of Class to the Evolution of Zimbabwe's Development Strategy, 1980–1991', *Journal of Southern African Studies*, 22 (1): 27–48.
EIU (The Economist Intelligence Unit) (various dates) *Country Report: Zimbabwe*, quarterly, London.
Gibbon, P. (ed) (1995) *Structural Adjustment and the Working Poor in Zimbabwe*. Nordiska Afrikainstitutet, Uppsala.
Hanlon, J. (1986) *Beggar Your Neighbours*. James Currey, London.
Jenkins, C. (1997) 'Post-independence Economic Policy in Zimbabwe – Lessons for South Africa, *Centre for Research into Economics and Finance in Southern Africa, Quarterly Review*, January: 2–14. London School of Economics, London.
Kisanga, E.J. (1991) *Industrial and Trade Co-operation in Eastern and Southern Africa*. Avebury, Aldershot.
Lines, T. (1988) 'Investment Sanctions and Zimbabwe: Breaking the Rod', *Third World Quarterly* 10(3): 1182–1216.

Mail & Guardian (1996) 'Zim Attacks SA on Trade Policies' report by Brian Latham, June.

Ncube, M. (1992) 'The Dynamics of Trade and Economics Relations in Southern Africa'. London School of Economics and Political Science. (mimeo).

Nyanguru, A. and Peil, M. (1991) 'Zimbabwe since Independence: a People's Assessment', *African Affairs* 90(361): 607–20.

Palmer, R. (1990) 'Land Reform in Zimbabwe, 1980–1990', *African Affairs* 89(355): 163–81.

Republic of Zimbabwe (1982) *Transitional National Development Plan, 1982/33 – 1984/85*, (TNDP). Government Printer, Harare.

Riddell, R. (1992) *Zimbabwe to 1996; At the Heart of a Growing Region*, EIU Special Report No. M205, Economist Intelligence Unit, London.

Southern African Development Coordination Conference (1988) *Southern Africa: Opportunities for Investment and Trade*, Gaborone.

Simon, D. (1995) 'The Medicine Man Cometh: Diagnoses and Prescriptions for Africa's Ills', *Third World Quarterly* 16(2): 319–25.

Stoneman, C. (ed.) (1988) *Zimbabwe's Prospects*. Macmillan, London.

Stoneman, C. (1990) 'Zimbabwe Opens Up to the Market', *Africa Recovery*, 4 (3–4): 18–23.

Stoneman, C. (1992) 'Policy Reform or Industrialisation?: the Choice in Zimbabwe', in Adhikari, R., Kirkpatrick, C. and Weiss, J. (eds) *Industrial and Trade Policy Reform in Developing Countries*. Manchester University Press, Manchester.

Stoneman, C. (1995) 'Can southern Africa be a NIC?', Paper delivered at a conference on 'Southern Africa Towards 2000: Investment and Trade Prospects for a Growing Region'. Dataworld, Harare.

Stoneman, C. and Cliffe L. (1989), *Zimbabwe: Politics, Economics and Society*. Pinter Publishers, London.

Tevera, D. (1995) 'The Medicine that Might Kill the Patient: Structural Adjustment and Urban Poverty in Zimbabwe' in Simon, D., van Spengen, W., Dixon, C. and Närman, A. (eds) *Structurally Adjusted Africa: Poverty, Debt and Basic Needs*. Pluto Press, London.

Thompson, C. (1988) 'Zimbabwe in SADCC: a Question of Dominance?' in Stoneman.

Weiner, D. (1988) 'Land and Agricultural Development'. in Stoneman.

World Bank (1992) *Investing in Health*. World Bank, Washington, DC.

7 Desert Enclave to Regional Gateway? Walvis Bay's Reintegration into Namibia

DAVID SIMON

Introduction

Over a decade ago, midway through the decade-long delay to Namibian independence which followed Ronald Reagan's inauguration as US President, I characterised the transport system in Namibia as being finely balanced in a 'noose or lifeline' situation (Simon 1986, 1989). The extremely tight physical and institutional integration of its rail, road, sea and air transport and telecommunications with neighbouring South Africa had provided high quality and well organised services along those routes and corridors which coincided with local settler needs and South Africa's commercial and strategic interests. However, in the event of independence under a government hostile to apartheid South Africa, this dependent situation could readily be used as a source of political and economic leverage. Not only was the railway network's sole international connection with South Africa but, crucially, the country's principal port of Walvis Bay formed a small enclave (Figure 7.1), over which South Africa claimed sovereignty on historical grounds and where it maintained a large military garrison. Since road connections with Namibia's other main neighbours, Angola and Botswana, had been negligible for many years, and no other direct links existed, the South African state would be able to exercise a stranglehold over all significant international traffic with consummate ease.

Its willingness to take such unneighbourly action had recently been demonstrated all too clearly by means of a total blockade in December 1985 against impoverished and landlocked Lesotho in order to precipitate the overthrow of the government of Chief Leabua Jonathan, whose political stance had come to anger Pretoria (Ferguson 1990). At that time, the apartheid government of President P.W. Botha was immersed in its 'total strategy' to counter what it portrayed as a 'total

This chapter represents part of the output from a research project, 'Restructuring the Postcolonial State in Namibia: Regional Councils and Local Authorities', funded by the British Academy and the Nuffield Foundation. Professor Chris Tapscott, then Director of the Social Sciences Division, Multi-disciplinary Research Centre of the University of Namibia, provided me with a base during August-September 1994. Without the co-operation of senior representatives of the Walvis Bay and Swakopmund Municipalities, Erongo Regional Council, the Ministry of Regional and Local Government and Housing, the Ministry of Works, Transport and Communications, TransNamib Ltd and the Namibian Port Authority (Namport), the research reported here would not have been possible. A particular debt is owed to Deputy Minister, the Hon. Dr Klaus Dierks, Captain Jens-Dieter von der Fecht, CEO of Namport, and Dr Nils Bruzelius, the transport consultant advising the Ministry, for data, insights into the complex negotiation process, and comments on a draft of this chapter. I am also grateful to Jonathan Leape, Jesmond Blumenfeld and Colin Stoneman for discussion of the implications of EPZ status in terms of the SACU. An earlier version of this chapter was presented in the panel on 'Crossing Borders: Boundaries of Change', at the biennial conference of the African Studies Association of the UK, University of Bristol, 9–11 September 1996; and published as CEDAR Research Paper 19, 1996.

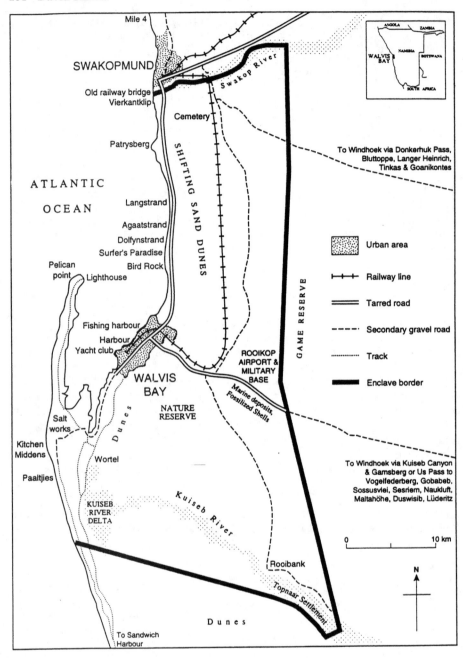

Figure 7.1   *The former Walvis Bay enclave*

onslaught' of communist and allied forces against it from beyond its borders, and an increasingly militant black majority seeking to make the country ungovernable from within. Notwithstanding the guerrilla war waged by the South West Africa People's Organisation (SWAPO) and international pressure, this embattled regime would clearly have a strong influence over whether, when and how Namibia ultimately gained independence. Since the late 1970s, it had sought to influence events so as to produce a settlement on terms favourable to itself, especially by establishing 'internal' client regimes hostile to SWAPO and its socialist political programme. Had these efforts finally failed, the blockade option might well have been deployed, with obvious consequences for Namibians.

It is a measure of the rapidity of change both in the region and globally, following the end of the Cold War and as a consequence of on-going international economic restructuring, that political relations in southern Africa have been transformed. As part of the transition to a post-apartheid order in the region, Namibia gained political independence on 21 March 1990, while Walvis Bay and the twelve offshore islands were reintegrated into Namibia on the night of 28 February – 1 March 1994, a few weeks before the equally historic non-racial election in South Africa which brought Nelson Mandela's African National Congress (ANC) to power. There is also now a new spirit of co-operation and development among the countries of the region. Naturally, and not a little ironically, South Africa's economic resources and new international status have put it firmly at the centre of such initiatives. This, in turn, is raising substantive questions regarding whether and to what extent the extreme existing inequalities between countries are likely to be reduced (Odén 1993; Du Pisani 1994; *Courier* 1995; Ramsamy 1995). Indeed, concerns are growing in some quarters at the speed with which South African companies are assuming dominant roles in various parts of Africa, often gaining control of local firms and driving inefficient or smaller competitors – not least state-owned or parastatal shipping or freight forwarding companies – out of business (Iheduru 1996).

I have analysed the geopolitics of Walvis Bay's reintegration into Namibia elsewhere (Simon 1996a; see also Evans 1993, 1994). Deploying critical geopolitical perspectives, I interrogated the conventional categories, assumptions and sources of international relations and political geography to inform the analysis based on in-depth interviews with key actors on both sides of the process as well as on both unpublished and published materials. This not only provides one of the first detailed post-Cold War case studies of statecraft deployed in peaceful international conflict resolution but also represents a significant addition to the literature on enclave geopolitics. The purposes of this companion chapter, which draws on the same foundations, are to examine the infrastructural and economic considerations at the heart of that process, to analyse the geopolitics of negotiations over the port and other assets, and to explore the immediate and likely longer-term economic potential of a reintegrated Walvis Bay for Namibia and the wider southern African region. In the words of the Namibian Deputy Minister of Works, Transport and Communications, Dr Klaus Dierks, who has adopted the 'noose or lifeline' analogy over the years, these developments are 'cutting the noose' (Dierks 1994a) both literally and symbolically. They also reveal very clearly how important the changing of borders, the crossing of boundaries, and the nature of international relations which bring these about, actually are for local societies and economies. To borrow the subtitle of a major recent book on the subject (Nugent and Asiwaju 1996), boundaries represent barriers, conduits and opportunities.

In researching this paper, I have been able to draw upon a wide range of secondary sources as well as extended interviews with many of the principal actors on both sides and access to primary material, some of which is not in the public domain. In order to preserve confidences, such sources have not been individually referenced.

Background

Historical Geopolitical Context
The centrality of reliable and rapid transport links in geopolitical strategies was well illustrated by the priority attached by South Africa to connecting its railway network with that of South West Africa after South African forces captured the territory from Germany in 1915. This suggested both that the territory was perceived as important to South Africa and that that country had long-term designs on its new conquest. So it proved. During South Africa's long occupation, progressively closer integration of the two economies and polities had been brought about with the eventual objective of integrating Namibia as a fifth province. South African policies of segregation and then apartheid were implemented, giving rise to indigenous opposition and eventually the protracted liberation struggle, supported by the United Nations and the international community. Even when Namibia finally became an independent state, South Africa refused to surrender the Walvis Bay enclave for a mixture of domestic political and especially regional geostrategic reasons.

At first sight, Walvis Bay is an unattractive, smallish, foggy and wind-blown town permeated by the pungent smell of fish processing factories, which lies huddled between high, ochre-coloured sand dunes and the cold Atlantic Ocean on the shores of the inhospitable Namib Desert. The rather tacky, end-of-the-world atmosphere on which many visitors over the years have remarked but which is at last changing for the better, belies its importance in terms of the geopolitical jigsaw of southern Africa. This, in turn, can only be understood in terms of its colonial history.

Since the eighteenth century, European and North American whaling ships were attracted to this bay, the only natural deepwater harbour on the coast of what is now Namibia, on account of the shelter it provided, the availability of fresh water and other supplies traded with the local indigenous communities, and because pods of Southern Right Whales frequented its waters. Herein lies the origin of the place's name in English, German, Dutch and Afrikaans (literally, Whale Bay). British and Dutch claims to the bay made in the 1790s were not exercised at the time. Only when its strategic importance during the European 'Scramble for Africa' in the late nineteenth century was appreciated, did Britain annex the bay and a small area of surrounding territory in 1878 to forestall German and Portuguese ambitions in the region. Given its isolated location, annexation of the enclave by the Cape Colony was authorised by Britain later the same year, but this took place only in 1884, shortly after Germany had proclaimed a protectorate over part of the southern Namibian coast centred on the shallow bay of Angra Pequena, then renamed Lüderitz. Already in 1874, twelve offshore islands between Walvis Bay and the Orange River (which formed the northern boundary of the Cape Colony) had been ceded to the Cape by Britain (Wellington 1976; Moorsom 1984a; Hangula 1993). These had been exploited for their rich guano deposits – hence their colloquial collective name of 'guano' or 'penguin' islands.

During the German colonial period in Deutsch Südwestafrika (1884–1915), use of Walvis Bay harbour was essential, and access appears to have been unrestricted for both military and civilian uses, at least until the outbreak of World War I. Following the formation of the Union of South Africa in 1910, a dispute over the enclave's boundaries arose with Germany. The matter was eventually settled by arbitration in

1911, giving it an area of 1,124 km². When South African forces ousted the Germans in 1915, Walvis Bay was quickly integrated into the new martial law regime established in South West Africa. South Africa was later awarded control over the territory as a C-Class Mandate by the League of Nations, and civilian rule was restored in 1921. The 1922 South West Africa Affairs Act, passed by the South African parliament to establish governmental structures and institutions, formalised Walvis Bay's position. It was henceforth to 'be administered as if it were part of the mandated territory and as if inhabitants of the said port and settlement were inhabitants of the mandated territory' (Moorsom 1984a: 14).

This remained the *status quo* until 1 September 1977 when South Africa reimposed direct rule over the enclave and reasserted its claim to sovereignty based on the original annexation, arguing that the arrangement during the previous 55 years had been one purely of administrative convenience. Walvis Bay was then designated part of the Cape Province, over 700 km to the south. The reason for this action was to avoid the enclave being 'lost', particularly to a hostile SWAPO government, in the event of Namibian independence, which then seemed imminent in the light of progress made in international negotiations. SWAPO and the UN Council for Namibia have always claimed the enclave as an integral part of Namibian territory. Naturally, the South African move, which some critics termed 'a second annexation' (Moorsom 1984a: 14–15), was not recognised internationally, and complex legal arguments ensued, based principally on the legal principle of *estoppel*, in terms of which one party could not belatedly assert a right of which it had been aware but which it had not exercised, if another party would be detrimentally affected by the belated exercise of that right (Moorsom 1984a: 15–21; Hopwood 1990; Berat 1990).

In order for this problem not to delay Namibian independence, UN Security Council Resolution 432 of 1978 was passed. While reiterating that the enclave formed an integral part of Namibia, the Resolution provided for bilateral negotiations between South Africa and a future Namibian government to resolve the matter. Hopes that South Africa would hand over the enclave as a 'birthday present' to Namibia at independence failed to materialise, so Resolution 432 provided the context for the process of negotiations which subsequently unfolded from 1991 to 1994. These talks and their geopolitical significance are dealt with in a separate paper (Simon 1996a; see also below).

Walvis Bay Town and Harbour

Above an impressive panoramic photograph of scores of workers busily erecting a 1,500-foot-long wharf along the foreshore, an enthusiastic article grandly entitled 'The Transformation of Walvis Bay' began by informing readers of South Africa's *Mining and Industrial Magazine* in 1926 that,

> To those who have not visited Walvis Bay for the last year or two the changes that have been brought about since the decision was taken to convert the place into an up-to-date port are astounding. The laying out of the township of Walvis Bay and the sale of building plots has not as yet resulted in a substantial increase in the number of buildings comprising the town, but the fact that a very large number of plots have been sold gives ground for the assumption that, with the completion of the harbour works, a much larger town will spring into being. It is in the direction of the actual harbour development, however, that the main changes are noticeable. ... It would be impossible in an article of this nature to convey a proper idea of the almost insurmountable difficulties that were experienced in the construction of the harbour wall (Lardner-Burke 1926: 29).

When the new harbour opened in 1927, its deepwater channels and wharves facilitated the growth and development of the small harbour and fishing settlement by several orders of magnitude. Nearby Swakopmund, the original German landing station some 30 km to the north, had already been eclipsed by World War I as it lacked the necessary draught or safety. Although subject to cyclical fluctuations in trade according to prevailing economic and farming conditions, Walvis Bay rapidly outflanked Lüderitz as the busiest port, as it was able to handle far larger ships and was substantially closer to Windhoek and to the principal commercial farming and major mining areas. Expansion in the post-World War II period was rapid, spurred by a substantial increase in white settler numbers in South West Africa and the development of new infrastructure. Moorsom (1984a) provides the most detailed survey of Walvis Bay's fortunes up to the early 1980s, with particular reference to its twin economic pillars of fishing and seaborne trade, with their associated service and supply industries.

Overfishing precipitated a crash in pelagic fish catches from 1975 onwards, leading to a severe local recession and the closure of several canning and fishmeal factories, despite some efforts to counter the impact by increasing the level of white fish caught (see also Moorsom 1984b). Black workers (i.e. Africans and Coloureds) bore the brunt of this. Numbering about 12,500 out of a total workforce of 16,000 in 1976, the peak year, over half had lost their jobs by 1981, when only 5,600 remained in employment. They therefore suffered about 86 per cent of the overall 8,000 job losses in the enclave over this period, most of which occurred during the three years after 1976. Since most African employees are migrant workers from northern Namibia, many returned to their homes, causing a temporary fall in the town's population (Table 7.1) and exacerbating the local recession.

A slow recovery of fish stocks began during the late 1980s but has accelerated since Namibian independence, with greater control over the issuing of catch quotas and licences, and the greatly enhanced ability to patrol and enforce the country's territorial waters and exclusive economic zone.[1] Together with increased trade through the hitherto underutilised harbour, prospects have improved markedly since 1990, despite the departure in 1993–4 of a substantial number of South African military personnel (some of whom have been replaced by Namibian Defence Force staff). When Walvis Bay was reintegrated into Namibia, its population was estimated at around 30,000 (Table 7.1), but it is generally thought to have increased significantly since then. Figures as high as 50,000 have been claimed, although this is almost certainly an exaggeration. Nevertheless, it is clearly now Namibia's second largest 'established' urban centre after Windhoek (200,000+), although two of the newly proclaimed towns in the northern communal areas, namely Oshakati (40,000) and Rundu (45,000), have comparable populations.

Until very recently, it was impossible to obtain harbour freight data on Walvis Bay, since South Africa regarded any accurate Namibian economic information as

Table 7.1   *Walvis Bay: population estimates by the municipality*

Year	Numbers	% Annual growth
1960	12,721	–
1970	21,917	5.6
1980	18,733	−1.6
1985	21,084	2.4
1990	29,950	7.3
1991	30,452	1.7
Growth rate 1960–90		2.9
Growth rate 1980–90		4.8

Source: Department of Regional and Land Affairs (1993).

potentially helpful to its opponents. Secondly, until 1995, no data were released on oil and other petroleum product shipments through any South African-controlled ports because oil was deemed a matter of critical state security in view of international sanctions against South Africa. Only after Walvis Bay's reintegration into Namibia were figures on trade volumes through the port made available, and only in late 1994 were petroleum cargoes disclosed by South Africa. Table 7.2 provides a breakdown of traffic for the period since the harbour's transfer to Namport. Substantial growth is evident. The 1993/94 data show only a small increase over the total of 1,595,471 tonnes recorded in the 1992/93 financial year, although this latter figure was substantially higher than the 1991/92 total of 1,483,624 tonnes.[2] Growth accelerated markedly in 1994/95 to 1.8 million tonnes, while the total tonnage handled in 1995/96 reached 1.9 million tonnes, of which petroleum product imports, the single largest commodity flow, comprised over 719,000 tonnes. The relative gap between imports and exports remains roughly consistent, although it is worth noting that total exports exceed imports of all commodities other than petroleum. Most of the traffic still represents Namibian import-export trade, although Zambian cop-

Table 7.2   *Walvis Bay Harbour: freight traffic 1993/94 – 1995/6 (tonnes)*

MAIN COMMODITIES: Landed Commodity	93/94	94/5	95/6
Petroleum	435,384	580,059	719,414
Fish products	61,291	106,650	108,062
Wheat	34,828	44,774	62,794
Maize	44,915	17,326	67,046
Sugar	39,344	45,045	50,741
Coal	147,859	154,315	47,070
Vehicles	4,226	10,609	19,129
Copper and lead	4,386	17,479	14,855
Cement	18,728	19,835	18,863
Malt	7,150	9,050	11,254
Wine	15,487	15,523	10,432
Other	88,582	89,718	85,229
Total	902,180	1,110,383	1,214,889
MAIN COMMODITIES: Shipped			
Salt	351,500	370,206	296,905
Manganese ore	–	29,360	104,096
Fish products	103,774	108,981	76,326
Copper and lead	50,956	38,516	37,844
Flourspar	32,434	52,782	34,732
Flat cartons	10,130	11,200	19,152
Marble and granite	20,169	13,760	11,244
Charcoal	2,820	5,400	14,191
Skins and hides	9,623	6,851	10,521
Fertiliser (guano)	3,271	1,764	2,412
Other	37,465	26,296	45,975
Total	622,142	665,116	653,398
TRANSSHIPMENT			
TOTAL	95,356	32,047	37,656
GRAND TOTAL	1,619,678	1,807,545	1,905,943

Note: Data refer to the periods 1 May – 30 April annually.

Sources: Chief Executive Officer, Namport, December 1995; Namibian Ports Authority 1996.

per exports and emergency food imports for drought-stricken southern Angola, in particular, are included (see below). Transshipment also contributes less than 40,000 tonnes per annum.

Since the annual capacity of the existing harbour facilities is estimated at about 2 million tonnes, only modest spare capacity currently exists. If growth continues at a rate comparable to that since 1991, the envisaged expansion and redevelopment (see below) will be needed quickly.[3] Meanwhile, the completion of a new bulk cargo terminal in late 1995 has enhanced its potential. Particularly in the early 1980s, despite the political and economic upheavals, considerable investment by the South African Transport Services (Transnet's predecessor) went into the port: three jetties and the small boat harbour were rebuilt and the tugs upgraded. Regular dredging is also required to maintain the depth of the sandy channels through the bay (Von der Fecht 1994). The existing harbour comprises eight berths with a total wharf length of 1,400 metres, container handling facilities, warehouses totalling 3,500m^3 of storage capacity, a mineral loading plant, a Dolphin-type tanker jetty with adjacent storage depot (Dierks 1994b; EIU 1996: 41) and the Synchrolift repair facility for vessels of up to 2,000 tonnes displacement and 70 m long. Although the cranes – all rail-mounted on the quayside – were between 19 and 35 years old in 1994, availability of over 90 per cent is maintained (Von der Fecht 1994).

Negotiating the Transfer of Walvis Bay and its Fixed Assets

During 1991, the Namibian Foreign Minister, Theo-Ben Gurirab, took the initiative in requesting that the South African and Namibian governments commence talks over the enclave's future. The first tangible result was the establishment, on 1 November 1992, of a Joint Administrative Authority (JAA) over Walvis Bay and the offshore islands, headed by a Chief Executive Officer from each country and charged with the administration of certain 'neutral' functions. Although the arrangement was open-ended in terms of duration, Namibia saw it very much as an interim stage leading to full Namibian sovereignty sooner rather than later (Simon 1996a). Indeed, the Ministry of Foreign Affairs' press release announcing the agreement to establish the JAA referred to it as 'an interim arrangement, pending the early resolution of the sovereignty issue' (MFA 1992). The wording of the formal agreement establishing the JAA was less specific: 'an interim arrangement, pending an *eventual settlement of the question of* Walvis Bay and the Off-Shore Islands' (Republic of Namibia and Republic of South Africa 1992; emphasis added). Publicly, however, South Africa continued to assert its sovereignty and claimed the JAA to be an indefinite arrangement – the latter fully justified in terms of the agreement.

Due primarily to the excellent personal working relationship built up by the respective Chief Executive Officers, Carl von Hirschberg (SA) and Nangolo Mbumba (Namibia), the JAA worked surprisingly well within its mandate, which required it to 'administer Walvis Bay in the best interests of its inhabitants' but excluded 'matters not considered susceptible to joint administration' such as diplomatic and other issues relating to the enclave's status (*ibid.;* Simon 1996a). Meanwhile, limited talks between the two governments on the sovereignty issue continued.

Inevitably, these essentially political negotiations on reintegration did not include the more practical issues surrounding Walvis Bay's transfer. During bilateral negotiations in Pretoria on 8 September 1993, political agreement was finally reached and the handover date set for 28 February 1994. This reflected not only the enclave's loss of strategic geopolitical significance for South Africa and the perceived benefits in terms of goodwill to be derived from its handover, but, crucially, also adroit Namibian diplomacy in raising the issue in South Africa's multiparty negotiating forum at a critical juncture (Simon 1996a). Only at this stage were senior officials of both sides instructed to begin discussions in November-December 1993 on the 'modalities', i.e. specific details and arrangements. The analysis in this section relies heavily on interviews with some of the senior officials, ministers and advisers on both sides who were directly involved in the process, and on confidential documentation produced pursuant to that process.

Areas of Substantive Disagreement
Two key issues of contention quickly emerged, both reflecting the specific geopolitical context. The first related to the protocol of the negotiations themselves. The Namibian government perceived these negotiations as an extension of the earlier process, and therefore insisted on their being conducted on a bilateral government-to-government basis. By contrast, the South African government's position was that a clear distinction existed between the government and state-owned (or, for that matter, private) companies. Pretoria saw its role as having been completed with the conclusion of the political agreement. Hence, except for a few small government properties, the modalities needed to be negotiated with its commercialised parastatal corporations which controlled the main relevant assets and operations, namely Portnet in the case of the harbour, the Telecommunications Corporation (Telkom) in relation to telecommunications facilities, and the Electricity Supply Commission (Eskom) in respect of the enclave's small power station and distribution grid.[4] Initially, rather awkward triangular meetings took place but, once the interim Namibian Ports Authority (Namport) board had been appointed in January 1994 (see below), bilateral negotiations between it and Portnet began and somewhat eased the tensions over the port, eventually facilitating a compromise 18 months after the official handover on 1 March 1994.

The second issue concerned the basis on which the assets would be transferred. The Namibian government took the view that it should inherit the assets in the same manner as those elsewhere in Namibia in 1990, i.e., in terms of the International Law of State Succession, as it was a new and legitimate government taking over from an illegal government of occupation which had constructed and used the facilities for its own ends and without consulting Namibians. Conversely, the official South African position was that it was transferring a piece of sovereign territory as a gesture of goodwill and that it should therefore be compensated at the appropriate commercial rate for the value of fixed and any moveable assets which Namibia wished to take over. Given the context, both positions were understandable, although such diametrically opposed starting positions, namely no versus full compensation, did not augur well for negotiations that were intended to be rapidly and successfully concluded before the actual transfer.

What Price for Principle and Pride? Negotiating a Compromise
The status of the Rooikop civilian airport terminal, itself a modest part of the larger military airport complex, did not present a significant problem. The military airport (minus equipment which had been largely removed or destroyed) was transferred to Namibia under the military agreement of February 1994 (Simon 1996a), while the civilian part, hitherto operated by the Municipality of Walvis Bay, became a Namibian state airport. One press report suggested that the Municipality were seeking a sum of N$2.2 million (*Namibian*, 5 November 1993), but I have found no evidence that money changed hands; the lease appears merely to have lapsed.

Other smaller items on the remaining agenda were resolved more quickly, albeit by no means easily. These included small government-owned premises and residential properties and the power station and associated electricity distribution grid, for which Namibia agreed to pay Eskom N$1 million. This left the harbour and its associated assets, and the telecommunications installations in the town as the bones of contention.

An additional, and initially seriously complicating, factor was that Namibia's multimodal parastatal transport corporation, TransNamib Ltd (TNL), had been negotiating with Transnet since 1992 when the JAA was inaugurated, about the establishment of a joint company to operate the port and railway in the enclave within the framework of the JAA agreement (Simon 1996a). These talks had apparently reached a relatively advanced stage by the time they were overtaken by the events under discussion here. Under a commercial agreement with SATS, Portnet's predecessor, in 1988, TNL already leased the railway track from the enclave's boundary to the port gate for a token R1 per annum but also took responsibility for its maintenance and operation. The track within the harbour was owned by Portnet but maintained and operated by TNL at Portnet's expense. In return, Portnet waived all charges for the movement of rolling stock and freight within the harbour (Uys 1994; Von der Fecht 1994). This arrangement continued after Walvis Bay's reintegration, as the payment/compensation issue had yet to be settled.

Particularly since TNL already owned and operated the small port of Lüderitz in southern Namibia,[5] but also for reasons of institutional politics[6] and the enlargement of its sphere of influence, TNL assumed that it would take over Walvis Bay as well, and the corporation's top management under Managing Director, Francois Uys, took rapid steps to try to ensure that they were a leading party in the negotiations. However, some key staff in the Namibian Ministry of Works, Transport and Communications (WTC) had had fundamental disagreements with TNL over policies, practices and attitudes, and were wary of such perceived empire building.

In any event, in line with international trends, the establishment of a separate ports authority was being actively considered in order to achieve an eventual separation of operations and ownership from regulatory functions. Indeed, the Namibian government evidently approved the establishment of such an authority with no link to TNL as early as 1 September. Nevertheless, these divergent views, and some ambivalence on the part of the Minister of WTC, Marco Hausiku, in particular, increased tensions and complicated the early negotiations until TNL had been definitively sidelined and excluded from the negotiations and the port authority model unambiguously approved at the end of the year.

Portnet saw the key issues at stake as comprising:

- that they, and not the South African government, would head the negotiations;
- the takeover and payment of compensation for Portnet assets tranferred, using a market value approach;
- the security of employment of staff and their transfer to Namibia if appropriate;
- the nature and terms of technical assistance to be provided by Portnet to Namibia;
- the future of the coastwise trade in salt produced in the enclave and which was shipped to Durban for use by South African industry. Walvis Bay had been designated a decentralisation point under South Africa's regional development programme, and as such local industry (most notably salt) received a subsidy. This put Walvis Bay salt at a great advantage over that produced across the enclave's border in Namibia (Mors and Swanepoel 1994).

Following familiarisation visits, the first formal negotiations took place in Windhoek on 16–17 November 1993. Because of the protocol problem (as no top South African government representative was present), these were heated, confused and inconclusive. The Namibian negotiating team was led by the then new Permanent Secretary of WTC, Frieda Williams. The South African team, headed by Portnet's Chief Executive Officer-designate, Neil Oosthuizen, included a senior official from the Ministry of Public Enterprises as well as Captain Jan Mors, Portnet's Executive Manager (Commercial) and the Port Manager in Walvis Bay, Captain Jens-Dieter von der Fecht. In late August, Von der Fecht had submitted a proposal for the takeover and running of the port to the Namibian Chief Executive Officer of the JAA, Nangolo Mbumba. This focused on depoliticisation and the operation of an integrated infrastructural system under a specialist authority, and corresponded quite closely to ideas obtained from an independent consultant.

With Namibian Cabinet approval, negotiations in what became known as the Technical Committee on the Port of Walvis Bay (TCPWB) pursued such possibilities and agreement on the broad basis for a transfer was reached with relative ease by mid-January. This involved Namibia making offers of employment to existing Portnet staff in Walvis Bay with a view to ensuring job security and the maintenance of smooth operations. Those wishing to return to South Africa would be transferred by Portnet or compensated if no suitable positions were available. Before the end of December, Von der Fecht, who wished to see out the few remaining years of his career in Walvis Bay, had tendered his resignation from Portnet with effect from 25 February 1994 and been offered employment by Namibia as from 1 March 1994 in order to head their nascent operation. Although kept confidential at the time, this appears to have been a crucial turning point and boost of confidence for Namibia's position and ability to ensure a workable transition.

Meanwhile, drafting of a Namibian Ports Authority Bill had commenced behind the scenes in early November, and the first draft was discussed by the Cabinet and consultants during late December and early January. Given the political uncertainties within Namibian government circles, the lack of movement on the assets question despite progress in drafting and agreeing both the South African and Namibian laws to give effect to the transfer (Simon 1996a), differences of view on the Ports Authority Bill and the extremely short timeframe available, the pressures and tensions were considerable, with frequent fears that the whole process could be scuppered.

An interim Namibian Ports Authority board of directors, headed by the Permanent Secretary of WTC (Williams) and including the Walvis Bay Port Manager (Von der Fecht), was appointed in mid-January and was able to pursue the negotiations with new vigour. Attempts to resolve the assets question were made at ministerial level, but by the end of January virtually no progress had yet been made, with each side reiterating its existing position, although South Africa is understood to have reduced its demand for R84.4 million compensation (calculated on a net present value basis of discounted future income flows) to R64.4 mn. Namibia indicated a willingness to consider recompense for Portnet liabilities but not the capital value of assets. The South African negotiators subsequently expressed some frustration at the lack of government support in the name of avoiding any further political controversy, claiming that they were left somewhat vulnerable and were not offered the possibility of a government 'subsidy' or compensation if it were deemed appropriate to waive some or all of the amount being claimed from Namibia (Mors and Swanepoel 1994; Van Eeden 1994).

In February 1994, South Africa's Ministry for Public Enterprises apparently indicated acceptance in principle of the use of the historical cost basis (from 1960) for calculating the value of assets rather than the net present value basis Portnet had been using until then. However, my informants are not agreed about this. Little further progress was achieved, except agreement that the transfer of Walvis Bay should go ahead on schedule with the issue of the assets to be resolved thereafter. This enabled Portnet staff formally to sign contracts of employment with the Namibians, something achieved under acute time pressure as the Ports Authority Bill finally completed its parliamentary passage on 24 February and was signed into law as an Act by the President the following day (Republic of Namibia 1994a). The three formal agreements on the use, transfer and secondment of Walvis Bay and relevant assets and staff were signed by Portnet and the Permanent Secretary of WTC on 27 February. Interestingly, only 15 of Portnet's 360 staff refused the offer of transfer to Namport, and remained in Walvis Bay on secondment pending redeployment to South Africa (Mors and Swanepoel 1994). Meanwhile, the assets remained on Portnet's books, with interest to be paid by Namport at a rate of 9–10 per cent on the disputed value of R64.4 mn, i.e. about R (or N$) 500,000 per month, although this would be reviewed once agreement had been reached (Von der Fecht 1994).

Walvis Bay was also declared to be a port of registry for ships as from 1 March 1994 (Republic of Namibia 1994a). The Ports Authority Act gives the Authority (Namport) fairly conventional powers and functions in respect of the management and control of ports and lighthouses, and the provision of related facilities and services. Importantly, it defines the boundaries of both Namibia's existing ports, Walvis Bay and Lüderitz, and makes provision for the future transfer of Lüderitz and the adjacent Diaz Point lighthouse from TNL (which owned and operated them) to Namport, which would then also manage and control them.[7] On 1 March 1994, Namport was to acquire and commence management of Walvis Bay and all lighthouses and navigational aids except that at Diaz Point (Republic of Namibia 1994a). Until that date, the lighthouses and navigational aids had been owned by TNL but operated by Portnet on their behalf (Nils Bruzelius, pers. comm.).

Naturally, given the rapid change in Walvis Bay's status, Namport's structure differs considerably from earlier ideas of a joint Portnet-TNL operating company under the Joint Administrative Authority, or TNL's subsequent intention of a straight takeover (see above, also *Lloyd's List;* 25 August 1993). Furthermore, senior Ministry of WTC sources still expected that, at some future point, ownership and operation of the ports and lighthouses would be separated from their regulation. This arrangement represents the so-called 'Continental Model', currently in vogue in many European and other countries. This duly happened to some extent in mid-1996, when Namport adopted a new internal structure which separated the 'Authority' from 'Service Providers' (e.g. Human Resources, Financial Services and Civil Engineering Services); the infrastructure was also divided into distinct 'business units' – namely Cargo Services, the Synchrolift and Technical Services (Jens-Dieter von der Fecht, pers. comm).

The momentous and ceremonial reintegration of Walvis Bay into Namibia took place on schedule at midnight on 28 February (Mulongeni 1994; Simon 1996a; *Southern African Economist* 1994; *Namibian,* 25 February 1994). Captain von der Fecht, who became Chief Executive Officer of Namport, was eventually able to collect the keys to the Synchrolift (small ship repair facility) and operations continued without interruption. The asset issue dragged on, with both parties agreeing to continue bilateral negotiations despite the passing of the agreed deadline for seeking neutral arbitration.

It is unclear to what extent the change of government in South Africa in May 1994 contributed to this delay. Despite the replacement of Pik Botha, the long-serving Foreign Minister, by Alfred Nzo, an ANC veteran, that Ministry's policies have been slower to change than almost any other's (Davies 1995; Evans 1995). There was probably little incentive to intervene directly in the Walvis Bay negotiations, which, by then, were being conducted by the respective port authorities and parastatals. However, the new Deputy Foreign Minister, Aziz Pahad, reportedly did not favour arbitration and was willing to have the assets in Walvis Bay transferred to Namibia without payment. When President Mandela announced, in December 1994, that South Africa had finally agreed to write off the roughly R800 million public debt which the Namibian government had inherited at independence from the South African-supported administrations, top-level officials remained unclear whether this included the Walvis Bay assets. Indeed, I initially received contradictory indications on this issue, until it emerged that negotiations were, in fact, continuing.

Eventually, in August 1995, Telecom Namibia agreed to pay its South African counterpart a total of N$5 million including interest for the telecommunications facilities, while in September/October 1995, Namport and Portnet agreed a capital sum of N$30mn, in addition to the interest already paid up to that date, in respect of the harbour assets and liabilities (Klaus Dierks and Jens-Dieter von der Fecht, pers. comm). The final agreement was hammered out by Transnet's General Manager Finance, Mr Schindehutte, and Namport, both working within limits mandated by their governments. The money, raised as a loan from a commercial bank, was handed over on the last working day of December 1995, while the official handover of the port took place at a high-level ceremony on 22 March 1996 attended by the responsible Cabinet ministers and heads of the parastatals from both countries (Von der Fecht, pers. comm). Thus, fully two and a half years after the bilateral agreement on Walvis Bay, and two years following the actual reintegration, the transaction was finally completed and Namibia's unimpeded sovereignty and ownership of the former enclave and its infrastructure assured.

Integrating Walvis Bay within Namibia's Restructured Internal Political Geography

One of the Namibian government's early priorities after independence was to formulate a new internal political geography that would signal a fundamental departure from previous apartheid policies and facilitate national integration and cohesion in line with government policies and constitutional principles. The Constitution stipulated that uniform regional and local authority structures were to be established throughout the country. The First Delimitation Commission was established for this purpose and its recommendations, tabled in mid-1991 (Republic of Namibia 1991), were duly accepted by the government and the boundaries of the 13 new regions gazetted in March 1992. Pursuant to the country's territorial limits as defined in the Constitution, Walvis Bay was included as one constituency within the adjacent Erongo Region, to come into effect as soon as circumstances permitted (Republic of Namibia 1991, 1992a; Sidaway and Simon 1993).

Following the subsequent promulgation of the Regional Councils Act, 1992 and Local Authorities Act, 1992 (Republic of Namibia 1992a, 1992b), elections for both sets of councils were held countrywide on 2 and 3 December 1992. Namibian residents of Walvis Bay, who comprise the majority of the local population, were not able to vote in the enclave which was still claimed as sovereign South African territory even under the newly established JAA. Instead, they were compelled to travel the 30 km to the neighbouring town of Swakopmund in Namibia. Obviously, no Namibian local authority could be elected, as the incumbent municipality existed under South African law, so voting was solely for the Regional Council constituency. This was duly won by SWAPO's Wilfried Emvula (now Deputy Minister of Trade and Industry), who polled 7,435 of the 8,228 votes cast (i.e. 90.4 per cent) in a 63.3 per cent turnout (Republic of Namibia 1992c). This provided an important barometer of Namibian opinion in Walvis Bay, signalling strong support for the government's policies in general and on the enclave in particular. It should be remembered that the majority of white residents were not eligible to vote on account of their South African citizenship.

As in most South African cities during the political transition of the early 1990s, a Local Government Negotiating Forum was established to work out plans to integrate the city council, which was still structured along apartheid lines. This proved problematic, not least because Namibians were not permitted to vote in any such elections, prompting the withdrawal of African participants (*Namibian*, 20 August 1993). Ultimately, as an interim measure, a Joint Town Council was formed on 1 November 1993, bringing together the three apartheid structures and the Walvis Bay Regional Services Council. In terms of the Interim Measures for Local Government Act, 1991 (Act 128 of 1991), they were formed into a single local authority, the Municipality of Walvis Bay, and all serving councillors of the respective bodies formed the new council (Cape of Good Hope 1993; *Namibian*, 14 and 21 February 1992, 12 November 1993).

Under an agreement between the two countries' Local Government ministers, the existing councillors would remain in office under existing South African legislation for up to six months following Walvis Bay's reintegration, and their salaries and pension benefits would be retained (*Namibian*, 18 March 1994). However, reincorporation into Namibia brought the municipality under the Namibian Local Authorities Act, 1992, which provides for a non-racial, integrated structure. A new Namibian municipality was duly elected on a universal adult franchise in August 1994. SWAPO gained 77.5 per cent of the vote and won 8 of the 10 seats in terms of the proportional representation system used for local authorities. The other two seats went to the official opposition, the Democratic Turnhalle Alliance (Republic of Namibia 1994c). One of the DTA councillors is the long-serving former town clerk. Despite its past racist record, the municipality has moved rapidly to reposition itself within its new Namibian context and to seize the initiative in promoting regional development in Walvis Bay, which is now Namibia's second largest urban centre. The politics of this are complex and centre on the establishment of an export processing zone (EPZ).

Walvis Bay as Gateway Port: Trade, an Export Processing Zone and some Wishful Thinking

Grand schemes to develop Walvis Bay as a key gateway for the southwestern segment of southern Africa, linked to major rail projects, have been mooted at various points since the late nineteenth century (Dierks 1993). On account of colonial geopolitics and then postcolonial conflicts centred on South Africa's apartheid policies and its continued occupation of Namibia, coupled with economic considerations, these proposals were all consigned to a transport historian's scrapbook of curiosities. The most recent non-starter was the 1980/81 proposal to construct a trans-Kalahari railway for the export of coal from an envisaged new coalfield around Palapye in eastern Botswana (Simon 1991). However, Namibian independence and the other regional realignments of recent years have transformed the prospects for new international surface transport routes. A new Trans-Kalahari Highway through central Botswana to the eastern Namibian regional centre of Gobabis, and then Windhoek and Walvis Bay, has been under construction and is due for completion in 1997/8, together with the Trans-Caprivi Highway linking Zambia and Zimbabwe with the Namibian road network (Dierks 1993; Simon 1991).

These schemes were designed to diversify the trade and transport options of Namibia and adjacent landlocked countries away from those under South African control. With the normalisation of relations with the newly non-racial South Africa, the political imperative for such measures has largely disappeared but diversification still makes logistical and economic sense. The new corridors are expected to promote development in outlying regions and will improve trade and the use of Namibia as a transit route for surrounding landlocked countries, despite fierce competition from South African and other regional rail and road transport operators. The precise size of these traffics remains unclear, however. On the other hand, the main immediate use of the Trans-Kalahari route will almost certainly be as a quick link between Johannesburg and Windhoek, as it shortens the existing road route by some 450 km.

The proposal for an Export Processing Zone (EPZ) in Walvis Bay represents another important strategy to generate employment, value added and trade in the light of the new circumstances in southern Africa. The context and evolution of this development will be explored in a broadly chronological manner in order to put it more fully in context.

An Enclave Economy, 1977–94
The business community in Walvis Bay had been in an ambivalent position since South Africa resumed direct control of the enclave in September 1977. Although many were South African citizens, predominantly conservative, happy to implement apartheid (which was traditionally strongly enforced in Walvis Bay) and profiting substantially from the heavy military presence in the enclave, they realised that the commercial future of the port city was ultimately bound up with conditions in the rest of Namibia. If transit traffic were to be substantially reduced or cut off by South Africa using Walvis Bay as a noose to pressurise Namibia, the town's economy would itself be strangled. Conditions had already been depressed for some years. A substantial contraction in the other pillar of the local economy, namely the fishing industry, in the mid-1980s, induced by overexploitation, had precipitated a major local recession and considerable net outmigration. The protracted uncertainty over Namibia's independence and then, after 1990, over the enclave's relationship to Namibia also affected business and investment confidence considerably. Many of the most prominent local business leaders therefore began exerting pressure on the South African authorities to resolve the issue in the early 1990s, with an increasing preference for formal reintegration into Namibia (e.g. NEPRU 1992), thus reinforcing the momentum on the Namibian side.

The Namibian independence process provided Walvis Bay's port and associated facilities with a much-needed boost as the UN shipped much of its heavy equipment and supplies for supervising the transition period (other than those procured from South Africa) through the port during 1989 and early 1990. This one-off flow was then replaced by increasing Namibian trade with the rest of the world. At least one important regional breakthrough was also achieved in late 1990, when TNL signed an agreement with Zambian Consolidated Copper Mines to transport 30,000 tonnes of copper per annum by road and rail to Walvis Bay for export (Simon 1991). This contract is still operative although only about one-tenth of the contracted amount was shipped during 1993/4 (Von der Fecht 1994).

On the political front, the establishment of the JAA in November 1992 implied that conditions were stabilising and that conflict was increasingly unlikely (Simon 1996a). This gave renewed impetus to hopes for investment and increased trade. The Walvis Bay Development Advisory Committee (established in 1982), representing various local interests from the private sector along with local and central government departments, pressed for a local economic development strategy geared to the promotion of the underutilised port's subregional role as a gateway for transit traffic to neighbouring countries and also as a potential entrepot.

The resulting document, produced in July 1993 by the South African government, took account of the JAA but restated 'Walvis Bay's constitutional association with South Africa' and made its first recommendation that 'the constitutional future of the Walvis Bay enclave as part of South Africa should be reconfirmed' (Department of Regional and Land Affairs, 1993: 2, 37). Much of the document comprised an overview and inventory of existing infrastructure, industry, employment and social facilities, but the final eight pages presented an evaluation of growth potential and proposed developments. The approach was framed by a 'SWOT analysis' (i.e. strong points, weak points, opportunities and threats), itself reflecting the disjuncture between economic contiguity and political separation. Most of the identified 'weaknesses' related to the problems this situation engendered and which were eliminated by the enclave's reintegration into Namibia nine months later. The entire document, in fact, was rendered obsolete by this process because it totally failed to consider alternative future scenarios, such as either reintegration (which was already then increasingly likely) or a new constitutional dispensation in South Africa (which was then under negotiation), and their implications for local development. The proposals were all made in terms of Walvis Bay remaining an enclave and were so self-evident and couched in such general terms as to be of little practical value anyway. This report therefore typified the head-in-the-sand attitude of many South African ministries and officials under the old regime, even as circumstances changed around them.

The period between independence and Walvis Bay's reintegration produced mixed fortunes for black Namibians, who form the majority of the enclave's population. It can perhaps best be described as a time of frustrating dynamic limbo, in the sense that change was uneven, sometimes non-existent, sometimes slow and then suddenly dramatic, while the uncertainties played on people's nerves and undermined economic confidence. Following the repeal, by mid-1991, of South Africa's most oppressive apartheid laws such as the Group Areas, Reservation of Separate Amenities and Population Registration Acts, freedom of movement and residence within the enclave eased considerably. On the other hand, workers continued to face racist hostility and exploitation in the workplace through practices such as unfair and summary dismissals and the refusal to recognise the main trade unions on the grounds that workers in South Africa should be represented by South African and not Namibian unions (*Namibian* 26 March 1993). Such matters fell outside the jurisdiction of the JAA, which was therefore unable to intervene directly. It was, however, able to reduce substantially the level of harassment facing black travellers, as the removal of border posts and checks between the enclave and Swakopmund was one of the first actions of the JAA (Simon 1996a).

The atmosphere changed dramatically with the announcement that Walvis Bay would be 'transferred' or 'incorporated' (according to South Africa) or 'reintegrated' or 'reincorporated' (according to Namibia).[8] While negotiations on the timetable continued, popular euphoria was clearly demonstrated by Namibians in the enclave, although many South African whites expressed anger at the 'sell-out' by Pretoria. The powerful civil servants' lobby, in particular, made frantic efforts to secure favourable terms for their continued residence and/or repatriation to South Africa (Simon 1996a). On the other hand, the response from the business community in the enclave, and those involved in trade and transport through it, was overwhelmingly positive. Newspaper headlines such as 'Walvis Bay, islands transfer "no threat" to diamond mining' (*Cape Times*, 21 August 1993), 'New horizons set to open up for Walvis Bay' (*Lloyd's List*, 27 August 1993) and 'Bay of Plenty?' (Murray 1994) were typical of local and overseas coverage of the economic implications.

The impact in the workplace was also tangible, with at least two important landmarks for workers' rights. At the beginning of November, South Africa's Industrial Court ruled that the dismissal in 1991 of 31 workers by a sugar company for taking part in a legitimate strike in support of demands that Walvis Bay be reintegrated into Namibia was illegal and that they would have to be reinstated with compensation (*Namibian*, 5 November 1993). The following week, a breakthrough was reached when the five largest fishing companies agreed to recognise the Namibian Food and Allied Workers' Union (NAFAU) as the exclusive bargaining agent for all their employees (*Namibian*, 12 November 1993).

Walvis Bay as Namibian Gateway and Export Processing Centre
Various development proposals were soon announced, as local, southern African and foreign firms sought to position themselves strategically to exploit the new opportunities. These reportedly included a Libyan bank willing to finance a luxury hotel, and unspecified interest by the ubiquitous Lonrho, which already has other Namibian investments (*Namibian*, 9 December 1993). However, the principal early player was the Projects, Industrial Development and Investment Company (Pidico), controlled by Egyptian interests but registered in the Isle of Man. This firm had entered Namibia with aplomb after independence, rapidly establishing good relations with senior members of the government and acquiring interests in farming, communications and printing in various parts of the country. It also claimed to have reached an agreement with the government to construct and operate a massive 20 km^2 free trade zone in Walvis Bay. Some land was secured from the Walvis Bay Municipality and a couple of steel structures erected in time for a grand opening ceremony on 1 March 1994, the day of Walvis Bay's reintegration into Namibia, at a claimed cost of N$3 million.

However, the company seems to have overplayed its hand, overextending itself, failing to consolidate early activity on many of its schemes and suffering deteriorating relations with the government. Whereas Pidico claimed the free trade zone as 'its' project, government ministers argued that it would merely be one of many investors and that legislation was being prepared to formalise and clarify Namibia's position on a free trade zone (*Namibian*, 22 April 1994). Questions about the company's pedigree and motives were soon being aired at the highest level, and the firm's representatives then disappeared without trace, abandoning equipment and unfinished projects. Although they evidently have successful operations elsewhere in the region, they have totally discredited themselves in Namibia in what appears to have been a rush to take advantage of inexperienced government ministers and officials in securing preferential treatment. The Walvis Bay Municipality eventually had to dismantle the useless and rusted structures erected by Pidico (*Namibian*, 13 April 1995).

Following the Pidico fiasco, the Municipality took its own initiative during 1994 in demarcating and preparing an export processing zone, planned to grow from an initial 20–30 hectares to 300 ha over a ten-year period. Both local and foreign investors were canvassed and although several expressions of interest and commitments regarding a hotel, garment factory, banking facilities and so forth were received, the lessons had been learnt the hard way, and the relevant legislation was awaited before the EPZ could be formally constituted (De Castro 1994; *Namibian*, 28 October 1994). The Export Processing Zones Bill was approved by the Cabinet in September 1994 and, following consultations, was submitted to parliament in early 1995, becoming law in April. In common with EPZs elsewhere, this Act provides exemption from corporation tax, sales tax, customs and import duties, and many worker rights, while also offering serviced sites and training grants.[9] Geographically, the scope of the Act has been widened from formally proclaimed EPZs, as originally conceived, to any part of the country, where individual companies can now apply for EPZ status provided that they comply with the formal prerequisites.[10] By the end of 1996, twelve firms had been granted EPZ status, while another 30 applications were being processed; one factory in the Walvis Bay EPZ was operational and exporting one containerload weekly (*Namibian*, 28 October 1994, 13 April 1995, 15 November 1996; Republic of Namibia 1995; EIU 1997; *Times*, 27 January 1997: 4).

Somewhat unexpectedly, the passing of this legislation sparked one of the most heated and politically important public confrontations over any law since independence. The National Union of Namibian Workers (NUNW), the previously SWAPO-affiliated umbrella federation, took exception to Section 8 of the Bill, which suspended the provisions of the Labour Act in EPZs, arguing that this represented a recipe for exploitative labour practices and for depriving workers of redress and protection. It mobilised support within the labour movement in a public campaign and, in the face of government refusals to back down, threatened court action. This was deferred, pending further negotiations, during which the government stood firm, citing the need to be internationally competitive, the importance of attracting manufacturing investment in order to create jobs, and common practice in EPZs in other countries. As provided for in Section 8 of the Act, it offered to draft regulations on basic conditions of employment, termination of contracts of employment, disciplinary actions, health, safety and welfare, in consultation with unions and the Offshore Development Company (ODC), which had been established in terms of the Act to promote and market Namibian EPZs (see below). By July, the unions seemed to be backing slowly away from their legal threats and in mid-September a compromise was ultimately reached in terms of which many provisions of the Labour Act were to remain in force, although strikes and lockouts would be banned. New regulations drafted by the Ministry of Trade and Industry stipulated a maximum 45-hour working week, paid holidays and sick leave (*Namibian*, 3 and 23 March, 13 April, 26 May, 7 July 1995; Economist Intelligence Unit 1995a: 9–10, 1995b: 11; *The Times*, 27 January 1997: 4).

An amendment to the Export Processing Zones Act became necessary to give effect to this agreement, and the relevant Bill passed its National Assembly stages in April and May 1996. This replaces Section 8 of the original Act and stipulates that the Labour Act will remain in force within EPZs, except for the right to strike or use lock-outs, for an initial five-year period. It also specifies special procedures to be followed in the event of a dispute arising, and penalties for contraventions (*Namibian*, 10 and 17 May 1996; Republic of Namibia 1996).

The importance of this struggle was twofold. First, it marked a political watershed, with the NUNW taking up the cudgels in defence of workers' rights against the government to which it had long been affiliated. Shortly after independence it had become apparent to the leadership that, with SWAPO now forming the government, disaffiliation might become necessary since the interests of the state and of labour would at some point diverge. The political revolution necessitated a new relationship. This was inevitably a hotly contested view but was ultimately carried and disaffiliation followed. However, this case marked the first substantial power struggle between the two, confirming their structurally induced conflicting interests. Secondly, despite the loss of some momentum and key leaders after independence (as a result of some worker indifference now that 'freedom had been achieved' and the appointment of key leaders to government posts), the NUNW was able to gain some notable concessions from the government, even after the main EPZ Bill had become law, and despite what militant workers felt to be a sell-out of their interests. Discontent among rank and file unionists with their officials and the government continued even after the compromise had been agreed and the Amendment Bill was debated in the National Assembly (*Namibian*, 12 April, 17 May 1996).

The Offshore Development Company was inaugurated in late June 1995 as a limited liability private company. Its six initial shareholders include the Namibian government (15 per cent) and Aaron Mushimba, the President's brother-in-law, although the three foreign investors (Saudi Arabian Sheikh Yamani's Hazy Investments, Transpolo of Taiwan, and a British oil consultant) hold over half the equity. A separate firm, the Walvis Bay Export Processing Zone Management Company, was also established to operate and manage the EPZ, in terms of the EPZ Act; the Walvis Bay Municipality were to hold a stake of 10–15 per cent, other local investors (by tender) up to another 45 per cent and foreign investors the remainder (EIU 1995a: 9–10; *Namibian*, 21 July 1995).

In recognition of these developments and the need for modernisation, expansion and reorganisation of parts of the port's operations to cope with increased trade flows and, in particular, increased competition for transit traffics against other southern African ports, Namport and the Ministry of WTC began preparation of a Walvis Bay Port Development Plan, to be undertaken jointly with private consultants under the terms of a German aid agreement. The objective is to capitalise on Walvis Bay's greater proximity to the major markets of Europe and North America than any South African or Mozambican port. This undertaking was then broadened into a Port Development Master Plan, to include Lüderitz and the potential of an envisaged third harbour at Möwe Bay on the northern coast (see below). The Master Plan, due for completion by the end of 1995 (Dierks 1994a: 22–23, 1995), was accepted in principle by the Namport board in early 1996 (Namibian Ports Authority 1996). Opinions on the extent of the regional traffic likely to be generated still differ, however. The Namport Chief Executive Officer, for example, is of the opinion that expansion should be planned with Namibian traffic as the backbone. Some foreign aid donors apparently had no idea of the quality and efficiency of Walvis Bay harbour and wanted to fund its 'rehabilitation', as has been necessary in Angolan and Mozambican ports. Other 'grandiose' schemes have been mooted, e.g. providing a new gantry crane for containers, although this would require an annual throughput of about 75,000 teu (twenty-foot equivalent units) compared with the 1993/4 and 1995/6 totals of 19,369 and 23,109 respectively (Von der Fecht 1994; *Lloyd's List*, 22 May 1996; *Namibian*, 15 November 1996; NPA 1996).

The possibility of installing a mobile shore crane on the quayside was investigated in 1994, but the existing quay was not strong enough to withstand the additional mass (Von der Fecht 1994). Namport's first significant new development in the port, a bulk cargo terminal, was completed in August 1995. A new Liebherr multi-purpose, mobile tower crane, with a capacity of 100 tonnes, was purchased for N$16 million in late 1996. Scheduled to start operations in January 1997, this crane is enabling direct ship-to-shore transfer of containers for the first time (*Lloyd's List*, 2 November 1996; NPA 1996). If fully implemented, the port development plan could raise annual capacity to as much as 10 million tonnes. However, this is certain to represent a long-term scenario, implementable only in phases, and involving major dredging works to increase the harbour's depth from 10 to 12.8 metres (EIU 1996: 41; Von der Fecht, pers. comm.; *Namibian*, 15 November 1996). This would enable ocean-going container and other large vessels to berth. By the end of 1996, then, the groundwork for Walvis Bay's envisaged role as a regional gateway had been completed, seeking to capitalise on the enclave's reintegration, the reputation of Namibia and the port of Walvis Bay for efficiency and reliability, and the changing conditions across post-apartheid southern Africa.

Evaluation

The specific issues and problems faced by Walvis Bay as a result of its particular geographical situation and politically contested status have now disappeared as a result of the enclave's reintegration into Namibia on 1 March 1994 and the eventual resolution of the dispute over the harbour assets in late 1995. In evaluating this process, two interesting and related issues should be addressed at the outset. First, the starting points of both parties on the asset issue appear, as would be expected, to have reflected their perceptions of their own material and strategic interests. Thus, the South African government was intent on being seen to make a generous political gesture to Namibia (and, indirectly, to the international community) on the sovereignty issue, in return for which it expected financial compensation for its previous material investment. Some sceptical observers and the Namibian government regarded this as a cynical manoeuvre to secure 'blood money' to which it had no right in view of South Africa's occupation and exploitation of Walvis Bay.

Conversely, Namibia sought 'free' transfer of the assets on the grounds of South Africa's illegal occupation and consequent moral debt, and the international law of state succession. Pretoria saw this as an attempt to squeeze something for nothing out of South Africa at a time of profound political flux. Indeed, it is noteworthy that the negotiations over the asset valuation continued for well over a year after the demise of National Party rule and accession to power of the ANC-dominated Government of National Unity. Although President Mandela moved relatively quickly to write off Namibia's pre-independence public sector debt to South Africa, that arrangement excluded Walvis Bay. It remains unclear whether this exclusion was made because capital assets were being transferred to independent Namibia or because Mandela was unwilling to intervene and overturn the previous government's position that authority in those negotiations rested with the commercialised parastatal corporations rather than the state itself. Either way, this provides a significant insight into the ANC government's early regional geopolitical perceptions.

The second issue is that Namibia ultimately agreed to negotiate over, and then pay, compensation, thereby effectively abandoning its claim for 'free' transfer in terms of the international law of state succession. The reason(s) for this appear to be pragmatic, an approach which has been the hallmark of Namibia's foreign policy since independence. This shift of position avoided the need to resort to cost-ly and time-consuming international arbitration, maintained the good working relations which had been built up with the South African government, *and* gained immediate use and secure tenure of the port. A modest payment (only about one-third of South Africa's original claim) was regarded as a price worth paying.

With the reintegration of Walvis Bay and final resolution of the asset issue, the political situation has now 'normalised', leaving Walvis Bay free to compete with other southern African ports for international transit traffic and with the overland road and rail routes from the Cape for a higher proportion of Namibia's imports and exports. Whereas South Africa has several major ports, and Mozambique and Angola three substantial ones each, Namibia has only one.[11] This may reduce Namport's flexibility in terms of port switching relative to the other national port authorities, but puts efficiency and reliability at a premium.

Walvis Bay is likely to experience a continuing increase in Namibian trade as overall volumes increase and Namibia continues its policy of diversifying the geog-raphy of its trade. However, the port's ability to attract significant new trade between South Africa and Namibia will almost certainly be limited to bulk freight (much of which, apart from a modest volume of petroleum currently sent by rail, already uses that route), on account of both cost and time considerations – as trans-shipment would be involved. Even for salt, which is produced in the immediate vicinity of the harbour, shipment to Durban for onward consignment to the Gauteng area – South Africa's economic heartland – holds a very thin advantage over direct transport by rail. Such traffics can readily be switched in response to a change in costs or the introduction or withdrawal of subsidies and other conces-sions, such as happened when Walvis Bay was reintegrated into Namibia.

Future prospects for the growth of regional transit traffic are difficult to predict with accuracy at this point, as relations across the region are still in transition. In particular, the three main regional economic organisations, the Southern African Customs Union (SACU), Southern African Development Community (SADC) and the Common Market for Eastern and Southern Africa (COMESA), are currently engaged in restructuring and rationalisation negotiations to accord more appropri-ately with post-apartheid conditions in southern Africa (e.g. Odén 1993; *Courier* 1995; Ramsamy 1995; Chapter 10). The outcome of this process will have some impact upon selective regional industrial investment programmes, possible infra-structural use policies and thus the extent of modernisation and upgrading under-taken with donor funding in individual ports.

Walvis Bay's principal advantages are its efficient record and good interchange facilities for both rail and road freight, and its location on the Namibian coast where there are no direct competitors. However, that may change relatively soon (see below). Moreover, it is not located on high volume routes, may soon be operating nearer to full capacity and, notwithstanding the current refurbishment and expan-sion programme, has limitations on ships' draught which preclude very large ves-sels from docking at present. It is far from clear that completion of the Trans-Kalahari Highway will lead to the diversion of significant Gauteng traffic to the Walvis Bay route from South African harbours, both because Durban and Richard's Bay harbours remain far closer and because Spoornet, the South African railway corporation, and South African road haulage companies offer very compet-itive rates. In addition, major expansion and development of the Maputo Corridor linking Gauteng to the port in Mozambique's capital city, which is now starting on a vastly greater scale than the Walvis Bay harbour and EPZ programmes (Chapter

9, this volume), will strengthen the eastward orientation of import/export traffics to/from South Africa's economic heartland. On the other hand, only if there is a substantial increase in the flow of containers through Walvis Bay (which is unlikely from purely Namibian traffic), would it be practicable for containerships to and from Europe or elsewhere to call en route. Currently, containers have to be shipped to Cape Town once per week for transshipment, increasing consignment times by several days.

As politically motivated or constrained decision-making has all but disappeared in the region, and liberalisation and privatisation have become the norm elsewhere in Africa and beyond, competition between ports and the railway systems which serve them is becoming increasingly based on considerations of cost, efficiency and reliability. Recent trends include the growing use of freight consolidation services (especially for containerised traffic) in one major hub port per (sub-)region, and the domination of major routes by a small number of shipping conference lines. Smaller ports and those with poor records or long rail distances, such as Dar es Salaam, have already begun to lose out and will be hard-pressed to raise their share of total traffic without predatory price cutting or the provision of subsidies, despite recent efforts to improve their images (*African Business* 1995; Hoyle and Charlier 1995; Iheduru 1996; Ngwenya *et al.* 1993). On grounds of efficiency and cost, Walvis Bay would seem likely to hold its own and increase its traffic somewhat. Even modest expansion of the new EPZ will assist this trend, although efforts to promote the port as a regional or subregional gateway for transit freight or as a major international free port linked to the EPZ are probably overoptimistic.

This point is underlined by the planned – and long delayed – rehabilitation of southern Angola's port of Namibe, which has long operated at a tiny fraction of potential capacity as a result of war and very old infrastructure. It is well located to serve a modest hinterland including northern Namibia, and is certain to feature in cross-border development initiatives. The Benguela Railway linking the Zambian Copperbelt to Lobito is also scheduled to return to service relatively soon, after lying idle since the mid-1970s as the Angolan hostilities raged across its route. Its rehabilitation has also suffered long delays to date.

Finally, Namibia has recently decided to proceed with a feasibility study for a third port, at Möwe Bay, on the northern Skeleton Coast. The study, costing over N$3.6mn, and funded mainly by Kuwait, was originally due for completion during 1996 but its commencement was greatly delayed (Nils Bruzelius, pers. comm.). It is now expected to be completed at the end of March 1999. Although the Möwe Bay plans had originally been conceived as an alternative to Walvis Bay if the latter remained in South African hands, certain politicians and senior officials in the Ministry of WTC and Namport continue to advocate the project as a fishing port in the first instance, to optimise development of that industry, and as a stimulus to regional development in Namibia's arid northwest. In 1994, construction of a fishing harbour was estimated to cost US$80mn, but road and/or rail links and the associated infrastructure would also have to be built through inhospitable terrain (Dierks 1995: 51–54; *Namibian*, 20 August, 26 November 1993, 24 November 1995; Stanley 1990). In the longer term, there is some hope for expansion on account of its relative proximity to the densely populated northern regions of Namibia and central southern Angola. However, such visions are likely to prove yet another unrealistic delusion of grandeur. It is far from certain that even the fishing harbour would represent an efficient or cost-effective use of scarce capital and skilled human resources.

Notes

1. The territorial waters were stipulated in Namibia's constitution and the EEZ was reproclaimed after independence. Both now have full local and international legal status. Previously, some foreign fishing boat operators claimed that they did not recognise the legitimacy of the original proclamation.
2. The commodity classification used by South Africa's Portnet parastatal (which provided the pre-1993/4 data) was different, thus making detailed comparison difficult. In addition, traffic was broken down into imports, exports, coastwise (to other South African-controlled ports), and petroleum products – the latter disclosed separately. I have thus had to calculate the overall totals from these separate headings. Furthermore, it appears that these data relate to the financial year (1 April-31 March) and are therefore not entirely comparable with the Namport data for the two most recent years. What is clear, though, is that the omission from previously published data of petroleum products has substantially understated the true levels of port usage in all South African-controlled harbours. In Walvis Bay, for example, petroleum products constituted 28.6 per cent of the total traffic in 1992/93. Under Portnet's management, Walvis Bay was its fifth busiest port after Durban, Cape Town, Port Elizabeth and Richard's Bay. Although handling a similar volume of freight to East London, Walvis Bay had been more profitable, generating 5–6 per cent of Portnet's total profits. In the words of the Portnet Executive Manager (Commercial), 'It ran itself nicely as a self-contained entity' (Mors and Swanepoel, 1994).
3. The port's maximum capacity is difficult to calculate precisely. The bulk terminal has a design capacity of 500 tonnes per hour (inward or outward), while the Tsumeb Corporation Ltd (TCL) ship loader can handle 500 tonnes of salt per hour. At present, however, the latter handles only 350,000 tonnes per annum. The tanker terminal is used on average for 4 days per month. Namport's Chief Executive Officer estimates that, with somewhat increased peak time delays, the port could handle 3 or 4 times its present freight tonnages, but that the main constraint is in the transport capacity of the rail and road hauliers, which have geared their fleets to average throughputs (Jens-Dieter von der Fecht, pers. comm.).
4. In early 1992, a gas turbine generator was removed to South Africa from Walvis Bay power station following negotiations between Eskom (the owners) and SWAWEK (the power station's operators). However, concerns that this represented asset stripping ahead of a settlement over the enclave, were denied on the grounds that it had been an unused back-up facility (*Namibian*, 16 April 1992).
5. This had been taken over from Portnet at the time of independence in 1990, but Portnet had subsequently provided assistance with the operation of the port and lighthouse (Mors and Swanepoel 1994).
6. These politics are complex, comprising a particularly aggressive, expansionist and entrepreneurial culture espoused by the South African-trained and largely Afrikaner top management, which emphasised multimodal growth ahead of consolidation and preached market competition but sought to maintain some aspects of state protection and previous privileges. It also acquired a bad reputation for labour relations which were out of tune with independent Namibia and more akin to traditional South African practice. In addition, it sought to avoid or minimise an affirmative action programme at senior level.
7. This transfer did then take place very quickly, i.e. before the end of May 1994.
8. The semantics of this terminology are both interesting and symbolically important, expressing and seeking to legitimise the respective governments' official positions (Simon 1996a). In this context, it is remarkable that the commemorative postage stamps issued by Namibia to mark the occasion bear the caption 'Incorporation of Walvis Bay'.
9. The Namibian government appears to have been rather ingenuously optimistic about the developmental potential of an EPZ. To some extent this probably reflected the persuasive powers of slick operators within Pidico and other vested interests. However, there was also a perception that such an initiative might facilitate competition with South Africa for foreign direct investment and thereby promote employment creation and, at least initially, a lack of awareness of the very mixed results of existing EPZs worldwide (only a minority, perhaps most conspicuously in Mauritius and China, have achieved spectacular success). In this context it is significant that several analyses of the potential benefits of establishing EPZs in South Africa have been less than enthusiastic. During the sanctions period, the idea was deemed inappropriate, but studies by parastatal corporations and urban local authorities in 1992 were optimistic. A recent impartial evaluation (Nel 1994) concluded that critical examination of EPZ experience and possible lessons for South Africa had been inadequate, and that more careful consideration of cost minimisation and recovery, locational optimality and political acceptability was essential before any implementation (cf. McCarthy 1986, 1991; Ligthelm and Wilsenach 1992; Nel 1994). It is unclear

how detailed an appraisal took place in Namibia, although it is certainly no coincidence that the person appointed as Chief Executive of the Offshore Development Company (see main text below) is Abdool Aboobakar, described in a recent newspaper survey as 'a Mauritian who had a high success rate in attracting investment to his native country' *The Times*, Namibia Special Supplement, 27 January 1997: 4).

10. Interestingly, although the duty-free nature of EPZ imports and exports infringes the regulations of the Southern African Customs Union (SACU), there appears to have been no opposition to Namibia's initiative from that body or its other members. Informed sources are also not aware of any discussion of the issue in the current SACU renegotiations (see below). Given the current small scale of Namibia's EPZ operations, the export duty revenues forgone on exports to non-SACU countries are likely to be small; the loss of revenue from import duties on inputs may be somewhat more significant. Declaration of the entire country as an EPZ would not seem appropriate at this stage, since few local firms export manufactured goods and the loss of revenue to the exchequer is likely to be relatively high. South Africa has also been considering introducing EPZs (Nel 1994; see also note 9), and it is worth pointing out that South Africa's Generalised Export Incentive Scheme (GEIS), now being phased out under World Trade Organization rules, also represents an infringement of SACU rules.

11. Lüderitz, on the southern coast, remains insignificant because of its distance from major nodes of economic activity or transport corridors, and the severe limitations on ship draught imposed by the solid rock seabed. Nevertheless, since Namport assumed control over the harbour, upgrading has begun and a N$68mn loan from the European Investment Bank was secured for this purpose in late 1996. The centrepiece of the work will comprise a new 300m multi-purpose quay (*Lloyd's List*, 2 November 1996; NPA 1996).

References

African Business (1995) 'New Head of Steam for TAZARA', *African Business*, No. 204, November: 22–23.

Berat, L. (1990) *Walvis Bay: Decolonization and International Law*. Yale University Press, New Haven, CT.

Cape of Good Hope (1993) Walvis Bay: agreement and measures in terms of the Interim Measures for Local Government Act, 1991 (Act 128 of 1991), Proclamation No. 122/1993, *Official Gazette of the Province of the Cape of Good Hope*, No. 4825, 29 October. Cape Town.

Courier, The (1995) 'Dossier: Southern Africa', September-October, No. 153: 47–78. Brussels.

Davies, R. (1995) *South African Foreign Policy Options in a Changing Global Context*. Working Paper 40, Centre for Southern African Studies, University of the Western Cape, Bellville.

De Castro, M. (1994) 'On the West Coast of Africa: the first EPZ in Namibia', *Namibia Yearbook*, No. 4, 1993/94: 8.

Department of Regional and Land Affairs (1993) *Enclave of Walvis Bay: Towards a Development Strategy*. Pretoria.

Dierks, K. (1993) *Namibia's Railway System – Future Link to Africa with Specific Reference to the Trans-Kalahari Railway*. Ministry of Works, Transport and Communications, Windhoek (October).

Dierks, K. (1994a) 'Cutting the Noose – Walvis Bay: Southern Africa's New Lifeline'. Paper presented at the First International Conference on African Maritime and Fisheries Expo for Walvis Bay, Walvis Bay, 22–24 October.

Dierks, K. (1994b) 'Walvis Bay Bids to Become a Regional Port', *Namibia Yearbook*, No. 4, 1993–4: 6–7 and 9–10.

Dierks, K. (1995) 'Guidelines for the Development Plan for Namibia's Ports with Special Reference to Walvis Bay' (Confidential Memorandum). Ministry of Works, Transport and Communications, Windhoek.

Du Pisani, A. (1994) 'South Africa and the Region', in Mills, G. (ed.) *From Pariah to Participant; South Africa's Evolving Foreign Relations, 1990–1994*. South African Institute of International Affairs, Johannesburg.

Economist Intelligence Unit (1995a) *EIU Country Report: Namibia; Third Quarter 1995*. EIU, London.

Economist Intelligence Unit (1995b) *EIU Country Report: Namibia; Fourth Quarter 1995*. EIU, London.

Economist Intelligence Unit (1996) *EIU Country Profile 1995–96: Namibia*. EIU, London.

Economist Intelligence Unit (1997) *EIU Country Profile 1996–97: Namibia*. EIU, London.

Evans, G. (1993) 'A New Small State with a Powerful Neighbour: Namibia/South Africa Relations since Independence, *Journal of Modern African Studies* 31(1): 131–48.

Evans, G. (1994) 'Across the Orange River: Namibia and Colonial Legacies', in Mills, G. (ed) *From Pariah to Participant; South Africa's Evolving Foreign Relations, 1990–1994*. South African Institute of International Affairs, Johannesburg.

Evans, G. (1995) 'South Africa in Remission: the Foreign Policy of an Altered State'. Paper present-ed at the Second Pan-European Conference on International Relations, Paris, 13–16 September (forthcoming in *Journal of Modern African Studies*).

Ferguson, J. (1990) *The Anti-Politics Machine: 'Development', Depoliticisation and Bureaucratic Power in Lesotho*. Cambridge University Press, Cambridge.

Hangula, L. (1993) *The International Boundary of Namibia*. Gamsberg-Macmillan, Windhoek.

Hopwood, G. (1990) *Walvis Bay: South Africa's Hostage*. Catholic Institute for International Relations, African-European Institute and Church Action on Namibia, London.

Hoyle, B. and Charlier, J. (1995) 'Inter-port Competition in Developing Countries: an East African Case Study, *Journal of Transport Geography* 3(2): 87–103.

Iheduru, O.C. (1996) Post-apartheid South Africa and Its Neighbours: a Maritime Transport Perspective', *Journal of Modern African Studies* 34(1): 1–26.

Lardner-Burke, J. D. (1926) 'The Transformation of Walvis Bay', *The Mining and Industrial Magazine* 2(1): 29–30.

Ligthelm, A.A. and Wilsenach, A. (1992) 'Special Economic Zones as an Instrument to Stimulate Export Production and Economic Growth within South Africa', *Development Southern Africa* 9(4): 397–410.

Lloyd's List (1993) 25, 27 August. London.

Lloyd's List (1996) 22 May, 2 November. London.

McCarthy, C.L. (1986) 'Export Processing Zones as an Element of Export Orientated and Regional Industrial Development', *Development Southern Africa* 3(3): 399–411.

McCarthy, C.L. (1991) 'Export Processing and the Economic Development of the Coastal Metropolitan Areas', *Development Southern Africa* 8(4): 459–465.

Ministry of Foreign Affairs (1992) *Press Release No. 49/92, Concerning Negotiations on Walvis Bay and the Off-Shore Islands*. Windhoek.

Moorsom, R. (1984a) *Walvis Bay: Namibia's Port*. International Defence and Aid Fund, London.

Moorsom, R. (1984b) *Fishing: Exploiting the Sea*. Catholic Institute for International Relations, London.

Mors, J. and Swanepoel, M. (1994) Interview with Executive Manager (Commercial) and Senior Manager (Corporate Marketing), Portnet Head Office, Johannesburg, 22 July.

Mulongeni, B. (1994) 'Walvis Bay Reintegration', *Namibia Review* 3(2), April: 1–19. Ministry of Information and Broadcasting, Windhoek.

Murray, R. (1994) 'Bay of Plenty?', *African Review of Business and Technology* 30(2): 29, 34.

Namibian Economic Policy Research Unit (1992) *Walvis Bay: Report of a Fact-Finding Mission, October 1990*, NEPRU Working Paper 13. NEPRU, Windhoek.

Namibian Ports Authority (1996) *Annual Report 1996*. Walvis Bay.

Nel, E.L. (1994) 'Export Processing Zones: International Experience and Applicability to South Africa,' *Development Southern Africa* 11(1): 99–111.

Ngwenya, S., Chipeta, H., Nkomo, J.C. and Banda, D.L. (1993) *The Transport and Communications Sector in Southern Africa*. SAPES Books, Harare.

Nugent, P. and Asiwaju, A.I. (eds)(1996) *African Boundaries: Barriers, Conduits and Opportunities*, Pinter, London.

Odén, B. (ed.) (1993) *Southern Africa After Apartheid; Regional Integration and External Resources*. Scandinavian Institute of African Studies, Seminar Proceedings 28, Uppsala.

Ramsamy, E. (1995) 'South Africa and SADC(C): a Critical Evaluation of Future Development Scenarios,' in Lemon, A. (ed.) *The Geography of Change in South Africa*. Wiley, Chichester.

Republic of Namibia (1991) *Report by the First Delimitation Commission of Namibia on the Determination of Regions, Constituencies and Local Authorities*. Windhoek.

Republic of Namibia (1992a) Regional Councils Act, 1992 (Act 22 of 1992), *Government Gazette* 469, 31 August. Windhoek.

Republic of Namibia (1992b) Local Authorities Act, 1992 (Act 23 of 1992) *Government Gazette* 470, 31 August. Windhoek.

Republic of Namibia (1992c) Government Notice No. 184 of 1992. Electoral Act, 1992: Notification of result of general election for regional councils, *Government Gazette* 545, 7 December. Windhoek.

Republic of Namibia (1994a) The Namibian Ports Authority Act, 1994 (Act 2 of 1994), *Government Gazette* 810, 28 February. Windhoek.

Republic of Namibia (1994b) Government Notice No. 24 of 1994. Merchant Shipping Act, 1951: Declaration of a port of registry for the registration of ships, *Government Gazette* 801, 24 February. Windhoek.

Republic of Namibia (1994c) Government Notice No. 157 of 1994. Electoral Act, 1992: Notification of result of the election for the Local Authority Council of Walvis Bay, *Government Gazette* 915, 9 September. Windhoek.

Republic of Namibia (1995) The Export Processing Zones Act, 1995 (Act 9 of 1995), *Government Gazette* 1069, 18 April. Windhoek.

Republic of Namibia (1996) National Assembly: Export Processing Zones Amendment Bill. Windhoek.

Republic of Namibia and Republic of South Africa (1992) *Agreement Between the Government of the Republic of Namibia and the Government of the Republic of South Africa on the Joint Administration of Walvis Bay and the Off-Shore Islands*. Windhoek, 30 October.

Sidaway, J.D. and Simon, D. (1993) 'Geopolitical Transition and State Formation: the Changing Political Geographies of Angola, Mozambique and Namibia,' *Journal of Southern African Studies* 19(1): 6–28.

Simon, D. (1986) *Noose or Lifeline? The Role of Transport in Independent Namibia*. Working paper 231. Institute for Transport Studies, University of Leeds.

Simon, D. (1989) 'Transport and Development in Independent Namibia: Noose or Lifeline?', *Third World Planning Review* 11(1): 5–21.

Simon, D. (1991) 'Namibia in Southern Africa: the Regional Implications of Independence,' *Tijdschrift voor Economische en Sociale Geografie* 82(5): 377–87.

Simon, D. (1996a) 'Strategic Territory and Territorial Strategy: the Geopolitics of Walvis Bay's Reintegration into Namibia', *Political Geography* 15(2): 193–219. An earlier version appeared under the same title as NEPRU Occasional Paper No. 1, May 1995, Namibian Economic Policy Research Unit, Windhoek.

Simon, D. (1996b) 'Restructuring the Local State in Post-apartheid Cities: Namibian Experience and Lessons for South Africa', *African Affairs*, 95(378): 51–84.

Southern African Economist, The (1994) April: 12–13. Harare.

Stanley, W. R. (1990) 'A Third Port for Southwest Africa/Namibia?' *GeoJournal* 22(3): 363-78.

Uys, D. (1994) Interview, Marketing Manager, TransNamib Ltd., at TransNamib Head Office, Windhoek, 28 July.

Van Eeden, E. P. (1994) Interview with Chief Executive, Office for Public Enterprises and Privatisation, Ministry for Public Enterprises, Pretoria, 22 July.

Von der Fecht, J-D (1994) Interview with Chief Executive Officer, Namibian Ports Authority, Namport Head Office, Walvis Bay, 4 August.

Wellington, J.C. (1976) *South West Africa and its Human Issues*. Oxford University Press, London.

8 The Changing Role of Sugar as a Vehicle for Economic Development within Southern Africa

STEVE ATKINS & ALAN TERRY

Introduction

In 1990, sugar accounted for US $8.6 billion in export income, or almost 10 per cent of the total value of agricultural exports of all developing countries, becoming their most important commodity export earner and for the first time exceeding coffee (FAO 1992). For the purposes of this discussion, the countries to be studied encompass the Southern African Development Community (SADC) region, nine of which produce significant quantities of raw sugar, all of it derived from sugar cane. Within the region sugar is currently attracting significant attention as it is a relatively easy crop to cultivate, under both estate and smallholder agricultural systems, and provides good returns and considerable potential for large-scale investors to participate in agricultural developments.

The sugar industry is therefore an important vehicle for rural development and illustrates many of the inter-related issues likely to impact upon the region as a consequence of the increasing economic links which are now possible between South Africa and its neighbours. These consequences may be summarised as, first, the likely impact on the South African sugar industry, second, the likely impact on the other regional producers and, third, the likely impact on the external sugar market. Many of the possible consequences of a greater integration of the region's sugar industries are closely interlinked. Thus, within South Africa, the sugar industry has been viewed as a key to a successful implementation of the Reconstruction and Development Programme (RDP), particularly within the politically sensitive KwaZulu-Natal province. However, large-scale South African sugar companies are beginning to exercise their greater freedom when making investment decisions, and this has opened up the possibility of their exploiting lower cost resources elsewhere in the region, which may undermine the prospects for achieving RDP targets involving the sugar industry. External to the region, the ending of apartheid has provided the opportunity for South Africa to begin to re-establish more formal ties with the European Union and the United States. Its current attempts to gain access to the Lomé Sugar Protocol indicate the potential strategic importance of the industry in levering access to a type of aid budget which could have a positive effect on rural incomes within the sugar producing areas. The sugar industry also provides an opportunity for South Africa to learn from the longer-established small-grower traditions of many of its neighbouring sugar industries as it seeks to increase the number of black small-scale sugar cane growers. Its willingness to seek advice may provide a pointer to its likely attitude towards its less economically and politically powerful neighbours. All of these developments are taking place against a background of internal deregulation within most of the regional sugar industries plus the consequences of increased trade liberalisation in agricultural products brought about by the recent establishment of the World Trade Organization (WTO).

The Role of Agriculture and Sugar in the SADC

There is a wide variation in the dependence of the SADC countries on commercial agriculture (Table 8.1). Botswana and South Africa have both been able to reduce significantly their dependence on the agricultural sector because of a diverse mineral base and substantial investments made in the mining and manufacturing sectors. In contrast, Mozambique and Tanzania have substantial mineral deposits but insufficient funds to exploit them, and are thus forced to rely upon agriculture for more than 60 per cent of GDP.

Sugar cane was introduced to the region by European farmers in the mid-nineteenth century, and for just over a century, outside the main centre of production in KwaZulu-Natal, the crop was grown on an insignificant scale, often for subsistence purposes, as in the case of Zambia, for example (Lombard and Tweedie 1974). Its the major expansion has occurred since the former colonial states acquired their independence in the 1960s. The same is also true for South Africa, where sugar cane production is estimated to have increased from 850,000 metric tonnes in 1961 to over 22.4 million metric tonnes in 1984/85 (FAO 1992).

In 1994/95, the SADC countries produced over 3.8 million tonnes of raw sugar, representing 55 per cent of the total for Africa, and 5 per cent of the world total (Table 8.1). Within the region, South Africa dominated with 47 per cent of the regional output, with three other countries, namely Mauritius, Swaziland and Zimbabwe, producing a further 39 per cent (Licht 1995). Regional sugar output peaked in the 1986/87 season at just over 4.2 million tonnes; since then the general trend has been down, reaching a low of 3.35 million tonnes (a 20 per cent fall) in 1992/93. South Africa accounted for 53 per cent of the decrease, and Zimbabwe a fur-

Table 8.1   *The role of agriculture and sugar within the SADC region*

Country	GNP per Capita 1992 US$*	Agriculture as a percentage of GDP 1992*	Agriculture's share of exports in GDP (%) 1992*	Sugar cane production 1994/95 '000 metric tonnes**
Angola	n/a	13	43	25
Botswana	2,790	5	n/a	0
Lesotho	590	11	19	0
Malawi	210	28	24	214
Mauritius	2,700	11	64	530
Mozambique	60	64	47	21
Namibia	1,610	10	14	0
South Africa	2,670	5	25	1,802
Swaziland	1,080	15	77	484
Tanzania	110	62	36	125
Zambia	290	9	26	168
Zimbabwe	570	20	22	465
SADC Average	1,153	21	36	3,834

Sources:* World Bank, 1994; ** Licht, 1995

Note: Average figures include Botswana, Lesotho and Namibia

ther 36 per cent. In both cases, the cause was the prolonged drought affecting the region in the early 1990s. The remainder was due to a variety of region-specific factors: economic constraints (Tanzania) (Sterkenburg and Van der Wiel 1995); civil war and economic stagnation (Mozambique and Angola); adverse climatic conditions including drought and cyclones, and competition for labour because of rapid industrialisation (Mauritius) (UNECA 1993).

Sugar varies considerably in importance to the regional producers. Revenue from sugar contributes around 60 per cent of Swaziland's GDP (ACP Secretariat 1996), but less than 1 per cent of South Africa's (Table 8.2). However, within South Africa, sugar is the major industry in KwaZulu-Natal and the lowveld of Mpumalanga (formerly the Eastern Transvaal) (Ridgway 1995). In general, however, it contributes less than 5 per cent of GDP to the SADC countries. The figure for Swaziland shown in Table 8.2 is misleading. In 1992 the contribution of agriculture to Swaziland's economy had fallen to 11.9 per cent (UnionBank of Swaziland 1994). However, by 1992, manufacturing was contributing 42 per cent to Swaziland's GDP, with the processing of sugar the largest single sector (EIU: 1995: 122-3). In 1987, soft drinks manufacturing had become the second largest export earner after sugar and by 1992 the contribution of sugar and 'miscellaneous edibles', made up predominantly of processed sugar products, contributed 55 per cent of the total value of exports (UnionBank of Swaziland 1994).

Structure of the SADC Sugar Sub-sector
Sugar is a major employer throughout the region (Table 8.3).

The employment figures include a very wide range of modes of employment from large-scale agri-industrial estates (miller-cum-planter) which predominate in Malawi, Swaziland, Zimbabwe, Zambia and Tanzania to large-scale commercial farms which have traditionally been significant producers in Swaziland and South Africa. Small grower and contract farming schemes are also widespread in Malawi, Zimbabwe, Zambia and Tanzania where they often form part of large-scale irrigated agri-industrial complexes. Notable expansion of small grower farming has taken place in South Africa and Swaziland in recent years, with Mozambique only recently experimenting with smallholder involvement. Within South Africa, a great deal of political pressure exists to include the rural black population in a successful industry. The Small Growers Development Trust (SGDT), established in 1992, has been set up on the lines of an ANC organisational structure to act as a model for

Table 8.2 *SADC sugar revenue as a percentage of GDP and total agricultural production, 1995*

Country	% of GDP	% of Agriculture
Angola	n/a	n/a
Malawi	18	55
Mauritius	7	66
Mozambique	n/a	n/a
South Africa	<1	7
Swaziland	60	65
Tanzania	3.1	5
Zambia	2.3	15
Zimbabwe	2	16.8

Sources: South Africa, Atkins 1996; the rest excluding Angola and Mozambique, ACP Secretariat, 1996.

Table 8.3   *Employment in the SADC sugar industries, 1995*

Country	Directly Employed	Indirectly Employed	Employment Total
Angola	n/a	n/a	n/a
Malawi	13,000	15,000	28,000
Mauritius	37,000	20,000	57,000
Mozambique	n/a	n/a	13,497
South Africa	130,000	12,000	142,000
Swaziland	9,000	20,000	29,000
Tanzania	32,000	20,000	52,000
Zambia	8,000	60,000	68,000
Zimbabwe	19,000	100,000	119,000
SADC Total	248,000	247,000	508,497

Source: All countries except Angola, Mozambique and South Africa. ACP Secretariat, 1996; Mozambique: Government of Mozambique 1996; South Africa: SASA, 1995.

Note: The ACP-derived figures for indirect employment probably relate to the total number of dependants rather than indirect employment; eg Jackson and Cheater (1994) indicate that in Zimbabwe, 22,000 permanent workers plus 3,500 seasonal workers are employed in the industry with a further 94,500 dependants. This equates very closely with the 119,000 shown above.

small farmer involvement in the Reconstruction and Development Programme (RDP). The SGDT has as its objectives the social and economic empowerment of small-scale cane growers and the development of viable, independent cane grow-ing communities by way of creating the required capacity, through institutional and community development, and agricultural and economic skills-based training (*SGDT Annual Review 1994–95*).

Although criticism has been levelled at the working and living conditions fac-ing workers, particularly on large-scale estates (Loewenson 1992), there can be lit-tle doubt that the introduction of the industry has had a major impact on all aspects of economic and social life in those regions where it has become estab-lished. Although it is possible to set up a sugar industry on a small scale, as was the case with the jaggery factories in Tanzania in the early part of the century (Sterkenburg and Van der Wiel 1995: 120), the normal model of development has centred upon a large-scale mill complex. This in turn requires the setting up of a sufficiently extensive sugar cane production system to satisfy the requirements of the mill for economic production. Thus the sugar producing areas, many of which were relatively isolated prior to the sugar developments, have become the hub of intense capital investment, involving the construction of agricultural estates, mills, housing, roads, schools and other support services. In most areas of the region outside KwaZulu-Natal, climatic conditions have also necessitated the development of large-scale irrigation systems. This is epitomised by the Swaziland sugar industry, which was developed in the virtually uninhabited semi-arid lowveld during the late 1950s. Between 1958 and 1960, sugar production from two mill complexes rose from less than 6,000 tonnes to more than 200,000 tonnes, with massive increases in employment and incomes. A similar transfor-mation occurred with the development of the Malawian, Tanzanian, Zambian and Zimbabwean sugar industries.

The geographic concentration of the industry within each of the countries can be seen from the relationship between the extent of the sugar cane estates and the numbers of mills, bearing in mind the relatively low economic distance for transporting the sugar cane (Table 8.4). The majority of sugar cane production lies within a 40 km radius of the mills, a situation which has tended to lead to marked differences in incomes and the provision of services between the core sugar producing regions and the surrounding rural areas.

The SADC Sugar Trade

In 1994, six of the twelve SADC countries were net exporters of sugar. Statistics relating to the net exporting and importing groups are shown in Table 8.5.

The three largest exporters, Mauritius, South Africa and Swaziland, account for 82 per cent of the total of the group. Although South Africa is the second largest exporter, exports represented only 23 per cent of its total production in 1994. This reflects the much larger domestic market within South Africa compared to the remainder of the region, accounting for 64.5 per cent of SADC's total consumption. However, of greater importance was the effect of the drought which had started to affect output in 1992/93. Production levels were still approximately only 74 per cent of the maximum of 2.3 million tonnes which had been attained before the onset of the drought. The South African sugar industry was forced to cut exports in 1992/93 in order to meet its domestic commitments. Exports, which had reached 969,000 tonnes in 1991/92, dropped by 87 per cent the following year and in 1993/94 were as low as 27,000 tonnes, when the country was forced to import 114,000 tonnes to make up the domestic shortfall. With the resumption of 'normal' production, South Africa would have an export availability of 850,000 to 1 million tonnes (SASA *Annual Report 1994/95*), over 50 per cent of the SADC total exports in 1994. For example, at the end of the 1995 milling season, over 1 million tonnes of sucrose were available for export following very favourable rains.

Table 8.4 *SADC: areas of sugar cane harvested and number of sugar mills, 1994/95*

Country	Area of sugar cane harvested (ha)	Number of sugar mills
Angola	n/a	n/a
Malawi	18,000	2
Mauritius	78,000	17
Mozambique	6,620	2
South Africa	289,000	16
Swaziland	38,000	3
Tanzania	18,000	5
Zambia	13,000	1
Zimbabwe	35,000	2
SADC Total	495,620	48

Sources: Mozambique, Government of Mozambique 1996; South Africa, SASA 1995. The rest, ACP Secretariat 1996

Note: In Mozambique only 2 mills are currently operating, a further 2 are capable of being rehabilitated, while 2 others have been completely written off following the deprivations of the civil war.

Table 8.5   *SADC: sugar trade balances (exporters and importers), 1994 (MT'000)*

Country	Domestic Consumption	Sugar Exports	Sugar Imports	% Exported	% Imported
Angola	95.0	0	42.4	0	44.6
Botswana	45.0	0	45.0	0	100
Lesotho	n/a	0	n/a	0	100
Malawi	164	48.2	0	23	0
Mauritius	38.9	535.4	0	92	0
Mozambique	72.5	25.5	104.9	100	100
Namibia	n/a	0	n/a	0	100
South Africa	1,262.2	419.7	11.9	23	0
Swaziland	144.3	299.7	1.0	65.8	0
Tanzania	166.2	17.4	51.4	0	31
Zambia	88.3	73.8	0	44.9	0
Zimbabwe	259.3	156.2	3.4	34.6	0
Total	1,957	1,533	16.3	47.2	

Source: Licht; Mozambique's exports, Ministerio do Comercio e Comissão Nacional do Plano (1996)

Note: For Mozambique and Tanzania, a proportion of total sugar stocks were (re)exported.

Total SADC sugar consumption in 1994 amounted to 61 per cent of production. Approximately 1.5 million tonnes of sugar therefore needed to be sold outside the region, although, as noted, South Africa could add at least a further 850,000 tonnes to this in an average year. Six of the region's sugar producers are members of the African Caribbean Pacific (ACP) Sugar Group and have a quota to export to the European Union under the Sugar Protocol attached to the Lomé Convention. Because of its financial importance and the current attempts by South Africa to participate in the Protocol, this will be referred to at greater length below.

In 1994, the intra-SADC market represented approximately 12 per cent of total SADC sugar exports. The largest single SADC exporter to other SADC countries was Swaziland, with 97,331 tonnes, although 47 per cent of this was sold to South Africa. South Africa has played little part in this intra-SADC trade in the past because of its political isolation; in 1991 for example, 72 per cent of its sugar exports were sold to Japan and South Korea, whilst none was sold to Africa (Licht 1995). Variations in the regional sugar market due to drought have provided opportunities for one-off sales. For example, in the 1993/94 season, South Africa and Zimbabwe imported a combined total of 210,000 tonnes because of drought-induced production shortfalls. Thus, in the 1993/94 season, Zimbabwe's imports were covered by Swaziland with 94,793 tonnes (51 per cent), with Brazil and Cuba providing 21 and 17 per cent respectively. The remaining 11 per cent was supplied by Zambia.

SADC sugar consumption averages 33.9 kg per head in raw value terms (Licht 1995 – no figures are available for Lesotho or Namibia). This compares with 13.4 kg for the whole of Africa and a global mean of 20.3 kg. However, the SADC figure is distorted by Swaziland's very high consumption of 169.5 kg per head, which was the highest in the world in 1994, due to the inclusion of sugar in exported foodstuffs (Licht 1995). If Swaziland is excluded, then the SADC average drops to 18.8 kg per head, ranging from 5.3 kg for Tanzania to 36.5 kg for South Africa. Excluding Swaziland, consumption per head dropped by 13.7 per cent between 1990 and 1994, with only Angola, Mozambique, Tanzania and Swaziland experiencing increases in their per capita consumption. Notwithstanding the disruptions due to war, we understand these recent Angolan and Mozambican data to be reliable.

The prospects for expansion of the SADC sugar market therefore rest upon a number of factors. For direct consumption, the main variables will be the rates of population and income growth. Given the low average income levels, the effect of the latter will be positive. For the industrial market, demand will depend upon the extent to which food and drink manufacturers expand within the region. The case of Swaziland provides an example of the extent to which this can lead to an increase in local consumption. Between 1990 and 1994, consumption per head rose by a factor of 1.7, mainly due to the establishment and expansion of the sugar processing sector, with large firms such as Cadbury-Schweppes, Nestlé and Coca Cola basing their regional production facilities within the country, in preference to investing in the then apartheid South Africa. For a more detailed discussion on demand elasticities, see Ortmann (1986, 1991) and DBSA (1993).

SADC Sugar Trade Through the ACP Sugar Quota

Under the terms of the Sugar Protocol agreed between the European Union and the ACP countries of the Lomé Convention, the EU applies to ACP sugar exporters' its internal sugar regime. They therefore not only escape import duty but also benefit from the subsidised prices paid to European sugar beet producers, which in general have been between twice and three times the free market prices for sugar during the 1980s and 1990s. Kerr and McDonald (1994) have estimated that the premium price resulted in an income transfer to the ACP sugar group of $US 5,153.5 million (1985 prices) between 1980 and 1990. For Mauritius, the premium was estimated to have been worth 9.52 per cent of GDP over this period, equivalent to an average transfer of $185.38 (1985 prices) per capita per annum. Table 8.6 indicates the current importance of the EU Sugar Protocol to each of the SADC ACP states.

The EU undertakes to import 1.3 million tonnes of sugar annually from the 16 ACP states, which have an obligation to supply this quantity. The result has been mutually beneficial to the ACP sugar industries and the EU sugar refiners. The former enjoy premium prices and a guaranteed market for a proportion of their exports, whilst the latter have a guaranteed source of supply. The 6 SADC ACP countries supply 52 per cent of the ACP quota, which along with the Special Preferential Sugars (SPS) represents an average of 28 per cent of their normal out-

Table 8.6   *Sugar statistics for SADC ACP states*

Country	EU protocol quota (tonnes)	SPS 1995/96 (tonnes)*	Protocol quota plus SPS as % of normal output	Average transfer per capita 1980-90 (US$)	Transfer as a % of GDP 1980-90
Malawi	20,824	13,972	14.8	1.41	0.56
Mauritius	491,030	93,667	90.0	185.38	9.52
Swaziland	117,845	52,480	35.2	80.28	6.97
Tanzania	10,186	1,943	10.1	0.19	0.06
Zambia	0	12,129	7.3	0	0
Zimbabwe	30,225	30,766	11.1	2.36	0.24
Total	670,110	204,957			
Average	111,686	34,160	28.1	53.9	3.47

Sources: ACP Aide Memoire 1996; Kerr, J. and McDonald, S. (ibid)

Note: (*) In addition to the EU Protocol quota, the EU has undertaken to import a variable tonnage of Special Preferential Sugars (SPS) up to at least 2001 at a price equivalent to 85 per cent of the guaranteed price.

put. Of more significance is the fact that the 875,067 tonnes represented 79 per cent by value of all exports for the SADC ACP countries in 1994.

The importance of the EU market to ACP exporters varies greatly (Table 8.7). Mauritius has been granted a combined ACP/SPS quota of 584,700 tonnes which represents 67 per cent of the SADC ACP members' total, and is the largest of the whole ACP group. Normally estimated at 90 per cent of the Mauritius output, in 1994/95 it was actually 49,300 tonnes above output and Mauritius had to import South African sugar on the open market for resale to the EU in order to fulfil its ACP obligations. In contrast, Zambia has no ACP quota but only a Special Preferential Sugar quota of 12,129 tonnes, representing 16.4 per cent of its 1994 exports.[1] It is therefore forced to seek markets elsewhere for the bulk of its exports. In 1995, SADC accounted for 14.3 per cent, but the single biggest market was the former Zaire (now Democratic Republic of Congo), with 44 per cent, whilst Burundi, Rwanda and Uganda together bought 22 per cent. The remainder was exported to the EU at the market price.

Access to the EU and to a lesser extent the US market has been of crucial importance to the expansion of both the Swazi and the Mauritian sugar industries, especially given their small domestic markets. In contrast, the other regional producers export a smaller but increasing proportion of their total production. Zambia now exports 44 per cent of its output, but has had to achieve this without reliance upon an ACP sugar quota, and, even now, has access to the EU market only through the less certain SPS (guaranteed only up to 2001). The ACP quota guarantees a market for the Protocol signatories in perpetuity, even if the Lomé Convention were to be rescinded. Article 1 of the Protocol states that,

> The Community undertakes for an indefinite period to buy and import, at guaranteed prices, specific quantities of cane sugar, raw or white, which originate in the African, Caribbean and Pacific states and which these states undertake to deliver to it.

The Sugar Protocol is of indefinite duration and cannot be changed unilaterally. Unlike the Lomé Convention to which it is attached, its text is not subject to rene-

Table 8.7   *ACP/SPS quota related to per capita incomes and direct employment in the sugar industries of SADC member states*

Country	GNP per capita (US$ 1992)	Average annual transfer per capita (1980-90) US$ 1985	ACP/SPS tonnes quota per worker (directly employed in the sugar industry)
Angola	n/a	0	0
Malawi	210	1.41	2.7
Mauritius	2,700	185.38	15.8
Mozambique	60	0	0
South Africa	2,670	0	0
Swaziland	1,080	80.28	18.9
Tanzania	110	0.19	0.38
Zambia	290	0	1.5*
Zimbabwe	570	2.36	3.21
SADC Mean	1,153	30	4.72

Sources: ACP Aide memoire 1996; Kerr and McDonald (1994)

* Zambia has no ACP quota. Figure based upon SPS only.

gotiation (ACP Secretariat, 1996). However, it might be argued that the terms 'in per-petuity' and 'for an indefinite period' are not entirely synonymous. The word 'indefinite' is ambiguous with respect to duration and the EU could argue in future that it does not represent an open-ended commitment to import within the terms of the Sugar Protocol.

Access to the EU market through the Protocol is currently one of the crucial issues facing the South African sugar industry. Although the relatively high average income per head of South Africa would appear to undermine its argument to join on an aid-related basis, a number of important factors will need to be considered before its claim for access to the preferential market can be dismissed. The average income figures for South Africa hide enormous variations between different ethnic groups. Whiteford and McGrath (1994) indicated a Gini-coefficient for the distribution of pre-tax income of 0.68, which is higher and therefore more unequal than they could find for any other developing country.

Developments within the South African Sugar Industry

The South African sugar industry has recently witnessed an unprecedented expansion of small grower sugar cane production through the SGDT. The majority of the 43,500 growers have low income levels, with an average farm size of only 2.5 hectares. Thus, the majority of the production comes from the large-scale commercial sector where, in 1994/95, 1,582 producers controlled 68 per cent of the cane producing area, although this was down from 83 per cent in 1980. The number of commercial growers declined by 13 per cent between 1980 and 1995. For much of this period, the trend was erratic, but since 1993/94, there has been a decline of 7 per cent (South African Sugar Association, 1995). A large proportion (65 per cent) of all small-scale sugar cane farmers are women:

> The industry's capacity to deliver community assets at a grassroots level has been recognised in the partnership recently announced between the Government's National Community Based Public Works Programme and the sugar industry. This programme, known as the Siyakha project, aims to provide basic needs as identified by the communities themselves while at the same time creating jobs in the sugarcane growing regions (*SASA Journal* 1995: 3).

Such factors support the South African case for access to the lucrative EU market on social grounds and help it expand its quota of 25,000 tonnes into the equally lucrative US market.

Although there has been very rapid expansion of the small-grower sugar cane sector in recent years, the SGDT faces major problems in achieving its objectives (Atkins 1996). These relate to the fragmented nature of the sub-sector, the low educational base, in both a technical and a business sense, of the majority of the participants, and a lack of finance. In addition, the black contractors who provide services to the smallholder cane growers, such as transport to the mill, also tend to have poor business and technical skills. There is the added difficulty in KwaZulu-Natal of the use of violence and intimidation of growers by contractors to obtain business. This is in addition to the political violence which is endemic in the province and has been cited by Ridgway (1995) as having a detrimental effect on development and investment in the region.

However, the SGDT has a well established committee structure centred on sixteen Mill Cane Committees. This gives the sugar sector a major strength and helps to explain the support of the ANC, and its expectation that the initiative will be able to deliver more broadly based rural development, thereby giving the RDP some much needed success. The SGDT is also aware of the need for a solid 'social contract' between the small growers and the industry, based upon equality between groups, educational provision and the application of good business principles. These tend to be lacking in nearly all smallholder contract schemes in other parts of Africa (Little and Watts 1994) and the SGDT may be a good model to export to other sugar industries where small growers predominate.

Many of the new small South African growers are developing sugar cane on marginal, steeply sloping, rain-fed areas with little prospect for irrigation, at substantial distances from mills. Moreover, many of the smallholders are opening up small plots, giving the sector a highly fragmented nature, and precluding economies of scale in managing and harvesting the crop. In 1994/5 some 400,000 hectares, of which 289,000 were harvested in that year, (Table 8.4), were under sugar cane in South Africa but only 15 per cent were irrigated. Rationalisation of the industry is one of the aims of the deregulation process currently being implemented. Thus by the end of the century, sugar production in South Africa may have become more consolidated on irrigated land, located close to the surviving mills. Expansion of small-grower cane farming in Mpumalanga has been based upon 100 per cent irrigation. In 1994 and 1995, much of the area suffered from a severe water shortage due to over-abstraction and low flow in the Komati River (*SASA Journal*, October 1995: 226). When the Driekoppies Dam is commissioned in 1998 and the Maguga Dam in 2001, the region should have excellent prospects for efficient production with similar relief and soils to the contiguous, low cost Swaziland industry. However, the urgency to develop impoverished former 'homeland' areas has resulted in an imbalance between the development of the sugar cane areas and associated mills, and the water resources on which they are dependent. As production switches to a greater reliance upon irrigation in an attempt to overcome the adverse effects of what appear to be longer and more intensive droughts in the rain-fed areas, the competition for the dwindling water supplies between different sectors within South Africa, and between South Africa and Swaziland and the southern region of Mozambique, is likely to intensify. This will therefore become a source of international tension in the absence of an agreed regime on the sharing of water resources.

Given these developments, it is perhaps understandable that the major South African millers are becoming more interested in establishing a presence in what might be considered less stressful environments in the region. Exchange controls limit the amount of outward investment that can be conducted by South African companies, but this is not a problem within the region. The potential for expansion of sugar cane production is huge. For example, Mozambique currently controls 30,000 hectares of irrigated farmland, much in need of rehabilitation, and a further 3 million hectares are estimated to be irrigable. Much of this could be supplied by low cost water from the Cahora Bassa Dam. Twenty-five perennial rivers cross the country from west to east. It is not surprising therefore that Tongaat-Hulett, a subsidiary of the giant Anglo-American Corporation, which processes 41 per cent of South Africa's internally produced sugar (DBSA 1993), is involved in the commissioning and management of the rehabilitated Mafambisse mill on the Pungwe River, inland from Beira, on the understanding that it will take a majority shareholding after three years. Although currently state-owned, the Mozambique sugar industry is to be privatised.

In addition, Illovo has purchased all Lonrho's sugar assets in Africa, which include Big Bend in Swaziland, Dwangwa and Sucoma in Malawi, estates south of Morogoro in Tanzania (*Financial Times*, 9 May 1997), and properties in Zambia and Zimbabwe. It has also purchased the mill and estate outside Maputo from the

Mozambique government (Booker Tate, pers. comm.). These acquisitions make Illovo, hitherto the second largest miller in South Africa, the largest actor in the region's sugar industry. Furthermore, the Tongaat-Hulett Group plans to build a R260 million sugar mill in Zimbabwe's Mazowe Valley, with a capacity of 140,000 tonnes per annum. This involves a link-up with the Lomaz farmers' co-operative. Ownership will vest in Tongaat-Hulett's wholly owned Zimbabwean subsidiary, Triangle Sugar Corporation, which already produces some 300,000 tonnes of sucrose annually. Expansion of Triangle's existing production combined with Mazowe is expected to bring its total capacity to 500,000 tonnes per annum (*Times of Swaziland,* 14 July 1997). In addition, it is in partnership with Tate & Lyle in the Zimbabwe Sugar Refineries Corporation.

South African transnational sugar producers seem to have positioned themselves well to take advantage of the opportunities, having the technical and financial capacity and first-hand knowledge of the region to provide the required services quickly. However, a major effect of such a strategy may be to undermine the ability of the South African sugar industry to sustain and enhance the incomes of the black communities in the least favoured sugar producing centres within South Africa, thereby undermining the RDP in a politically sensitive province. Nevertheless, where water is available, expansion is possible, with up to 6,000 hectares likely to be developed for small growers in the Makatini Flats area in north eastern KwaZulu-Natal. A new mill is planned for this development, which is likely to be the first black-owned and managed complex in the country.

Challenges and Opportunities for the Regional Sugar Industry

Recent developments indicate the opportunities for the expansion of South African sugar exports. Coca Cola purchases 45,000 tonnes of South African sugar for export to its East African bottlers. This decision was made because

> locally produced sugar has often failed to meet the required standards. The benefits for Coca Cola include considerable cost savings and improved economies of scale (Carl Ware, Coca Cola Africa Group President, quoted in *Sunday Times* (Johannesburg), 23 June 1996.

This indication of the relative strength of South African producers is further enhanced by the merger between the South African Bottling Company and Coca Cola. Coca Cola has swapped its bottling plants in Kenya, Tanzania, Uganda and Namibia for a 14 per cent stake in the new company. There is a new bottling plant at Beira in Mozambique and the existing plant in Maputo has been rehabilitated and expanded. There are also new plants under construction in Dar es Salaam and in Uganda. The company's sales and distribution infrastructure in Tanzania, Kenya and Uganda is also to be expanded in anticipation of increased consumer spending. The significance of such developments lies in the ability of a large-scale South African-based company to exploit its economies of scale and superior marketing expertise over its regional competitors. The implications for the latter are that, now that South Africa has access to the regional market, it is likely to be proactive and aggressive in its attempts to seek new opportunities for its products. The Coca Cola contract represented 5 per cent of South Africa's expected exports of 1.1 million tonnes in 1996/97. By linking up with the established market leader in the soft drinks sector, the South African producers are beginning to create forward links with industrial consumers within the regional market.

The extent to which the domestic South African sugar industry will be able to compete successfully against its regional rivals will depend partly upon the relative costs of sugar production. These were estimated by Landell Mills (commodity researchers) for 1994/95 as US$248 per tonne. Whilst this compares favourably with Kenya ($251), it is higher than Swaziland ($233), Zambia ($230), Malawi ($195), and Zimbabwe ($189) (Government of Mozambique 1996). Whilst costs are important, other factors such as quality and reliability of supply are also significant. The Coca Cola contract gives the company supply priority in times of crop shortage and provides for a more stable pricing structure than is currently the case in East Africa where prices are determined by the volatile world market and subsidised EU exports. The last of these factors is significant in the light of South Africa's reliance on rain-fed cane for the bulk of its production, in contrast to the irrigation which is used by most other regional producers. Given the rapid increase in sales in recent years, demand is expected to increase. For example, in the first nine months of 1995, East Africa had become Coca Cola's global sales leader in terms of growth rate (*SASA Journal*, October 1995: 239).

Similar developments have taken place in Tanzania, where Tanzanian Breweries has been taken over by South African Breweries (SAB). As part of the agreement with the South African Reserve Bank to release funds for the takeover, the new company has had to use as many South African raw materials as possible. One main benefactor of this policy is the South African sugar industry, which supplies refined sugar (*SASA Journal*, October 1995).

In contrast to the advance of South African sugar into East African markets, industry spokesmen have become increasingly concerned at the growth of competition in the home market from Swaziland and, to a lesser extent, Zimbabwe. Ardington (1995) cites competition from Swaziland as 'one of the three most pressing problems facing us', along with the need to establish a Sugar Agreement within the region of southern Africa and to maintain and improve cost competitiveness. Swaziland, as part of the Southern African Customs Union (SACU), faces no import barriers into South Africa or the other member states, Botswana, Lesotho and Namibia. Savage (1996), Managing Director of the Tongaat Hulett group, one of South Africa's largest sugar producers, believes that Swaziland and Zimbabwe are able to operate at a lower price than South Africa because of their more productive growing conditions and lower labour costs. Atkins and Terry (1995:241) have shown that wage rates in South Africa were 48 per cent higher, diesel fuel costs 15 per cent higher and electricity 37 per cent higher than in Swaziland. Swaziland is therefore able to deliver sugar to Durban at a lower price than South African producers. 'It is not impossible to envisage one third of domestic sales in South Africa being supplied by Swaziland and Zimbabwe' (Savage 1996). Swazi competition is not, however, confined to the direct sugar market. All 180,000 tonnes of refined sugar produced in Swaziland are allocated to sugar processing companies within the country but much of the finished product is sold to the South African market. Uncorroborated reports also indicate that some of this refined sugar is sold direct to processors within South Africa. The implication of more value added manufacturing occurring in Swaziland is that the competition which has been adversely affecting South Africa is likely to intensify still further.

Ironically, such competition, when linked to a lack of irrigated sugar cane land in KwaZulu-Natal, is catalysing a corporate exodus from the South African sugar industry, with investment into neighbouring states. The range of such developments is broad. Apart from the case of Mozambican associations such as the Tongaat-Hulett example mentioned above, the SASA is currently exploring the possibility of setting up partnership agreements with Kenya, Madagascar and Zimbabwe, and further association with Mozambique.

South African sugar millers like Anglo Vaal and Tongaat-Hulett seem to be adopting an appropriationist policy, moving out of home-based sugar cane production and looking to invest further north, particularly in Zimbabwe, where they are able to take advantage of cheaper labour rates and obtain access to water. If production can be secured via management contracts in the first instance, it will entail relatively little direct investment by South African companies. These management contracts will benefit from subsidised development finance capital, which will considerably reduce their exposure to risk. The contracts will earn foreign exchange for South Africa, and are likely to stipulate that the foreign cane producers become more tied into the South African agricultural input system. The raw sugar produced could then be exported to South African refineries to meet the needs of the rapidly increasing black population whose standard of living is expected to rise.

Savage's warning to the South African industry that one-third of domestic demand may be supplied by Swaziland and Zimbabwe may not therefore be such a problem for the millers who may, in fact, be major suppliers themselves and therefore competitors with purely South African producers. The opportunities created by the ending of South Africa's political isolation are therefore enabling its major agri-industrial players to begin to strive for internal efficiency, and to acquire regional economic leadership and control of resources in other SADC countries. Opportunities exist outside of the traditional sugar producing regions. Thus, the pilot Caprivi Sugar Project in Namibia, which had been under the control of Lonrho since its inception shortly after Namibian independence in 1990, was taken over by the Namibia Development Corporation in 1995 (*The Namibian*, 18 August 1995). Although the original intention had apparently been to develop the Caprivi region to supply a joint Namibian/Zambian refinery, little development has occurred since the transfer of what was never likely to be a successful venture in this relatively dry area. It has never progressed beyond the pilot stage of being a seed cane farm.

Conclusions

Since 1993, the regional sugar industry has faced unprecedented changes caused by the liberalisation of international trade and political changes within South Africa. In addition, many of the region's industries are undergoing a period of deregulation, with the objective of achieving a more rational use of the resources on which their sugar industries have developed. In this context, the term 'rational' relates to the lowering of production costs, which will have the consequence of seeing production relocate to the most profitable locations. For much of this period, the heartland of the sugar industry in South Africa and Zimbabwe has been slowly recovering from the adverse effects of a drought which may be related to longer-term changes in the regional climate. Given the uncertainties which all of these events have generated, it becomes difficult to attempt to predict how the national industries may develop by the end of the century and to pinpoint those changes which may be caused specifically by the entry of the South African industry as a competitor or partner to its SADC neighbours.

One of the consequences of the closer ties already beginning to develop between South Africa and some of the SADC countries is the reassessment of the whole area as a regional producer on a global scale. A potential combined sugar output close to 4.5 million tonnes would make the region one of the big players in the global market, comparable to Australia or Thailand. The rationale for this arises from the increasing concentration of exports amongst a smaller group of producers: in 1970, the top five exporters accounted for around 35 per cent of total world exports; in 1995, the top five, namely, the EU, Brazil, Australia, Thailand and Cuba, accounted for over 70 per cent. Cuban production dropped by 58 per cent, from 8.2 million tonnes to 3.4 million tonnes between 1988/89 and 1994/95, due to the loss of markets in the former Soviet bloc countries. In contrast, Thailand's output has more than doubled, from 2.7 million tonnes to 5.5 million tonnes (Licht 1995).

Bromfield (1995) points to the growth of regional customs unions as a development for the future (see also Chapter 10, this volume). This would involve the opening up of markets within their regional boundaries and the elimination of tariffs as an essential element in the creation of a large supranational trading bloc. The consequence would be for pressure to develop to equalise costs across countries within the customs union, with high-cost producers being forced to become more efficient or lose market share.

The customs union should therefore help to rationalise costs and create a more competitive sugar industry. It should also link the region's producers more closely to resources such as research and development, technical training and finance which have been developed by SASA to sustain and improve its own industry. Such links are already beginning to appear, especially in the private sector, with the lead being taken by large-scale South African agri-businesses which are moving in to manage, and in some cases acquire, control of important resources within the region. However, evidence is also emerging that SASA is beginning to withdraw access to previously shared resources from what it increasingly sees as its major regional competitor. Thus it has withdrawn some of the infrastructural, technological and educational support which it previously made available to the Swazi sugar industry (*Times of Swaziland,* 12 August 1996), including the use of its Durban port facilities from 1 April 1997 with the expiry of the contract, and access to the SASA Sugar Milling Research Institute and the Research and Extension Facilities at the SASA Experimental Station. The Swazi industry now exports through Maputo, which had been the main export link before disruption caused by the Mozambican civil war, and has begun to seek alternative agronomic, technical and training facilities in Mauritius, Zimbabwe and Australia. This action of SASA against the Swazi industry tends to reinforce the view that South Africa's inclusion within the wider regional structure is regarded by South African interests primarily as an opportunity to enhance the position of their own industry rather than as a means to encourage their regional competitors.

Whether or not a SADC customs union will emerge which allows for free trade in sugar between member states depends upon the perceptions of the regional producers as to the likely costs and benefits of such a strategy. Under the GATT Uruguay Round, the region's least developed countries, Malawi, Mozambique, Tanzania and Zambia, do not have to dismantle their import tariffs (Stevens 1996: 78). But entering a customs union would entail their opening up their domestic markets to competition from larger-scale producers such as South Africa, Swaziland, Zimbabwe and Mauritius. However, Malawi and Zambia have a cost advantage over all SADC competitors apart from Zimbabwe, and so ought to be able to benefit from improved access to the regional market.

Evidence is emerging of the ability of South African agri-businesses to exploit their more sophisticated financial and marketing resources to move into regional markets by allying themselves with large-scale industrial purchasers of sugar such as Coca Cola. With good port access via Durban, and soon also Maputo, to the main sugar producing areas, this gives South Africa an important competitive advantage in a continent with notoriously poor internal communications. Given the political and philosophical will which exists in many of the region's sugar industries to deregulate, this provides the opportunity for such companies to gain control over resources such as land, labour and government subsidies (McMichael and Raynolds 1994:316). More importantly, it may also enable South African companies to gain access to the premium prices available to the region's ACP producers. Given the fact that these industries are already generally large-scale, often in the private sector, or mixed between public and private, this cannot be considered as a process of incorporation into a capitalist system. However, it does indicate that, in the sugar industry, the South Africans are willing and able to take a leadership role and are beginning to realise their regional economic potential. The ending of the apartheid era may, therefore, herald a period when the former pariah state becomes a major economic beneficiary as a consequence of its domestic political transformation.

The evidence from SACU also points to potential problems facing any large-scale expansion of the customs union. South Africa is deeply concerned about the growing competition from the expanding and lower-cost, 100 per cent irrigated, Swazi industry. A fundamental principle of SACU is unrestricted tariff-free movement of goods between member countries, but the sugar trade between South Africa and Swaziland has always been regulated. This regulation has been unofficial and arose out of the agreement between the two countries which allowed Swaziland to acquire a share of South Africa"s Commonwealth Sugar Agreement quota during the early period of expansion in 1960. It is difficult to see how this can be justified, given the fact that Swaziland is the lower-cost producer and has a large negative trade balance with South Africa. However, as Westlake points out (1995:61), a complete opening up of South Africa would not be in Swaziland's interests. This is because, in all but the most severe drought years, SACU's sugar production exceeds its sales into the higher priced domestic and concessional markets. Under a completely free market, open competition would drive the SACU internal price down to the much lower world market price. Atkins and Terry (1995: 238) have shown that, at such prices, small grower sugar developments in Swaziland are uneconomic.

Thus the creation of a customs union is no panacea for the region's producers, and the complexities of a larger organisation would multiply the problems to an enormous extent. Although, in a strict financial sense, production within the region should be located in the lowest-cost areas, when the full economic costs of such developments are taken into account, the position becomes more complicated. Especially when the political necessity of creating development opportunities for South Africa's rural black population is added to this, the financial argument is weakened still further.

With respect to its current attempts to gain access to the ACP Sugar Protocol, South Africa would, in principle, like to carry out such discussions as a regional bloc. The ACP countries are unlikely to support South Africa's application as it would dilute their own quota and SPS, given the unlikelihood of the EU increasing the global ACP preferential imports. Moreover, one of the consequences of the Maastricht Agreement is that the EU is likely to focus aid on the poorer ACP and other developing countries. The probability of South Africa being given a preferential quota would therefore seem to be further diminished. In contrast, the least developed ACP countries within SADC may receive special benefits under the World Trade Organization (WTO), while those with a higher GDP per capita might be 'graduated out of the trade agreement' (Hewitt and Koning 1996: 101). This could have serious consequences for Mauritius and to a lesser extent Swaziland (McDonald 1996: 145).

This indicates that external factors could well create internal tensions in any customs union where income disparities are as large as those which exist within SADC. Possible ways in which South Africa may advance its case for an ACP quota may be in emphasising that the benefits of the quota would go exclusively to small growers. In Swaziland and Zimbabwe, many of the benefits of the quota have gone to the large-scale agri-businesses which dominate production. Perhaps the ACP should refine the scale on which it evaluates access to the ACP quota so that regional or social variations are taken into account rather than the national picture. However, as Hewitt and Koning (1996: 101) state:

> ACP states need to focus on their comparative advantage and know that they should rely less on the EU preferential market. This means diversifying the structure and destination of their exports.

Although containing a myriad of production systems and with great variations in their economic importance to each of the individual countries, the SADC sugar industries are nevertheless central to many of the wider rural development issues affecting the region. These include the types of production systems, whether small- or large-scale; the ownership of the assets, whether state or private, local or transnational; the control of transnational resources such as rivers; the role of cash versus subsistence crops; the environmental impact of the sugar cane monoculture; the ability of the RDP within South Africa to spread the benefits of a 'successful' industry so that the majority of the rural poor achieve greater benefits. As Bromfield (1995) states, 'The future for sugar is promising but complex'. This seems to be particularly germane for sugar producers within the SADC region, where the economic, political and environmental factors affecting the industry are both immensely challenging and closely interlinked.

Note

1. Zambia was not a signatory of the original Sugar Protocol. The only way new signatories can acquire quota is if existing signatories fail to deliver their quota consistently. This shortfall can then be reallocated to a new member. Zambia has not been able to benefit from this. In contrast, Zimbabwe has acquired 30,225 tonnes of quota since joining.

References

ACP Secretariat (1996) 'Aide Memoire on ACP Sugar', Brussels, April.

African Development Bank (1988) *Appraisal Report for the Mafambisse Sugar Rehabilitation Project.* Abidjan.

Ardington, T. (1995) 'Highlights from the Vice-Chairman's Address', in South African Sugar Association, *Annual Report 1994/95*, Durban.

Atkins, S. (1996) *Management Priorities for the Small Growers Development Trust, South Africa.* Report prepared for the SGDT, SASA, Mananga Management Centre, Swaziland.

Atkins, S. and Terry, A. (1995) 'The Economics of Sugar Cane Production in the Northern Lowveld of Swaziland', *Quarterly Journal of International Agriculture* 34(3): 224–47.

Bromfield, F. (1995) 'The Changing World Sugar Market and Outlook', *South African Sugar Journal* 79 (12): 294–5.

Czarnikow (1993) quoted in Stoneman C. and Thompson C., *The GATT Uruguay Round: Implications for the Agricultural Sector in Zimbabwe.* Catholic Institute for International Relations and the Sustainable Agriculture Food and Environment Alliance, London.

Development Bank of Southern Africa (1993) *A Sugar Commodity Perspective.* DBSA, Pretoria.

Economist Intelligence Unit (1995) *Swaziland Country Report 4th Quarter, 1995.* EIU London.

Financial Times, The (1997) 9 May, London.

Food and Agriculture Organization (1992) *The World Sugar Market: Prospects for the Nineties.* Commodities and Trade Division, FAO, Rome.

Food and Agricultural Organization (1995) *Impact of the Uruguay Round on Agriculture*. Commodities and Trade Division, FAO, Rome.

Government of Mozambique, INA (1996) *Proposta De Politica, Estrategias E Programas Para O Desenvolvimento Do Sector Acucareiro*. Ministry of Agriculture and Fisheries, Maputo.

Hewitt, A. and Koning, A. (1996) 'The Survival of Special Preferences under the Lomé Convention: The ACP Countries and the European Union after the Uruguay Round', in Sander, H. and Inotai, A. (eds) *World Trade After the Uruguay Round: Prospects and Policy Options for the Twenty-first Century*. Routledge, London.

Jackson, J.C. and Cheater, A.P. (1994) 'Contract Farming in Zimbabwe: Case Studies of Sugar, Tea, and Cotton', in Little and Watts.

Kerr, J. and McDonald, S. (1994) 'Developed Country Sugar Policies and the ACP Countries'. Paper presented to the Agricultural Economics Society Annual Conference, Exeter University, April.

Licht, F.O. (1995) *World Sugar and Sweetener Yearbook 1995*. FO Licht Gmbh, Ratzeburg, Germany.

Little, P. D. and Watts, M. J. (eds) (1994) *Living Under Contract: Contract Farming and Agrarian Transformation in Sub-Saharan Africa*. University of Wisconsin Press, Madison, WI.

Loewenson, R. (1992) *Modern Plantation Agriculture: Corporate Wealth and Labour Squalor*. Zed Books Ltd, London and Atlantic Heights, NJ.

Lombard, C.S. and Tweedie, A.H.C. (1974) *Agriculture in Zambia since Independence*. Neczam, Lusaka.

McDonald S. (1996) 'Reform of the EU's Sugar Policies and ACP countries', *Development Policy Review*, 14(2), 131–49.

McMichael, P. and Raynolds, L. (1994) 'Capitalism, Agriculture and the World Economy, in Sklair, L. (ed.) *Capitalism and Development*. Routledge, London.

Ortmann, G.F. (1991) 'Viewpoint: Short and Long Term Prospects for Sugar and Forestry in South Africa', *Agrekon* 30(3).

Ortmann, G.F. (1986) 'Regional Development Effects of a Free Market for Sugar in South Africa', *Development Southern Africa*, 3 (3): 411–22.

Republic of South Africa, Ministry of Agricultural Development (1994) *Agriculture in South Africa*. Van Rensburg Publications, Johannesburg.

Ridgway, D. (1995) 'Chairman's Address to the South African Sugar Association' in *South African Sugar Association Annual Report 1994/95*, Durban.

Savage, C. (1996) 'Address to the Annual Congress of the South African Sugar Technologists Association', *The Swazi Observer*, 11 June, Mbabane.

South African Sugar Association (1995) *Siyakha: Building Together*. SASA, Durban.

Sterkenburg, J. and Van der Wiel, A. (1995) 'Structural Adjustment, Sugar Sector Development and Netherlands Aid to Tanzania' in Simon, D., Van Spengen, W., Dixon, C. and Närman, A. (eds), *Structurally Adjusted Africa: Poverty, Debt and Basic Needs*. Pluto, London.

Stevens, C. (1996) 'The Consequences of the Uruguay Round for Developing Countries', in Sander, H. and Inotai, A. (eds), *World Trade After the Uruguay Round: Prospects and Policy Options for the Twenty-First Century*. Routledge, London.

UnionBank of Swaziland (1994) *Swaziland in Figures*, Mbabane.

United Nations Economic Commission for Africa (1993) *Survey of Economic and Social Conditions in Africa 1990–91*. Addis Ababa.

World Bank (1994) *World Bank Atlas 1994*, Washington, DC.

Westlake, M.J. (1995) *Prospects for Swaziland's Sugar Industry in SACU*. Ministry of Finance, Kingdom of Swaziland, Mbabane.

Whiteford, A. and McGrath, M. (1994) 'Distribution of income in South Africa', quoted in Nolan B. (1995) 'Poverty, Inequality and Reconstruction in South Africa', *Development Policy Review* 13 (2): 151–71.

9 Powering the Region: South Africa in the Southern African Power Pool

TORE HORVEI

Electricity in Southern Africa: Self-interest or Counter-productive Dominance?

Current disparities between South Africa and the rest of southern Africa are rooted largely in differential growth rates of economic output over extended historical periods. Two observations can be made on these historical experiences. First, and most important, the process of economic development in the region is uneven, across countries and over time. Second, there is a certain conditional convergence over time, i.e., the developing economies are determined to 'catch up' with the industrial ones. This is clearly reflected in the energy sector, and is particularly evident in the widely divergent patterns of electricity availability and use.

The availability of energy is crucial to every country's economic, social and cultural development. The southern African region stands out for its abundant variety of energy resources, both renewable and non-renewable, namely, mineral coal, hydrocarbons, and biomass as well as hydro, wind and solar energy resources. It is every government's stated objective to expand popular access to these resources, in safe conditions of usage, as economically as possible and whilst conserving the environment.

In the institutional domain, the governments of the region have implemented legislation which will stimulate the participation of private economic agents, both national and foreign, in order to complement and expand the governments' efforts to make the use of electrical energy ever more accessible to their populations to support economic development. These efforts are further enhanced by increased regional co-operation and integration. President Mandela himself at the SADC heads of state summit in September 1994 stated that: 'the challenges South Africa faces are equally those of the region. ... For us, integrated development of the region as a whole is a priority of the highest order.' This is the context in which regional co-operation in the electricity sector should be discussed and analysed.

Profound Regional Imbalances and Disparities

In the context of the expanding regional electricity grid, and the newly established Southern African Power Pool (SAPP) in particular, it is important to include the former Zaire – now the Democratic Republic of Congo (DRC) – because of its tremendous potential for generating hydro-electric power from the Congo River, and its membership of the SAPP. The southern Africa region is marked by profound imbalances in the electricity sector, with regard to not only the availability and composition of energy sources but also the size and composition of electricity demand, the population's access to electricity, and the availability of technology and the necessary human and financial resources. In most instances the imbalance is in South

Africa's favour. While South Africa contains about 23 per cent of the population of southern Africa (including the DRC), its GDP accounts for more than 75 per cent of the regional total. In the electricity sector, in 1996 South Africa accounted for: 78 per cent of installed power generating capacity; 84 per cent of the regional peak load; and 85 per cent of the electricity distributed and sold. About 50 per cent of the population had access to electricity, while the regional average was about 10 per cent, as illustrated by Figure 9.1. The national power utility, Eskom, is ranked among the five largest utilities in the world, with annual sales of US$4.8 billion, net income of US$800 million, total assets of US$14.4 bn, annual investments of US$1.4 bn, almost 40,000 employees, and a research and development department whose size and annual budget approximate the total staffing and budget of several of the other regional power utilities.

The above data clearly illustrate the dominant position of South Africa (and Eskom) in the regional electricity sector. It is obvious that Eskom's strong technical and financial situation has many advantages for the region, e.g. through contributions to technical planning and development of appropriate local technical solutions in areas like electrification, as well as augmentation of a regional transmission system and investments in new capacity when and where required. However, the huge disparity between Eskom and the situation in most of the other utilities also poses problems for balanced and efficient co-operation at the regional level. Handling this disparity is one of the key challenges for the SAPP, which will be examined in detail below.

The most notable exception to South Africa's dominant position is the relative abundance of hydro power resources, and to a certain extent natural gas, in the region outside of South Africa. This imbalance in favour of the northern part of the region creates substantial scope for increased regional trade in electricity, thereby fostering economic integration and closer co-operation in the electricity sector.

Regional Electricity Demand

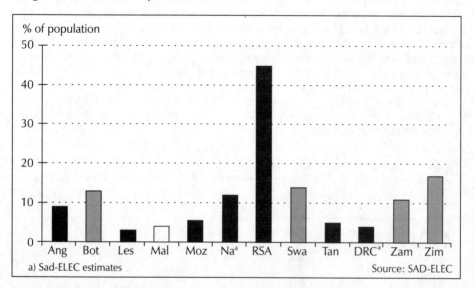

Figure 9.1 *Access to electricity, 1995*

Since the early 1990s, economic growth in the Southern African Development Community (SADC) has exceeded the annual population growth rate and in 1995 reached an average level of around 5 per cent. This trend is likely to continue well into the next decade. At this stage of development in most southern African countries, energy demand tends to grow at a higher annual rate than the economic growth rate, with the exception of South Africa, where the energy intensity of the economy is already high.

Substantial social and economic development is expected in southern Africa during the next ten years, particularly in South Africa, Angola, Botswana, Mozambique, Namibia and Zimbabwe. This would represent a welcome and much needed post-apartheid and post-Cold War peace dividend. In several of these countries the economic growth rates are already at or near 'take-off' levels and there is no compelling reason to exclude future successful economic development. South-east Asia and Latin America provide useful examples in this respect, where 10–15 years ago few people would have ventured to suggest that 10 per cent growth rates were achievable (Mills 1996).

A Shift Towards Electricity

The most important aspect for electricity lies in what may happen on the demand rather than the supply side. By 2020 the share of non-commercial final energy is expected to decrease to around 15 per cent, compared with some 43 per cent in 1990 (Table 9.1). There is already a continuing and pervasive shift from energy used in its original form – such as traditional direct uses of coal and biomass (wood, charcoal, dung, crop residues) – to manufactured energy like electricity and liquid fuels. This shift is taking place in all the countries of southern Africa and is defining the need for increasingly sophisticated/higher quality energy carriers. The share of electricity is increasing. While electricity in 1990 accounted for about 26 per cent of total final commercial energy demand, this is expected to increase to 30–34 per cent by 2010 (SAD-ELEC & MEPC 1996).

The main consumers or end users of electricity are industries and the public and domestic sectors. Historically, the emphasis has been on access to secure, adequate and cheap electricity by industry, mining, commerce, the railways, commercial agriculture and mid- to high-income households. Consequently, despite extensive over-investment in generation capacity, the majority (about 80 per cent) of households in the region remain unelectrified. Throughout the region there is a wide supply-demand imbalance and substantial suppressed demand. Until the 1990s, no national policies existed to provide wider access to electricity. The new focus on improved access for the region's population, not least by means of the Reconstruction and Development Programme (RDP) in South Africa, is already contributing to the increased electricity demand.

Table 9.1   *Final energy use by carrier – SADC and South Africa, 1990/91*

| | SADC excl. SA | | South Africa (SA) | | SADC incl. SA | |
	TJ	%	TJ	%	TJ	%
Electricity	78	5.0	455	25.8	533	16.1
Liquid fuels	202	13.0	523	29.6	725	21.9
Biomass	1,178	76.0	239	13.5	1,417	42.7
Coal and coke	91	6.0	547	31.1	638	19.3
TOTAL	1,549	100.0	1,764	100.0	3,313	100.0

Source: SAD-ELEC & MEPC (1996)

The RDP set a target of 2.5 million households to be connected to the electricity grid in the five-year period, 1995–9; Eskom's share of the total is 1.75 million (African National Congress 1994; Republic of South Africa 1994). In both 1995 and 1996, the 478,000 and 307,047 new connections achieved exceeded the annual targets of 450,000 and 300,000 respectively. By the end of 1996 there were estimated to be more houses in South Africa with access to electricity (54.63 per cent) than without (45.37 per cent) for the first time in the country's history (National Electricity Regulator 1997: 12). If this rate can be maintained, by 2000 over 70 per cent of all South African households will have direct access to electricity, in line with the government's RDP target.

Botswana, Namibia, Swaziland and possibly Zimbabwe are also making serious progress, but elsewhere in the region the picture is less optimistic. For example, following an earlier initiative (Kalapula 1987), Zambia has embarked on an electrification programme of 150,000 urban households by 2000. With an average of six persons per household, this would provide a further 900,000 people with electricity. However, since population growth over the same period is expected to be approximately 1.2–1.4 million, even such large electrification programmes are not enough to make inroads into the backlog.

Urbanisation

Demographic changes associated with urbanisation reinforce the trend. In southern Africa, annual population growth rates are high, at 3 per cent or more. Declining growth rates are expected only well into the next century, although the impact of HIV/AIDS will be felt increasingly from now on (Chapter 13). Nevertheless, urbanisation is a strong trend across the region, despite some slowing down or reversals during recent hard times (Potts 1995). More than 35 per cent of the population of the region already live in urban or peri-urban environments; 60 per cent can be expected to live in urban environments by 2020. An increasing proportion will live in metropolises such as Kinshasa, Luanda, Johannesburg, Cape Town, Durban and Greater Harare. Per capita electricity use in urban areas is much higher than the rural average, largely as a result of higher urban incomes as well as the greater availability of supply.

Rural areas

In the rural areas, the emphasis was previously placed on decentralised, small-scale, renewable sources for satisfying energy/electricity requirements. It was believed that this would provide a basis for slower rates of urbanisation and improved food production at relatively lower costs. Experience indicates that this has seldom been the case, and that such solutions should be regarded as interim measures. Emphasis is now shifting to the extension of grid electricity through the expansion of transmission and distribution networks to rural communities (SAD-ELEC & MEPC 1996). In a special programme aimed at providing basic electricity services to a large number of rural schools, Eskom continues to pursue the use of renewable technologies in the form of solar systems (Eskom 1997b: 4). However, in the total energy scene, biomass – particularly fuelwood and charcoal – and, to a lesser extent, paraffin, will continue to fill the gap.

Regional electricity demand scenarios

There are large uncertainties as far as future electricity consumption is concerned. Although actual demand will be greatly affected by the levels of economic growth achieved and the electricity tariff policies to be pursued in the region, high rates of population growth are likely to exert enormous pressure on demand, particularly with the continued trend towards urbanisation. Increasing foreign investment should further contribute to high electricity growth rates. Forecasts for the region suggest an average annual growth rate of 4.0–4.5 per cent, and thus demand is expected to double in less than 20 years, as illustrated in Figure 9.2.

South Africa constitutes about 85 per cent of the electricity market in southern Africa. Despite higher forecast growth in several other countries, the historical legacy of South Africa's dominant position is unlikely to undergo significant change in the next 10 years. For example, although a proposed aluminium smelter in Mozambique would require an annual 850 MW of electric power, thereby increasing demand in that country by some 450–500 per cent, such a project would only amount to some 3 per cent of South Africa's power demand and would therefore not change the regional situation in any major way. Initially, demand would be met from the existing surplus in the South African system, which will increase in the short term by the reinstatement of supplies from the Cahora Bassa dam on the Zambezi River. Exports to South Africa from the 2,075 MW Cahora Bassa hydro plant resumed during the second half of 1997. Reconstruction of the transmission line, which had been sabotaged during the war in Mozambique, was financed by Portugal, the European Union and Eskom (backed by South African government guarantees), and scheduled for completion in August 1997. In the longer term, demand will need to be met by new developments, such as the proposed Mepanda Uncua hydro scheme, involving a third dam on the Zambezi (Eskom 1997a: 2–3).

Managing the Supply Side

At present the southern African region has a surplus of available generating capacity of approximately 9,000 MW. Most of this is in the South African and DRC systems. Of the other countries already interconnected via the SAPP transmission grid, only Zambia is self-sufficient in meeting its demand for electricity. The regional

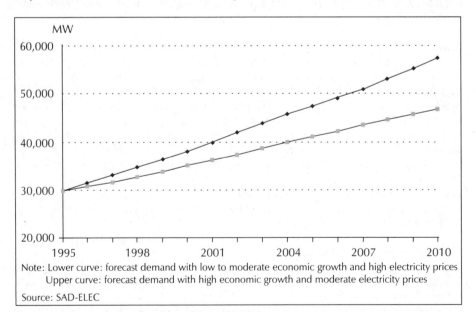

Note: Lower curve: forecast demand with low to moderate economic growth and high electricity prices
      Upper curve: forecast demand with high economic growth and moderate electricity prices

Source: SAD-ELEC

Figure 9.2 *Regional power demand scenarios, 1995–2010*

demand for power is increasing by about 1,200–1,300 MW a year, indicating that new supply capacity is needed within the next 6–8 years on a regional basis (SAD-ELEC & MEPC 1996).

Generation: an Abundance of Water and Coal

Installed generating capacity in the various countries is shown in Table 9.2. Thermal generation accounts for close to 80 per cent of the installed capacity and is the principal form found in South Africa, Zimbabwe and Botswana. The other countries are generally dependent on hydro power, supplemented by imports in some cases, to meet their electricity demand.

South Africa has the largest known coal reserves on the African continent, estimated at 55,000 million tonnes. This compares with an annual production of 194 million tonnes, giving a reserve:production ratio of more than 280 years at present production levels. The country is the world's third largest exporter of coal, with a global share of exports of 14 per cent (SADC 1996), the principal destinations being the European Union and the Far East.

On the hydro side, the potential of the SADC region is estimated at about 48,000 MW, of which only about 6,000 MW has been developed so far. This potential is increased considerably when the DRC is included. The DRC has a hydro potential of 90,000–100,000 MW, of which some 45,000 MW could be at the Inga dam site on the Congo River alone. Only 2,500 MW of the DRC's potential has been developed so far (SADC 1996; SAD-ELEC & MEPC 1996).

Diversification of supply

Much of the future demand will be met through the development of new hydro-electric schemes, the largest most likely being located in Mozambique, Angola, Zambia and the DRC. Natural gas will play an increasing role based on offshore gas resources in Mozambique, Namibia and Angola (see below). The possibility also exists for increased gas production from the Mossgas field off the southern Cape coast, aimed at piping the gas to the Cape Town area for use in power generation and industrial applications. Major new coal developments are likely to be limited, particularly because of increasing environmental concerns that will require mitigation measures through costly carbon, sulphur and nitrogen cleaning, but also because of rising production costs. However, with South Africa's large existing

Table 9.2   *Installed generating capacity, 1994 (MW)*

	Hydro	Thermal	Total	% hydro
Angola	300.9	267.0	567.9	53.0
Botswana	0.0	197.0	197.0	0.0
Lesotho	3.3	1.6	4.9	67.4
Malawi	219.1	25.1	244.2	89.7
Mozambiqu	2,181.6	205.4	2,387.0	91.4
Namibia	240.0	147.0	387.0	62.0
South Africa	2,000.0	35,840.0	37,840.0	5.3
Swaziland	40.5	9.5	50.0	81.0
Tanzania	381.7	195.8	577.5	66.1
DR Congo	2,442.2	37.8	2,480.0	98.5
Zambia	1,670.0	129.0	1,799.0	92.8
Zimbabwe	666.0	1,295.0	1,961.0	34.0
TOTAL	10,145.3	38,350.2	48,495.5	20.9

Sources: Eskom, *Statistical Yearbook 1994*; SAD-ELEC & MEPC (1996)

installed capacity, coal will remain the dominant source well into the next century. Botswana's proposed coal-fired export power station (using coal from the vast Palapye reserves) is not deemed economically viable compared with South African power generation costs and the region's hydro options.

Despite the dominance of coal, the electricity supply structure after 2010 is best characterised by likely supply diversification, in which no single technology or fuel will truly dominate regional electricity generation. Non-fossil technologies, particularly hydro, but also solar and possibly wind generation, will make increasing inroads into both new capacity and replacement markets. Remote area power supplies (RAPS), such as solar power and wind technology, can assist in meeting basic household electrical needs for lighting, TV and small-scale water supply. For example, 10,000 households in Zimbabwe will be supplied with solar technology with support from the United Nations' Global Environmental Facility (GEF/UNDP). South Africa is in the process of establishing a Rural Electrification Fund (REFSA) for the same purpose. However, it is generally accepted that such non-grid solutions will make only modest contributions for the foreseeable future.

Nuclear power is totally off the development agenda at present. Apart from the high capital and operating costs, feeling in South Africa runs contrary to the likelihood of any new nuclear generation plant, although the existing Koeberg station near Cape Town will continue to operate. In addition, it is also likely that Africa's poor track record in maintenance could cause international anxiety.

End-use efficiencies and other changes within the industry

Extensive cost-effective, end-use efficiency improvements, e.g. hot water load management, interruptible load management, and time-of-use tariffs implemented by Eskom, have been introduced in the region, particularly in South Africa (Eskom 1996). Nevertheless, energy efficiency and conservation programmes have limited success: capacity expansion through supply diversification will therefore remain the principal characteristic for the future.

An increasing trend is expected in favour of those energy suppliers most successful in switching from selling just kWh to selling energy services as a whole. The power utility industry will become flatter, in particular as renewable technologies enter the generating market. First, the number of independent producers is likely to increase. Second, production will probably become decentralised. And third, deregulation and common carrier rights will transform energy production, transmission and distribution into separate businesses. Another profound transformation taking place is the increasing degree to which electrical energy is delivered by dedicated transport systems. This enhances trade possibilities and promotes similar end-use patterns across the sub-regions with fundamentally different primary energy supply structures.

Regional Power Trading through the SAPP

While increasing demand may tempt the power system planners to be generation-oriented, the immediate emphasis in southern Africa is on the expansion of the regional transmission network, to access surplus and permit electricity trade. Cross-border trading in electricity is expected to increase substantially under the auspices of the SAPP. Strengthening the transmission system within countries and the interconnectors between them will be required not only to integrate the new supply sources, but also to wheel traded power across countries. A map of the existing and proposed southern Africa grid is shown in Figure 9.3.

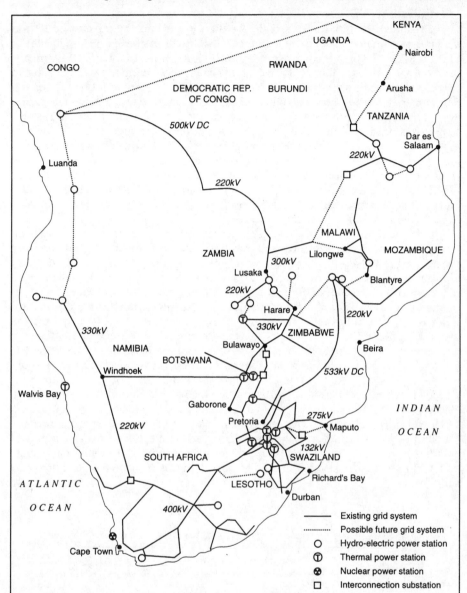

Source: SADC (1996)

Figure 9.3 *The southern African power grid*

Investment needs and sources

The investment required to meet rehabilitation needs and the forecast growth in demand is estimated to be in the region of US$15bn for the period 1996–2005 (SAD-ELEC & MEPC 1996). A breakdown per country is provided in Table 9.3. This means that southern Africa will have to invest an average US$1.5bn per year in expansion of the power sector infrastructure. Of this, about 75 per cent would be for generation and transmission projects, while 25 per cent would be for rehabilitation and extension of the distribution system. Further investments would be required for customer connections and wiring the premises of new customers.

Since the early 1990s, it has been recognised that such large investment requirements cannot be met solely by public resources. Historically, state-owned enterprises had captured a disproportionate share of credit and had contributed to large fiscal deficits. Furthermore, the self-financing capability of most of the regional utilities, although improving in many cases, is limited and would at best contribute some 25 per cent of the financing required.

Funds from multilateral and bilateral development financing agencies are used to support power sector reform programmes in several countries, but can only provide a limited (5–10 per cent) contribution towards the overall investment requirements of the region. Based on the above, the private sector contributions required amount to about US$9bn, or about 60 per cent of the investment requirements up to 2005. Regional governments and the international financial institutions see private funding as necessary for infrastructure projects to get off the ground. Initially, the need for private participation in the development of the power sector infrastructure reflected the budgetary constraints imposed by the World Bank and the International Monetary Fund on most southern African governments. The budgetary disciplines emphasised limits on public expenditure as part of structural adjustment and economic recovery programmes (Simon *et al.* 1995).

However, there is a growing recognition that the private sector can contribute the kind of sophisticated management skills essential for the success of large and complex infrastructure projects. The private sector, and the international private sector in particular, is also better able to provide a range of modern technological solutions.

Table 9.3 *Power sector investments (in US$ m), 1996 – 2005*

	1996 – 2000	2001 – 2005	TOTAL
Angola	350.0	250.0	600.0
Botswana	75.0	100.0	175.0
Lesotho	125.0	75.0	200.0
Malawi	250.0	150.0	400.0
Mozambique	100.0	2,200.0	2,300.0
Namibia	200.0	500.0	700.0
South Africa	4,000.0	3,000.0	7,000.0
Swaziland	50.0	25.0	75.0
Tanzania	500.0	200.0	700.0
DR Congo	300.0	400.0	700.0
Zambia	150.0	200.0	350.0
Zimbabwe	800.0	1,000.0	1,800.0
TOTAL	6,900.0	8,100.0	15,000.0

Source: SAD-ELEC & MEPC (1996)

Recent Developments

Despite awareness of the vital role of the private sector, its participation in electricity sector infrastructure development was very limited until 1996, particularly with regard to equity contributions. Many memoranda of understanding had been signed, but only a small fraction had reached the stage of actual development because of the slow rate of contract completions. Reasons for this include:

- delays in public sector reform/privatisation/changes to the regulatory framework;
- underestimation of approval processes in many countries;
- underdeveloped local debt markets/lack of guarantee schemes;
- uneconomic electricity prices; and
- incomplete understanding of the local political and economic environment by sponsors and international lenders.

This situation is now undergoing a quantum change. In Zimbabwe, a Malaysian company has bought 51 per cent of the Hwange coal-fired power station in a deal aimed at expanding the capacity of the station by some 660 MW (*Financial Gazette*, 10 and 17 October 1996), and in Tanzania, Canadian investors are involved in the development of the US$300 mn Songas project to use natural gas for power generation and industrial applications. In Zambia, the Power Division of the Zambia Consolidated Copper Mines (ZCCM) was privatised in mid-1997, with the UK's National Grid Co. and Midland Electricity being the new owners. In Mozambique, an American company was undertaking a study during 1997 with a view to building, owning and operating (BOO) a proposed 80 MW hydro plant as an independent power producer (IPP). Also in Mozambique, several potential international developers have expressed keen interest in the proposed 1,700–2,000 MW Mepanda Uncua hydro scheme aimed at export to South Africa and possibly Zimbabwe. In Namibia, development of the Kudu offshore gas field for power generation purposes is exciting similar interest: in May 1997, Shell Exploration and its partners (Eskom and the Namibian electricity utility, NamPower) agreed in principle to develop a 750 MW combined cycle power plant provided that technical, financial and economic investigations prove favourable. This followed confirmation that reserves in the Kudu field were adequate to supply the plant for at least 20 years. Production could begin in 2000 or 2001 (*Lloyd's List*, 6 February 1997; NamPower 1997). Meanwhile, several prospective developers are seeking entry to the Pande gas field in Mozambique (*Business Day*, 5 December 1996). Zambia's Kafue Gorge Lower and Ithezi-thezi hydro projects are also being considered by prospective American and European investors, and the giant potential of Inga in the DRC is recognised as pivotal in any long-term development plan for the region (SAD-ELEC & MEPC 1996).

Another important recent development has been the establishment of Southern African Development Through Electricity (SAD-ELEC), an independent, self-financing development agency. Founded in 1994 by southern Africans for southern Africans, its operating office is in Johannesburg, and its geographical focus is the SADC region plus Kenya and Uganda. SAD-ELEC has a two-tier organisational structure. The first tier comprises a high-level Board of international and regional members with comprehensive experience and influence in the energy and electrification sectors. The second tier is the core organisation based in Johannesburg, which is led by a three-person Management Committee. The professional staff are sourced mainly from southern Africa, and are well experienced in the electricity industry.

SAD-ELEC has an active regional involvement. Its principal activities include power utility support and advisory services, project identification and promotion, mobilisation of technical assistance, seeking investors for development, facilitating business relationships (both regional and international), and co-ordinating research and consulting services. It has been appointed to manage a UK government-financed technical and human resources support programme for the SAPP, and is in discussion with the SAPP and international financiers about further support programmes in the environmental and human resource areas. SAD-ELEC's activities are complementary to the efforts of other organisations active in the region and are geared to increased use of regional competence through collaborative undertakings with such organisations.

South Africa: the pull factor

There is no doubt that many outsiders still see southern Africa as a high investment risk, but South African involvement is already helping to change that perception. South Africa represents a viable market, as well as a credible source of financing for new investments. However, involvement of other regional players is also needed to balance the South African position.

Nevertheless, South Africa represents the primary future market for electricity from new power projects. In addition to its expected growth in demand in absolute terms, and therefore absorption by 2005–7 of its present nominal over-capacity, the changes already taking place in demand patterns indicate that its requirements for peak power will soon become urgent. For this reason, tapping into the hydro resources of the region is a very attractive prospect for South Africa. Eskom is keen to start imports as soon as possible, and is actively engaged in promotion of and participation in developments elsewhere in southern Africa, including rehabilitation of the power line from Cahora Bassa (see above), construction of new interconnectors to facilitate imports to South Africa and increased power trading in the region.

An Enabling Regional Investment Climate

To ensure improved private sector funding of infrastructure projects, which by their very nature are complex and have long gestation periods of 8–10 years to develop and 20–25 years or more to yield a sufficient return, most of the national governments are in the process of taking the steps necessary to create attractive investment conditions.

In general, the revised policies exhibit a clarity of government sector objectives and strategies – including social and environmental aims. Less complex regulatory codes, structures and administrative procedures are being put in place. These provide transparency in areas such as the awarding of contracts, resolution of disputes, repatriation of invested funds and profits, guarantees against nationalisation and seizure of assets, and similar requirements. Procedures are being developed for the distribution of risks and their allocation to those best able to manage them: government, sponsors, suppliers and financiers. For example, a Bill providing a legal framework for private involvement in electricity production and distribution passed through the Mozambican parliament in July 1997. The words of the Deputy Minister of Mineral Resources and Energy, Castigo Langa, in introducing the Bill, are indicative of current thinking:

> The epoch in which the state, either directly or through public corporations, held a monopoly on the generation, transmission and distribution of electricity is giving way to another, in which private initiatives are increasing[ly] called upon to contribute to the development of new and large projects in the areas of generation and distribution, while in general the state retains control over the transmission systems (Mozambique News Agency 1997: 2).

Specifically to assist investments in the energy sector, initiatives are in progress for the harmonisation of legislative and regulatory regimes among countries in the region. Although in some countries these are still in their infancy, there has been substantial progress in the development and strengthening of domestic financial and capital markets to mobilise resources and develop the instruments required for risk dispersion. Although international investors/lenders like 'local' involvement, there is as yet limited capacity for long-term lending in the region, and even less for equity involvement in major infrastructure projects. Once again, South Africa stands out as a notable exception.

Moreover, uneconomically high interest rates in the region make local options unattractive to borrowers. There is also limited experience of project finance. But governments are increasingly open to new and innovative structures, and other, non-financial forms of local support and participation are also coming to be regarded by international investors as viable alternatives.

The Southern African Power Pool – A Formula for Success

The creation of the SAPP in 1995 was a major event in the new era of co-operation in the regional electricity sector. This new organisation has been established to foster and develop a regional electricity infrastructure of mutual benefit to all the countries involved and to the benefit of the population and the economies of the region through lower electricity prices.

The process of creating the SAPP was led by the power utilities of the region, not by governments or outside players. As such it is a home-grown solution for the region by the region. Support was provided by the SADC Energy Sector's Technical and Administrative Unit (TAU). The utilities recognised the need for closer regional co-operation, particularly after the tough lessons learned from the 1992 drought, which clearly demonstrated the vulnerability and high cost to the overall economy of pursuing a policy of self-sufficiency in the area of electricity supply (SAPP 1995a, 1995b).

Compelling arguments for stronger regional co-operation include: demand/supply imbalances, economies of scale, considerations of security and quality of supply, financial constraints on utilities and national governments, system operation benefits from joint thermal/hydro system operations, different shapes of the demand curves and the level of environmental degradation and pollution in various parts of the region. Interdependence (within limits) is therefore accepted as a way forward. Supply and demand imbalances throughout the region, being a major rationale behind the SAPP, are illustrated in Figure 9.4, depicting the situation in 1995.

The creation of the SAPP took place through a three-year process culminating in the signing of the Inter-Governmental Memorandum of Understanding in late August 1995. The negotiations began well before the 1994 elections brought the ANC-dominated government to power in South Africa. The SAPP agreement includes all the SADC countries including the DRC. The power utilities later signed several inter-utility agreements formalising their co-operation and operations. The SAPP organisational structure is illustrated in Figure 9.5. The Chief Executives of the various power utilities form the Executive Committee, which has responsibility for important policy decisions and the future development of the SAPP. A Management Committee oversees the management of the organisation, with three different sub-committees – the Operating, Planning and Environmental Sub-Committees – reporting to it. The Operating Sub-Committee members are those power utilities that are already interconnected and exchange power on a major scale. A Co-ordi-

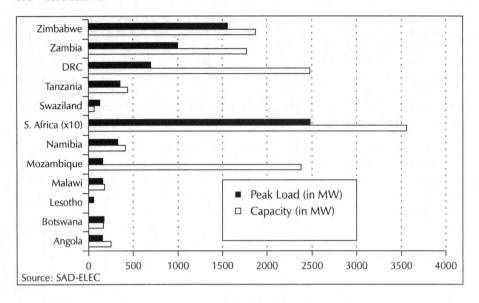

Figure 9.4   *Power supply and demand balances in southern Africa, 1995*

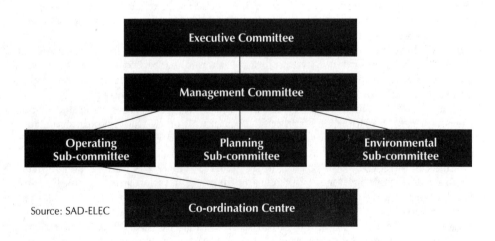

Figure 9.5   *The Southern African Power Pool organisational structure*

nation Centre is being established in Harare, Zimbabwe, to monitor and control the various power exchanges taking place in accordance with agreed procedures and guidelines. The SAPP will initially be operated as a loose type of co-operative arrangement, while future developments might include a firming up towards centralised dispatching based on order of economic merit and efficiency.

Key challenges facing the SAPP include how to handle different political agendas to achieve the best result for the region; harmonisation of national frameworks to serve both national and regional objectives; improvement of utility finances; and development of constructive approaches and methods for the integration of international and private involvement in the regional electricity sector.

The SAPP is attracting considerable interest, both in the region and internationally. If successful, and at present there is every reason to believe that the SAPP will be a success, it can serve as a model for enhanced regional co-operation and integration in other sectors. The SAPP model is a good example of how possible dominance by one or a few players can be counteracted. Although Eskom is by far the largest player in the SAPP, it is only one of 12 participating utilities, and as such has to proceed carefully so as to ensure that whatever initiatives it puts forward are acceptable to the other utilities.

Powering the Region: How South Africa Can Contribute

Of course, southern Africa still faces major problems. There are political complexities over regional domination and hegemony. The agendas of the various countries are not always consistent. There are national interests to keep tariff levels high in order to protect domestic industries which do not yet exist in other member states. Such a tendency is exacerbated by overvalued exchange rates which encourage imports unless tariffs are raised. However, this situation will soon change as a result of the implementation of the GATT/WTO international trade regime (Chapter 10). Finally, the whole process of regional integration clearly hinges on continued national economic growth and stability – traits for which southern Africa has not been renowned until recently.

South Africa: the Elephant in the Canoe
Post-apartheid South Africa is striving to balance the demands of global economic integration with the need to strike bilateral agreements, such as that with the European Union as well as regional and domestic demands. But there are still some political difficulties relating to South Africa's regional economic pre-eminence, and sensitivities about its domination of the southern African region; the South African economy is 20 times the size of the next largest SADC member, and 4 times the size of the then 11 other member states put together. There is suspicion that South Africa has everything to gain by pushing for the ratification of regional protocols such as those on energy, while it has nothing to gain from protocols on trade (Mills 1996).

South Africa's exports to the surrounding region are rising fast, with US$2.8bn exported in 1995, whereas imports remained relatively stable at US$0.4bn. The South African Department of Trade and Industry says that this trade gap is not sustainable and that the country's economic future lies in developing the prosperity of the region as a whole. If the region's economy does not grow, the South African economy will remain too small to become a significant player globally. Regional economic development must go beyond purely trading considerations: there is an investment and industrial tapestry that can unite the region (Mills 1996; Chapters 5 and 10).

The new gas policy now being drafted in South Africa specifically promotes the use of gas from Namibia's Kudu and Mozambique's Pande gas fields for power generation and industrial use, although Eskom may not make such purchases for several more years (*Lloyd's List*, 6 February 97). Such developments would help the gas fields' developers in both countries to market their output. Because of economies of scale, the volumes of gas that they have to produce are far too high for Namibian and Mozambican domestic consumption alone. South Africa's Minister for Minerals and Energy Affairs, Penuell Maduna, declared that the new energy policy would be aimed at promoting gas development on a regional basis. 'It is obvious that there will never be movement unless South Africa becomes available as a market', he said, adding that the government was committed to ensuring that the resources would be used for the development not just of South Africa but of the whole sub-region (*Africa Energy and Mining* 1996).

The South African involvement is investment-inducing for another reason. Southern Africa has depended on development assistance for many years, and is relatively unknown to commercial investors and financiers. In contrast, despite its years of isolation during sanctions imposed in the 1980s, South Africa continued to maintain a generally sound reputation for the sanctity of contracts, payment of fees, interest, and dividends, and acceptable levels of return on equity. South African involvement in regional developments is therefore seen to remove complexities in evaluating cash flow uncertainty.

In the 1970s, the Cahora Bassa hydro scheme in Mozambique was made possible because of a South African market for the electricity produced and South Africa's participation in the financing of a portion of the associated high voltage transmission system. The same is true of the present rehabilitation of the transmission lines from Cahora Bassa to South Africa. South Africa's more recent involvement in the region has already extended to a range of multi- and transnational infrastructure projects: water sector developments such as the Lesotho Highlands Water Project, the plan to construct a major dam in Swaziland, the Matimba-Bulawayo high voltage transmission line linking South Africa and Zimbabwe, as well as the multi-sectoral Maputo corridor development.

The Maputo Corridor Development: a Blueprint to be Followed?

The Maputo corridor development provides an important example for the process of regional economic integration, and will significantly enhance the underlying conditions for economic growth and development along the entire length of the corridor. The scope of the project is enormous, extending to a number of economic sectors including tourism, agriculture and forestry, mining, construction, energy, finance and services, and possibly totalling some US$20bn on the South African side of the border. The extent of private and public sector commitment to the project heralds a new era of cross-border co-operation in trade and investment in the region after years of dependence on foreign aid (Mozambique News Agency 1996; Smith 1996). The approach could be a useful model for future developments in the power sector.

A key feature of this development is that the financing issues were addressed at a very early stage of the planning process. Investments of about US$5bn are planned on the Mozambique side, of which the aid component is likely to be only US$150 million, directed mainly at the upgrading of Maputo's port facilities. A large portion of the investment will be made by South African entities. Over an expected five-year period, annual expenditure of US$77 mn on telecommunications and US$67 mn on electricity distribution is expected in the sub-region. The whole project is expected to create some 100,000 jobs. The regional governments of

Mozambique, South Africa, Zimbabwe, Swaziland and Botswana have set up the Maputo Corridor Company (MCC) with an office in Nelspruit in South Africa's Mpumalanga Province.

The development of the Mepanda Uncua hydro scheme could very well follow a similar path, and ultimately also form the basis for developing the DRC's Inga scheme. A similar approach may be possible also for transmission projects, e.g. the DRC-Zambia interconnector. Gas from both Namibia's Kudu and Mozambique's Pande fields also needs anchor clients in South Africa, and any downstream development will probably result from a combination of public and private money. The official South African stance is that the government's job is to open up the way and leave investors to make the decisions.

Proposals are also under consideration to reduce Mossgas's synthetic fuel output and turn the plant into a higher value, gas-based petrochemical feedstock producer. The South African petrochemicals industry is facing a shortage of olefins, and will soon have to decide on a new source to support further expansion of the downstream plastics industry. Mossgas has tabled a plan for its site to be considered for the next naphtha cracker, which will use imported naphtha to produce olefins (Rosenthal 1997).

Southern African governments are under heavy pressure to reduce state expenditure and their levels of long-term borrowings. Simultaneously, however, populist pressure is being exerted on them to allocate scarce capital to social projects, such as housing, water, electricity and health services, that have an immediate and obvious impact. Faced with this dilemma and cognisant of the need to sustain and enhance the basic infrastructure, governments are increasingly following the contemporary trend of placing the development in the hands of the private sector, while at the same time acting in a facilitating role, as is the case with the Maputo Development Corridor, where the governments still set policy (on energy, transport, etc.), but the private sector is now the partner of government in implementing that policy. This works only where the projects are financially viable. For example, in the case of the road transport routes, the levels of traffic and the toll rate should render sufficient returns to allow the private investors to realise a level of return commensurate with the risk borne. The analogy for the power sector is an obvious one. The novelty of this approach to the financing of infrastructure has forced local companies to re-evaluate their reasons for tendering to build and operate concessions.

Spin-offs
South Africa has an industrial policy that is moving away from dependence on the production of primary commodities towards downstream production – moving from a low wage/low consumption economy to a high wage/high consumption economy. As a result, there will have to be some degree of segmentation of production within the region. This will lead to increased demand for energy, particularly electricity, in those countries which are able to benefit from such segmentation.

As the major portion of South Africa's imports comprises capital goods, such as machinery used to produce goods, so its exports to the region contain a significant capital goods element. During the sanctions era, equipment suppliers were unlikely to be able to offer supply and support from the natural operational base provided by South Africa, and products were routed directly from the exporting country, such as the US or Japan. Now there is a tendency for such products to move through South Africa, and to be supported by a South African-based subsidiary, which reduces the cost of support and supply to the region as a whole. This is increasingly becoming a feature in the power sector, with the added advantage that back-up facilities such as spares, repair services, and operating and maintenance training are more readily available.

South Africa in the Region: a Healthy Self-interest

Until recently, South Africa's commitment to southern Africa may have been far less altruistic than it appeared. Regional issues rarely feature in public debate in the country. South Africa has limited capacity to deal with its own challenges of economic and social restructuring, and it would be arrogant to claim that it has sufficient skills and largesse to share with southern Africa. There is also the view that South Africa is, to some extent, on the horns of a dilemma: if it ignores the region, it is seen as callous; if it becomes actively involved, it is seen as returning to the domineering ways of the past.

While these points indicate that a more active role in southern Africa will be difficult, they do not alter the reality that South Africa may have very little option but to engage in the region, and that it will need to accept substantial costs in time, money and people. An obvious issue is the limited potential of trade opportunities in southern Africa so as long as its foreign exchange supplies remain scarce. Business with these states will not reach its potential levels if their development remains limited.

It can also be argued that South Africa will expend great effort on the region's future only in so far as there is directly demonstrable benefit to itself, and that such involvement will generally be at a level which entails only relatively short-term costs. This does not, however, in any way negate the net benefit to be derived by the region from South Africa's involvement (Friedman 1996).

The power sector is a useful case in point. Eskom has obtained approval from the relevant authorities to invest in electricity infrastructure development in the region, provided that there will be demonstrable benefit to South African electricity consumers. Examples of projects where Eskom involvement is being considered include the Mepanda Uncua hydro project in Mozambique, rehabilitation and upgrading of facilities for the export of power from Inga in the DRC to southern Africa, and a study of the creation of a 'western corridor' for the transport of power from Inga to South Africa, through Angola and Namibia (Figure 9.3). A South African involvement is also possible in new regional interconnector projects aimed at linking Malawi and Tanzania to the SAPP's integrated electricity network.

Eskom is in a strong position technologically and through its balance sheet, and could play a useful role in levering financing for the region. Clearly, investment in securing least-cost options meets the stated requirement, while, at the same time, providing 'comfort' to potential international co-investors in such schemes, as well as opportunities for other countries in the region to earn royalties and create employment and other spin-offs.

A South African lead in regional integration of the power sector through the SAPP will reduce risks for investors, governments and end-users alike. It will stimulate national efforts in the important area of widening access to electricity. Prerequisites for this to happen are that national governments throughout southern Africa should take the necessary steps to modernise their legal and regulatory frameworks and continue the process of commercialising power utility operations, moving towards cost-reflective and market-based electricity tariffs, and stimulating private sector involvement in the power industry. Under such a scenario, South Africa can certainly contribute to 'powering the region' in a constructive manner.

References

Africa Energy and Mining (1996) 'Kudu-4. Successful', No. 193: 4.

African National Congress (1994) *The Reconstruction and Development Programme*. Umanyano, Johannesburg.

Eskom (1996) *Integrated Electricity Planning, Revision 5.* Johannesburg.

Eskom (1997a) 'Feasibility Study: New Hydro Plant in Mozambique', *Eskom Newsbrief* 20: 2–3. London.

Eskom (1997b) 'Utilisation of Renewable Energy Sources', *Eskom Newsbrief* 22: 4. London.

Friedman, S. (1996) 'Engagement with Africa is Not a Choice', *Business Day*, 25 November: 11. Johannesburg.

Government of Zambia (1993) *Investment Act.* Lusaka.

Horvei, T. (1996), *Electricity – Engine for Growth and Regional Integration in Southern Africa.* Energy Symposium of the Europe-South Africa 1996 Business and Finance Forum, Cannes, June 17–19.

Horvei, T. (1995), *Regional Co-operation and the Need for Reform.* World Bank symposium on Power Sector Report, Johannesburg, December 5-7.

Horvei, T. (1995), *The Scope for Regional Co-operation in Electricity Generation and Distribution.* Dataworld/Financial Gazette conference on Southern Africa Towards 2000, Harare, November 6–7.

Kalapula, E.S. (1987) 'Electrification of Peri-urban Areas in Lusaka, Zambia', *Geography* 72(3): 243–6.

Mills, G. (1996) 'A Blueprint to Meet the Challenge of Africa's Regional Demands', *Business Day*, (Johannesburg) 31 October: 16.

Mozambique News Agency (1996) *AIM Reports*, Nos. 77 (8 February 1996), 91 (21 August 1996), 99 (12 December 1996). London.

NamPower (1997) 'Press Release: Kudu Combined Cycle Gas-fired Power Plant'. 14 May. Windhoek.

National Electricity Regulator (1996) *Annual Report 1995/96.* Pretoria.

National Electricity Regulator (1997) *Annual Report 1996/97.* Pretoria.

Potts, D. (1995) 'Shall We Go Home? Increasing Urban Poverty in African Cities and Migration Processes', *Geographical Journal* 161(3) 245–64.

Republic of Mozambique (1995) *Programme of the Government of Mozambique approved by Parliament for the period 1995–2000.*

Republic of South Africa (1994) *The Reconstruction and Development Programme White Paper.* Cape Town.

Rosenthal, J. (1997) 'Mossgas to Crack its own Future', *The Star Business Report*, 10 February. Johannesburg.

Simon, D., Van Spengen, W., Dixon, C. and Närman, A. (eds)(1995) *Structurally Adjusted Africa; Poverty, Debt and Basic Needs.* Pluto, London.

Smith, J. (1996) 'Mozambique's Lifeline Revived', *The Star*, 1 May. Johannesburg.

SAD-ELEC & MEPC (1996) *Electricity in Southern Africa.* Financial Times, London.

Southern Africa Development Community (1996) *SADC Energy Cooperation Policy and Strategy*, SADC Energy Sector – TAU, Luanda.

Southern African Power Pool (1995a) *Inter-utility Memorandum of Understanding.* Pretoria, 16 May.

Southern African Power Pool (1995b) *Agreement between Operating Members.* Pretoria, 31 May.

Star, The (1996) Business Report: 'Maputo Development Corridor', 28 August. Johannesburg.

10 SADC, COMESA, SACU: Contradictory Formats for Regional 'Integration' in Southern Africa?

JAMES D SIDAWAY & RICHARD GIBB

Introduction

An avowedly *postcolonial/post-apartheid* southern Africa contains three intergovernmental organisations associated with projects of regional integration: the Southern Africa Development Community (SADC), the Common Market for Eastern and Southern Africa (COMESA) and the Southern African Customs Union (SACU) (Figure 10.1). The modest (but by no means straightforward) purpose of this chapter is to look critically at the operations of each and some significant elements of the relations between them, as well as something of the way that these relations mediate a variety of social interests.

A central contention underpinning the chapter is that regional integration in southern Africa is characterised by an institutional *vulnerability* to a variety of pressures. In turn the chapter examines the ways in which the practice of regional integration is locked into a set of ideologies of *development* and *statehood*. It begins with a contextual review of SADC, proceeds to look briefly at COMESA (and the uneasy relationship between SADC and COMESA), before examining SACU, and in particular its current renegotiation and how the terms relate to a colonially generated history of dependency and uneven development. Where necessary, the chapter points to the significance and complexity of the impacts of outside pressures on southern African regionalism. Throughout it draws upon a mixture of sources: interviews, official documentation, academic and popular literatures (including journalism).

From SADCC to SADC

Since the Southern African Development Co-ordination Conference (SADCC) was founded in 1980, a substantial critical literature[1] has documented the evolution of an organisation which (nominally) brought together Zimbabwe, Mozambique, Angola, Swaziland, Lesotho, Botswana, Malawi, Zambia, Tanzania and Namibia (which joined SADCC on independence in 1990) 'out of a common awareness of common

James Sidaway would like to acknowledge support from the Economic and Social Research Council (ESRC) (Research Fellowship Award H536 27 500595 on the Geography of Southern African Transitions). Richard Gibb acknowledges support from the Nuffield Foundation for his research on SACU, together with the support and time of numerous interviewees in southern Africa. Responsibility for any errors or misinterpretations is the authors'.

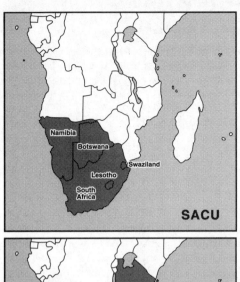

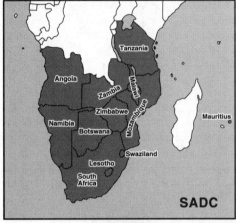

Figure 10.1 *Member states of SADC, SACU and COMESA, 1996*

interest' (President Masire's address to the SADCC summit in 1992, cited in Mandaza and Tostensen, 1994: 72)). Critics have not been reluctant to draw attention to the failures of SADCC – particularly in its declared terms – to pursue the objectives of:

a) the reduction of economic dependence, particularly but not only, on the Republic of South Africa;
b) the forging of links to create a genuine and equitable regional integration;
c) the mobilisation of resources to promote the implementation of national, interstate and regional policies;
d) concerted action to secure international co-operation within the framework of a strategy for economic liberation. (SADCC 1981a).

The year 1992 saw SADCC transform itself into a 'Development Community' (SADC) and in 1994 South Africa became its eleventh member state (Mauritius also joined in 1995 followed by the Seychelles and the Democratic Republic of Congo in 1997). But the conclusion of a considerable weight of journalistic (*Africa Confidential* 1995) and academic (Mfone 1993; Maasdorp 1993; Maasdorp and Whiteside 1993) commentary is that the old SADCC had never been able to fulfil its stated aims of reducing dependence on South Africa and that the new SADC will not deliver much 'development' or 'regional integration'. Most sharply, when SADC invited member states to submit suggestions for a SADC logo, a satirical commentary in Zimbabwe's weekly *Financial Gazette* suggested (with due reference to the organisation's dependence on Western aid for project finance) that SADC could be best symbolised by;

> a begging bowl [For] What has SADC achieved apart from mugging gullible Scandinavian countries? SADC members are today more dependent upon South Africa than they were in the early 1980s (*Financial Gazette*, 3 February 1994).

That calls have been made for the revival of apartheid-era electrified border fences between South Africa and some of its erstwhile SADC partners,[2] plus the way that the possibility of *integration* presupposes formal state sovereignty (of which the least that must be said is that it is somewhat tentative[3] in some SADC members), reinforces those who are sceptical regarding SADC's claims to achievements and prospects.

Although there is a small permanent secretariat located in Gaborone, Botswana, all SADC development programmes function on the basis of external aid and are managed by sectoral co-ordinating units (each member state has at least one of these). Critically, only two sectors[4] enjoy the status of a regional commission, with staff recruited at a regional level and funded by all member states. In all the other cases, the sectoral co-ordination staff are also civil servants in their respective countries, and SADC affairs are usually just one (and frequently not a very prominent element) of their responsibilities. SADC therefore remains mostly intergovernmental, with a small and relatively powerless secretariat dependent on the good offices of civil servants and politicians in all the member states.

Statements by member-state politicians reinforce the point about the decentralised (and relatively *ad hoc*) nature of SADCC/SADC. As Julius Nyerere explained in 1985, SADCC:

> ...does not consist of a Headquarters and Secretariat which initiates and organises everything, with member countries trying to direct and keep budgetary control through periodic Ministerial and Summit meetings. Instead, all members are actively concerned in the initiation and implementation of all SADCC projects, with each having the responsibility for co-ordinating and promoting a particular sector. This structure enables the Secretariat to remain small and effective,

while monitoring and co-ordinating the work of the co-ordinators. Even more important, this structure enhances the active involvement of all member states in both the work and benefits of co-operation (cited in Mandaza and Tostensen 1994: 70).

Very often, however, such 'active involvement' has been consciously absent. The basic formal structures of the organisation remain more or less as they were defined in the Memorandum of Understanding signed by member heads of state in 1980. Reproducing the sense of this founding moment, an annual summit of heads of state is the supreme body responsible for 'overall policy direction and control of the functions of SADC'.

SADCC's acknowledged successes are in some of the domains of sectoral co-ordination (notably food security and transport), in mobilising aid, and – not least – in holding together within the contexts of a history of uneven regional development, political fracture and ideological diversity. Superimposed on an already fractious late colonial history,[5] there were not only the divide and rule strategies of South African economic power juxtaposed with destabilisation in the 1980s, but also a diversity of internal and international ideological orientations. These ranged from the avowed Marxism-Leninism (albeit not domestically hegemonic) in Angola and Mozambique (and at one time a similar claim, though never formally constituted, in Zimbabwe) through formal democracy in Botswana to the veteran one-party 'African socialisms' in Tanzania and Zambia, the conservative monarchy in Swaziland and the proto-fascist state of Hastings Kamuzu Banda in Malawi.

Within these contexts, SADCC's cohesion has been well aided by a certain formal political *performativity*. For example, in the earliest days, the slogan, *a luta continua* ['the struggle continues'], adopted from the self-proclaimed Marxist-Leninist ruling parties in Angola and Mozambique, was often in evidence. Even a minister of the Malawian government, notorious for its blend of conservatism and despotism and for its uniquely open and subordinate relationship with Pretoria, could refer to 'continuing struggle':

> There are countless pot-holes on the road to economic liberation and what SADCC has managed to achieve so far is only a very short distance on the long road to economic independence. But united as we are, and with the support received from many governments and organisations, we are confident that we will, with good intentions win the battle. As our brothers and sisters in the People's Republic of Mozambique say, "A Luta Continua!" – "Let us fight on!" (L Chakakala Chaziya, Malawian Minister of Finance, cited in SADCC 1981a: 7).

Key features of SADCC/SADC practice have all hinged on the unwritten rules of diplomatic performance, especially what the founding Treaty codifies as 'consensus'. Within these interlocking sets of norms, a number of components may be disaggregated. First, no substantial critique of other member states is expected. As Weisfelder (1991: 7) notes:

> SADCC deliberations have a consensus building function not easily comprehensible to those accustomed to decisive confrontations among sharply defined alternatives.

This goes hand in hand with minimal granting of powers to institutional structures (most notably the secretariat) to produce an atmosphere of ritualised diplomatic politeness and *protocol*. This has been most evident at the annual summits of heads of state or government of the member countries. Until 1992, this body (and the entire SADCC structure) operated solely on the basis of custom codified in the original 'Memorandum of Understanding' which established SADCC's institutions in 1980. In other words, they had no formal legal existence other than as a *de facto* extension of member states. It may be the case, as Lipson (1991: 500) argues, that: 'Informality [in international agreements] is best understood as a device for minimising the impediments to co-operation, at both the domestic and international levels'. But it also profoundly shapes the modes, formats and limits to such co-operation. In the case of SADCC, the decentralised and *ad hoc* structure which evolved from the original memorandum of understanding has provided the basis around which the organisation has been able to evolve. In turn, however, this structure has come to constitute a key internal tension now that the old SADCC is formally transformed into the new SADC. An interviewee[6] in the SADC secretariat could describe how '[Ministers and Heads of] member states have not really appreciated in full what they have [now] signed up to'. More particularly, at the annual summits of heads of states/governments which (according to the 1992 SADC Treaty) are responsible for the overall policy, direction and control of SADC; 'heads of state never really engage each other'.[7] Such meetings remain high on formal content and protocol, speeches and dinners, interspersed with photo opportunities. As an observant journalist was led to comment on the 1993 Annual Summit:

> Last time they met in Gaborone it was to convert the Southern African Development Co-ordination Conference to Southern African Development Community. Last week in Mbabane they met to confer the chairmanship of the community on Sir Ketumile Masire. But what a farce it turned out to be.

> It was as if the august gathering had been drugged. I saw at least five eminent members asleep, their heads thrown recklessly far back as if they wanted to break their necks. One could not resist a cynic's observation that if these people's servants were so tormented with drink from their sinecures, it is only fair to retrench them. What message did these sleeping servants carry home to their paymasters? Was the dreary litany of self-praise itself [so] soporific that none of the members cared to convey it to anyone (*Financial Gazette*, 3 February 1994).

The answer might be found in the comment in 1991 of the then SADC Executive Secretary to the effect that:

> lack of continuous involvement in SADC...[meant] that government officials thought about the movement only when they were en route to its meetings and forgot about it when they returned to their countries (cited in Mandaza, 1991: 9).

Meetings of the Council of Ministers[8] tend to be considerably more animated. Whilst its decisions are formally taken by 'consensus', arriving at such a condition involves a variety of conflicts and stresses. A secretariat employee[9] described how the reception of proposals formulated in the secretariat at Council of Ministers meetings

> is a disincentive to do anything [which might be even mildly controversial]....your skin will be quite safe if you do not propose changes [to established ways of doing things]...even if you are acting in good faith.

He noted how his initial assumptions that ministers and/or sectoral co-operation staff might have had prior consultations, or even worked out positions on issues to be discussed at Council meetings, were rapidly challenged:

> one assumes that member states have had thorough consultations – but this is not necessarily true. [Only] when you produce an instrument to operationalise [a proviso already formally accepted by heads of state] then eyes open...[and] the atmosphere can become very negative...People in sectoral co-operation whom you have earlier communicated with [and apparently had supported an initiative] put on a different hat and [now] agree with their ministers [who oppose it]

This structural contradiction (or 'bottleneck' as some interviewees characterise it) runs through the core of SADCC and has become more acute as the organisation has taken on a new formal role and a key new member.

According to the text of the declaration by the SADC heads of state at their 1992 summit, something called 'effective and self-sustaining regional development...requires political commitment and effective institutions and mechanisms to mobilise the region's own resources' (SADC 1993: 4). The formal establishment of SADC and its embodiment in a treaty are represented in the text of the Treaty itself as symbols of this commitment. The declaration also makes reference to the transformed regional situation; to the end of South African regional destabilisation which had characterised the 1980s; to Namibian independence; and to the transition in South Africa.

One of the proclaimed achievements of the transformation from SADCC to SADC is that the institution has written into its own treaty the possibility of legally binding protocols that 'once approved by the Summit on the recommendation of the Council...shall thereafter become an integral part of this treaty' (SADC 1993: 19). To date, however, protocol negotiations have been slow, albeit, in part, because the secretariat initiated a process of consultation/workshops to broaden the initial drafting processes. Achievements in the relatively non-controversial domains of shared water resources and control of narcotic trafficking have occurred against the backdrop of drawn-out and contentious negotiations concerning proposals (emanating from the secretariat) on regulating the movement of migrants, on trade and on security. The first of these is widely dismissed in the media and diplomatic-state apparatus of member states as a virtual non-starter (unless in some watered-down form) and the security/military co-operation theme is seen as something that is beyond the SADC remit (Cilliers 1995). A Political, Defence and Security Department (to be presided over by Robert Mugabe) was in fact approved at the 1996 SADC summit, but the department stands aside from the secretariat.[10]

The key trade protocol has been hostage to many interests and unresolved questions, including South Africa's relations with the European Union (Bhatia 1995; Campbell and Scerri 1995; Holland 1995a, 1995b) and with other extra-regional partners, and the negotiations about the future of SACU (to be detailed below). After much hard work by the secretariat, a draft trade protocol was signed (with only Angola opting out) in August 1996, although at the time of writing it had not yet been ratified by the member states. The protocol specifies the creation of a 'free trade area' by 2005. The protocol was described[11] by the Zimbabwean Industry and Commerce Minister as 'a major achievement for Southern Africa' and as 'an exciting breakthrough' by South Africa's Trade and Industry Minister. The Botswanan President, Ketumile Masire, was more precise when he declared: 'By signing these protocols, we have not only demonstrated our unwavering commitment to regional integration, but we have also set a daunting task for ourselves'.

Certainly the diversity of formal state-diplomatic apparatuses and the varied social interests in and across them will make implementation of the 'free trade' proposal rather tricky. These positions and interests must perforce remain largely outside our scope here, but a few observations are in order. In the first place, unease regarding SADC trade negotiations is felt particularly in Zimbabwe, the largest economy and military power in SADCC prior to South African accession: it was also Zimbabwe's own transition to black majority rule in 1980 which made possible a subcontinental economic-political bloc against apartheid. A series of worsening trade disputes between South Africa and Zimbabwe since 1992 has enhanced the latter's perception that the mercantilist policies of the new South Africa pose a new kind of threat to its business and diplomatic interests (Chapter 6; see also Polhmus 1992; Peta 1996; Gqumbule 1996; Hartrack 1996; Iheduru 1996). A decade of IMF World Bank-directed structural adjustment has increased the sense of local vulnerability in states like Zimbabwe with respect to South African (and other foreign) capital.

For these reasons, a certain ambivalence regarding SADC is also evident in Zambia, where (aside from the fact that Lusaka hosts the COMESA secretariat) there is also a strong perception that the country has not received due recognition and recompense for its long-term practical support for southern African liberation. Similar sentiments are evident in Tanzania, which is now seeking to reinforce its relationships with Kenya and Uganda. Zimbabwean President Robert Mugabe has also suggested that these states could become SADC members. To the extent that it could reinstate Zimbabwe's relative centrality, this would act as a (small) counter to the South African relative (economic) dominance of SADC. At the same time, however, South African civil servants and diplomats have proposed for some time that the Democratic Republic of Congo (the former Zaire) join SADC. As was noted in the *Indian Ocean Newsletter*, at the 1995 heads of state SADC summit, held in Johannesburg:

> Although SADC executive secretary Kaire Mbuende publicly admitted that with twelve members SADC was 'a complete number', closed-session discussions in Johannesburg uncovered a sharp divergence of viewpoints over the Republic of South Africa's insistence that Zaire should be admitted as a member too. In fact, observers point out, Pretoria wants to diversify its energy supplies and also wants the Southern African Development Community to base its planning on South Africa's project for a major electricity grid which includes the Zaire. The South African state-owned utility Eskom is highly interested in the Zaire's hydroelectric resources. Angola and Mozambique's delegates at the Johannesburg summit did not see things that way at all and strongly opposed any idea of Zaire being admitted. (*Indian Ocean Newsletter* 1995: 7)

All this occurred despite the fact that, earlier in the same year, the Council of Ministers had formally accepted a proposal from the secretariat concerning 'Guidelines, Criteria and Procedure for the Admission of New Members' (detailed in SADC 1995b: 19–22) which specified that applicants must fulfil all of the following criteria:

a) geographical proximity to the SADC region;
b) commonality of political, economic, social and cultural systems with the systems of the SADC region;
c) feasibility of cost-effective and efficient co-ordination of economic, social and cultural activities under the SADC framework of co-operation;
d) absence of a record of engagement in subversive and destabilisation activities, and territorial ambitions against any SADC, or any of its member states [sic];
e) must be a democracy, observing the principles of human rights and the rule of law;
f) must share SADC's ideals and aspirations.

Whilst the notion of 'democracy' being invoked seems flexible enough to include rather anti-democratic Swaziland, its meaning would indeed have been stretched if Mobutu's Zaire had also been described as 'democratic'. Following his departure, the new regime in the renamed Democratic Republic of Congo (DRC) applied to join, together with the Seychelles. The admission of both was duly approved at the 1997 summit. The SADC executive secretary noted how the DRC could 'serve as a gateway between central and southern Africa', and how SADC must 'strengthen the democratic process' there. He had earlier been rather less positive regarding the application from the Seychelles, contrasting the DRC's geographical proximity to the existing SADC members with the fact that the 'Seychelles appears to be next to India, but they have applied'.

Whilst SADCC has become SADC and gained new members, many of the structural contradictions identified in the mid-1980s remain unresolved. In particular, formal procedure often remains all important, and the success of a SADC meeting will still be registered by the extent to which delegates are happy with procedural issues at least as much as with the content. Conduct is content. One of the results is that, at SADC functions, positions on a theme are often coded, unstated or expressed primarily through a later non-compliance with a decision taken. This is exemplified in the relations between SADC and COMESA.

COMESA versus SADC?

COMESA formally came into existence in December 1994. Following initiatives from the UN Economic Commission for Africa (Asanke 1991; Anglin 1983), COMESA began life as the Preferential Trade Area for Eastern and Southern Africa (PTA) in 1981. Of the original eight states (Comoros, Djibouti, Ethiopia, Malawi, Mauritius, Somalia, Uganda and Zambia) that signed up to the PTA in Lusaka in December 1981, all (except Somalia and Djibouti) have become members of COMESA, together with Angola, Burundi, Eritrea, Kenya, Lesotho, Madagascar, Mozambique, Namibia, Rwanda, Sudan, Swaziland, Tanzania, the Democratic Republic of Congo and Zimbabwe – which had joined the PTA subsequent to its establishment (Figure 10.1). This grouping includes, as a report on integration in southern Africa by the African Development Bank recognises, 'countries with exceedingly diverse characteristics and economic interests: several are in a state of considerable internal turmoil' (African Development Bank 1993: 9).

For although SADC is massively heterogeneous in terms of economic and political conditions, most of its members are linked through a certain functional unity, derived from the (colonial) network of labour migration, trade and communications that was centred on the industrial, minerals-energy economy of South Africa. COMESA does not enjoy even this asymmetric and uneven set of linkages. The African Development Bank (1993) carefully suggests that the tighter and more limited structure and scope of SADC makes it a stronger basis for future 'integration' than COMESA. Encouraged by this judgement, the SADC secretariat has moved from a stated position in 1992 that 'the two Organisations had distinct objectives and mandates and they must, therefore, continue to exist as autonomous, but complementary entities' (SADCC 1992: 75), to a resolution, agreed at the 1994 heads of state summit, declaring that SADC members should withdraw from COMESA. After a considerable delay, a joint SADC-COMESA ministerial committee in August 1996 advocated the continued separate existence of the two organisations.[12] Yet by April 1997, only two countries – Mozambique and Lesotho – had formally announced their intention to withdraw. As a secretariat employee explained:[13] 'Formal withdrawals do not take place...Members let fees and participation etc. lapse. They don't need to say "we are pulling out"'. Indeed, Zambia (where the COMESA secretariat is located) and Malawi (from where COMESA's secretary-general originates (Ndovi 1996)) have registered a commitment to COMESA, even if SADC's former secretary-general[14] complains of 'two cancers...[of] bad blood between the two secretariats and inconsistencies implicit in states being members of both'. Furthermore, SADC members are also entangled in other (frequently contradictory) regional commitments.[15] The most significant of these is SACU: an organisation that predates SADC and COMESA by the best part of a century.

Fourteen into Five? SACU and SADC

SACU is a revenue-sharing agreement between South Africa, Botswana, Lesotho, Swaziland and Namibia.[16] In its original form, it dates from agreements negotiated in the late nineteenth and early twentieth centuries by Britain, which, along with

South Africa, then considered that Bechuanaland (Botswana), Basutoland (Lesotho) and Swaziland would ultimately be incorporated into South Africa. SACU is a product of its imperial times. It has therefore embodied a complex, but nevertheless profound and enduring, dependency relationship between South Africa and its near neighbours – although the shifting terms of this dependency have been expressed in periodic renegotiations of the treaty, notably in 1969, 1976 and again since 1994. SACU can therefore be traced to the 1889 Customs Union Convention signed by the British Colony of the Cape of Good Hope and the Orange Free State Boer Republic (Maasdorp 1989). In 1893, Bechuanaland and Basutoland – both under the direct administrative control of the British High Commissioner – joined the 1889 Customs Union Convention, albeit with significantly diminished rights (Ettinger 1974). Although a second customs convention was negotiated in 1898, the Anglo-Boer war and British conquests further north resulted in British colonial rule throughout the present-day South Africa, Bechuanaland, Basutoland, Swaziland and the Rhodesias (Zambia and Zimbabwe). This made negotiating a customs union less onerous and in 1903 a Customs Union Convention was signed between the Cape, Natal, Orange River Colony, Transvaal and Southern Rhodesia. Again, Bechuanaland, Basutoland and Swaziland were admitted as members under a protocol, effectively categorising them as second-class members with diminished rights (Maasdorp 1989). The formation of the Union of South Africa just seven years later resulted in the termination of all previous customs union arrangements. However, because the Union excluded the three High Commission Territories, a new customs union agreement was negotiated in June 1910 (Walters 1989).

The 1910 Agreement: Dreams of Colonial Incorporation

The 1910 Customs Union Agreement was the direct forerunner of the present-day SACU. It was negotiated by Britain which, along with South Africa, intended to incorporate the High Commission Territories into South Africa (McCarthy 1992). The fact that the Territories did not then have their own customs administrations was, as a consequence, interpreted to be of little consequence. Furthermore, as noted by Walters (1989), the ability of the Territories to manage their economies was not really considered, as economic development beyond extraction of resources for overseas markets was not envisaged.

The 1910 Agreement provided for the free movement of manufactured products, plus a common external tariff and a revenue-sharing formula. Revenue was to be divided among the four signatories in proportion to the level of their external trade between the years 1907 and 1910 (Cattaneo, 1990). The agreement resulted in South Africa receiving 98.7 per cent of the joint revenue, whilst the High Commission Territories received collectively 1.3 per cent: Bechuanaland, 0.27 per cent; Basutoland, 0.88 per cent; Swaziland, 0.15 per cent (ibid). Although the 1910 Agreement lasted for almost 60 years, there were many unsatisfactory and contentious operating procedures that put the Customs Union under strain. Of particular dissatisfaction to the postcolonial states that emerged from the High Commision Territories was the fact that the revenue-sharing formula remained static, unaffected by levels of imports and exports. As far as South Africa was concerned, the revenue-sharing formula was regarded (like the wider set of structural dominations of which it was a part) as indefinite (Walters 1989).

Like a number of other peripheral states (notably in Latin America) in the mid-1920s, the South African regime framed an attempt to promote local industrial capital through the adoption of an import substitution programme. This resulted in high protective tariff barriers being imposed around the Customs Union (McCarthy

1992). For the High Commission Territories this had two negative impacts. First, the tariff barriers promoted trade diversion as the Territories were forced to purchase relatively high-cost (and relatively low-quality) South African produce. Secondly, the overall level of customs revenue as a proportion of GDP began to fall. Together these reinforced the relative underdevelopment of the Territories. Compounding this, South Africa's (unilateral) decision to follow a policy of import substitution highlighted the fact that the Territories had no local fiscal discretion and virtually no influence over the direction of South Africa's fiscal policy changes affecting them.

From the 1930s onwards, British pressure to renegotiate the revenue-sharing formula and the 1910 Agreement intensified. Furthermore, it became apparent that, following the coming to power of the National Party in 1948, Britain no longer intended to allow the incorporation of the Territories into South Africa. Negotiations for a new agreement, although started in 1963, were delayed pending the independence of the three BLS states; Botswana and Lesotho in 1966 and Swaziland in 1968. Negotiations then began in earnest and an agreement was signed on 11 December 1969, establishing SACU in its contemporary format. Although the 1969 Agreement has been amended on various occasions, it remains largely intact and forms the basis of the current renegotiations.

Before assessing further the characteristics of the 1969 Agreement and the renegotiations, it is necessary to emphasise a number of key issues emerging from our historical review. First, the SACU has its origins in a colonial policy that sought to incorporate the High Commission Territories into South Africa. Until the 1950s, London turned a blind eye to South African designs on them and governed the Territories with due regard to what was generally seen as a quite natural dependence on South Africa. Secondly, up to the 1910 Agreement, Custom Union Conventions peripheralised the Territories, placing them in a marginal position subordinate to the principal signatories. Thirdly, ever since 1889, the BLS states have belonged to a regional trading arrangement of a fairly substantial character, with a common external tariff, free trade between the parties, an integrated infrastructure and, for the most part, a common currency. In turn, all this meant that the 1910 Customs Union differed from later Third World customs union 'models' in which 'integration' is discursively linked with development. The economic development of the Territories was accorded *minimal* priority. As McCarthy (1992) notes, the 1910 agreement was 'essentially a revenue device'. He explains how any analysis of the SACU must bear in mind that it was an arrangement to distribute revenue among territories whose colonial 'integration' was a *fait accompli*.

Therefore comparisons with text-book schemes which describe states moving from a 'free trade area' to an 'economic union' via a customs union and common market would be rather futile (Gibb and Michalak 1994). No autonomous state-elites were voluntarily ceding elements of their sovereignty to a higher joint authority. Until the late 1960s, the High Commission Territories were under colonial rule and no one from them had real influence in the organisation and policies of the Customs Union Agreement.

The 1969 Southern African Customs Union Agreement, Renegotiations and the Rise of 'Development'
The 1969 Agreement (now under renegotiation) has been subject to several minor amendments since its inception, most notably in 1976, with the introduction of a stabilisation factor into the revenue-sharing formula. However, since the 1980s, all the parties have become – for different reasons – increasingly dissatisfied with the operating procedures, implementation and impacts of the Agreement. Although several

attempts were made in the latter part of the 1970s and throughout the 1980s to rene-gotiate it, regional tensions over South Africa's so-called 'independent' homelands (which were – as far as South Africa was concerned – separate members of the SACU) and regional policies (in particular, the havoc generated by South African destabilisation) resulted (as destabilisation intended more widely) in a broad preser-vation of the *status quo*.

It is notable, however, that unlike the 1910 Agreement – which felt no need to emphasise either economic development or integration (Walters 1989) – the 1969 Agreement set out clearly the claim that it would promote economic *development* throughout all member states on the basis of what it called 'equitable benefits':

> ...to ensure the continued economic development of the customs union area as a whole, and to ensure in particular that these arrangements encourage the development of the less advanced members of the customs union and the diversification of their economies, and afford all parties equitable benefits arising from trade among themselves and with other countries (Republic of South Africa 1969: 2).

This re-inscription, and the accompanying shifting formats of power and hege-monic discourse in the region (away from 'trusteeship' towards 'development'), took shape in a number of novel provisions. The most important of these relate to an adjusted revenue-sharing formula to apportion the Common Revenue Pool, intra-regional trade and infant-industry protection. These provisions have since become the principal sources of discontent and form the key issues in the current renegotiations.

The revenue-sharing formula is the single most important source of dissatis-faction (Thomas 1995). The technicalities and operational equation of the rev-enue-sharing agreement have been analysed in detail elsewhere (Walters 1989; Maasdorp and Whiteside 1993) and will be dealt with only briefly here. At the most basic level, the SACU Agreement provides for the pooling of customs, excise, import surcharges and sales duties among the five member countries. The South African Reserve Bank manages this so-called Common Revenue Pool and, in the first instance, divides the Pool according to annual imports, production and consumption of dutiable goods. A compensation factor is then added to the above which provides for a 42 per cent loading in favour of the BLSN countries.[17] In 1976, the formula was amended so as to provide a 'stabilisation factor' in the levels of revenue received by the BLSN. Throughout the 1970s, these revenues fluctuated markedly, registering both the accelerating global economic disorder, the crises experienced by South African capitalism after the Soweto uprising and the 'shocks' to the old regional 'order' delivered by the collapse of the Portuguese empire. The stabilisation formula guarantees that the BLSN receive between 17 and 23 per cent of the value of their imports of durable goods and duties paid and thereby represents a shift towards readdressing their marginalisation (Table 10.1).

For the BLSN states, the revenue-sharing formula offers a trade-off between re-lative fiscal autonomy and an income to state coffers. In this respect it represents the relative ascendancy of a rentier class in the BLSN states and cements their (some-times uneasy) relationship to the dominant strata in South Africa. Perhaps the most significant factor here is the substantial contribution to state revenue provided by the Revenue Pool. In 1992, SACU receipts accounted for between 11 and 20 per cent of GDP, and 22 and 47 per cent of government revenue (Table 10.2). This represents not only a significant percentage of state revenue, but also a secure source of (ren-tier) income. Other major benefits include relief from the burden of having to oper-ate an independent customs service and associated administrations, free access to

Table 10.1   *The Common Revenue Pool, 1994/95*

	Basic Revenue Share	Compensation adjustment by 1.42	Stabilisation adjustment	Actual total Revenue Share (1994/95)
Total SACU Revenue	8918			
SACU Imports and Excisable Production	102786			
Botswana	5382	467	196	252	915
Lesotho	3656	317	134	171	622
Namibia	4705	408	172	220	800
Swaziland	2541	220	93	119	432
Sub-Total	16284	1413	595	762	2770
RSA's Share	86502	7505	−595	−762	6418
Total	102786	8918			8918

supplies from South Africa and access to foreign exchange and a semi-convertible currency (all high on the agendas of the holders of state power – and associated elites – in the BLSN states) along with the prospects for accumulation, enrichment and speculation offered by the relatively sophisticated South African financial infrastructure, which in turn is plugged into global circuits.[18]

The obverse of this is the limits to fiscal autonomy codified by the Union. Article 4 of the 1969 Agreement stipulates that, with limited exceptions, the customs tariff, excise and duties in force in South Africa 'shall be applied to goods imported into the common customs area' (Republic of South Africa 1969: 6). Thus, the BLSN states are legally obliged to apply a common external tariff determined unilaterally by South Africa. Although Article 5 stipulates that South Africa must consult with them before changes in duty, consultation does not imply consent. Article 5 stipulates that:

....the Government of South Africa shall give the other contracting parties adequate opportunity for consultations before *imposing, amending or abrogating* any customs duty....(emphasis added)(*ibid.*).

In practice, the South African Board of Tariffs and Trade, on which the BLSN countries have no representation, adopts tariffs and duties unilaterally (see Mayer and Zarenda 1994). Whilst the 1969 Agreement does make provision for 'infant-industry' protection (Article 6), the protection of industries of 'major importance' (Article 7), and the right to impose tariffs 'for economic, social and other reasons' (Article 11), any action has to be agreed by South Africa and is likely to be of limited use as South Africa can still deny market access to the products of such industries. Although

Table 10.2   *BLSN SACU receipts as a share of national income revenue/grants*

Country	Financial Year 1988		Financial Year 1992	
	% GDP	% of Revenue	% GDP	% of Revenue
Botswana	5.4	11.5	11.2	21.6
Lesotho	9.8*	41.5	15.6	47.2
Swaziland	10.3	37.2	14.0	40.3
Namibia	12.3	31.9	20.5	32.1

* = GNP

SACU does in theory, therefore, allow for some protection for industrial production in the BLSN states, there are numerous instances where this has been withheld (Davies 1994).

Furthermore, at the start of the 1990s, it was revealed that a secret memorandum (see Maasdorp and Whiteside 1993) attached to the 1969 Agreement requires an 'infant industry' requiring protection to be able to supply at least 60 per cent of the demand of the customs union before it is eligible for protection. As Mayer and Zarenda (1994) note, the memorandum represents an almost insurmountable obstacle to new industrial development in the BLSN countries. In addition to these impacts of the SACU on the BLSN states (which, it should be recalled, are supposedly compensated for by the revenue-sharing formula), there is one other major impact: the effect of the two-year time lag in payments from the Common Revenue Pool. In practice, this gives South Africa an interest-free loan and, as a result of high inflation (averaging 15 per cent in the 1980s), loss of interest and exchange-rate depreciation, significantly undermines the enhancement/stabilisation factor.

None of this has been enough to produce the unravelling of SACU. But – together with the wider shift accompanying Namibian independence and the issues which its membership raised (Simon 1991), as well as the South African political transition – it has been enough to produce a certain pressure from within the BLSN states for a further renegotiation of SACU's terms.

South Africa and the SACU: terms of renegotiation
In the context of the commitments associated with the Reconstruction and Development Programme (RDP) and the longer-term fiscal crisis of the South African state, South African complaints about SACU focus on the argument that the growing burden of the compensatory revenue-sharing payments has become 'unaffordable' (Davies 1994). In basic material terms, South Africa's residual share of the Common Revenue Pool has been falling consistently. According to figures provided by the South African Department of Trade and Industry (Lagardien 1995), the South African share of the Common Revenue Pool in 1969/70 stood at 97.4 per cent, with the remaining 2.6 per cent distributed among the three BLS states. By 1984, the BLS share had risen dramatically to 12.2 per cent, reducing South Africa's residual share to 87.8 per cent. More recent figures illustrate a continuation of this trend (Figure 10.2). By 1990/1, the BLS countries' share of the Pool accounted for approximately 18 per cent and, with newly independent Namibia included, the total BLSN share rose to 26 per cent. By 1991/2 this had further increased to 32 per cent. This increase in the BLSN states' collective share is, in part, a product of the relatively high growth rates experienced by Botswana, which, after South Africa, currently commands the largest portion of the Pool (15 per cent of total SACU revenue in 1992/3). Another significant factor behind South Africa's declining share is the impact of changes in the domestic tax structure, with a move away from sales taxes (included in SACU) towards value added tax (excluded from SACU).

Furthermore, the crises of the 1980s have meant that the overall size of the Pool has been relatively stagnant over the recent past, a trend that has not yet been substantially reversed in the 1990s. This situation is exacerbated by planned reductions that will take place in the Common External Tariff, necessitated by GATT/WTO agreements.[19] Under the existing SACU Agreement the impact of these reductions, in terms of loss of revenue, will not be passed on to the BLSN states which would be protected by the stabilisation factor.

Against the increasing share of the Common Revenue Pool accruing to BLSN must be weighed the substantial benefits that South Africa derives from its mem-

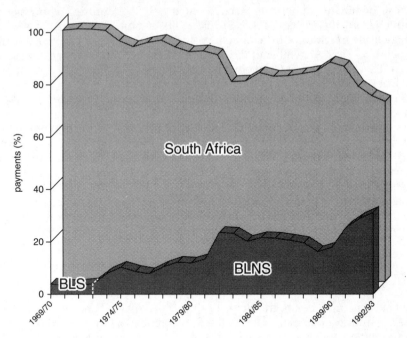

Figure 10.2   *Percentage of SACU revenue accruing to each member state*

bership of the Union. During the latter years of the apartheid era the single most important advantage of the SACU was the (geo)political dividend of South Africa having established and formal links with independent African states (Gibb 1997). In addition, the SACU was a major conduit for 'sanctions-busting'. With these factors no longer relevant, the biggest benefit to South Africa today arises from the existence of a captive market for its internationally uncompetitive exports. Although two studies commissioned by the South African government (Margo Commission 1987; McCarthy 1985) argue that there is little economic justification for the continuation of the SACU, most commentators disagree (Mayer and Zarenda 1994). The Union remains vital to South African capital, accounting for approximately 25 per cent of manufacturing exports (Gibb 1993). Furthermore, total South African exports to SACU in 1994 amounted to R13.8 bn whereas imports stood at only R3.4 bn (Burton 1995). South Africa therefore ran a trade surplus with the SACU of over R10 bn, which compares with its overall national deficit of R2.1 bn (*ibid.*).

The negotiations for a reconstituted SACU began in November 1994. A Customs Union Task Team, consisting of officials from all five member states, was mandated to negotiate on behalf of the ministers of SACU (Thomas 1995). Not unsurprisingly, the principal difficulty concerns renegotiating the revenue-sharing formula (*Business Day* 1995: 3). The South African Department of Finance has called for a 'clean formula', with any additional payments destined for the BLSN countries coming from the South African budget as regional aid (*Cape Times* 1995). In other words, the BLSN states would receive only their portion of the Revenue Pool with no enhancement factor. Pretoria has argued that an industrial development strategy should replace the revenue contributed under the enhancement/stabilisation agreements. However, the proposal for a development fund threatens the interests of those dominant rentier-elite fractions in the BLSN countries who have long accommodated themselves to the SACU, whilst simultaneously being read as a strategy likely to reinforce the competitive edge of South African capital. It is therefore being resisted. A member of the South African negotiating team complained to us that 'They [the other SACU members] have the world of time...they are dragging their feet because the old formula is advantageous to them'.[20]

There is more common ground on the question of institutionalising and democratising SACU. At present, it is administered on an informal and *ad hoc* basis with no permanent secretariat or officials. The BLSN states justifiably complain that they have no power or even influence in the formulation of policies regulating industrial and trade issues. Whilst the conversion of SACU into a formal organisation with some kind of permanent secretariat has been supported by all five member states, the contentious issue here rests with the level of autonomy and the formal powers to be granted to such an authority (as well as its location). In this context, the BLSN countries are demanding an arrangement under which all SACU governments have an *equal* say in the governing body (see Leistner 1995).

Conclusions

It will be some time before the shape of the arrangements between SACU, SADC, COMESA and external blocs such as the European Union are worked out (and no such 'resolution' will ever be total or able to contain all the historically derived disputes). In particular, the extent to which the formal fiscal integration represented by SACU might be extended to the region as a whole, and the future possibility of SACU as some kind of potential 'integration core' to SADC, remain open questions. What can be noted is that, until the on-going SACU renegotiation is settled, implementation of the SADC trade protocol will be impeded. This chapter has emphasised that regional integration in southern Africa is hostage to certain contradictions and vulnerabilities. In turn, these are elements of the wider regional conjuncture that have been well documented by historians – a legacy of profoundly uneven development and the drawn-out and violent struggle for decolonisation in southern Africa. To these should be added the (congenitally partial and incomplete) nature of the South African transition and the existence of a regional and global political economy in which conspicuous consumption, corruption and a certain (neo-liberal) version of 'development' are hegemonic.[21]

Furthermore, in southern Africa the discourse and practice of integration are (as elsewhere) largely the product of certain fractions of the state elites. This shapes its parameters and much of its substantive content. We have already noted that the discourse of integration presupposes sovereignty. Although taken for granted or naturalised in many accounts, the claim by states that they possess something called sovereignty must be continuously reinforced by a set of actions. Actions as diverse as the policing of borders, participation in international fora, recognition, 'development' and education all play their role in this social activity. Amongst other things, our brief review of SADC, COMESA and SACU indicates that a formal commitment to, and participation in, 'integration' might be read as a part of the set of processes by which *sovereignty* is *confirmed*. Recognition of this enables a richer understanding of SADC in particular.[22] Specifically, the way that diplomatic activity (the *perfomativity* mentioned earlier in this chapter) aids the reproduction-legitimisation of the state is striking. For example, at a SADC summit, Angolan ministers are uncontested embodiments of the Angolan government's sovereignty. But within the geopolitical space called Angola, government forces, the insurgent movements of UNITA and FLEC,[23] foreign oil companies, mercenaries and, at various times, Cuban and South African troops have all invoked sovereign authority. This tension (between *de jure* and *de facto* sovereignty) is particularly evident in such a case. But Angola should be seen as an extreme form of a wider phenomenon, whereby, as Weber (1995: 129) argues, sovereignty should be thought of not as an essential, fixed category but rather as operating within the logics of discourse and simulation. She notes how:

> In an order of simulation, what a state must do in order to be sovereign is control the simulation of its 'source' of sovereign authority and simulate a boundary...which marks the range of its legitimate powers and competencies.

As a key example, she cites the way diplomatic cultures claim to be sovereign voices of states:

> Implicit in the notion that diplomats offer justifications to interpretive communities is the assumption that the state for whom the diplomat speaks is also already fully constituted as a sovereign identity (Weber 1995: 5).

Therefore, in so far as the discourse/practice of regional integration in forms such as SADC diplomacy presupposes the existence of sovereignty, the latter is inscribed (or, as Weber would claim, *simulated*) through it.

This means that the widespread idea that regional integration is a challenge to state sovereignty, or that the persistence of the latter limits the scope for integration, requires considerable revision. Our examination of SADC shows how the converse can be the case; that is, formal participation in SADC is another way whereby states seek to confirm, fix and secure the appearance and power of 'sovereignty'. Rather like the boundaries and colour schemes of political maps, participation in fora such as SADC is a way in which the state is actively *represented* as a real, solid, omnipresent authority. In doing so, the fact that it is a contested, socially constructed (not simply natural) object is obscured, and states would have us take them for granted as the natural objects of governance and politics. The reality, of course, is that the state may best be understood less as a pre-given and omnipresent thing than as itself the consequence of the repeated performances which seek to impress the tangibility of states on subject populations. Sometimes this performance takes the form of quite straightforward domination: the actions of police, armies and tax inspectors. More often, though, it is much more subtle and requires ideological mobilisation, the construction of hegemony and a sense of legitimacy. It is in this respect that we can make better sense of the participation of southern African states in a 'collective' development community.

We have also noted that it is possible to discern a history (or genealogy) of the different formats that integration has taken. Our work on SACU – one of the longest established regional trade formations in the world – indicates how its rhetoric and claim of development evolved from an imperial discourse of trusteeship. A significant feature of this is that the discourse of development – as articulated by SACU after 1969 – proclaims its *difference* from colonial discourse (i.e. SACU prior to the independence of Botswana, Lesotho and Swaziland) whilst structurally reproducing many of the colonially derived relations. Revealed quite starkly in our analysis of SACU, such a strategy has been a much wider feature of discourses of development.[24] In this respect, we join those, such as Crush (1995) and Tapscott (1995), who argue that historicising 'development' in southern Africa can cast its claims, ideological occlusions and amnesias into critical relief. At the least, such a history can remind those who would narrate the story of southern African integration that it still tends to have a plot from which the mass of the people are excluded.[25]

Notes

1   The best overall guide to the literature is the comprehensive annotated bibliography in Pennetta and Di Statsi (1995). Amidst many accounts of aspects of SADCC/SADC, a few do stand out for theoretical and empirical contents: Anglin (1983); C. B. Thompson (1985, 1986); L. Thompson (1991); Tsie (1996) and Lee (1989). Although quite brief, Weisfelder's (1989, 1991) accounts have proven suggestive for our analysis. Two quasi-official but useful accounts, published by the secretariat, are Chipeta and Davies (1993) and Mandaza and Tostensen (1994). For an attempt to think about SADCC through the framework of integration theory (functionalism, neo-functionalism, etc.), see Abegunrin (1990).

2   South Africa has an electrified fence (constructed in the 1980s) along its border with Mozambique and along part of its Zimbabwean border. Until 1990 both fences carried a lethal voltage; they have since been turned down to a painful, but non-lethal 'detection mode'.

3   Though it must be largely beyond our scope here, the foundational status of sovereignty inside notions of integration demands critical scepticism. For a deconstruction of sovereignty's self-claims and foundations, see Weber (1995). In a related sense, we must recognise (as this chapter does) that 'regional integration' is a project of state elites. Regionalism may also be read – in post-structuralist terminology – as a *discourse*. Therefore, a *genealogy* of regionalism becomes possible. For a primer on this, see Jayasuriya (1994). We shall comment again on the discourse of regional integration in the conclusion.

4   These are the Southern African Centre for Co-operation in Agricultural Research (SACCAR) in Botswana and the Southern African Transport and Communications Commission (SATCC) in Mozambique. The distribution of sectoral co-ordination in 1996 was as follows: Botswana – agriculture and natural resources research and training plus livestock production and animal disease control; Mozambique – culture and information; Zambia – employment and labour plus mining; Angola – energy; Lesotho – environment and land management plus tourism; South Africa – finance and investment; Zimbabwe – food, agriculture and natural resources; Swaziland – human resources development; Tanzania – industry and trade; Malawi – inland fisheries, forestry and wildlife; Namibia— marine fisheries and resources. Mauritius joined SADC in 1995 and was allocated the tourism sector in early 1997. In turn, Lesotho,which had previously been responsible for this sector, has been allocated the new sector of water. However, in the main, the current sectoral portfolios reflect continuity with those under SADCC.

5   Although the mid-twentieth century colonial economy of southern Africa was (in certain respects) more functionally integrated than today's, its operation and slow disintegration, including the establishment and then break-up of the Central Africa Federation (1953–63) left bitter legacies and bolstered disparities. Amongst these were a reinforcement of the relative underdevelopment of Northern Rhodesia and Nyasaland at the expense of Southern Rhodesia and an enhancement of white Southern Rhodesian political confidence (see Bowman, 1968, 1971; Martin, 1990). On the legacy of resentments generated by the Federation (which was, of course, swiftly followed by Rhodesian UDI), a Zimbabwean diplomat recounted the anecdote about a Zambian politician visiting Harare, who, when shown around the parliament building said: 'It's our parliament! We built it!'. 'Such mentalities', we were informed; 'play a very important role' (interview, Gaborone, 11 March 1996). See Sidaway (1998) for more on SADC in colonial and post-colonial contexts.

6   Interview, Gaborone, 13 March 96.

7   *ibid.*

8   In the terms of the 1992 treaty, the Council of Ministers is responsible for the oversight of 'the functioning and development of SADC' and 'the implementation of the policies of SADCC and the proper execution of its programmes'.

9   Interview, Gaborone, 13 March 96.

10   An initial meeting of the Department – attended by regional heads of state and the SADC Executive Secretary – took place in Luanda in October 1996. It was hoped that Jonas Savimbi would attend and the Angolan 'peace process' move forward. Savimbi did not show up (see: *Summary of World Broadcasts* AL/2733 A/1 3 Oct 96). See Cilliers (1995) for an account of debates in South Africa and SADC following the dissolution of the Frontline states. The article includes a brief but informative account of the Inter-State Defence and Security Committee, first established in 1983 as an informal structure within the Frontline states, but which has survived the latter and now includes Lesotho, Malawi and Swaziland. Specific instances of co-ordinated diplomatic action between South Africa, Botswana and Zimbabwe (following the 'royal coup' in Lesotho in August 1994 and during Renamo's threatened withdrawal from the Mozambican elections in October 1995) indicate a working – if not always smooth – capacity for 'crisis' mediation.

11 This and the following two quotations are taken from the text of a report by the South African news agency SAPA. *Summary of World Broadcasts* AL/2701 A/2, 27 August 1996.

12 See *Summary of World Broadcasts* LW/0488 WA/1, 13 August 1996.

13 Interview, Gaborone, 6 March 1996.

14 Quoted in *Business Day*, Johannesburg, 16 February 1996.

15 For example, South Africa has made overtures towards the possibility of an Indian Ocean Community. For press coverage, see AFP (1995) and Bhatia (1995). A more detailed account of the history of the proposal and its prospects is given in Campbell and Scerri (1995). Although it does not cover the Indian Ocean ideas, Mwase (1995) provides a valuable overview of the array of Southern (and Eastern) African regional schemes and the relationships between them. For accounts of the relations between the EU, SADC and South Africa, see Holland (1995a, 1995b) and Kibble *et al.* (1995).

16 The literature on SACU is enormous. As with SADCC/SADC, Pennata and di Statsi (1995) is a useful guide. Particularly useful accounts are Cobbe (1980), Gibb (1997), Maasdorp (1982), Guma (1987) and Kumar (1990).

17 We adopt the convention of using the abbreviation BLSN to refer to Botswana, Lesotho and Swaziland and (after 1990) Namibia.

18 See Ellis (1996) for some reflections on corruption mediated through South Africa.

19 Under the terms of GATT and WTO agreements, South Africa is now obliged to make a number of tariff adjustments. These include the rationalisation of its tariff structure from 10,000 tariff lines to 6,000; the replacement of all remaining quantitative and quota regimes with *ad valorem* duties; reduction of the maximum tariff from 100 per cent to 30 per cent (with the exception of motor cars – from 100 to 50 per cent – and textiles). In addition, the GATT/WTO requires export subsidies to be phased out, resulting in the termination of the General Export Incentive Scheme (GEIS), a central plank of South Africa's export-orientated policy in the 1990s. Although these changes will be phased in over a transition period of between 5 and 8 years, they nonetheless represent a significant commitment to reduce overall levels of protectionism and reinforce the pressure on the South Africans to squeeze the best possible terms out of the SACU renegotiation.

20 Interview, Pretoria, 1 April 1996.

'21 For further reflections on this in southern Africa, see Saul (1993), Sidaway and Power (1995, 1998), Sidaway (1998), plus Ellis (1996).

22 Sidaway (1997) offers a deeper exploration of this than we are able to develop here.

23 UNITA: The *Uniao para a Independencia Total de Angola* (an insurgent movement operating mostly in southern Angola which received large-scale South African and CIA support in the 1980s) and FLEC: *Frente de Libertação do Enclave de Cabinda* (a group of insurgent movements that operate in the oil-rich enclave of Cabinda).

24 General accounts of this are Cowen and Shenton (1996) and Escobar (1995). For a stimulating evaluation of both, see Brown (1996). A good critical account of the South African conjuncture, which reads development as both the possibility of progressive transformation and a hegemonic discourse, see Bond and Mayekiso (1996).

25 Vale (1996: 18) makes some suggestive comments on what he terms 'regionalism from below', noting how, for example:

> Well-organized social movements have recognized the power of regional links. When, for instance, Zimbabwe's President Robert Mugabe savaged the common law rights of gays in that country, South Africa'a vociferous and confident gay community took to the streets. Their organized protests in Johannesburg during the SADC heads of government meeting almost entirely silenced Mugabe...'.

For Vale, 'A nascent regional civil society is developing a transnational momentum' and:

> By offering solutions to people on the ground, the myths which created the region's current maps are being destroyed; new forms of regionalism are being probed; and the maps which have defined and dominated the lives of the region's people are being challenged. (pp 17–19).

A fuller account of this would require a nuanced treatment of a variety of pre-colonial, colonial, anti- and post-colonial linkages and transformations.

References

Abegunrin, O. (1990) *Economic Dependence and Regional Co-operation in Southern Africa: SADCC and South Africa in Confrontation*. Edwin Mellen Press, New York.

AFP (1995) 'India Backs Ocean-rim Trade Bloc', *Star*, 8 Johannesburg. 13 December 1995.

Africa Confidential (1995) 'Still the Boss: Regional Co-operation, Economic and Military, Will Continue to be Dominated by South Africa', 36(17): 3–4. London.

African Development Bank (1993) *Economic Integration in Southern Africa*, Vol. 1, African Development Bank, Abidjan.

Anglin, D.G. (1983) 'Economic Liberation and Regional Co-operation in Southern Africa: SADCC and the PTA', *International Organisation* 37(4): 681–711.

Asanke, S. K. B. (1991) *African Development:. Adebano Adedeji's Alternative Strategies*. Hans Zell, London.

Bhatia, S. (1995) 'Trade Focus for Indian Ocean Bloc', *Star*, Johannesburg, 19 July.

Bond, P. and Mayekiso, M. (1996) 'Developing Resistance, Resisting 'Development': Reflections from the South African Struggle', in Pantitch, L.N. (ed.) *Socialist Register 1996*. Merlin Press, London.

Bowman, L. C. (1968) 'The Subordinate State System of Southern Africa', *International Studies Quarterly* 12: 231–61.

Bowman, L. C. (1971) 'Authoritarian politics in Rhodesia', PhD thesis, Department of Politics, Brandeis University.

Brown, E. (1996) 'Deconstructing Development: Alternative Perspectives on the History of an Idea', *Journal of Historical Geography* 22(3): 333–9.

Burton, J. (1995) 'Short Paper on the Renegotiation of SACU and the Free Trade Area between RSA and the EU'. Overseas Development Agency, Pretoria, unpublished.

Business Day (1995) 'South Africa Drags Feet on Customs Reform', 14 June.

Campbell, R. G. and Scerri, M. (1995) 'The Prospects for an Indian Ocean Rim (IOP) Economic Organisation', *The South African Journal of International Affairs*, 19: 11–37.

Cape Times (1995) 'Customs Union Talks Stall', 8 June.

Cattaneo, N. (1990) 'Piece of Paper or Paper of Peace: The Southern African Customs Union Agreement', *International Affairs Bulletin*, 11: 543–64.

Chipeta, G. and Davies, R. (1993) *Regional Relations and Cooperation Post-Apartheid: A Macroframework Study Report*. SADC, Gaborone.

Cilliers, J. (1995) 'The Evolving Security Architecture in Southern Africa', *African Security Review* 4(5): 30–47.

Cobbe, J. H. (1980) 'Integration Among Unequals: the Southern African Customs Union and Development', *World Development* 8(4): 329–36.

Cowen, M. P. and Shenton, R. W. (1996) *Doctrines of Development*. Routledge, London.

Crush, J. (1995) 'Introduction: Imagining development' in Crush, J. (ed.) *Power of Development*. Routledge, London and New York.

Davies, R. (1994) '*The South African Customs Union (SACU): Background and Possible Negotiating Issues Facing a Democratic Government*', Working paper, Centre for Southern African Studies, University of Western Cape, South Africa.

Ellis, S. (1996) 'Africa and International Corruption: the Strange Case of South Africa and Seychelles', *African Affairs* 95, 165–96.

Escobar, A. (1995) *Encountering Development: The Making and Unmaking of the Third World*. Princeton University Press, Princeton, NJ.

Ettinger, S. J. (1974) 'The Economics of the Custom Union between Botswana, Lesotho and Swaziland;, Unpublished PhD Thesis, University of Michigan, Ann Arbor, MI.

Financial Gazette, The (1994) 'Media Circus with Muckraker', Harare, 3 February.

Gibb, R. A. (1993) 'A Common Market for Post-apartheid Southern Africa: Prospects and Problems', *Southern African Geographical Journal*, 75: 28–35.

Gibb, R. A. (1997) 'Regional Integration in Post-Apartheid Southern Africa: the Case of Re-negotiating the Southern African Customs Union', *Journal of Southern African Studies*, 23(1): 67–86.

Gibb, R. A. and Michalak, W. (eds) (1994) *Continental Trading Blocs: the Growth of Regionalism in the World Economy*. John Wiley, Chichester.

Gqumbule, D. (1996) 'Row Looms over SA's Regional Trade Surplus', *Star*, Johannesburg, 12 February 1996.

Guma, X. P. (1987) 'The Revised Southern African Customs Union Agreement: An Appraisal', *South African Journal of Economics* 58(1): 63–73.

Hartrack, M. (1996) 'SA 'May Ruin its Markets', *Business Day*, Johannesburg, 16 February 1996.

Holland, M. (1995a) 'South Africa, SADC, and the European Union: Matching Bilateral with Regional Policies', *Journal of Modern African Studies*, 33(2): 263–83.

Holland, M. (1995b) *European Union Common Foreign Policy. From EPC to CFSP. Joint Action and South Africa*. St Martins Press, New York.

Iheduru, O. (1996) 'Post-apartheid South Africa and its Neighbours: a Maritime Transport Perspective', *Journal of Modern African Studies* 34(1): 1–26.

Indian Ocean Newsletter, The (1995) 'Southern Africa: Sparks fly at Summit', No. 683 September, Paris.

Jayasuriya, K. (1994) 'Singapore: the Politics of Regional Definition', *The Pacific Review,* 7(4): 411–20.

Kibble, S., Goodison, P. and Tsie, B. (1995) 'The Uneasy Triangle – South Africa, Southern Africa and Europe in the Post-Apartheid Era', *International Relations* 12(4): 141–161.

Kumar, U. (1990) 'Southern African Customs Union and BLS-countries (Botswana, Lesotho and Swaziland)', *Journal of World Trade,* 24(3): 31–53.

Lee, M.C. (1989) *SADCC: The Political Economy of Development in Southern Africa.* Winston-Derek Publishers Ltd, Nashville, TN.

Leistner, E. (1992) South African Chamber of Business discussion document commissioned by the SACOB on South Africa's options for future relations with Southern Africa and the European Community. Annex in Club de Bruxelles (ed.) *The Future of Relations between the EC and Southern Africa.* Club de Bruxelles, Brussels.

Leistner, E. (1995) 'Renegotiating the Southern Africa Customs Union (SACU)', *Africa Institute Bulletin* 35(2): 4–5.

Lipson, C. (1991) 'Why Are Some Iinternational Agreements Informal?', *International Organisation* 45(4): 495–538.

Maasdorp, G. (1982) 'The Southern African Customs Union: An Assessment', *Journal of Contemporary African Studies* 1: 81–112.

Maasdorp, G. (1989) 'A Century of Customs Unions in Southern Africa', paper presented at a conference of the Economic Society of South Africa, Johannesburg, 6–7 September.

Maasdorp, G. (1993) 'The Advantages and Disadvantages of Current Regional Institutions for Integration', in Baker, P.H., Boraine A. and Krafchik W. (eds) *South Africa and the World Economy in the 1990s.* David Philip, Cape Town.

Maasdorp, G. and Whiteside, A. (1993) *Rethinking Economic Co-operation in Southern Africa: Trade and Investment.* Konrad-Adenauer Foundation, Johannesburg.

Mandaza I. (1991) 'Did Chogm Undermine SADCC?' *Southern African Political and Economic Monthly* 52: 3–9.

Mandaza, I. and Tostensen, A. (1994) *Southern Africa: In Search of a Common Future,* SADC, Gaborone.

Margo Commission (1987) *Report of the Commission of Inquiry into the Tax Structure of the Republic of South Africa,* WPC-88. Government Printer, Pretoria.

Martin, W. G. (1990) 'Region Formation Under Crisis Conditions: South vs Southern Africa in the Interwar Period', *Journal of Southern African Studies* 16(1): 112–38.

Mayer, M. and Zarenda, H. (1994) *The Southern Africa Customs Union: A Review of Costs and Benefits.* Development Bank of Southern Africa, Policy Working Paper 19, Halfway House, South Africa.

McCarthy, C. L. (1985) 'Southern African Customs Union', report prepared for the Central Economic Advisory Service, South Africa, unpublished.

McCarthy C. L. (1992) 'Revenue Distribution and Economic Development in the Southern African Customs Union', *The South African Journal of Economics.* 62(3): 167–87.

Meyns, P. (1995) 'Time to Decide: Rethinking the Institutional Framework of Regional Co-operation in Southern Africa', in Spanjer, H.J. and Vale, P. (eds) *Bridges to the Future: Prospects for Peace and Security in Southern Africa.* Westview Press, Boulder, CO.

Mfune, P. (1993) 'The Future of SADCC' in Siddiqui, R.A. (ed) *Sub-Saharan Africa: Sub-continent in Transition.* Avebury, Aldershot.

Mwase, N. (1995) 'Economic Integration for Development in Eastern and Southern Africa: Assessment and Prospects, *The Round Table,* 336: 477–93.

Ndovi, V. (1996) 'Another View: Malawi's Diplomatic Quandary', *Daily Times* 7, Blantyre, 2 May 1996.

Pennetta, P. and Di Statsi, A. (1995) *'Le Organizzazioni Economiche Regionali Africane: Commenti, Documenti, Bibliografia 1. Le Organizzazioni dell'Africa Australe',* (S.A.C.U and S.A.D.C.), Edizioni Scientifiche, Naples.

Peta, B. (1996) 'SA Punitive Duty on Transit Cargo Illegal', *The Financial Gazette,* 14 March 1996: 2.

Polhmus, J. H. (1992) 'Zimbabwe's Response to Change in South Africa', in Etherington, N. (ed.) *Peace, Politics and Violence in the New South Africa.* Hans Zell Publishers, London.

Republic of South Africa (1969) *Customs Union Agreement, and Memorandum of Understanding, between the Governments of the Republic of South Africa, Botswana, Lesotho, and Swaziland.* Republic of South Africa Treaty Series No. 8/1969, Pretoria.

SADCC (1981a) *Memorandum of Understanding on the Institutions of the Southern African Development Co-ordination Conference.* SADCC, Salisbury.

SADCC (1981b) *Southern African Development Co-ordination: from Dependence and Poverty Toward Economic Liberation.* SADCC, Gaborone.

SADCC (1992) 'SADCC/PTA Cooperation'. Note from the secretariat [SADCC/CM/2/92/3], SADCC, Gaborone.

SADC (1993) *Declaration Treaty and Protocol of the SADC.* SADC, Gaborone.

SADC (1995a) *SADC – Procedures, Organisation and Consultative Agreements. Note from the Secretariat.* SADC, Gaborone.

SADC (1995b) *Report of the Council of Ministers meeting held in Lilongwe, Republic of Malawi, 31 January 1995.* SADC, Gaborone.

Saul, J. S. (1993) *Recolonization and Resistance: Southern Africa in the 1990s.* Africa World Press, Trenton, NJ.

Sidaway, J. D. (1998) 'The (Geo)politics of Regional Integration: the Example of the Southern African Development Community after the new South Africa', *Environment and Planning D: Society and Space.*

Sidaway, J. D. and Power, M. (1998) ' "Sex and Violence on the Wild Frontiers": the Aftermath of State Socialism in the Periphery,' in Pickles, J. and Smith, A. (eds) *Theorizing Transition: the Political Economy of Transformation in Post-Communist Societies.* Routledge, London.

Sidaway, J. D. and Power, M. (1995) 'Sociospatial Transformations in the 'Postsocialist' Periphery: the Case of Maputo, Mozambique', *Environment and Planning A* 27: 1463–91.

Simon, D. (1991) 'Namibia in Southern Africa: the Regional Implications of Independence', *Tijdschrift voor Economische en Sociale Geografie* 82(5): 367–76.

Summary of World Broadcasts, (various issues) BBC monitoring, Caversham.

Tapscott, C. (1995) 'Changing Discourses of Development in South Africa' in Crush.

Thomas, R. (1995) 'South and Southern Africa: Restructuring Economic Co-operation Initiatives to Encourage Growth and Diversity', Development Bank of Southern Africa, Halfway House, South Africa, unpublished.

Thompson, C. B. (1985) *Challenge to Imperialism: the Frontline States in the Liberation of Zimbabwe.* Zimbabwe Publishing House, Harare.

Thompson, C. B. (1986) 'Regional Economic Policy under Crisis Conditions: the Case of Agriculture within SADCC', *Journal of Southern African Studies* 13(1): 82–100.

Thompson, C. B. (1986) *Harvests under Fire: Regional Co-operation for Food Security in Southern Africa.* Zed, London.

Thompson, L. (1991) 'SADCC: Part of a Whole or Whole of a Part?', *International Affairs Bulletin* 15(1): 59–71.

Tsie, B. (1996) 'States and Markets in the Southern African Development Community (SADC): Beyond the Neo-liberal Paradigm', *Journal of Southern African Studies* 22(1): 75–98.

Vale, P. (1996) *Southern Africa: Exploring a Peace Dividend.* Catholic Institute for International Relations, London.

Walters, J. (1989) 'Re-negotiating Dependency: the Case of the Southern African Customs Union', *Journal of Common Market Studies* 28(1): 30–52.

Weber, C. (1995) *Simulating Sovereignty: Intervention, the State and Symbolic Exchange.* Cambridge University Press, Cambridge.

Weeks, J. (1996) 'Regional Co-operation and Southern African Development', *Journal of Southern African Studies* 22(1): 99–117.

Weggoro, N. C. (1995) *Effects of Regional Economic Integration in Southern Africa and the Role of the Republic of South Africa: a Study of Project Co-ordination Approach in Industry and Trade in SADCC/SADC'.* Verlag Koster, Berlin.

Weisfelder, R. F. (1989) 'SADCC as a Counter-dependency Strategy: How Much Collective Clout?' in Keller, E.J. and Picard, L.A. (eds) *South Africa in Southern Africa – Domestic Change and International Conflict.* Lynne Rienner, Boulder, CO.

Weisfelder, R. F. (1991) 'Collective Foreign Policy Decision-making within SADCC: Do Regional Objectives Alter National Policies', *Africa Today* 38(1): 5–17.

C.
Population and Mobility

11 Obscuring History? Contemporary Patterns of Regional Migration to South Africa[1]

SALLY PEBERDY

'Aliens put big strain on SA' (*Sowetan*, 11 January 1995); 'Closing door on illegals: "Back-door" aliens pouring in' (*Star*, 11 August 1995); '28500 illegal border crossers held in '95' (*Star*, 23 January 1996); 'Move on illegals triggers fear of huge influx' (*Business Day*, 5 June 1996); 'SA – twilight world for many: There has been criticism that the Government is hard only on Africans' (*Sowetan*, 1 July 1996); 'SADC rush for permanent residence in SA' (*Star*, 16 September 1996); 'ID documents: reports of police extortion, beatings in Sandton' (*Star*, 18 October 1996); 'Influx of illegal immigrants demands active SA control' (*Sowetan*, 23 October 1996); 'And still aliens flood SA' (*Star*, 14 November 1996); 'Electric border fence is no deterrent to desperate Mozambicans' (*Star*, 6 December 1996); '135,000 illegals sent home, but more stay' (*Star*, 9 January 1997); 'Authorities battle to stem flow of illegals who flock to SA for better life' (*Star*, 20 January 1997).

Introduction

> This situation has been further aggravated by the influx of illegal aliens from the neighbouring countries in particular, where conditions of economic deprivation and depression occur and who are consequently prepared to work for meagre wages... With whatever empathy and understanding one may judge the underlying reasons and motivation why people are compelled to leave their fatherland and to seek refuge here, the interests of the RSA and her citizens and legal residents must be our first and foremost consideration... (Mangosuthu Buthelezi, Minister of Home Affairs, 10 March 1995).

The words of the Minister of Home Affairs and the selection of headlines above illustrate the current language, content and tone of popular public debates on regional immigration to South Africa. Regional immigrants are portrayed as unskilled, impoverished peasants seeking gold on the streets of Gauteng. At the same time, immigration to South Africa is presented as a new, growing, illegal and negative phenomenon, and largely (southern) African. The 'influx' is linked to political liberalisation in 1990 and the formation of the 'new' South Africa in 1994. However, these public debates obscure how the historical legacy of the structures governing immigration, and the legislation, have shaped patterns of regional migration. They also fail to acknowledge the nature and extent of immigration from the region and, more recently, the rest of Africa.

Surprisingly little research has been undertaken on immigration and regional migration to South Africa (other than to the gold mines). Studies of the history of documented immigration to South Africa, with the exception of Bradlow (1978), are essentially descriptive accounts of the immigration of particular white population groups.[2] A number of largely speculative studies and papers on contemporary immigration patterns have been published in the past two years.[3]

This chapter will look at the history of the legislation that currently governs immigration to South Africa as the nation redefines itself and its relationship with southern Africa. It argues that the legislative frameworks which have governed and govern immigration, as well as the patterns of immigration that have emerged from them, are deeply rooted in South Africa's history. The chapter concludes with an exploration of the impact of this legislative history on contract, documented and undocumented migration from the region.

The Contemporary Legislative Framework

Immigration to South Africa in 1997 is regulated by the Aliens Control Act, 1991 (Act No. 96). In an attempt to remove the more draconian sections and to bring it, at least partially, in line with the new Constitution the Act was amended in 1995 (Act No. 76, Aliens Control Amendment Act, 1995)(Klaaren 1996, forthcoming; Katz 1997; Kotzé and Hill 1997). South Africa has no statute governing the admission of refugees. They are currently admitted on special permits issued under the 1991 Aliens Control Act (Section 41). A refugee Bill is currently being drafted by the Department of Home Affairs.

In what has been called the 'two gates' policy (Cooper 1995 cited in Crush 1997), im/migrants from the region can 'legally' enter South Africa under the Aliens Control Act 1991 as contract workers or on temporary or permanent residence permits.[4] Contract workers are allowed to enter for fixed, but usually repeated, periods under agreements and treaties with neighbouring states and are mainly employed in the mining and agricultural sectors. Documented im/migrants may also enter on immigration permits (previously permanent residence permits) or temporary residence permits issued for visitor, business, work, work seeking, study, or medical purposes. People living close to the borders may hold 'local passports' which allow movement within specified distances of the border.

Non-South Africans may also be in South Africa as undocumented im/migrants (usually referred to as 'illegal immigrants' or 'illegal aliens').[5] These are people who have crossed the border without having their documents approved, without documents, or who have overstayed or exceeded the terms of their permits.

The Genesis of Legislation

The introduction of the Aliens Control Act in 1991 was, like many statutes introduced in the closing years of apartheid, an attempt to entrench the past in the future (Crush and Peberdy forthcoming). The Act is drawn directly from the 1913 Immigrants Regulation Act (Act No. 22), as amended in 1972, and the 1937 Aliens Act (Act No. 1), and their amendments. The intent of both of these Acts was to exclude specific 'racial' groups from entering South Africa and to set frameworks for control and regulation of the immigration process.[6]

The 1913 Immigrants Regulation Act[7]
Following the formation of the Union in 1910, the new government sought to introduce immigration legislation. After three years of wrangling with the provinces and the colonial British government, the 1913 Act was introduced to provide compre-

hensive legislation to deal with all aspects of immigration. It was intended to facilitate white immigration and provide a means to prevent non-white immigration, particularly from India and Mauritius. The growing Indian population in the Union was a cause of concern to the government, and attempts by provincial governments to discourage Indians from remaining in, and coming to, South Africa had been unsuccessful.[8] Introducing the Bill, the Minister said:

> It was no use hiding their light under a bushel, for they all knew it was the intention of South Africa to exclude Asiatics [Indians]...they must make it clear that they deemed the European civilisation the desirable one from which to seek progress and advancement of the country (*Hansard* 30 April 1913 col. 2050–51)

To ensure the exclusion of non-whites, the Act stated that the Minister could deem 'any person or class of persons...on economic grounds or on account of standards or habits of life to be unsuited to the requirements of the Union' (Section 4(1)(a)). The day the Act was passed, the Minister deemed all non-white immigrants to be 'unsuited to the requirements of the Union' and thus prohibited them (Bradlow 1978).

The Act also set out other criteria to determine whether a (white) person would be allowed entry or be denied entry and declared a prohibited immigrant (Section 4). Criteria of exclusion included being: likely to become a charge on the state; undesirable for political reasons; having a criminal record; a prostitute or living off the earnings of prostitution; mentally or physically disabled; or the carrier of a 'loathsome' or 'contagious' disease. Potential immigrants were also required to read and write a European language (which after lobbying by the Jewish Board of Deputies, included Yiddish).

To ensure the supply of black contract labour from the region to the mining industry, an exemption clause was introduced (Section 5(d)). This allowed the Minister to exempt people entering under treaties or agreements with other states or territories (who came from South of latitude 22 degrees South) from meeting the terms of Section 4. Those allowed entry to South Africa under this clause were not allowed to claim domicile, permanent residence or to change employers (under later amendments). The clause established that non-white regional migration could persist, as long as it was not permanent and was in the interests of the South African state and industry. At the same time it entrenched and formalised the migrant labour system in South Africa's legal framework (Crush and Peberdy, forthcoming).

The 1913 Act therefore established that immigrants to South Africa could only be white, making it impossible for non-whites, regardless of their country of origin, to formalise their status in South Africa unless they entered as contract workers. The criteria of exclusion have essentially, with the exception of Section 4(1)(a) and the requirement to speak a European language, been retained in the 1991 Act.

The 1930 Immigration Quota Act (Act No. 8)
Following the end of World War I, new racial fears emerged, focused on the Jewish community. At the end of the war Jewish immigration from Eastern Europe started to increase (Office of Census and Statistics (OCS) 1922: 163; 1924: 169).[9] Anti-semitic fears of an 'influx' of Jewish immigrants were strengthened by the introduction of a Quota Act in 1921 by the United States, which restricted immigration from Eastern and Southern Europe.

Between 1920 and 1924 the Union government secretly used administrative means and Section 4(1)(a) of the 1913 Act to exclude East European Jewish immigrants, as the government 'was against any migration of fresh Jews'.[10] Although these restrictions were effective, they were lifted prior to the elections of 1924 as parties vied for the Jewish vote. Anti-semitic fears did not abate, but were bolstered by a subsequent increase in Jewish immigration from Eastern Europe and the introduction of a more restrictive Quota Act in the United States in 1924.

The government responded in 1930 by introducing the Immigration Quota Act. This allowed unlimited (white) immigration from West and Northern Europe, Spain, Portugal and North America. East European and other countries were given a quota of 50 places a year, allocated by an Immigrants Selection Board. The 1930 Act was effective. In 1929, about 2,438 East Europeans had entered South Africa, by 1932 new arrivals had fallen to 636 (OCS 1936: 938).

The 1937 Aliens Control Act

The rise of fascism in 1930s Europe led to a new wave of Jewish immigration from Germany and Holland to South Africa. These immigrants met the criteria of the 1913 Act and were not excluded by the 1930 Act. In 1935, led by the head of the South African Legation in Berlin, the Ministers in Europe (the equivalent of Ambassadors) initiated a discussion around the increasing number of applications to emigrate to South Africa that they were receiving from Jewish people. In 1935 they sent a memorandum to the Prime Minister calling for greater restrictions on 'unassimilable immigrants' (BLO 321 PS/17/49 1935). In a private communication, the High Commissioner in London made it clear who they considered unassimilable. He stated that their intent was 'aimed at meeting the problem of the Jewish emigré...' (*ibid.* 17 January 1936).

Although the government agreed that Jewish immigration should be curtailed, it wanted to find a way to exclude German and Dutch Jews without excluding non-Jews. It did so in the 1937 Aliens Act. Under the Act, applicants had to meet certain criteria to be issued a permit which allowed them to enter South Africa and be considered for permanent residence under the 1913 Act. Applications were judged by an Immigrants Selection Board appointed by the Minister.

The most important of the criteria required the potential immigrant to be 'of good character', and 'readily assimilable with the European population of the Union', and be likely to become 'a desirable inhabitant of the Union within a reasonable period'. The use of the word 'European' excluded all non-white people from applying for a permit. Jewish immigrants could be excluded from the Union, as they were, for the most part, considered 'unassimilable'.

The Act was used immediately to deny applications from German Jews. In 1936 almost 5,500 people had arrived in South Africa from Germany and Holland, by 1938 less than 1,500 people were admitted (OCS 1940: 1046). Again, the Union government had succeeded in introducing racially exclusionary legislation which did not explicitly state its intent.[11] The conditions for a permit for permanent residence laid out in the 1937 Act, with the exception of the word European (removed in 1986), are found in the 1991 Act, and Immigrants Selection Boards continue to adjudicate applications. The Act also entrenched the word 'alien' in the vocabulary of official and public discourse to describe non-South Africans.[12]

Four issues emerge from these statutes. First, they established that legal immigration to South Africa would be white as the legislation was racially exclusionary in its intent, practice, and effect. Second, they established the procedures and Boards which would govern immigration into the 1990s. Third, they made it clear that potential immigrants did not have the same rights as citizens. Finally, they laid the basis for all subsequent legislation, including the 1991 Aliens Control Act, setting out the criteria for admission and exclusion and the relevant procedures, most of which (with some alterations) are still present in today's legislation.

The Apartheid Years

The apartheid years were marked by attempts to recruit British and European (and ironically in later years East European) semi-skilled and skilled immigrants, by fears of increasing disparities in the black:white population ratio, and by growing concern over the impact of political resistance on patterns of white emigration and immigration. Immigration fell and emigration rose in coincidence with periods of unrest, and particularly following the Sharpeville Massacre in 1960 (and the Treason Trials and imposition of the State of Emergency); the Soweto Uprising of 1976; resistance in 1986; the political changes following the unbanning of the ANC and PAC in 1990; and the elections of 1994.

No major changes were made to existing legislation in the post-war period until the 1991 Aliens Control Act was introduced (although the 1913 Act and its amendments were consolidated in the 1972 Admission of Persons to the Republic Regulation Act). However, mirroring the extension of state power in the apartheid years, amendments to the 1913 and 1937 Acts gave the state increasing control over non-South Africans living in the country ('legally' and 'illegally'). The Minister was given greater discretionary powers, particularly over deportation and the appointment of persons with the same powers of arrest, detention and removal as immigration officers, and control over movement across the border was enhanced.

The tightening of restrictions on the rights of immigrants plus the control of the state not only affected white immigrants. The introduction of the 1960 Immigration Amendment Act (Act No. 60) stipulated that legal entry could only be through a recognised border post and that all entrants must hold a passport. This mainly affected non-white migrants from the region who were less likely to have formal travel documents, could not easily enter legally and were more likely to cross the border away from official posts. The Minister's powers of delegation allowed him to designate railway officials, among others, as immigration officers (Act No. 38, 1969 Admission of Persons to the Republic Amendment Act). This assisted the control of regional migration as railways were a common means of transport for regional im/migrants entering South Africa.

In 1986, the introduction of the Admission to and Residence in the Republic Act (Act No. 53) made a major change in South Africa's immigration legislation. It removed the word 'European' from the assimilation clause of the 1937 Aliens Act, allowing non-white people to be admitted under the Act. However, the removal of the word European reflected the government's attempts to entrench apartheid rather than dismantle it, as they wanted to encourage African professionals to come in to work in the hospitals and universities of the 'homelands' (Crush and Peberdy, forthcoming).

Two other statutes passed in the apartheid years had an impact on regional im/migrants. The 1950 Population Registration Act laid the infrastructure for subsequent apartheid legislation. It compelled people to carry identity books which stated their race, and date and place of birth. Introducing the Act, the Minister stressed that it would assist in the control of illegal immigrants (Brownell, private papers). The legacy of the 1950 Act persists in post-apartheid South Africa as ID books are used by police and other officials seeking to identify undocumented im/migrants (Crush and Peberdy forthcoming; Peberdy 1997b).

The Union of South Africa declared itself a Republic in May 1961 and left the Commonwealth. In 1962 the Commonwealth Relations Act was promulgated. This redefined the term 'alien' as 'a person who is not a Union national', thus bringing British and Commonwealth citizens under the 1937 Aliens Act. The declaration of the Republic also affected the citizens of Botswana, Lesotho and Swaziland (BLS).

Previously they had been treated, and had the same rights, as Union citizens (according to 'race'). In 1963, these rights were renegotiated and citizens from the BLS states had to meet the terms of the 1913 and 1937 Acts unless they were contract workers. This led to the forced removal of women migrants from Botswana (Crush and Peberdy forthcoming: Chapter 12). Nonetheless, to maintain the supply of labour and consumers to the farms and shops of the Orange Free State, Northern Transvaal and Natal, agreements were reached regarding the movement of people in border areas (KGT 92 N9/22/2, 14 June 1963).

The legislation passed in the apartheid years reflected the centralisation of state power; eroded even further the already minimal rights of im/migrants; continued to entrench the contract labour system; was increasingly directed at the control of non-white regional im/migrants; set in place a system of identification (ID books); and radically changed the status of people entering from Botswana, Lesotho and Swaziland.

The Legislative Legacy

The majority of the criteria of inclusion and exclusion laid out in the 1913 and 1937 Acts have been retained in the 1991 Act, as have the procedures for application and adjudication and appeal, as well as arrest, detention and removal. The Immigrants Selection Boards established under the 1937 Act continue to adjudicate applications. ID books are still used to identify non-South Africans. Although the 1995 Aliens Amendment Act went some way towards bringing the Act into line with the new Constitution, the rights of im/migrants, particularly in regard to arrest, detention and removal procedures, are challenged (Klaaren forthcoming, 1996; Katz 1997; Peberdy 1997b). The new Constitution will provide some protection once challenges have been mounted, but, like the legislation, it makes distinctions between the rights of citizens and non-citizens.

Furthermore, the history of South Africa's exclusionary immigration legislation has defined the relationship of im/migrant southern Africans to the South African state. At the same time, this history has defined the processes of contract, documented and undocumented migration.

Contract Migration

Southern African contract workers have worked in South Africa's mines and farms since the turn of the century. Agreements, treaties and conventions between the South African government, the sending states and, in the case of the mining industry, the Chamber of Mines, have governed the numbers recruited and their conditions of recruitment. The distinctiveness of contract migration, and the importance of its history to the economic development of South Africa, make it difficult to do anything but provide a cursory overview.[13]

Southern Africans have been employed in South Africa's mining industry for over 150 years. Initially they came as individuals to work in the diamond mines. As the mining industry developed and diversified, workers were recruited under contract by recruiting agencies and the Chamber of Mines (Crush 1997). Since the turn of the century over 40 per cent of the labour working in South Africa's gold mines have come from outside South Africa (ibid.), the majority of them from Mozambique, Lesotho and Swaziland. In the past miners have also been recruited from Tanzania (halted at independence), Zimbabwe and Zambia (recruitment falling off in the 1960s). Malawians have also played a significant role in the mine labour force. In 1974 the Malawian government halted recruitment and withdrew almost all of the approximately 120,000 Malawians working in the mines, allowing recruitment to recommence only in 1977. By this time other sources of labour had been found and recruitment was therefore less than 20 per cent of the pre-1974 levels (Crush *et al.* 1991; Simon 1989).[14] Recruitment from Malawi was stopped again in 1988 after Malawian miners were erroneously and irrationally accused of bringing AIDS to South Africa (see Chirwa 1994).

In 1994, over 150,000 of the more than 250,000 workers in the gold mines came from outside South Africa (Crush 1997: 20). Most of them were recruited in Mozambique, Lesotho and Swaziland. This migration is significant not only for the mining industry but also for the economies of the sending countries in the region. A system of deferred pay for miners from Mozambique and Lesotho has meant that a proportion of their pay has been remitted to their government and paid to the miner on his return home. The government has accrued interest on this, and the system has ensured that a proportion of a miner's salary will be spent in his home country. In 1993, miners' remittances to Lesotho constituted over half the country's GNP. The earnings of Mozambican miners made up approximately a third of foreign exchange earnings (De Vletter 1995: 22).

Most of the southern Africans working in the agricultural sector are from Mozambique, Zimbabwe and Lesotho. The majority are undocumented migrants or use 'local passports'. The South African Labour Commission has estimated that about 100,000 non-South Africans are working in the agricultural sector (Toolo and Bethlehem 1995: 18). However, De Vletter (1995: 27) says that as many as 150,000–200,000 Mozambicans alone may be working on South Africa's farms. Little information on the employment of contract workers in the agricultural sector is available. The majority of agricultural contract workers are Mozambican. In 1994 the Mozambican Labour Office stated that approximately 20,000 Mozambicans were working under contract on the farms of the Mpumalanga and Northern Transvaal (*ibid.*)

The 1913 Immigrants Regulation Act formalised and entrenched the migrant labour system (which has sustained the mining industry) in South Africa's legislative framework (Crush and Peberdy, forthcoming). The 1991 Aliens Control Act retains the exemption clause and so continues to enshrine the contract labour system in law. Until 1986, this was the only 'legal' way for non-white people from the region to enter South Africa to work. However, unlike white people on temporary permits or on contract to the mines and other industries, these contract workers were (and are) not allowed to claim domicile, apply for permanent residence or change employers.

In 1995, the government offered mineworkers the option of applying for permanent residence. Miners who had been working in South Africa since 1986 and who had voted in the 1994 elections were offered permanent residence by the government. Of the estimated 130,000 mineworkers eligible, only 47,364 have applied for permanent residence (Crush 1997: 8). A study of the attitudes of Lesotho mineworkers to claiming permanent residence showed that there was confusion about eligibility and the rules of qualification. More importantly, however, the study showed that only 18.7 per cent of the sample said that they wanted to claim permanent residence if eligible, although they wanted to be allowed to work in the mining industry (Crush 1997: 9). The research indicated that the majority of miners had strong links to Lesotho which they wanted to maintain: 63.3 per cent of those miners who wanted to take permanent residence also said they would maintain another home in Lesotho (*ibid*). This indicates that, contrary to public opinion, Lesotho mineworkers may want to continue working, and in some cases living, in South Africa but are not anxious to settle themselves or their families permanently there.[15]

Thus the legislative legacy of contract labour persists, and is entrenched in the economies of South Africa and those countries providing labour as well as in the domestic economies of the households supplying labour. South Africa has a historical obligation to the hundreds of thousands of men (and their families) from the region who have played an enormous part in developing its wealth, and who have paid a high price in terms of separation, low wages and poor health (see also Crush 1997).

Documented Migration
Immigration permits

Documented migration encompasses people holding temporary and immigration permits. Since the formation of the Union in 1910, Britain has been the primary source of immigrants, or permanent residents. Attempts were also made to recruit from Germany and Holland, and Portuguese and Italian immigrants came in significant numbers in the 1960s. East Europeans arrived during the 1920s and, following the collapse of communism, were actively recruited by the National Party in the 1980s (personal communication, Polish Ambassador, January 1997).

Although Africans were not legally welcomed in South Africa, whites fleeing the black governments of the newly independent states of East and southern Africa were. From the late 1950s and early 1960s, white immigrants from Kenya, Tanzania, Uganda and Zambia arrived in significant numbers. They were followed in the 1970s by whites leaving Angola and Mozambique after the Portuguese revolution of 1974, and from Rhodesia following the declaration of UDI in 1976 and in the 1980s after Zimbabwe gained independence.

As the genesis of the Aliens Act 1937 shows, not all whites were welcome. The 1930 Quota Act and the 1937 Aliens Act were both designed to exclude Jewish immigrants. In the 1960s and 1970s, to placate opposition to immigration from Afrikaner cultural groups, administrative restrictions (on religious and cultural grounds) were placed on the immigration of Portuguese, Italian and Greek immigrants (Brownell 1985; Brownell, private papers). Thus, white migration to South Africa has also been shaped by the racial, religious and cultural prejudices of the South African state.

The number of immigrant/permanent residence permits issued each year is recorded. Since 1990 there has been a significant drop in the number of permanent residence permits issued, from 14,499 in 1990 to 5,064 in 1995. Of the 58,850 people granted permanent residence from 1990 to 1995, just under 20 per cent (11,090) came from Africa, 27 per cent from Asia and 47.1 per cent from Europe (Bouillon 1996a: 4). Although the numbers of permits issued each year could give an indication of patterns of immigration, they do not show how many of these people may have subsequently left South Africa. It is therefore impossible to know how many southern Africans hold permanent residence in South Africa at any one time.

Since 1995, emphasis has been placed on securing employment for South Africans and excluding new immigrants. Furthermore, since 1 July, 1996 all applicants must pay a R 5,580 non-returnable fee (raised to R7,130 on 1 April 1997) which is particularly onerous for applicants from the region. Thus, patterns of applications are likely to change as the requirements for permanent residence become more stringent.

Temporary residence permits

Statistics provided by the Central Statistical Services record how many temporary permits are issued by nationality, but do not indicate either the length of time for which they are issued, or whether they are renewals or reissues to the same individual. Moreover, the conditions applicable to the various temporary permits mean that many regional im/migrants apply for or are issued with permits which do not necessarily correlate with their intended activity in South Africa. For instance, informal cross-border traders are usually issued with single entry visitors permits even if officials know that the purpose of the visit is to trade (Peberdy 1997a). Hence these figures give little indication of either patterns or intent to visit, work or trade in South Africa.[16]

Since 1 July 1996 non-returnable fees of R360 (increased to R460 on 1 April 1997) are required for certain temporary permits. Deposits may also be demanded before a permit will be issued. It is reported that people applying for visitors permits in Maputo are required to pay US$30 (personal communication, February 1997). These fees and deposits are onerous for regional applicants (and people from countries with weak currencies), and especially for students and visitors.

The brain drain

Over half of the southern Africans who have entered as permanent residents or on work permits have come to work as professionals, the majority in South Africa's hospitals, universities and schools (De Vletter 1995: 28). Over 50 per cent of the doctors working in government hospitals are non-South Africans. A significant number of these medical professionals come from southern Africa. In 1991 alone, 200 Zimbabwean doctors left for South Africa and Botswana (ibid.). Although the employment of southern African professionals contributes to the skills base of South Africa, their loss is of considerable concern to the sending countries.

Undocumented Im/migration

Between 1913 and 1986 (and from then only at the discretion of the Immigrants Selection Board and immigration officials), non-whites were not eligible for temporary or permanent residence permits. Non-white people could only enter South Africa illegally or as contract workers. Once there, as contract or undocumented workers, they were still unable to regularise or make their positions permanent.

However, archival evidence from 1910 onwards shows that people from all over southern Africa have been coming to South Africa in significant numbers (and in smaller numbers from the rest of Africa) since at least the turn of the century.[17] These im/migrants arrived in South Africa to work on farms, in industry, homes, restaurants and shops; to trade; and to seek opportunities for self-employment.

The attitude of the South African government appears to have veered between encouragement, acceptance, ambivalence and hostility. The evidence also suggests that the Departments of Labour, Agriculture and Native Affairs adopted differing attitudes according to their competing interests. Although regional im/migrants were removed under the 1913 Act, for the most part their movements were controlled by the 1925 Natives (Urban Areas) Act, the 1937 Native Laws Amendment Act, and, in the postwar period, by the 1945 Urban Areas Act and their amendments (Davenport 1969).[18] The use of these Acts reflects the accepting and/or ambivalent attitudes of the government to the presence of regional migrants in South Africa.

Records show that, until 1928, the government had no objections to giving permission to stay to those without criminal records.[19] Instead, objections were received by the Union from the governments of Nyasaland (Malawi), Southern Rhodesia (Zimbabwe) and Mozambique. They objected to the numbers of non-mine migrants that South Africa was allowing to enter and remain in the country, arguing that the Union was undermining their development by depleting the labour force of their countries by allowing 'clandestine' migration.[20] This correspondence not only indicates that the Union government was willing to accept regional im/migrants, but that these migrations involved significant numbers of people.

In 1928, South Africa and Mozambique renegotiated the Mozambique Convention governing labour migration and trade between the two countries (see Katzenellenbogen 1982 for a study of the genesis and practices of the Convention). At the same time South Africa was entering a period of economic recession. Between 1928 and 1935 there seems to have been an unwillingness to openly sanction 'clandestine' or undocumented im/migration from the region.[21] However, pressure from the agricultural sector led to the establishment of a system in the 1920s whereby the government supplied farmers with regional im/migrants apprehended crossing the border and in urban areas. These im/migrants were given the option of being returned to their home country or being given temporary permits to work on farms. The system was maintained with varying degrees of vigour at least until the 1960s (Bradford 1993).[22] Toolo and Bethlehem (1995: 18) report that in 1993, in recognition of a *de facto* situation, the government issued temporary permits to farm workers in Northern Transvaal and Eastern Transvaal (Mpumalanga) who had entered illegally.

Departmental correspondence from the 1940s and 1950s shows a return to the ambivalence of the early years of the Union.[23] The declaration of the Republic in 1961, the formulation of the 'homelands' policy and stricter application of pass laws appear to have coincided with a hardening of attitudes against 'clandestine' regional migrants. In 1961, the government appointed the Froneman Commission to inquire into the presence of 'foreign Bantu in the Republic'. Using data gathered from censuses, the police and District Commissioners, the Commission estimated that there were 836,000 'foreign-born' Bantu in the Union. It cited that 53,281 'foreign Bantu' were registered as working in urban areas (Froneman Commission 1962: 165). It further estimated that at least 420,000 non-South Africans from the region were employed in rural areas (*ibid.*: 166).

Despite the apparent concern over the number of regional im/migrants in the country, the renegotiation of the Mozambique Convention in 1963 led to an 'Exchange of Notes' between the two governments relating to clandestine immigration. This exchange allowed undocumented migration to continue until or unless either government decided to halt it (BAO 2323 C28/6 1962–1965). The evidence gathered by the Froneman Commission also shows that, by the early 1960s, non-South Africans who had migrated from the region were entrenched in every sector of South Africa's labour force. They not only worked in private homes and industries, but for the government as well, reflecting the ambiguity and passivity of the government's attitude to regional immigration.

Archival records for the 1970s are still closed. Available evidence suggests that the increasing isolation of South Africa and increased tension between the Republic and neighbouring states led not only to growing internal repression and the development of a police state, but to a reduction in the numbers of southern Africans living in the Republic – at least in urban areas (Brownell, private papers). This is possibly because the increasingly repressive practices of the state not only made arrest more likely and life much harder, but also led to a hardening of attitudes towards im/migrants arriving from neighbouring states as government paranoia about terrorism, black nationalism and communism grew.[24]

It is difficult to know how many people came, since the available figures are as ambiguous as those cited by the Ministry of Home Affairs today. Documents refer to numbers which are little more than guesses, or rely on anecdotal evidence, and with no reference to concrete research. Like those of today, they seem to be influenced by the prevailing attitude of the government to undocumented migration from the region.

Census data could provide an indication of the number of regional migrants in the Union. However, it is probable that the population has been undercounted (particularly in later censuses which did not venture into many township areas). The creation of 'homelands' further complicates the numbers. From 1980, people born in Bophuthatswana, Ciskei, Transkei and Venda were counted as 'foreign Bantu'. The unreliability of census data can be seen in the 1990 census: an estimated 350,000 Mozambican refugees were living in South Africa but the census recorded just over 190,000. The problematic nature of the censuses from at least 1970 makes them undependable and largely useless.

Popular debates around immigration to South Africa tend to imply (if not argue) that undocumented migration from the region is a new and rapidly growing phenomenon. Yet people have been coming to South Africa from the region since before the turn of the century (e.g. Chapter 12). There may be an increase in the rate of undocumented regional migration, but it must be recognised that not only have people been unable to formalise their status in South Africa, but also that movement through the region to South Africa has a long and substantive history.

'Amnesty'

On 1 July 1996, the government started an 'amnesty' programme for people from SADC countries who had entered South Africa 'illegally'. The amnesty period ended on 30 September 1996. Citizens of SADC countries who had been continually resident in South Africa for five years or longer prior to 1 July 1996; were engaged in productive economic activity or were maintaining a relationship with a South African citizen or had dependent children born in South Africa; did not have a criminal record; and would be 'desirable inhabitants of the Republic' were eligible to apply for permanent residence. Documentary proof was required. Contract workers (including miners) were not able to apply. The government estimated that it would receive up to 2 million applications. Of the 192,422 applications received, 21,572 had been approved, and 6,396 rejected by 1 January 1997 (*Star*, 13 January 1997).

Refugees

Since the beginning of 1994, South Africa has granted refugee status under the United Nations Convention on Refugees (1951) and the OAU Convention (1969). Although refugees are not immigrants, the refusal of the government to accord refugee status in the past has left its own legacy.

As a result of civil war (promoted and sustained by South Africa) and drought, approximately 350,000 Mozambican refugees arrived in South Africa in the 1980s and early 1990s (Dolan 1995: 54). Although South Africa refused to recognise these refugees, the former homelands of Gazankulu and KaNgwane gave refugee status to approximately 120,000 (Brunk 1996: 4). These people were given refugee status by South Africa in 1993. Unable to get support from international refugee agencies, many others arrived in South Africa's cities seeking work. As they were not recognised as refugees, they were classified as undocumented or 'illegal' immigrants.

In 1994, the UNHCR and the South African government started a voluntary repatriation programme. Just over 31,000 refugees returned to Mozambique under the programme (Dolan 1995: 53). Some may have returned of their own accord. In March 1995 all Mozambican refugees remaining in South Africa lost their refugee status. Thus many Mozambicans were denied the opportunity to claim asylum, or to become legal immigrants, while South Africa also bears responsibility for the political and economic destabilisation which has pushed many of them to seek employment in South Africa.

'New' Immigrants

While this chapter has focused on regional im/migration, im/migration from the rest of Africa has also grown since racially exclusionary statutory restrictions were removed in 1986. The first to arrive were West African (usually English-speaking) professionals who came to work in the hospitals, schools and universities of the 'homelands' and rural areas. During the 1990s, immigrants from East, Central and West Africa have become increasingly visible in South Africa, encountered in shops, vending on the streets, as doctors and nurses in government hospitals, as teachers and students, etc. Particularly visible in recent years (possibly because of linguistic differences and African francophone fashion) has been the increase in immigration from francophone West and Central Africa. Bouillon (1996b: 1), saying that it is difficult to know the exact number, estimates that there are between 15,000 and 30,000 French-speaking African immigrants in South Africa, the majority (he estimates over 15,000) from Zaire.

Given the history of South Africa's isolation, links between South Africa and the rest of Africa and particularly French-speaking countries may appear obscure, yet relatively strong trade links developed with many African countries during the 1980s. Despite economic sanctions, trade with non-SACU African countries increased from 6.5 to 10 per cent between 1984 and 1988. In 1988 these countries received 12 per cent of all South African direct foreign investment, and South Africa had become the seventh largest commercial partner of the rest of Africa. By 1989, one third of all South African manufactured export goods went to other African countries (Bouillon 1996b: 4). Including SACU countries, trade with other African countries in 1995 amounted to 31.7 per cent of South Africa's total trade, and 12.8 per cent excluding the SACU countries (Davies 1997: 1).

The governments of Zaire, Côte d'Ivoire, Gabon and the previous South African government established political relationships in the 1980s, for which economic relationships emerged. By 1988, Zaire had become South Africa's second largest trading partner in Africa (Bouillon 1996b: 4). Thus the first significant movements of traders, business people and goods between South Africa and the rest of Africa dates back to the 1980s. While the volume may have increased, this immigration may not be as 'new' as it first seems.

Counting the Uncountable

It is difficult, or even impossible, to estimate accurately the numbers of people from the region and the rest of Africa who arrive and live in South Africa with or without documents. Despite this, the articles attached to the headlines quoted at the start of this chapter, and other commentaries, do not hesitate to quote figures provided by the Ministry of Home Affairs, the South African Police Service (SAPS) and the South African National Defence Force (SANDF) on the numbers of regional im/migrants living in South Africa. Over the past three years, estimates by the Department of Home Affairs of the number of undocumented regional im/migrants in the country have ranged from 2 million to 12 million. In 1996 the figure of 2.5 to 4.5 million was quoted (*Star*, 4 December 1996). The range of official estimates indicates that these numbers have little basis in researched reality.

The increasing numbers of people arrested and removed (or deported), and the numbers of people detected crossing the border outside official border posts are often cited as indicators that regional immigration is growing. The SAPS and the Department of Home Affairs both provide data showing the numbers of people deported from the country. There is no recognition that these figures may include people who have been deported more than once within the year, and that the numbers of people deported largely depends on the enthusiasm with which they are sought by the police and Home Affairs officials. In 1994 the number of people repatriated was 90,962, in 1995 it reached over 157,000 and in 1996 fell back to 135,408 (Brunk 1995: 3; *Star*, 14 November 1996; *Star*, 9 January 1997). Of those repatriated the majority (about 80 per cent) are from Mozambique, and approximately 98 per cent are from SADC countries.[25]

The SANDF record the number of people arrested crossing the border and/or detected by the electric fence which runs part way along the border of South Africa. In 1996, 17,967 people were detected trying to cross the fence and apparently 36,362 people were arrested at the border (*Star*, 6 February 1997). These counts (usually particularly high in January, after people have been home for Christmas) do not recognise that many im/migrants may leave through the border posts but re-enter over the fence. Again, the number arrested is also affected by the priority accorded by the SANDF to apprehending people 'jumping' the fence. Thus these figures cannot indicate whether numbers of people entering South Africa over the border are increasing.

The number of people overstaying the time limits on their visas may also provide an indication of the number of undocumented non-South Africans in the country. However, again, this number is both fluid and difficult to disaggregate. Combined with removal figures it is perhaps more useful in determining the priority given to undocumented im/migrants from Europe and Africa. From January to April 1996, over 130,000 visitors had overstayed. The majority were from southern Africa, but 12,000 came from the UK, 11,000 from Germany and 3,000 from the United States. Yet in the whole of 1995, only 28 people were deported to the UK, 13 to Germany and 8 to the US (*Star*, 14 November 1996).

Because the available figures are so dubious it is not possible to quantify contemporary patterns of migration from the region. Until more thorough research has been undertaken it would be foolhardy to make any claims to concrete knowledge. Furthermore, until the legislative history of immigration in South Africa is understood, any such figures (even if they were authoritative) are likely to present a dehistoricised and inaccurate picture of current migration patterns, whatever they may be.

Im/migrants and Crime

The SAPS also intermittently provide data on the numbers of 'illegal immigrants' arrested in 'crime swoops'. Although these figures may improve the arrest rates of the SAPS, the conflation of arrested criminals and arrested illegal immigrants creates spurious links between crime and undocumented im/migrants. For instance, according to Col. Van Niekerk of the SAPS, 'Swoops on illegal immigrants also accounted for 20 per cent of all arrests made by police in the Witwatersrand operational area in June 1995'. While this may indicate the seemingly skewed priorities of the SAPS in the area, it does *not* indicate a connection between the presence of undocumented im/migrants and crime, as such press articles would have us believe.[26]

Indicative of the dubious association in contemporary debates between criminal activities and specific immigrant communities was a headline reading 'Nigerians arrested in drug raid on city hotel' (*Star*, 14 February 1997). The text of the article, having listed the large amount of drugs found in the raid (which searched all the rooms in the building), then continues '[w]hile no drug related arrests were made...two Nigerian nationals were arrested for being in the country illegally'. The headline, however, had already made the connection. These associations tend not only to create spurious linkages between undocumented im/migrants and crime and create national stereotypes, but also reflect and feed a seemingly growing xenophobia about African im/migration (see also Dolan and Reitzes 1996).

Conclusion

The history of the 1991 Aliens Control Act not only reflects South Africa's racially exclusionary past, but also sets in place the structures and processes which still govern immigration and which have shaped patterns of migration from the region. The 1913 Immigrants Regulation Act entrenched the regional migrant labour system in legislation. It secured a supply of cheap labour (without the overheads of a permanent workforce) for the mining industry, and to a lesser extent the agricultural industry. Simultaneously, it denied miners and farm workers from the region the opportunity of permanent employment and/or residence in South Africa.

The 1913 and the 1937 Aliens Acts made it impossible for regional im/migrants to enter South Africa on temporary or permanent residence permits until 1986. Semi-skilled and skilled black workers from the region, who would have been actively recruited to South Africa had they been white Europeans, have been denied the opportunity to enter legally. Consequently, regional im/migrants denied the opportunity to enter 'legally' have arrived without documents. For the majority of this century they were tacitly (and explicitly) allowed to enter 'clandestinely' to work in South Africa.

The lack of recognition given to the long and substantial, but hidden, history of regional im/migration in contemporary debates obscures the migratory relationships which have been built in the region over the past century. No recognition is made of the substantive trade relationships with other African countries. The uncritical use of dubious statistics allows the 'flood' to grow. The association between 'illegal immigrants' and illegal activities in the crime statistics creates both national stereotypes and an artificial connection between crime and im/migrants. It is only with an understanding of the effects of South Africa's im/migration history on patterns of regional im/migration, which recognises the problems of quantification, that informed debate will be able to take place.

It has not been possible to explore here the impact of South Africa's political and economic links to the region on immigration patterns. South Africa is currently reintegrating itself in the region. Trade and other agreements are being renegotiated within SADC (see Chapter 10) and South Africa is taking an increasing role in mediating regional conflicts (for instance in Zaire and Lesotho). Economic links are also strong. SADC states are among South Africa's major trading partners. Trade with non-SACU SADC states amounted to R9.7 billion in 1995 and trade with SACU countries to over R15 billion in 1993 (Davies 1995: 1). The proposed development of the Maputo corridor and bilateral trade talks with neighbouring states may influence future migratory patterns. South Africa may also be under an obligation to neighbouring states which bore the brunt of destabilisation campaigns, military incursions and economic disruption in the 1980s and 1990s and which provided sanctuary to South African exiles and refugees.

Reflecting regional relationships, regional migration is not just a one-way street leading to South Africa, but is made up of a complex network of routes that criss-cross the borders of the region (Peberdy 1997b). While popular debates may be counting the costs and benefits of regional migration to South Africa, it should be remembered that sending countries also incur costs and benefits, and that South Africa is just one country in the migratory network of the region. In addition, there is some migration from South Africa to countries of the region, comprising both a return migration of workers, e.g. on the mines, who have been retrenched (an increasing problem for Lesotho during the 1990s), and also a very small but politi-cally significant group of white farmers being encouraged into Zambia, Mozambique and potentially other countries also to undertake commercial farming. However, these counterflows have not been examined in this chapter, which has been concerned with South Africa's policy and record in respect of inward migrants.

The exclusionary history of South Africa's immigration legislation as well as the history of trade and political relationships and present developments have implica-tions not only for patterns of regional im/migration but also for policy development. It is doubtful if the use of legislation with roots in racially exclusionary statutes designed with only white immigration in mind is appropriate for South Africa today (Crush and Peberdy forthcoming; Peberdy 1997a). Any policies developed to con-trol, limit or allow free movement should take cognisance of the past. While it may not be possible to right all past wrongs, the exclusion of black im/migrants from South Africa should be recognised, as should the long-standing links between South Africa and the rest of the region and the continent.

Notes

1 This chapter draws on research conducted for my doctoral thesis and research undertaken for a Research Fellowship held with the Southern African Migration Project which is funded by the Canadian International Development Agency. The author wishes to thank CIDA for their finan-cial support provided through the Fellowship.
2 See for instance Akenson (1991); Bradlow (1978); Brownell (1985); Cox (1970); Donsky (1989); Hockley (1952); Stone (1973).
3 Brunk (1996); Bouillon (1996a; 1996b); Crush and Peberdy (forthcoming); De Villiers and Reitzes (1995); De Vletter (1995); Dolan and Reitzes (1996); Hough (1995); Reitzes (1995a; 1995b; 1997); Minaar (1995); Minaar and Hough (1996); Peberdy (1997a; 1997b); Van Neikerk (1995).
   It is hoped that new research initiatives will provide a more solid base from which to draw conclusions. The Southern African Migration Project, a joint initiative between Queen's University, Canada and the Institute for Democracy in South Africa (IDASA) (with partners in Mozambique, Zimbabwe and Lesotho) funded by CIDA, is a three-year project which is estab-lishing a database exploring perceptions and behaviours of migration, and examining the par-ticipation of regional immigrants in the South African economy. IFAS/ORSTOM is initiating research into francophone migration to South Africa. Klaaren (1996, forthcoming) has examined the implications of the new Constitution for the present legislative framework and the rights of im/migrants.
4 Perhaps clumsily, im/migrant will be used to describe immigrants and migrants, unless intent to reside permanently or temporarily is clear. Immigrant implies permanence and migrant tran-sience. In the past black people from the region entering South Africa have largely been referred to as migrants and whites as immigrants. Yet neither word may adequately describe the intent to remain permanently of either white or black arrivals. Hence the use of im/migrant.
5 Although undocumented im/migrants are usually referred to as illegals, illegal immigrants or illegal aliens, the use of the word illegal implies criminality which may not reflect the intent of the immigrant. The use of undocumented also reflects common international terminology (Cohen 1997). The use of 'alien' implies that immigrants are strange or extra-terrestrial – or both – and is dehumanising.
6 The use of the term 'race' is problematic. This chapter is based on the understanding that race is a socially constructed category and is therefore mutable (see Gates 1986; Jackson and Penrose

1993). Not surprisingly, the term race in the South African context is associated with colour. However, as Malik (1996) argues, race has been and may still be associated with cultural difference and not just perceived physical differences. This chapter uses or refers to race in the ways it was constructed during the period under discussion. It is apparent that Jewish people were regarded as belonging to a separate racial category from other white South Africans, and that race was often conflated with nationality, culture and religion.

7   See Bradlow (1978) for a detailed study of the development of the 1913 Act and the exclusion of Indian immigrants.

8   For accounts of Indian immigration see Bhana and Brain (1990) and Arkin *et al.* (1989). Indians first arrived in South Africa in 1860 to work as indentured labourers on five-year contracts in the Natal sugar industry. By 1911 the Indian population had grown to over 152,000 (Brijlal 1989: 26). Over 40,000 had been born in South Africa or were 'free' immigrants from India and Mauritius (mainly as traders). The reluctance of indentured labourers to return to India on completion of their contracts, and the arrival of 'free' immigrants led provincial governments to introduce measures to discourage Indians from staying. These included restrictions on movement in and between provinces as well as on trading, and the hated Natal Head Tax. These measures (and the 1913 Act) were resisted by the Indian community and the Natal Indian Congress (Bradlow 1978; Brijlal 1989).

9   Jewish immigrants had been coming to South Africa since it was first settled in the 1600s (Shain 1994). Between 1880 and 1911 the Jewish population of South Africa grew from about 4,000 to almost 50,000, or 3.7 per cent of the white population (Boiskin 1993: 40; Bradlow 1994: 103). Most arrived as immigrants from Russia, Lithuania and Eastern Europe.

10 BNS 1/1/380 200/74 vol. 1, 30 July 1920; *ibid.* 16 May 1921; BNS 1/1/380 200/74 vol. 4, 12 December 1922.

11 See also Note 6. The exclusion of potential Jewish immigrants may have hinged on their religious affiliation. However, at this time the conflation of culture and race meant that their exclusion was couched in racially and not culturally exclusionary language. See Malik (1996) for a discussion of the conflation of race, culture and religion; Dubow (1995) for a discussion of constructions of race in South Africa in the 1920s and 1930s; and Gilman (1985).

12 I am indebted to Jonathan Crush for this point.

13 For gold mining see for instance: Crush (1997, 1987); Crush and James (1995); Crush *et al.* (1991); James (1992); Jeeves (1985); Moodie (1994). For coal mining see First (1983). For migration from Mozambique between 1860 and 1910 to mines and farms see Harries (1994). Little is written on non-South African contract workers in the farming industry, but for historical perspectives see Bradford (1993); Jeeves (1992).

14 Recruitment was halted in 1974 following an air crash which killed 74 miners returning to Malawi. President Banda immediately called for the withdrawal of all miners and the halting of recruitment. It is thought that demands for labour in Malawi also underlay his response to the accident (Crush *et al.* 1991; Simon 1989).

15 The number of eligible miners may have been over-estimated, and there seems to be some confusion over the implications of taking up permanent residence among possible applicants.

16 The issue of permits is also subject to administrative measures. In October 1996, the South African High Commission in Zimbabwe said that it would not issue visas to people who were unemployed, had no family ties in Zimbabwe or who did not have enough money to cover the cost of their stay in South Africa (*Star* 22 October 1996)

17 This includes the archives of the Departments of the Interior, Native Affairs, Labour and Public Health held in the State Archives, Pretoria.

18 See also NTS 2072 144/280 vol. 5; BAO 3208 C43/1; BAO 3210 C43/1/1/1 vols. 1–2; BAO 3211 C43/2 vol. 1; NTS 2092 216/280.

19 See GNLB 407 60/17–66; BNS 1/2/57 A2225-A3900.

20 See, for instance, GNLB 406; GNLB 407; BNS 1/1/359 1/123/74; BNS 1/1/377 194/74.

21 BNS 1/1/377 194/74A; BNS 1/1/359 1/123/74; NTS 2077 172/280.

22 See also NTS 2093 222/280 vol 1–23. Jeeves (1992) explores the supply of non-South African labour to the sugar estates.

23 See, for instance, BAO 2323 C/28/6; NTS 2077 172/280.

24 The electric fence was built in 1976 and was turned up to lethal voltage for much of the 1980s and early 1990s, providing an obstacle to border crossers.

25 The large proportion of Mozambicans amongst those removed may not just reflect the numbers in the country, but that they are more easily identified by accent, command of English and vaccination marks found on their forearms (unlike South Africans and others from the region who are vaccinated on the upper arm).

26 Other headlines included '451 illegals held in city' (*Star 21 September 1994*); 'Crime wave "imported"' (*City Press* 11 December 1994); 'Over 300 illegals arrested in swoop' (*Star 28 February 1996*).

References

References BLO (Dept of Foreign Affairs), BNS (Dept. of Interior/Home Affairs), NTS (Department of Native Affairs), BAO (Department of Bantu Administration) are from the State Archives, Pretoria. References GNLB are from the Transvaal Archives held at the State Archives, Pretoria. Papers presented to the Green Paper Task Group on International Immigration can be found on the internet.

Akenson, D. (1991) *The Irish in South Africa*. Occasional Paper. Institute of Economic and Social Research, Rhodes University.

Arkin, A., Magyar, K. and Pillay, G. (eds) (1989) *The Indian South Africans*. Owen Burgess, Durban.

Bhana, S. and Brain, J. (1990) *Setting Down Roots: Indian Migrants in South Africa, 1860–1911*. Witwatersrand University Press, Johannesburg.

Boiskin, J. (1993) 'Beinkinstadts, 1903–1933[prime], *Jewish Affairs*, Spring: 39–42.

Bouillon, A. (1996a) 'South Africa and International Migration in Transition'. Unpublished paper, Migration Research Program, Institut Francais d'Afrique du Sud (IFAS/ORSTOM), Paris.

Bouillon, A. (1996b) '"New" African Immigration to South Africa'. Revised version of a paper presented at the South African Sociological Association Conference, Durban, 7–11 July.

Bradford, H. (1993) 'Getting Away with Murder: 'Mealie Kings', the State and Foreigners', in Bonner, P., Delius, P. and Posel, D. *Apartheid's Genesis, 1935–1962*. Ravan Press and Witwatersrand University Press, Johannesburg.

Bradlow, E. (1994) 'The Anatomy of an Immigrant Community: Cape Town Jewry from the Turn of the Century to the Passing of the Quota Act', *South African Historical Journal* 31: 103–27.

Bradlow, E. (1978) 'Immigration into the Union 1910–1948: Policies and Attitudes', PhD Thesis, University of Cape Town.

Brijlal, P. (1989) 'Demographic Profile', in Arkin *et al.*

Brownell, F. (1985) 'British Immigration to South Africa, 1946–1970', M.A. Thesis, UNISA, 1977, published in *Archives Year Book for South African History*, 48(1): 1–196.

Brownell, F., private papers. Mr Brownell kindly gave me permission to read his collection of documents from his years with the Department of Home Affairs.

Brunk, M. (1996) *Undocumented Migration to South Africa: More Questions than Answers*. IDASA, Public Information Series, No. 4, IDASA, Cape Town.

Buthelezi, M. (1995) 'Address to the National Union of Mineworkers' Annual Central Committee Meeting', 10 March.

Byarugaba, J. (1994) *Mozambican Refugees in South Africa: Special focus on vulnerable groups*. UNHCR/UNICEF Report, Johannesburg.

Chirwa, W. (1994) 'Malawian Migrant Labour and the Politics of HIV/AIDS, 1985–1993'. Paper presented at conference on Transforming Mine Migrancy in the 1990s: Southern Africa', 27–29 June.

Cohen, R. (1997) 'International Migration: Southern Africa in Global Perspective'. Briefing paper for the Green Paper Task Group on International Migration, Cape Town, 13–14 January.

Cooper, C. (1995) 'Labour Migration in Southern Africa'. Submission to the Labour Market Commission, 1995.

Cox, K. (1970) *Immigration into South Africa, 1940–1967: A Bibliography*. University of Cape Town Libraries, Cape Town.

Crush, J. (1997) 'Contract Migration to South Africa: Past, Present and Future'. Briefing paper for the Green Paper Task Group on International Migration, Cape Town, 13–14 January.

Crush, J. (1987) *The Struggle for Swazi Labour, 1890–1920*. McGill-Queen's Press, Kingston and Montreal.

Crush, J. and Peberdy, S. (forthcoming) 'A Brief History of South Africa's Immigration legislation', in Crush, J. and Mojapelo, R. (eds) *The Aliens Control Act: A Review and a Critique*. IDASA, Cape Town.

Crush, J. and James, W. (1995) 'Mine Migrancy in a Democratic South Africa', in *Labour Migrancy in Southern Africa: Prospects for Post-apartheid Transformation*. Southern African Labour Monographs No. 3/1995, Labour Law Unit, University of Cape Town.

Crush, J., Jeeves, A. and Yudelman, D. (1991) *South Africa's Labour Empire: A History of Black Migrancy to the Gold Mines*. Westview and David Phillip, Boulder, CO and Cape Town.

Davenport, T. (1969) 'The Triumph of Colonel Stallard: The Transformation of the Natives (Urban Areas) Act between 1923 and 1937', *South African Historical Journal* 2: 77–96.

Davies, R. (1997) 'Impact on Migration', briefing paper for the Green Paper Task Group on International Migration, Cape Town, 13–14 January.

De Villiers, R. and Reitzes, M. (1995) *Southern African Migration: Domestic and Regional Policy Implications*. Centre for Policy Studies, Workshop proceedings, No. 14, Johannesburg.

De Vletter, F. (1995) 'The Implications of Changing Migration Patterns in Southern Africa', in *Labour*

Migrancy in Southern Africa: Prospects for Post-apartheid Transformation. Southern African Labour Monograph No. 3/1995, Labour Law Unit, University of Cape Town.

Dolan, C. (1995) 'Policy Challenges for the New South Africa', in De Villiers and Reitzes.

Dolan, C. and Reitzes, M. (1996) *The Insider Story? Press Coverage of Illegal Immigrants and Refugees, April 1994–September 1995.* Research Report No. 48, Centre for Policy Studies, Johannesburg.

Donsky, I. (1989) 'Aspects of the Immigration of Europeans to South Africa, 1946–1970', M.A. Thesis, Rand Afrikaans University, Johannesburg.

Dubow, S. (1995) *Illicit Union: Scientific Racism in Modern South Africa.* Cambridge University Press and Witwatersrand University Press, Johannesburg.

First, R. (1983) *Black Gold: The Mozambican Miner, Proletarian and Peasant.* St. Martin's Press, New York.

Friedman, S. and Reitzes, M. (1996) 'Immigration and Human Rights in South Africa', paper prepared for the Human Rights Commission, Centre for Policy Studies, Johannesburg.

Froneman Commission (1962) *Interdepartmental Commission of Inquiry into Foreign Bantu.* Government Printer, Pretoria.

Gates, H. (ed.) 1986. *'Race', Writing and Difference.* University of Chicago Press, Chicago.

Gilman, S. (1985) *Difference and Pathology: Stereotypes of Sexuality, Race and Madness.* John Wiley, New York.

Harries, P. (1994) *Work, Culture and Identity: Migrant Laborers in Mozambique and South Africa.* Heinemann, New York.

Hockley, H. (1957) *The Story of the British Settlers of 1820 in South Africa.* Juta, Cape Town and Johannesburg.

Hough, M. (1995) 'Illegal Aliens in South Africa: Causes and Facilitating Factors', *Strategic Review*, Institute for Strategic Studies, University of Pretoria.

Jackson, P. and Penrose, J. (eds.) (1993) *Constructions of Race, Place and Nation.* University College London Press, London.

James, W. (1992) *Our Precious Metal: African Labour in South Africa's Gold Industry, 1970–1990.* David Phillip, James Currey and Indiana University Press, Cape Town, London and Bloomington, IN.

Jeeves, A. (1992) 'Sugar and Gold in the Making of the South African Labour System: The Crisis of Supply on the Zululand Sugar estates, 1906–1950', *South African Journal of Economic History* 7(2): 7–33.

Jeeves, A. (1985) *Migrant Labour in South Africa's Mining Economy: The Struggle for the Gold Mines Labour Supply.* McGill-Queen's Press, Kingston and Montreal.

Katz, A. (1997) 'Reform of Administrative Justice'. Briefing paper for the Green Paper Task Group on International Migration, Pretoria, 12 March.

Katzellenbogen, S. (1982) *South Africa and Southern Mozambique: Labour, Railways and Trade in the Making of a Relationship.* Manchester University Press, Manchester.

Kotzé, H. and Hill, L. (1997) 'Emergent Migration Policy in a Democratic South Africa', *International Migration* 35(1): 5–35.

Klaaren, J. 1996. 'So Far Not So Good: An Analysis of Immigration Decisions under the Interim Constitution'. Draft of unpublished paper.

Klaaren, J. (forthcoming) 'Is Constitutionality Catching?: A Survey of South African Immigration Legislation and Some Constitutional Issues', in Crush, J. and Mojapelo, R. (eds) *The Aliens Control Act: A Review and a Critique.* IDASA, Cape Town.

Malik, K. (1996) *The Meaning of Race: Race, History and Culture in Western Society.* Macmillan, Basingstoke, UK.

Minaar, A. (1995) 'Ours for the Taking? Crime and Illegals', *Social Update*, 4.

Minaar, A. and Hough, M. (1996) *Who Goes There? Perspectives on Clandestine Migration and Illegal Aliens in Southern Africa.* Human Sciences Research Council, Pretoria.

Moodie, D. (1994) *Going for Gold: Mine, Mines and Migrancy in South Africa,* University of California Press, Berkeley, CA.

Office of Census and Statistics (OCS) (1922) *Official Year Book of the Union, and of Basutoland, Bechuanaland Protectorate and Swaziland, 1921.* Government Printer, Pretoria.

Office of Census and Statistics (OCS) (1925) *Official Year Book of the Union, and of Basutoland, Bechuanaland Protectorate and Swaziland, 1924.* Government Printer, Pretoria.

Office of Census and Statistics (OCS) (1936) *Official Year Book of the Union, and of Basutoland, Bechuanaland Protectorate and Swaziland, 1934–1935.* Government Printer, Pretoria.

Office of Census and Statistics (OCS) (1940) *Official Year Book of the Union, and of Basutoland, Bechuanaland Protectorate and Swaziland, 1940.* Government Printer, Pretoria.

Peberdy, S. (1997a) 'Cross Border Trading in South Africa'. Briefing paper for the Green Paper Task Group on International Migration, Pretoria, 12 March.

Peberdy, S. (1997b) 'A History of South Africa's Immigration Legislation'. Briefing paper for the Green Paper Task Group on International Migration, Cape Town, 13–14 January.

Reitzes, M. (1997) 'Undocumented Migration: Dimensions and Dilemmas'. Briefing paper for the Green Paper Task Group on International Migration, Pretoria, 12 March.

Reitzes, M. (1995a) 'Divided on the 'Demon': Immigration Policy since the Election', *Policy: Issues and Actors*, 8(9): 1–26.

Reitzes, M. (1995b) 'Insiders and Outsiders: The Reconstruction of Citizenship in South Africa', *Policy: Issues and Actors*, 8(1): 1–36.

Shain, M. (1994) *The Roots of Antisemitism in South Africa*. Witwatersrand University Press, Johannesburg.

Simon, D. (1989) 'Rural-urban Interaction and Development in Southern Africa: the Implications of Reduced Labour Migration', in Potter, R.B. and Unwin, T. (eds) *The Geography of Urban-Rural Interaction*. Routledge, London and New York.

Stone, J. (1973) *Colonist or Uitlander? A Study of the British Immigrant in South Africa*. Clarendon Press, Oxford.

Thomas, R. (1995) 'South Africa is no island...', in de Villiers. and Reitzes.

Tomlinson, M. R., Bam, S. and Mathole, T. (1995) *More than Mealies and Marigolds: From Homeseekers to Citizens in Ivory Park*. Centre for Policy Studies, Johannesburg.

Toolo, H. and Bethlehem, T. (1995) 'Problems, Issues, and Possible Approaches for Organised Labour', in de Villiers and Reitzes.

Van Niekerk, B. (1995) 'The Impact of Illegal Aliens on Safety and Security in South Africa', *ISSUP Bulletin*.

Wilson, F. (1972) *Labour in the South African Gold Mines*. Cambridge University Press, Cambridge.

12 Gender, Labour Markets and Female Migration in and from Botswana

KAVITA DATTA

Introduction

We live, according to some, in the 'age of migration' (Castle and Miller 1993). Migration literature, however, remains curiously fragmented and diverse in terms of both its theoretical underpinnings and methodological considerations. A more recent cause of concern has been the relative neglect of gender. While it is generally accepted that specific cultural groups differ in their attitudes towards 'place', a less acknowledged fact is that men and women within the same cultural group also experience 'place' differently because of their relative positions in social, economic and ideological hierarchies. Migration studies, which are fundamentally concerned with this experience, have exemplified this preoccupation with the male norm, and women have been largely treated as passive participants, or even victims, either moving as dependants of men or being 'left behind' in the rural areas. Women, as *migrants,* have become visible fairly recently due to the efforts of feminists from various disciplines who have illustrated their historical and contemporary participation in the migration process as well as the significant differences in the motives and patterns of movements of men and women migrants (Bozzoli 1990; Chant and Radcliffe 1992; Walker 1990; Izzard 1985).

The relatively new focus on gender has led to a re-examination of traditional migration theories and methods within a feminist framework. In the context of southern Africa, hitherto the structural debate has reigned supreme. The creation of impoverished reserves has been attributed to the penetration of capital into peasant societies, the undermining of the self-sufficiency of these societies and their subsequent transformation into labour exporting peripheries (Wolpe 1972; Parson 1985). This strategy is seen as being part and parcel of the logic of colonial capital accumulation. Feminist researchers have criticised this theoretical perspective on various fronts (Bozzoli 1983, 1990; Walker 1990). First, they have argued that structuralism only provides a partial explanation of women's subordination: for example, there is little explanation of why, over much of southern Africa, women remained on the land and men left for the mines. As Bozzoli (1983: 143) argues, 'there is no logic in the fact of proletarianisation which determines that men should be first off the land, as historians of 19th century African societies are well aware'. Second, the structuralist debate totally ignores the machinations of patriarchy. Women in southern Africa faced a struggle on two fronts: between women and capitalism *and* between women and men. The third criticism of this theoretical perspective is that it treats the migration experience of southern African societies as homogenous. Walker (1990) has pointed out that African societies (and I would add men and women within these societies) responded to the penetration of capital in a variety of ways and were actively engaged in shaping the migration process. They were not passive participants in or victims of the process of proletarianisation.

This chapter will start by exploring the manifestations of this debate in the context of the historic and contemporary migration of men and women from Botswana to South Africa. It will illustrate the response of Tswana communities to, and interaction with, the evolving South African capitalist system from the 1880s to the present day. The forces shaping the gendered nature of the migration flows from Botswana to South Africa will be identified in order to determine why men dominated as migrants. It will then identify the women who *did* migrate and point out the important differences between the movements of men and women. The section will end by addressing recent radical changes in the political environment of southern Africa which have once again changed the context within which international migration is taking place.

The focus of the chapter will then shift to address specific methodological considerations. Migration studies have been caught in the dilemma of 'articulating the particular and the general' experience of migration (Izzard 1985: 259). Empirical studies have been vital in outlining trends and making women more visible in migration flows. Yet, at the same time, they have regarded women migrants as a homogenous category so that generalisations about the migration of women have persisted without qualification. An increasing appreciation of the importance of human agency and the complexity of human existence has resulted in feminist geographers calling for the use of new methods. It is in this context that the use of narratives (such as oral histories, biographical interviews, life histories) has gained currency, as they are seen as being more meaningful and representative of the individual 'interior' experience of migration and the new 'places' that migrants come to occupy (Miles and Crush 1993; Vandsemb 1995). By drawing on biographical interviews with women who had moved from rural areas to Gaborone,[1] the second section of this chapter will deconstruct the category 'women migrants' and highlight some of the critical factors which have a fundamental impact on the experience of the 'urban'.

International Migration

Historical Observations
The southern African migration system has been described as one of the 'modern world's most enduring, organised and rapacious system[s] of international labour movement' (Crush 1995: 229). In the context of Botswana (or Bechuanaland[2] as it was known at that time), the earliest records of migration to South Africa come from the 1880s, pre-dating the discovery of minerals there. These movements vividly illustrate the *active* participation of men and women and were largely in response to the imposition of a border which divided the Tswana community between Bechuanaland and South Africa. Border communities in the Protectorate often owned land and cattle on the other side which necessitated daily trips to the land as well as social trips to maintain ties with kin (Cockerton 1996). Women were particularly important participants in these movements because of prescribed gender roles – they were primarily responsible for subsistence production as well as sustaining social and cultural ties.

By 1880, two interrelated events changed the context within which migration was occurring between Bechuanaland and South Africa. The first was a widespread rinderpest epidemic in 1886–87 followed by a famine and the introduction of a 'hut tax' in 1899. The epidemic was one of the most catastrophic events in the recorded history of the Tswana and resulted in a huge loss of cattle, on which the livelihood of many households depended (Jones-Dube 1995). Drought and famine intensified levels of rural poverty which were further exacerbated by the introduction of the 'hut tax' which was later converted to a poll tax. The fact that the poll tax (unlike tribute to chiefs) was calculated on the potential, as opposed to actual, productive capacity of a household intensified the pressure on households to seek waged employment so that they could buy food, rebuild their lost herds and pay the tax (Walker 1990).

Unfortunately, such opportunities did not exist in the Protectorate and two contrasting arguments have emerged to explain this lack of 'development' in Bechuanaland (although see also Steenkamp 1991). The first is that the British regarded Bechuanaland as a 'worthless strip of territory' and, having protected their access to the interior of Africa, were content to do 'as little in the way of administration or settlement as possible' (Campbell 1980). The alternative view is that this neglect was anything but benign. Parson (1985) argues that coercive capitalism undermined the self-sufficiency of Tswana societies in the interest of development at the centre – namely, South Africa. It is estimated that only one-tenth of the total labour force was able to find employment (usually short-term and temporary) within the Protectorate during British rule. This lack of local employment opportunities coincided with the establishment of deep-level mining in South Africa which created an immense demand for cheap labour. Thus, the discovery and mining of diamonds in Kimberley and then gold in the Witwatersrand area in 1886 engendered the creation of a steady stream of emigrants heading for the mines.

Although these structural forces changed the context within which movements were taking place, there is archival evidence that the ethnic groups in Bechuanaland responded differently to the demands of capitalism. The fact that land alienation in the Protectorate did not exist at the same level as it did in other southern African countries meant that most groups maintained their control over productive resources and could therefore determine the pace at which they were being integrated into the capitalist economy. Thus, there is evidence of labourers moving of their own volition (with the support of their chiefs), spurred on by the desire to obtain firearms and other Western goods. Research from elsewhere in southern Africa also supports this view. For example, Bozzoli (1990) argues that young men in the Phokeng region chose to migrate in order to escape the tedium of rural life as well as the pressure placed on them to become good husbands and fathers and provide for their families.

However, this was also undeniably the start of the period of forced migrations as the early 1900s saw the establishment of recruitment centres, particularly in or near the border districts. The recurrence of droughts and famines and the loss of cattle led to sharp declines in the subsistence economy. Significantly, the migrants began to lose control over the decision-making process. Now they were expected or indeed forced to take up employment at the mines by various colonial laws and pressures from tribal authorities. Gender differences were immediately apparent in recruitment drives, as it was men who were selected. The poll tax, for example, was administered on men (in their capacity as heads of households) so as to engender their movement to the mines. The demand for male labour was part of an imperial ideology which viewed women primarily as wives and mothers: an ironic fact in the face of women's considerable labour input into rural subsistence economies (Bozzoli 1983).

By 1880, 2,135 Tswana men from Bechuanaland were in South Africa (Schapera 1947). Moreover, the extent of male migration to South Africa grew so rapidly that, by 1924, the tribal authorities were perturbed by its incidence and its subsequent impact on the welfare of the tribal group. It is estimated that there were four times as many Tswana men in South Africa (totalling 18,400) in 1940 as ten years previously (Schapera 1947; Kerven 1982). These migrations were largely circular in nature[3] – a reflection of both colonial and traditional preferences. Chiefs were keen to retain control over their young men as well as their earnings so that male privileges over rights to rural land were maintained (Walker 1990; Bozzoli 1990). The colonial authorities also ensured that African men went back by issuing two-year contracts which deterred them from attempting to set up a permanent abode in South Africa. The impact and scale of male emigration on traditional Tswana society can be gauged by the fact that migration to the South African mines assumed the form of an initiation rite necessary to prove both adulthood and manhood. More often than not, the adult working lives of men began with migration to the mines (Field 1982). Coplan (1987) notes how, in the case of Basotho, migration to South Africa was seen as a test of male courage and endurance comparable to the cattle raiding and warfare activities of earlier generations.

Thus, by the 1900s, the migration of men was increasingly reflecting the impact of structural forces which were constraining the opportunities available to them. What about women migrants? The first fact which is immediately noticeable is that, historically, the migration of women was never numerically equal to that of men. However, it was still significant. In vivid contrast to the movements of men, considerable pressure was exerted on women to stay and not participate in migration flows. This in itself was because of both the nature of capitalist expansion in the region *and* the subordination of women in the traditionally patriarchal Tswana society. Capitalism called for labour and structures of patriarchy determined that it was male labour that was released from the rural areas.

The idea that African women were expected to remain in the rural areas, maintaining a continuous set of social relations to which men could expect to return, was a common thread in European writings. There was also an underlying political and economic motive for this separation of men from their families. It was recognised that workers constantly on the move between home and the mines would find it difficult to overcome barriers of geography, nationality and language and would consequently find it difficult to organise themselves against employers or the government (Brown 1983). Moreover, rural women employed in subsistence agriculture were an important aspect of the strategy to transfer the cost of reproduction and the maintenance of labour power on to the labourer's family so as to minimise the cost of mine labour (Nelson 1992). Massey (1980) argues that this strategy allowed mining corporations to maintain the same low real wage for over fifty years.

Women were virtually excluded from formal wage labour opportunities in South Africa and there were few opportunities to earn a living outside of the household (Sharp and Spiegel 1990; Walker 1990). The combination of contracts and the pass system meant that black workers were under incredible pressure to find work within a period of six days or face fines, imprisonment and expulsion – and women were not even engaged on labour contracts (Pycroft and Munslow 1988; Bell 1986). Moreover, male miners in South Africa were expressly forbidden from providing accommodation for their wives/partners, with most of them being housed in single-sex hostels. Gugler and Ludwar-Ene (1995) note that the gold mines in South Africa were only legally obliged to provide family accommodation for a mere 3 per cent of their African workforce right up to 1986 (although some mines had exceeded this level some years earlier), when it was proposed that the pass laws should be abolished.

But perhaps more important in determining the gender of migrants were the structures of patriarchy within Tswana society and the household economy which strove to keep women at home while releasing male labour. Ultimately societies like the Tswana were able and willing to export male labour because the system of household production was managed by women and these societies possessed the capacity to subordinate women's labour (Walker 1990). Thus, for example, in the struggle over domestic resources such as land and labour, women usually lost out. This in turn increased their dependence not only on men but also on the older women in their communities (Kinsman 1983). Initially, agricultural production was regarded as being more important than the remittances of migrant labour to sustain traditional communities, so that it was vital that it survived. As the contribution of women to subsistence agriculture was crucial, it was indispensable and so it was that redundant male labour was released or able to respond to the labour demands of the mines.

Furthermore, as Bozzoli (1983) argues, kinship and 'purity' ideologies provided a system for the control of women. The Setswana word for woman is *mosadi* which, literally translated, means one who stays or remains. Traditional initiation rites imbued women with an acceptance of both their subservience to men and the importance of communal good (Kinsman 1983). Perhaps the underlying fear of women's migration was that it would result in their sexual emancipation. The official European view in colonial societies was that 'pure' African societies were in fact rural communities and even the thought of African men as permanent urban residents was distasteful, hence the short-term contracts. More importantly, it was, in particular, believed that 'proper' female behaviour included a rural residence, which reflected a view widely held by both African men and European settlers that African women in towns were 'trouble'. Thus, women who migrated were portrayed as being morally loose and trying to behave like men.

Hence, there were strong legal and social sanctions in Bechuanaland right up to the 1940s which prevented any significant movement of women.[4] Women who wished to migrate were expected to obtain the express permission of their chiefs. Schapera (1947) notes that, among the Ngwato group in the Protectorate, Chief Khama introduced a law that no women could leave Bechuanaland by rail without the chief's permission, and his representatives were placed on railway stations to ensure that the law was implemented. This was an effective deterrent as migrants could take several weeks to reach their destination on foot. Further, two sub-chiefs in the Tati region decreed that women who left would not be allowed to return home, so as to discourage the further movement of women.

Yet, in spite of all these deterrents, women *did* move to South Africa. It is not possible to judge their numbers accurately as much of their migration took place outside the recorded and regulated migrant labour system. In fact, it was not until the 1930s that women and children were required to acquire passes to move to South Africa, which made their migration more visible. Schapera (1947) postulates that by the 1940s, 4.3 per cent of the total adult female population in the Protectorate had migrated to South Africa. One has to consider here why these women migrated in the face of strong social and legal deterrents. The majority of women who moved were single, abandoned or divorced. The migration of men and the consequent separation of families precipitated the process of the social disintegration of Tswana society. Already by the 1930s, there was an increased incidence of de facto female-headed households in the Protectorate and it was rare for married couples to live together for more than two months at a time (Schapera 1971). There are records, dating back to the early 1900s, of abandoned women who went to South Africa to look for their husbands with whom they had lost contact and some of whom had set up second households (Schapera 1947). Divorced women migrated as they were particularly stigmatised in Tswana society as being morally unstable. Thus, if they remained at home, they were subject to irksome restrictions. Moreover, an increasing number of women were either opting, or being forced, to remain single for longer periods of time.

Thus, in one way or another, these women were already defying culturally accepted norms of 'proper' female behaviour. Schapera (1947) notes that, under traditional law, unmarried women and women whose husbands had migrated remained legal minors under the care of a male relative. As such, these women effectively lost their access to the means of production and became dependants of the extended family. Rural lives were (and it can be argued still are) very hard on women. Women living with their parents were not treated as adults, irrespective of their age (Enge 1982). Often most of the domestic work fell on the daughter: for as long as a mother had a grown daughter in the yard, she would not touch the pots and pans. Moreover, as male migration to South Africa was closely linked with economic stress, the remittances sent by migrants were vital for the survival of poor households (Bell 1986). Since it was primarily male migrants who sent these remittances, their position within the household was further exalted. Both household structure and organisation were profoundly influenced by this penetration of capital (Bell 1986). Differences between households and individuals within households were accentuated. Generally, female-headed households and women living within nuclear and extended households were marginalised in this process.

Moreover, as Coplan (1987) argues, male migrants were humiliated and dehumanised by a cruel system which issued number tags to replace names. Male migrants themselves made an important distinction between the work they performed at the mines and that which they did at home. Mine labour was associated with wage labour and with destruction, while the latter was linked with the enduring value of cattle and self-construction (Comaroff and Comaroff 1987). The meaningful social and cultural existence of migrants was very much in the village, and the idea of a home to return to was central to their existence in the mines (Coplan 1987; Crush 1995). As such, on their return, these men were eager to reassert their undisputed control over their wives and homesteads – a position which could lead to resentment as the women's labour on the farms was unrecognised and marginalised.

In such a context, while working on the mines may have been forced on men through economic necessity, for women the story could be very different. For them, migrating to South Africa was an opportunity, a choice and an avenue for greater independence. By the 1930s, women had developed their own networks which provided information about far away and strange places as well as about accommodation, which was crucial while they searched for jobs. Spurred on by the perceived greater spending power of returned migrants, women expressed a strong preference to engage in wage labour (Bozzoli 1990). Progressively, parental and societal disapproval of female migration was tempered by a knowledge that male migrants were failing to return home or send regular remittances, which were crucial for household survival as traditional African societies were laid to waste by the forces of capitalism. With the relative disintegration of the extended family and kinship systems, waged employment was recognised as being more likely to provide women with an independent source of income as opposed to the customary gifts and compensation that they would receive for working on their husbands' or male relatives' farms (Dennis 1988).

Having migrated, women tended to adopt two types of movement which were significantly different from those of their male counterparts. They either migrated seasonally or stayed in South Africa for longer periods of time. The occupations they took up in South Africa were affected by their ties with their villages as well as by established gender roles. Tswana women were largely employed either as urban domestic servants or as farm workers. Domestic jobs afforded women the flexibility to return home when their parents demanded that they contribute their labour to agricultural production or for community obligations such as funerals. Longer-term migration was a response to the realisation that there were few prospects for women in the rural areas.

I want to end this section by looking briefly at the women 'left behind' or the women who never participated in these migration flows – the so-called victims. One could argue that these women were themselves engaged in forms of resistance to rural patriarchy. In the case of rural Tswana society, in the absence of a fairly large number of men, women were able to renegotiate their position in their communities in terms of both their access to resources and gender roles. Independent Botswana, for example, had to recognise the significance of women in rural production and decreed that rural women would now also be allocated land. Moreover, traditional gender roles were constructed around two ideals: being a wife and a mother – in that order. However, the high incidence of male emigration had a definite impact on sexuality, with an increase in pre-marital sexual relations, a larger number of sexual partners as well as a relative decline in marriages. Obviously women responded to these changes in different ways. While some undoubtedly rued the decline in marriage and the supposed security it offered them, other women came to realise that they experienced far greater levels of independence as single women (Datta 1995).

Post-Colonial Relations with South Africa

Few countries had such dismal prospects at independence as Botswana in 1966 (Picard 1987; Hartland-Thunberg 1975). It was one of the poorest countries in the world, a situation worsened by yet another long and severe drought in the 1960s which left 100,000 people existing on drought relief programmes and killed one-third of the national herd (Sillery 1974). The country was heavily dependent on British aid for both investment and recurrent expenditure. In addition to this, it had practically no infrastructure and inherited an economy which was extremely under-developed (Harvey and Lewis 1990). Surrounded by hostile white minority states, the country was widely believed to be incapable of surviving as an independent nation and it was thought that at the very least it would be a South African puppet, a functional 'bantustan'. The continued lack of employment opportunities as well as the widespread loss of cattle had a particular impact on men, as they were once again superfluous to agricultural requirements. Hence, the migration of men to South Africa continued unabated, reaching a peak in 1976, when 40,000 male Batswana labourers were recruited by the South African mines. Migration levels were particularly high in the districts bordering South Africa, such as Kweneng, where one-third of households had a father or brother employed on the mines in 1984 (Ingstad 1994). There is anecdotal evidence that older men, in particular, exerted a great deal of pressure on younger male kin to emigrate to the mines.

However, the numbers of Batswana migrating to South Africa began to decline after this date, due to two related developments. The first was the growth and expansion of the domestic labour market. By the late 1970s, Botswana was being hailed as one of Africa's few success stories. According to World Bank figures, the country was the best economic performer in Africa between 1970 and 1980, with a growth rate of 16.1 per cent (Picard 1985). Government revenue had increased more than tenfold and infrastructure had expanded (Hartland-Thunberg 1978). The mining sector in the country contributed significantly to this economic success. By 1975, the diamond mine in the town of Orapa was fully operational and was rumoured to be among the largest producers of industrial diamonds worldwide. The mining sector is now the largest private sector employer in the country (Ministry of Finance and Development Planning 1991). With the growth of other industries (both formal and informal), employment opportunities were beginning to appear in the country. This had a particular impact on women's migration flows, as a demand for female labour emerged and women have been particularly dominant in migration flows to the urban areas.

Perhaps a more significant reason for the decline in recruitment of mining labour was the South African decision to undertake a 'comprehensive planned disengagement of non-South African labour' (Taylor 1986: 35). Since the 1970s, the South African mines have pursued a policy of using more accessible sources of labour from within the country in order to reduce its dependence on foreign black workers who were reputed to make up 80 per cent of the total labour force in the early 1970s. In part, this was a response to the growing politicisation of this workforce as well as a realisation that the now independent (in some cases Marxist) black countries surrounding South Africa were not as pliant as the former British colonies had been.[5] In effect, it was recognised that South Africa's *cordon sanitaire* was disintegrating (Pycroft and Munslow 1988). Thus, a Government Commission of Inquiry set up in 1975 decreed that reliance on foreign labour had become too risky. The decision to use internal labour coincided with the demand for a more stable workforce. Consequently, mines began to issue longer contracts as well as to reduce the length of time miners spent at home, through initiatives such as 'valid re-engagement certificates' and 'early return bonus schemes' (Pycroft and Munslow 1988). Moreover, mine wages were raised to a level which would make them competitive with the lower ranks of industrial employment. It is estimated that between 1970 and 1982 black mineworkers' wages were increased fourfold in real terms so as to make them comparable with those in the manufacturing and agricultural sectors (Pycroft and Munslow 1988). Growing levels of mechanisation and a recession ensured that the labour demands of the mines could now be met internally and from the 'independent' homelands of Transkei and Bophuthatswana.

Hence, unlike their predecessors belonging to an earlier generation, Batswana migrants now found that opportunities to work in South Africa were declining significantly. Patterns of male migration to the mines were changed from being an intermittent occupation for a majority to a more permanent job for a smaller group of migrants (Harris 1982). Female migration, however, did not decline as significantly. This can be attributed to the fact that women's employment opportunities in the farms and homes were not subject to the same stringent restrictions. By 1981, however, the number of male and female migrants to South Africa had fallen to 32,576 men and 9,439 women (Central Statistics Office 1988). The Botswana government tried to cope with reduced numbers of migrant labourers by encouraging people to set up viable businesses within the country or to engage in agriculture with government help (*Daily News*, 7 August 1984). Efforts were made to lure multinational corporations away from South Africa to the more stable Botswana with the argument that it would hasten the demise of apartheid (*Daily News*, 9 April 1985).

Botswana's relationship with South Africa in this period was a mixture of bravado and realism, the latter based on the knowledge that South Africa possessed not only a larger and more sophisticated economy (on which Botswana was heavily dependent) but also a formidable army. For their part, the South African authorities undertook armed incursions into Botswana to weed out political refugee activists who had fled South Africa. These destabilisation activities are rumoured to have cost the SADCC region $10 billion between 1980 and 1985 (*Daily News*, 23 July 1985). Ever aware of its heavy reliance on South African mines to absorb its surplus labour, the South Africans exerted political pressure on Botswana in the 1980s to sign a non-aggression pact which would effectively deny a safe haven to fleeing political refugees. Botswana's refusal to do so was bitterly condemned and the government was accused of seeking economic co-operation with South Africa while 'terrorist' acts were being launched from its territory. As a show of its superior might, around 30,000 Batswana migrant workers were repatriated from South Africa (*Daily News*, 8 September 1984). Again, this had a particular effect on male migrants as Batswana women were invisible in the farms and homes.

Hence, the increasingly strained relationship between the two countries had a direct impact on migration flows. By 1991, an official total of 30,998 people from Botswana were in South Africa. The gender bias of this migration has continued, with 77 per cent of the migrants being men and 23 per cent women. In total, there were close to 6,700 Batswana women working in South Africa in 1991, the majority of them single (Central Statistics Office 1991). While male immigrants were predominantly employed in the mines, women were still largely working as domestic servants. The majority of migrants (both men and women) had been in South Africa for less than one year.

South Africa's first all-race elections took place in April 1994. While these elections were welcomed by the neighbouring countries, there were certain reservations as the realisation dawned that the geopolitical order in the region was going to be altered dramatically. There was an expectation that democratic South Africa would make amends for the widespread destabilisation in southern Africa during the years of apartheid, which had had serious political, economic and social consequences. Botswana's foremost concerns were the fate of its migrant workers, the future of the Southern African Customs Union and the impact of admitting South Africa to the Southern African Development Community (see Chapter 10). The Reconstruction and Development Programme of the newly elected South African government allayed some of these concerns, as it argued that sustainable reconstruction and development in South Africa could only be achieved through developments in the *whole* of southern Africa. Furthermore, President Mandela specifically drew attention to foreign workers in his address at the opening of Parliament in May 1994, when he stated that the government should deal sensitively with the issue of foreign workers in order to protect South African workers, to guard against the exploitation of foreign workers and to ensure friendly relations with other countries. Indeed, in the early months of 1994, the President of the National Union of Mineworkers argued that long-term African migrants should be granted citizenship in order to enable them to participate in the April elections. This was to address an injustice to African miners who were employed on successive short-term contracts under the apartheid regime, while their white counterparts were granted citizenship after five years of residence in South Africa (South African Institute of Race Relations 1995).

However, this rhetoric has to be evaluated against concrete actions. National newspapers and public opinion have become increasingly xenophobic as the newly legitimate South Africa has attracted a growing number of foreign workers, predominantly from the African continent. The 1991 Population Census revealed that there were 906,000 foreigners in the country, a significant proportion of them illegal immigrants. These immigrants are blamed for high levels of unemployment, for depressing already low minimum wages and for exacerbating the housing crisis. Moreover, the *South African Yearbook* (1995) reported that the international demand for minerals had fluctuated seriously, necessitating the restructuring of the industry. The cost of this restructuring has been borne mainly by the mineworkers, one-third of whom have been retrenched. The majority of these were foreign workers.

As David Simon pointed out in Chapter 1, South Africa's neighbours have yet to be convinced that the new South Africa is not continuing simply to regard the markets of its neighbours as dumping grounds for its manufactured goods, since it has made little effort to reduce existing trade imbalances. Botswana has a R3 billion annual trade deficit with South Africa, which looks set to continue as South Africa continues to pump manufactured goods into the market. Meanwhile, the fate of Botswana's emigrants – men and women – hangs in the balance.

Methodological Considerations

Urban Immigration and the Experience of Migration

By the mid-1970s, twice as many migrants in Botswana were heading for towns and mines within the country as for South African destinations. Women have been particularly dominant in these movements, and by 1991 it was estimated that they made up 49 per cent of the total migrant flow to the capital city, Gaborone (Women's Affairs Unit 1991). In the early years, much of this migration occurred within nuclear households, with married women either accompanying or joining their husbands/partners. More recently, however, the independent migration of women has gained momentum as the migration process has built up. Links between the villages and the city have spread information about urban opportunities while at the same time rural disenchantment has increased the desire to move. A lament often heard is that young women are not interested in agriculture as their mothers and grandmothers were a generation ago (Kinsman 1983).

It has been argued that the city can be empowering for migrant women as the responsibilities and initiatives that they take on there can undermine patriarchal privileges (Erman 1994). Thus, migration empowers women by emancipating them from male oppression. The opposing argument is that migration erodes the powerful position that rural women occupy, particularly in traditional African societies, and that it increases their dependence on men because of the inequitable and unfavourable distribution of educational and employment opportunities and destination areas (Hallos 1991). Both these arguments illustrate the earlier point of the homogenisation of women migrants: they are either victims or heroines. This view, in turn, is attributable to the empirical methods which are traditionally used to study migration. The narrow focus of these methods on the categories and 'laws' of migration fails to illustrate the differences in the migration experience of women, due to their neglect of both the importance of the individual migrant and the inherently fluid nature of the migration process. It is in this context that the use of biographical approaches has been advocated. They are seen as being particularly suited to illustrate differences and they provide 'the ground level context within which migration takes place' (Vandsemb 1995: 415).[6] By drawing on three specific biographical interviews (which will be supplemented by other related interviews and survey data), I want to illustrate some of the factors which are critical in determining whether migration to urban areas results in women's empowerment or not.

Kebonye and Tsholofelo:

> Kebonye is 21 years old, single with no children. She was born in the village of Mochudi. She attend-
> ed school for a few years but eventually dropped out before she could complete primary school. In
> 1988, her elder sister decided to migrate to Gaborone to find a job. She was the first person in the
> household to move to the city. Within a few years, she had two children and early in 1995 she asked
> Kebonye to come to Gaborone to help her look after her children as she was now employed as a
> full-time shop assistant. After some discussion, it was decided that Kebonye would move to the city
> to live with her sister. In return for looking after the children, doing most of the domestic work and
> cooking, her sister provides her with accommodation (in her two-roomed rented accommodation),
> pays all the bills and buys the food. Kebonye sleeps in the sitting room which she shares with anoth-
> er relative who has recently moved to Gaborone. Kebonye did not know how long she would be
> staying in Gaborone because her sister was talking about sending the children back to the village,
> in which case she felt that she would have to go with them (1995 field interviews).

Young, single women like Kebonye are often absorbed into the households of urban
based kin, and their migrations can be taken as an illustration of how the extended
household continues to function over geographical distances. The experience of
people like Kebonye of the urban 'place' is largely dependent on the power relations that exist within the extended household. It is quite common for older relatives to be able to call on their younger kin for domestic help, and in so doing they
are drawing on surplus labour which is not required in the rural areas. As a provider
of accommodation (in itself a very significant fact in the face of a growing housing
shortage and escalating rents) *and* jobs, urban kin can exert a great deal of control
over the lives of the young, single women who have migrated.

While Kebonye was quite happy with her life in Gaborone, this is not always the
case. Like Kebonye, Tsholofelo, another migrant, was looking after her sister's children in return for lodgings and food. She, however, was unhappy with her situation as she thought that her sister 'was bossy and shouted at her if the children cried
or if she beat the children for being rude to her' (1995 field interview). Tsholofelo
came to Gaborone in search of a job and lived with her sister while she looked for
one. On failing to find employment, she reluctantly agreed to look after her sister's
children as she had thought that she would get a 'better' job in the city. Her main
reason for looking after her niece and nephews was because her sister was providing her with accommodation. While this may seem a fair exchange, the fact that
Tsholofelo was not paid a wage and was expected to look after the children during
the day meant that her chances of finding a job were slim. In effect, women like
Tsholofelo and Kebonye become domestic workers for their families. This raises the
question of the exploitation of these women by their 'trust groups'. Moreover, their
situation can be even more precarious because of the changing natures of households. If urban sisters acquire male partners, the pressure on sharers like Kebonye
and Tsholofelo to find their own accommodation increases owing to lack of space.
This in turn increases the pressure to obtain a job so that they can pay rent.

Manyana:

> Manyana is single and eighteen years old. She comes from the village of Tonota where her par-
> ents still live. She has one daughter whom she has left behind in Tonota with her parents.
> Manyana came to Gaborone to look for a job as there were few such opportunities at home. She
> has no formal education. After hunting around for a job for four months in Gaborone, during
> which time she was able to live with her cousin, Manyana finally found a job as a housemaid.
> She was able to move into the servant's quarters where she lives rent-free. She gets paid P70[7]
> per month. She tries to send money home to her mother when she can but this is not always
> possible because Gaborone is such an expensive place. Manyana would prefer not to live with
> her employers because that would effectively shorten her workday. By living on the plot, she is
> asked by her employer to work at any time of the day or night – but she is not earning enough
> to be able to rent her own place. She had felt guilty sharing with her cousin before she got this

job because her cousin had had to support her fully – pay her rent and even buy her food. Her cousin did not complain but she felt bad, and so she took this job when it came along. She is also fed up with being shouted at by her employer for no good reason. However, she has to work to earn a living. She hopes that her daughter will come to live with her some time in the future but is not sure whether her employer will allow this (1995 field interviews).

Women with young children face greater problems in gaining access to accommodation with their relatives – largely due to the lack of space in urban dwellings rather than any stigmatisation of single mothers. Thus, the most common strategy employed by unmarried mothers is to migrate to the towns, leaving their children behind in the care of their grandmothers at least until they can find jobs and accommodation, and in some cases even longer. The 1995 field interviews revealed that nearly half of the mothers interviewed said that their children were living in the rural areas with their grandmothers. The incidence of children born out of wedlock is on the increase in Botswana due to the declining importance of marriage but also the continued value attached to motherhood. Tswana society has responded in a variety of ways to this increase, but in general it is true to say that there is limited legal obligation on fathers to support their illegitimate children. Ingstad (1994) further illustrates that not only are legal obligations weak, but men's relatives (specifically their mothers) also frequently discourage them from claiming these children as it weakens their right to their sons' income and support. Thus, increasingly, women like Manyana are having to support their children by themselves and in order to do this, they have to call on their mothers for help. It is important to remember that this is not a novel situation as, even in rural areas, children live in the villages where the schools are located, under the supervision of an elder sibling or grandparents, while their own parents spend most of their time on the land and at the cattleposts. What has changed recently is that the contact between the mothers and their children has become less frequent, especially if the villages are located at a considerable distance from Gaborone. One of my respondents sent her child to her mother-in-law during the period that I was visiting her in 1995 and she thought that, in all probability, she would not see her daughter for at least six to nine months. As children grow older and start to attend school, some mothers (depending on their income and residential status) are able to take them to Gaborone to attend school, as Manyana hopes to do. Domestic work is advantageous in this respect as it gives women the opportunity of combining their productive and reproductive duties.

The pressure to obtain a job so that they can support their children is immense on women like Manyana. The search for a job is often long and disappointing, partly due to low educational achievements but also to the prevailing attitudes about women's role in society. The significant incidence of women's unemployment in the sample is supported by national figures stating that 73 per cent of the unemployed population are women (Central Statistics Office 1991). The higher wages earned by men and the concentration of women among the unemployed reveal the persistence of an ideology that men are the main breadwinners, in spite of the high incidence of female household heads in the city as well as changing views on work among women themselves. Manyana, who has no education, can only hope to get a job in the informal sector where, as illustrated above, salaries are low and levels of control are high. Domestic service is not covered by minimum wage legislation nor the provision of mandatory holidays. At the same time, the experience of other women suggests that domestic work does have its advantages. First and foremost, it is usually accompanied with 'servant's quarters' which provide women with the essential accommodation that they need as soon as they move to the city. In addition, it requires few skills which these women do not already have. Moreover, some women prefer domestic service as it gives them the opportunity to pursue part-time courses. Charity, for example, was able to negotiate her working hours with her employer and thus attend an evening secretarial course (1995 field interview). In time, she hoped to be able to get a job in a company which would be a more stable occupation and provide her with a higher wage. There *are* success stories, like Dimpo, who came to Gaborone in 1986, took a part-time course in accountancy and now has a job in a company which brings her in a wage of P700 per month. She is married and lives with her husband and two children in their own house.

Pondi:

> Pondi is 54 years old and comes from the village of Mashunga. She came to Gaborone in the late 1960s. On her arrival in the city, she was able to occupy some land in Old Naledi (then an unauthorised settlement). She found it difficult to get a job because she was not educated and there were few opportunities open to her. When Old Naledi was upgraded, she was granted a plot in a new settlement, New Stands, in 1974. By this time she had started a hawking business which was located on her plot and she sold vegetables, drinks and fruit. She built a temporary house which she consolidated as money became available. In 1976, she decided to let a couple of rooms to supplement her income. By this time, her family had grown in size and she had four children so she needed the extra money. Over the years, she was able to raise the rent as the housing shortage in the city got worse. By 1992 her children had grown up and her family had increased in size again, now incorporating six grandchildren and one son-in-law. All her children work (two in government offices) and they now help her a lot as they buy the food and have assumed responsibility for other household expenses. She was still continuing to rent and run her hawking business as she wanted some money of her own (1992 field interview*)*.

Pondi's story illustrates the initiatives and strategies that 'women on their own' adopt to create new lives for themselves in the city. Pondi was quick to grasp the opportunity of obtaining a (illegal) plot of land which gave her access to a cheap dwelling. Subsequently, she again seized the opportunity to obtain a legal plot from the government on which she built her house. Thus, she was able to take advantage of a government-subsidised home ownership scheme which lowered her housing costs considerably. However, she arrived in Gaborone when there were very few employment opportunities open to women. This can be attributed to the fact that the proletarianisation of women followed that of men, so that the latter tended to dominate not only the traditionally 'male' employment sectors like mining and construction but also modern industrial and manufacturing enterprises. Older women like Pondi were further disadvantaged in formal labour markets because of their low educational attainments. Although a third of all men in formal employment have no education, a far smaller proportion of uneducated women are found in this sector. Pondi did find other ways of earning, and supplementing her cash income, by first setting up a hawking business which she could operate on her plot and later letting rooms. The money earned from rent or informal activities is vital for the survival of these women, particularly those who live in female-headed households. By the time of the interview, although Pondi was continuing her activities, her children were providing important support. The growth of Pondi's household is a vivid illustration of the dynamic nature of households. Pondi herself lived with a man for some time but then went back to living with her children. Now, she is the head of an extended household in which not only her children but also her grandchildren (whose mothers are not married) stay. Interestingly, this type of household is now located in the urban area.

Conclusions

Starting from humble beginnings, the migration of women in Botswana has gained momentum over time. Arriving at South African destinations, the older generation of Tswana women carved a 'new' life for themselves in spite of a great deal of social pressure from both the traditional and the colonial authorities. However, this migration did not necessarily lead to greater freedom. It has been argued that freedom in the migration process is only associated with the actual movement from one place to another – arriving in a new place is the end of that freedom. So it was for women who went to South Africa. They freed themselves from the traditional rules and regulations of Tswana communities but found themselves enmeshed in a more sinister, stricter environment. Yet, even here they found ways and means of (re)creating their communities and identities. Embellished accounts of life in this land of gold created myths and stories which successive generations of women migrants reinvented.

In the postcolonial period of Botswana's history, women have been particularly prevalent in migration from rural to urban areas. This migration runs counter to the conservative rhetoric of the state which is trying to preserve the 'traditional' way of life by keeping people, especially women, in the villages. However, rural disenchantment and urban promise are powerful forces. Like their mothers and grandmothers before them, women migrate in search of greater freedom and opportunities. For some, however, Gaborone is not dissimilar to the villages they have left behind – for here too there are restricted employment markets, biased housing policies and a male-dominated society. These constraints, however, have a different impact on women migrants because of inherent differences amongst female-headed households. Thus, while some continue to eke out an existence, others capitalise on the limited opportunities available to them.

Notes

1   I would like to thank the Nuffield Foundation for an award which enabled me to undertake research in Botswana in 1995. A total of 115 interviews were conducted with male- and female-headed households living in low income areas in Gaborone. These interviews are supplemented by a further 80 interviews conducted in 1992 in Gaborone.
2   Botswana was a British Protectorate (the Protectorate of Bechuanaland) from 1885 to 1966.
3   To the extent that miners returned to their country of origin if not their villages. Research from Lesotho shows how progressively miners spent their holidays in Maseru and went back to the mines without visiting their homes (Crush 1995).
4   It is important to note here that ethnic groups in Botswana are not homogenous and they did and do practise female subordination in different ways and to a varying extent (See Schapera 1947).
5   For example, President Banda's decision to stop miners from Malawi from emigrating to South Africa in 1974 as well as the riots and associated walkouts among the Lesotho workforce cost the South African mines dear at a time when the price of gold was on the increase. In this year alone, there were 26 riots and strikes in South African mines – the first since 1946 (Massey 1980).
6   The use of biographical methods has been criticised on various fronts. Peters (1983) argues that their focus on difference can lead to a proliferation of 'types'. Moreover, they have been criticised for presenting people, and their lives, as being frozen in time and space.
7   A Pula is worth £0.23 (late 1996).

References

Bell, M. (1986) 'Migration and Rural-urban Interactions', in Bell, M. *Contemporary Africa: Development, Culture and the State.* Longman, Harlow.
Bozzoli, B. (1983) 'Marxism, Feminism and South African Studies', *Journal of Southern African Studies* 9 (2): 139–71.
Bozzoli, B. (1990) *Women of Phokeng: Consciousness, Life Strategy and Migrancy in South Africa, 1900–1983.* James Currey, London.

Brown, B. (1983) 'The Impact of Male Labour Migration on Women in Botswana', *African Affairs* 82: 367–88.

Campbell, A. (1980) *The Guide to Botswana*. Winchester, Gaborone.

Castle, S. and Miller, M. (1993) *The Age of Migration: International Population Movements in the Modern World*. Macmillan, Basingstoke.

Central Statistics Office (1988) *Household Income and Expenditure Survey, 1985/86*. Government Printer, Gaborone.

Central Statistics Office (1991) *1991 Population and Housing Census: Administrative/Technical Report and Statistical Tables*. Government Printer, Gaborone.

Chant, S. and Radcliffe, S. (1992) 'Migration and Development: the Importance of Gender' in Chant, S. (ed.) *Gender and Migration in Developing Countries*. Belhaven, London.

Cockerton, C. (1996) 'Less a Barrier, More a Line: the Migration of Bechuanaland Women to South Africa, 1850–1930', *Journal of Historical Geography* 22 (3): 291–307.

Comaroff, J. and Comaroff, J. (1987) 'The Madman and the Migrant: Work and Labour in the Historical Consciousness of a South African people', *American Ethnologist* 14: 191–209.

Coplan, D. (1987) 'Eloquent Knowledge: Lesotho Migrants' Songs and the Anthropology of Experience', *American Ethnologist* 14: 413–33.

Crush, J. (1995) 'Vulcan's Brood: Spatial Narratives of Migration in Southern Africa' in King, R, Connell, J. and White, P. (eds) *Writing Across Worlds: Literature and Migration*. Routledge, London.

Datta, K. (1995) 'Rural Homes and Urban Dwellings? Gender, Migration and the Importance of Tenure in Gaborone, Botswana', *International Journal of Population Geography* 1 (2): 183–96.

Dennis, C. (1988) 'Women in African Labour History', *Journal of Asian and African Studies* 23 (1–2): 125–40.

Enge, M. (1982) *Women in Botswana: Dependent yet Independent*. SIDA Report.

Erman, T. (1994) 'The City as Land of Promises? A Turkish Women's Perspective', Paper given at the International Conference on Gender, Urbanisation and Environment, Nairobi.

Field, R. (1982) 'Batswana Labour in South Africa: Migration to the Mines' in Central Statistics Office, *Migration in Botswana: Patterns, Causes and Consequences* Vol.3. Government Printer, Gaborone.

Gugler, J. and Ludwar-Ene, G. (1995) 'Gender and Migration in Africa South of the Sahara' in Baker, J. and Aina, T.A. (eds) *The Migration Experience in Africa*. Nordiska Afrikainstitutet, Uppsala.

Hallos, M. (1991) 'Migration, Education and the Status of Women in Southern Nigeria', *American Anthropologist* 93: 852–70.

Harris, J. (1982) 'Economic Effects of Mine Labour Migration' in Central Statistics Office, *Migration in Botswana: Patterns, Causes and Consequences* Vol. 3. Government Printer, Gaborone.

Hartland-Thunberg, P. (1978) *Botswana: An African Growth Economy*. Westview, Boulder, CO.

Harvey, C. and Lewis, S. (1990) *Policy Change and Development Performance in Botswana*. Macmillan, Basingstoke.

Ingstad, B. (1994) 'The Grandmother and Householdviability in Botswana' in Adepoju, A. and Oppong, C. (eds) *Gender, Work and Population in Sub-Saharan Africa*. James Currey, London.

Izzard, W. (1979) 'Rural-urban Migration of Women in Botswana' in Central Statistics Office, *National Migration Study: Patterns, Causes and Consequences* Vol. 3. Government Printer, Gaborone.

Izzard, W. (1985) 'Migrants and Mothers: Case Studies from Botswana, *Journal of Southern African Studies* 11 (2): 258–80.

Jones-Dube, E. (1995) 'Non-metropolitan Migration in Botswana with an Emphasis on Gender' in Baker, J. and Aina, T.A. (eds) *The Migration Experience in Africa*. Nordiska Afrikainstitutet, Uppsala.

Kerven, C. (1979) *Urban and Rural Female-headed Households Dependence on Agriculture*. Government Printer, Gaborone.

Kerven, C. (1982) 'The Effects of Migration on Agricultural Production' in Central Statistics Office, *Migration in Botswana: Patterns, Causes and Consequences* Vol. 3. Government Printer, Gaborone.

Kinsman, M. (1983) 'Beasts of Burden: the Subordination of Southern Tswana Women ca. 1800–1840', *Journal of Southern African Studies* 10: 39–54.

Massey, D. (1980) 'The Changing Political Economy of Migrant Labour in Botswana', *South African Labour Bulletin*, 5 (5): 4–26.

Miles, M. and Crush, J. (1993) 'Personal Narratives as Interactive Texts: Collecting and Interpreting Migrant Life Histories', *Professional Geographer*, 45: 84–94.

Ministry of Finance and Development Planning (1991) *National Development Plan VI*. Government Printer, Gaborone.

Momsen, J. (1993) *Women and Development in the Third World*. Routledge, London.

Nelson, N. (1992) 'The Women who have Left and Those who have Stayed Behind: Rural-urban Migration in Central and Eastern Kenya' in Chant, S. (ed.) *Gender and Migration in Developing Countries*. Belhaven, London.

Parson, J. (1985) 'The Labour Reserve in Historical Perspective: Toward a Political Economy of the Bechuanaland Protectorate' in Picard, L. (ed.) *The Evolution of Modern Botswana*. Rex Collings, London.

Peters, P. (1983) 'Gender, Developmental Cycles and Historical Process: a Critique of Recent Research on Women in Botswana', *Journal of Southern African Studies* 10: 100–22.

Picard, L. (1985) 'From Bechuanaland to Botswana: an Overview' in Picard, L. (ed.) *The Evolution of Modern Botswana*. Rex Collings, London.

Picard, L. (1987) *The Politics of Development in Botswana: A Model for Success*. Lynne Rienner, Boulder, CO.

Pycroft, C. and Munslow, B. (1988) 'Black Mine Workers in South Africa: Strategies for Co-option and Resistance', *Journal of Asian and African Studies*, 23 (1–2): 156–79.

Schapera, I. (1947) *Migrant Labour and Tribal Life*. Oxford University Press, London.

Schapera, I. (1971) *Married Life in an African Tribe*. Penguin, London.

Sharp, J. and Spiegel, A. (1990) 'Women and Wages: Gender and the Control of Income in Farm and Bantustan Households', *Journal of Southern African Studies* 16 (3): 527–49.

Sillery, A. (1974) *Botswana: A Short Political History*. Methuen, London.

South African Institute of Race Relations (1995) *South African Yearbook*. Pretoria.

Steenkamp, P (1991) '"Cinderella of the Empire?" Development Policy in Bechuanaland in the 1930s', *Journal of Southern African Studies*, 17 (2): 292–308.

Taylor, J. (1986) 'Some Consequences of Recent Reductions in Mine Labour Recruitment in Botswana', *Geography* 71: 34–45.

Vandsemb, B. (1995) 'The Place of Narrative in the Study of Third World Migration: The Case of Spontaneous Rural Migration in Sri Lanka', *Professional Geographer*, 47 (4): 411–25.

Walker, C. (1990) 'Gender and the Development of the Migrant Labour System c.1850–1930: An Overview' in Walker, C. (ed.) *Women and Gender in Southern Africa to 1945*. James Currey, London.

Wolpe, H. (1972) 'Capitalism and Cheap Labour Power in South Africa: From Segregation to Apartheid', *Economy and Society*, 1 (4).

Women's Affairs Unit (1991) *Women and Men in Botswana: Facts and Figures*. Government Printer, Gaborone.

13 The Sexual and Economic Politics of (Re)integration: HIV/AIDS and the Question of Stability in Southern Africa

DOUGLAS WEBB

The reintegration of southern Africa after decades of conflict presents a host of opportunities to establish political and economic stability. The HIV/AIDS pandemic, however, represents one of the principal threats to the realisation of this stability. The complex linkages between HIV/AIDS and development rarely allow for generalisation, but in the case of southern Africa two distinct, but interrelated, processes are emerging: (i) the process of reintegration has in part shaped the epidemiology of HIV in the region, and has contributed to its continued spread, and (ii) the impact of AIDS in the region will create negative forces which will counteract the process of regionalisation. This chapter seeks to examine these two opposing processes and their wider implications, using Zambia as a case study.

Macro studies of HIV/AIDS in southern Africa rarely address the complex issues of political economy, but focus instead on the more tangible outcomes of sectoral impact projections using mathematical simulation models (Doyle 1993; Cuddington and Hancock 1995). The understanding of the relationships between macro-political and economic processes and HIV epidemiology is also poorly developed. Links are alluded to, but rarely, if ever, do the assertions that are made go beyond implication. The reasons for this reflect the rapid progression of the epidemic in southern Africa which has not allowed for serious reflection on its socio-epidemiological determinants. Instead, the focus has been limited to the viral epidemiology itself. In addition, the rapidly changing socio-political environment contextualising the epidemic has again not permitted the analysis of their complex interrelationships. The dynamism of both the epidemic and its socio-political context has left researchers constantly conducting retrospective analyses, while accurate foresight to date has been surprisingly lacking.

The regionalisation processes currently under way, however, now allow for the analysis of the epidemiology of HIV/AIDS and its broader political economy, in a single frame of reference. Previous (and ongoing) macro-events, such as drought and structural adjustment, have been heterogeneous in nature and differential in impact. As a result, their interrelationships with HIV epidemiology were place-specific and generalisations to regional level proved untenable (Webb 1997). With the focus on the new Southern African Development Community (SADC) and associated regional economic processes, a macro perspective is now possible and is attempted here.

Thanks to Alan Fleming, Theo Bull, Gaudenzio Rossi and David Simon for comments on earlier drafts of this paper and to Justin Jacyno for assistance with the graphics.

The Extent of HIV/AIDS in Southern Africa

The Joint United Nations Programme on HIV/AIDS (UNAIDS) estimates that there had been around 7.7 million cumulative AIDS cases globally by July 1996, with around 22 million people living with HIV/AIDS worldwide. Of these 90 per cent are in the developing world (AIDSCAP 1996). Projections for the number of infections by the end of the decade range between 30 and 40 million. In sub-Saharan Africa in mid-1996, an estimated 13.3 million adults were HIV-infected. Of the five countries with the highest HIV prevalence in the world, four are in southern Africa. Figure 13.1 and Table 13.1 show recent working estimates of HIV prevalence within the region's sexually active population. The estimates from the WHO are considerably lower than those produced by the countries themselves, reflecting different estimation techniques, and the WHO figures can be considered very conservative estimates.

Just why the seroprevalence figures in the region are amongst the highest in the world is a matter of conjecture. Suffice it to say that the region provides ideal conditions for the spread of HIV, namely, chronic widespread poverty, a high prevalence of other sexually transmitted diseases (STDs), poorly developed health systems (some of which have contracted recently as a result of structural adjustment policies), high levels of circulatory migration, rapid urbanisation creating gender biases, and chronic levels of violence. Further analysis would reveal the adverse influences of drought and structural adjustment (Webb 1997; Chalowandya et al. 1996), which exacerbate the processes which marginalise people and make high-risk sexual behaviour more likely. In addition, recent work on the genetic diversity of HIV has revealed that the subtypes found in sub-Saharan Africa, especially HIV-1 A and HIV-1 C, are more easily transmitted than variants found in other areas (Hu et al. 1996).

The wide variety in the seroprevalence figures subdivides the region into high and low prevalence areas. The distinction between the two zones is closely linked to male circumcision patterns (Caldwell and Caldwell 1996; World Bank 1996), although clear acceptance of this relationship is limited amongst analysts. Within

Table 13.1 *HIV/AIDS in southern Africa*

Country	Estimated HIV prevalence in the sexually active population (aged 15–59), January 1995 (%)[a]	Number of reported AIDS cases (last report date)
High prevalence countries		
Botswana	16.5–23	3,110 (Aug 1995)
Zimbabwe	15.9–22	54,744 (Aug 1995)
Zambia	15.8–20	36,894 (Apr 1995)
Malawi	12.3–20	39,989 (Sep 1995)
Low prevalence countries		
Namibia	5.8–15	5,101 (Dec 1993)
Tanzania	5.8	45,968 (Jun 19954)
Mozambique	5.1	1,815 (May 1995)
Swaziland	3.4	413 (Feb 1994)
South Africa	2.9–10.4	3,847 (Dec 1994)
Lesotho	2.7	515 (Dec 1994)
Angola	0.9	895 (Mar 1995)

Sources: WHO Website, July 1996; Whiteside, 1995; *SAFAIDS News*, Vol. 3, No. 2, June 1995 and Vol. 4, No. 1, March 1996.

[a] Initial figure represents the 1995 WHO estimate; the second figure represents the estimate from the country's National AIDS Control Programme.

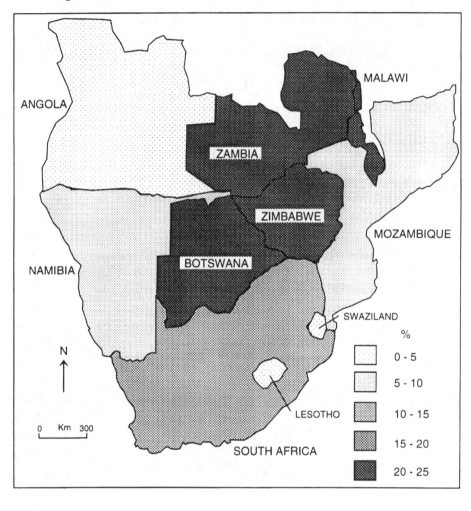

Figure 13.1 *Estimated HIV seroprevalence amongst the sexually active population, southern Africa, 1995*

the South African context the relationship is clearly demonstrated through infection patterns, which peak in KwaZulu-Natal: 18.2 per cent in 1995 compared with the national average of 10.4 per cent.[1] KwaZulu-Natal is the only region in the country where male circumcision is not traditionally practised (Webb 1994a). Conversely, lower than average levels of infection in Zambia's North Western Province may be linked to the fact that the ethnic groups in this area, especially the Luvale, are the only groups in Zambia who consistently circumcise their males.

Great heterogeneity across the region is therefore matched by marked intra-country differences in seroprevalence levels. In Zambia, sero-surveillance data from antenatal clinics in 1994 show a great diversity in the spread of HIV across the country, the range being from 1.6 to 31.9 per cent at clinic level (Fylkesnes 1995). As in other countries of the southern African region, there is a marked urban/rural differentiation in infection rates; in rural areas the average is around 10–15 per cent while in urban areas it is higher, at 25–30 per cent. For Zambia, evidence suggests that rates are still rising in rural areas while in urban areas they have stabilised. In 1994 the total number of HIV-infected adults was between 600,000 and 700,000, equivalent to between 14.4 and 16.5 per cent of the adult population.

Within the sexually active population, HIV prevalence across the region is highest in 20–30-year-old women and 30–40-year-old men. In the younger age cohorts, HIV prevalence is far higher in females; HIV infection rates for 15–19-year-old females in Zambia are seven times those of males in the same age cohort, indicating the high incidence of inter-age cohort sexual mixing and the fact that by far the highest number of new infections is in adolescent girls. Of additional concern is the strong positive correlation between educational status in females and seropositivity. Women with over twelve years of education show the highest HIV rates; those with none show the least (Fylkesnes 1995). This counter-intuitive finding could relate to the sexual networking of these women, whose partners are more likely to be affluent, in formal employment and have high access to other sexual partners. In addition, many of these women would have been infected before the onset of mass media prevention campaigns, and this correlation is likely to be reversed in coming years, as more affluent women have greater ability to effect appropriate behavioural change. In Zambia, infections are concentrated in the urban centres, being highest in Livingstone and Chipata (both border towns) and the capital, Lusaka, where prevalence in 1994 averaged around 28 per cent. A similar spatial distribution, i.e. a rural/urban differential, is to be found in neighbouring Malawi, with estimated rates of 12.3 per cent and 30.5 per cent respectively (*World AIDS*, July 1994:9).

Within Botswana, HIV infection is concentrated on the eastern side of the country, where population densities are highest and most of the urban areas are situated. The urban/rural differential is again apparent, with the highest rates of infection in 1995 in Francistown (39.6 per cent), Lobatse (38.9 per cent) and Chobe (37.9 per cent). Overall it is estimated by the Ministry of Health that 23 per cent of the sexually active population (aged 15–49) are seropositive.[2] The situation in Mozambique is not as severe as in neighbouring Zimbabwe, Zambia and Malawi, but the potential is there for a rapid increase in incidence rates. Nearly 25 per cent of its total population of 16 million people were displaced during the war and their reintegration is now almost complete. Many of the returnees following the ending of the civil war were refugees in the neighbouring high prevalence countries. There are an estimated 800,000 HIV-positive people in Mozambique, while antenatal prevalence rates within the country in 1994 ranged from 2.7 per cent in Maputo to 18.1 per cent in Tete. The high rate in Tete can be attributed to the high level of interaction with Malawi to the east and Zimbabwe to the west, as the main international trunk road runs through this 'Tete corridor'.[3] Both South Africa (Table 13.2) and Namibia (Table 13.3 and Figure 13.2) have seen a rapid increase in seroprevalence during recent years, and South Africa can almost be considered as the southern extension of the AIDS belt, with infection concentrated in the north and east of the country.

Reintegration and HIV Movement

The reintegration process was heralded by the ending of conflicts in the region which caused a massive movement of returnee migrants. In Namibia, the crucial event was the ending in 1989 of the war for independence between the South West Africa People's Organisation (SWAPO) and the South African Defence Force (SADF), soon to be followed by Namibian independence in March 1990. Within a period of eight months, 43,387 registered exiles returned to Namibia and, for the most part, resettled in their home locations, the majority of which are in the large northern communal area formerly known as the Owamboland bantustan (Simon and Preston 1993). Of these returnees, more than 28,000 were aged over 18, and it is reasonable to assume that a significant minority of this group would have been infected during their time in exile. This would represent a sudden influx of the virus into a low prevalence population, so distorting the epidemiology by staggering a smooth progression. Once returned to Namibia, the repatriates proved to be relatively mobile in their search for work, and were found to be twice as likely to move to seek work as the 'stayers' (Preston 1993). In Oshakati in 1996, HIV prevalence rates amongst the sexually active population were about 22.4 per cent, having risen from 3.6 per cent in 1992 and 14.2 per cent in 1994 (Table 13.3). Pre-independence seroprevalence was negligible.

The political and economic reintegration process itself is represented by a freer movement of people and goods within the region. The implications of this for increased HIV spread are considerable. The development of the regional market for South African, and to a lesser extent, Zimbabwean goods has opened up previously unexploited areas. Improvements in transport infrastructure, very often with South African or other bilateral aid investment, have allowed the flow of goods and people to increase markedly over recent years. Localised cross-border movements, in particular, are crucial. A case study area can illustrate the point.

Table 13.2 *HIV seroprevalence amongst antenatal clinic attenders in South Africa (%)*

Province	1990	1991	1992	1993	1994	1995
Western Cape	–	–	–	–	1.2	1.7
Eastern Cape	–	–	–	–	4.6	6.0
Northern Cape	–	–	–	–	1.8	5.3
Free State	0.6	1.5	2.9	4.8	9.2	11.0
Kwazulu-Natal	1.6	2.9	4.8	9.6	14.4	18.2
Mpumalanga	–	–	–	–	12.2	16.2
Northern Province	–	–	–	–	3.0	4.9
Gauteng	–	–	–	–	6.4	12.0
North West	–	–	–	–	6.7	8.3
South Africa	0.8	1.4	2.4	4.3	7.6	10.4

Sources: Department of Health (1995); *Epidemiological Comments*, 22, 5, Department of Health, August 1996.

Table 13.3   *HIV prevalence amongst antenatal clinic attenders in Namibia (%)*

Locality	1992	1994	1996
Windhoek	4.2	6.8	16.0
Oshakati	3.6	14.2	22.4
Katima Mulilo	13.7	24.5	24.2
Otjiwarongo/Grootfontein	1.9	8.9	n/a
Rundu	4.1	8.4	8.4
Swakopmundó	2.9	7.3	17.4
Keetmanshoop/Lüderitz	4.3	8.4	n/a
Namibia	4.7	8.4	15.4

Sources: National AIDS Control Programme (1995), *Results of National HIV Sero-Survey in Pregnant Women 1994*, Press Release, 10 February, 1995; National AIDS Control Programme (1996) *National HIV Sentinel Survey*, Ministry of Health and Social Services, Windhoek.

Arguably the highest area of seroprevalence in the world at the present time is the nexus centred on Lake Kariba on the Zambia/Zimbabwe border (Figure 13.3). This area encompasses the Southern Province of Zambia up as far as Lusaka and Mongu in Western Province, western and central Zimbabwe, northern Botswana and the Caprivi Strip of Namibia.

The area is characterised by large movements of people involved in formal and informal sector trading of either manufactured goods such as soap and household goods or agricultural products such as fish and maize meal. A high adult seroprevalence in Francistown, Botswana (39.6 per cent) strongly implicates cross-border movements with nearby Bulawayo in Zimbabwe. Francistown attracts many traders (mainly female) from Zambia and Zimbabwe, who are reputedly exploited sexually by police at the border post at Plumtree, who demand sex from women they catch crossing the border illegally. As a local magistrate commented, 'only the ugly ones come to court'.[4] Similarly high prevalences are found in the border town of Livingstone in southern Zambia (32 per cent in 1994), where many women make a living by crossing over to Victoria Falls in Zimbabwe, purchasing goods to sell at a marginal profit back in Livingstone. Children are increasingly entering this trade, and young girls are especially vulnerable to sexual exploitation which is closely related to informal sector trading. Interviews with streetgirls in Lusaka, for example, have shown the high level of casual sex which takes place between the girls and older men, who prey on their economic vulnerability and destitution (*Frontlines* 1995). Sexual exploitation of young girls at truck stops is also commonplace, with girls from around the age of twelve upwards involved (Shinkanga 1996). It is no surprise that by far the highest HIV prevalence rates in Namibia at present are in Kutima Mulilo in the Caprivi Strip (24.2 per cent in 1996, 24.5 per cent in 1994). Highly localised cross-border movements such as these create foci of infection, which are linked into other such foci by the extensive and improving transport networks. In Zambia, the highest prevalence figures follow the line of the road/rail networks closely but figures peak at the borders, where truckers and other itinerants are very often forced to spend more time than necessary owing to staggered border opening hours. The important factor of high traffic densities which is linked to HIV seroprevalence (Webb and Simon 1993), combined with the propensity of traffic to stop, make border crossings in the region classic 'high risk situations' for infection.

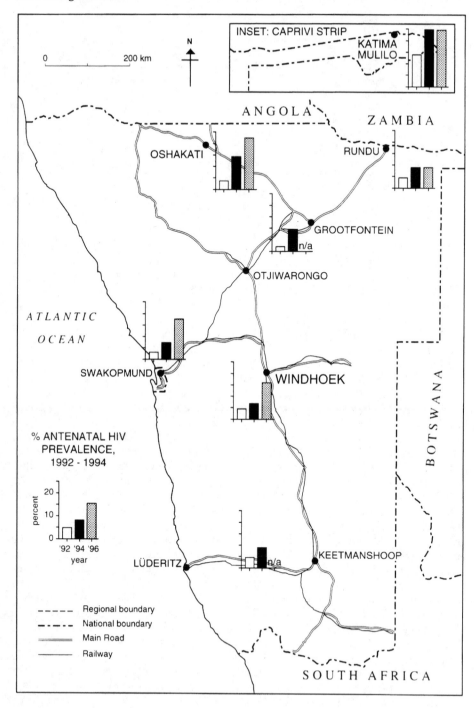

Figure 13.2   *HIV seroprevalence amongst antenatal clinic attenders in Namibia, 1992–6*

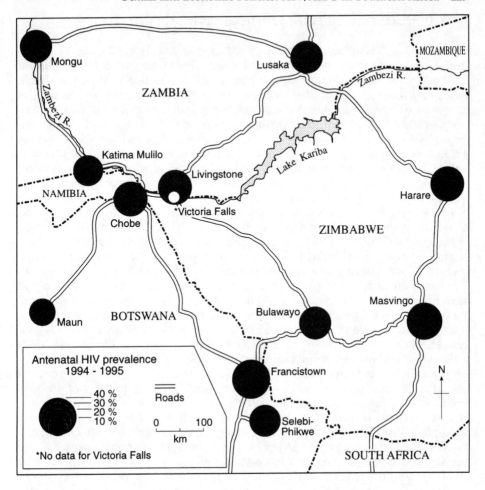

Figure 13.3   *Lake Kariba HIV/AIDS nexus: antenatal seroprevalence 1994–5*

The Nature of Regional Demographic Restructuring

The societal and economic impact of AIDS will be considerable and the manifestations of demographic change are not yet recognised (United Nations 1994). Population growth rates in some high prevalence countries will decline to almost zero, while the demographic structure will alter dramatically. In South Africa, projections suggest that there will be a reduction in the population growth rate to a minimum of 1 per cent by 2005 (Doyle 1993). Life expectancy is predicted to drop to around 45 (from the present 49) in Zambia, while fewer people will enter middle and late age (Fylkesnes 1995). This 'reverse ageing' process indicates that the proportion of 15–25-year-olds will double over the next few decades. Long-term demographic impact shows that, assuming no change in the total fertility rate (TFR), the population growth rate in Zambia might drop from 3.5 per cent in 1990 to 2.6 per cent. The effect on the growth rate when assuming a decline in fertility is clearly more significant, and the results show that by the end of the period (in 2030) the growth rate could be below 1 per cent (Fylkesnes et al. 1994). The TFR will in fact probably decline. Baylies's (1996) study of the impact of AIDS on fertility in Zambia suggests that AIDS will reinforce the existing trend toward having lower preferred numbers of children.

More immediately, the rising number of AIDS orphans across the region will stretch both extended families and government structures to the limits. The spatial variability of the epidemic means that orphan numbers are highest and most concentrated in the urban and peri-urban centres. As far as the status of orphans is concerned, several enumeration studies have been completed. McKerrow (1996) estimated that 51 per cent of children across four sample communities in Zambia were orphaned. In this case an orphan is defined as a child below the age of 18 who has lost one or both parents. This very high figure represents a virtual doubling of previous estimates, and suggests that the situation is extremely dynamic. This survey of nearly 1,000 households also indicated an average of 72 per cent of households caring for an orphan. This also represents a doubling of previous estimates; Mulenga (1993) estimated a national figure of 37 per cent of households in Zambia caring for an orphan. In Zambia, an estimated 500–600,000 children will have been orphaned by AIDS by 2000 (Fylkesnes et al. 1994). Overall, planners in high prevalence countries can expect an average of 20 per cent of children under 18 to be without one or both parents by 2000. In these areas, adult mortality rates stand at an estimated 3–5 per cent per year within the formal sector and are still rising (Baggaley et al. 1994).

The dependency switch in the household as parents fall ill is offset to some extent by help from other family members, but the impact of this reverse in the dependency relationship will become more severe over time as family support is stretched further. Evidence suggests that extended families are still managing to cope with the burden of orphans at this stage (McKerrow 1996; Foster 1996), with the caring function remaining with the mothers and maternal relatives. A distinct but still poorly understood coping mechanism is the migration of adults and children related to the morbidity and mortality of adult household members. Evidence suggests an urban-rural movement of children in particular, causing an extra strain on selected rural households through adverse changes in dependency ratios (Baylies 1996; McKerrow 1996; Poulter 1996).

The Sectoral Impact of AIDS in Zambia

The translation of demographic change into the assessment of sectoral impact within the region is a new subdiscipline within social science and economics in particular (Cross and Whiteside 1993; Whiteside 1995; Webb 1996b), which is still imprecise and in need of methodological strengthening. To date, emphasis has been placed on economic studies focusing on the impact of increasing morbidity and mortality on sectoral activity. On the whole, because of incomplete data sets and poor records, the research has not yielded concrete results but has alluded to widespread, but as yet undramatic, impacts on the Zambian economy.

The overall finding that there is an increasing loss of person-hours and growing costs related to absenteeism, training and ex-gratia payments to the ill and dying and their families, does not conflict with intuition, yet the widespread responses from sectors that might be expected are not apparent. Planning horizons are short and consequently are reactionary in nature; the experience of AIDS to date has been an aggravation rather than the cause of a wholesale shift in management practice. The unstable economic environment in Zambia, combined with the incidence of recurrent drought in recent years, has negated the potential for foresight in planning. The abundance of low-cost labour in the agricultural and primary sectors relieves the economic responsibility or need to make any major changes in production practices. The differential impact of AIDS in terms of worker mortality is now being recognised and is potentially the most serious aspect of the epidemic. As more companies recognise the importance of the loss of skilled labour, one of the worst hit cohorts, the real impact on company practice will begin to be seen. At the present time the tangible impacts are still essentially limited.

The most comprehensive macro-impact study of AIDS in Zambia has been that by Forgy and Mwanza (1994), who attempted to forecast the impact of AIDS on the development of the economy. Two scenarios are presented; one with the supplementation of foreign aid and one without. The worst case scenario envisaged is one in which Zambia is forced to absorb internally the costs accrued through AIDS. In this case, gross domestic product (GDP) is projected to fall by 9 per cent below the non-AIDS baseline projection by 2000. This represents a figure of $5 billion compared with the non-AIDS projection of $5.5 billion. Per capita income at the end of the decade would be only $494, or about 4 per cent lower than the baseline simulation. If foreign resources were made available to compensate for the loss (i.e. to cover costs of medical fees, worker shifts and retraining) then the GDP would fall to only $5.2 billion by 2000 (a drop of only about 5 per cent). This loss would be due solely to the absolute reduction in the predicted size of the workforce.

Specific impacts on industrial activity have been estimated through the analysis of medical records kept by companies, although these records on the whole are incomplete. Ching'ambo (1993) reviewed records of urban companies in Kitwe, Ndola and Lusaka for 1984 and 1992. Records indicated that 96 per cent of deaths were in the 15–40 age range and that there was an increasing trend in mortality. Over half (50.7 per cent) of employees who died were below 20 years of age. HIV/AIDS was implicated in 62 per cent of the deaths. Data from Barclays Bank, however, show peak mortality in the 30–39 age range (Keembe 1993). Estimation of impact is also possible through the analysis of trends in ex-gratia payments. At Barclays Bank the death rate rose from 0.4 per cent in 1987 to 2.2 per cent in 1992, and the Bank paid out more than ZKw 10 million (US$ 12,700) in the form of ex-gratia payments to the bereaved families in 1992. Medical expenses and training costs were on the increase while person-hours were reduced. How companies are responding to rising mortality and increasing costs was studied by Ching'ambo *et al.* (1995). The potential impact of rising mortality was mitigated by the finding that, in virtually every establishment studied, the lower strata of management and general workers were more affected than top management, even in proportional terms. In looking at various sectors, including finance and tourism, it was clear that direct costs, i.e. medical benefits, funeral grants and terminal benefits, had all increased substantially since the late 1980s. At the same time, however, they concluded that HIV/AIDS had not played a major role in management's decisions on staffing levels, and that market conditions were the crucial determining factors. There had been little change in training or recruitment procedures, although companies were tending to recruit already trained personnel rather than intensifying corporate training efforts. In conclusion, it was posited that planning horizons were still very short-term and that HIV/AIDS was not a factor in management decisions.

The analysis of the impact of HIV/AIDS on agricultural systems in Zambia is complicated by the occurrence of drought in three of the last four years. Dissociating the effects of drought, structural adjustment and the impact of illness is therefore subject to speculation and reliance on anecdote. Several attempts have been made to focus on the impact of AIDS, but a clear picture has yet to emerge. Drinkwater (1993) assessed the impact on agricultural systems in Ndola Rural and Serenje districts. At the time of the fieldwork the impact appeared to be limited, yet the predictions related to an overall increase in food insecurity and social dislocation, as urban residents returned to rural areas to die. The differential impact of AIDS in rural areas, given assumed homogeneous infection patterns, would result from variable degrees of capacity to cope with labour loss. Larger and more affluent farmers can rely on hired labour and draft power in the early stages of impact (*ibid.*), whereas smaller households would suffer to a greater degree. Baylies (1996) reported from fieldwork in agricultural households in Eastern and Lusaka Provinces that AIDS-affected households tended to concentrate on maize production at the expense of non-staple foods, once labour loss was a factor. In addition, livestock and other assets would be sold and the area under cultivation would be reduced. In her field areas, 16–20 per cent of households reported an AIDS death, and the crippling effect of the disease was exacerbated more by the long periods of morbidity of the patients than by the cumulative impact of deaths and changes in household composition. She noted that there was a tendency to underestimate the impact of AIDS on agriculture in the case study communities;

> there seems to be a partial denial of the impact of AIDS on agriculture, or at least of its systematic significance. Particularly in Chipapa [Lusaka Rural] there was a tendency to see the drought as far more responsible for declines in agricultural output than illness. (Baylies 1996:74)

In the commercial (estate) sector, the impact of AIDS is limited so far, and is concentrated on the supply of skilled and educated members of the workforce (Barnett 1994). A case study of Nakambala Sugar Estate in Mazabuka district (Haslwimmer 1994) revealed that the impact of AIDS was so far restricted, even though the person-hours lost due to TB/AIDS accounted for 50 per cent of the total. It was suspected that 75 per cent of deaths on the estate between 1992 and 1993 were HIV-related (NASTLP 1994). Haslwimmer noted that in 1992/93 the sale of sugar reached its peak since the founding of Nakambala, implying that AIDS had so far not had a serious impact on production. Indeed, the apparent impact of AIDS is mitigated in its severity through the perception of many involved in the sector that other pressures on production such as drought and morbidity caused by malaria and diarrhoea are far greater problems than HIV/AIDS. Baggaley's (1996) interviews with 23 farm owners/managers, also in Mazabuka, revealed reluctant acknowledgement that the number of deaths and the level of absenteeism were increasing in the sector, but these were only compounding the impact of drought and pre-existing health problems, especially malaria. The only tangible impact of the epidemic was the fact that some farmers had taken to hiring more labour to compensate for the increasing sick leave, absenteeism and funeral attendance. Only in passing did farmers mention the impact on production through the increasing loss of skilled personnel, a factor echoed in a separate study by Mwanza (1995).

The economic impact within the sector is still inconsiderable, and related to increasing benefit payments rather than lost production (*ibid.*). Calculations at Nakambala for the costs generated by HIV/AIDS during 1992–93 (based on lost workforce, extension of expatriate contracts, medical fees, funerals, pensions, repatriation and training) totalled $473,000, representing a mere 2 per cent of total costs (Haslwimmer 1994). At the present time in Zambia, the costs of the epidemic in the commercial sector are being borne mainly by households and farm workers, with minimal impact on production itself.

The impact of HIV/AIDS on the health sector in Zambia has been an area of much concern, due to the potentially enormous costs that it will have to bear without a massive restructuring of service provision. The envisaged transfer of costs of AIDS management from the higher-level institutions (i.e. the three major hospitals in Lusaka, Kitwe and Ndola) to lower-level institutions, such as rural health centres and finally the communities/households, is a recurring theme. Current reforms within the health sector are devolving funding and accountability to the district level to ease the burden on the higher-level institutions. Health-seeking behaviour in this respect has yet to follow suit, and patients are still seeking care at secondary and tertiary level institutions, in particular.

The major study in this area (Foster 1993) suggests that planning and providing care for people with HIV disease in Zambia is still considered a major problem. Care continues to be offered, regardless of the cost. The present situation indicates that the entire burden of providing care is falling on hospitals such as the University Teaching Hospital (UTH) in Lusaka and on families themselves, with the health centres experiencing a dearth of AIDS cases. The current status of about 15,000 hospital beds in 82 hospitals and 6,000 health centre beds in 950 health centres still shows that most of the health centre beds are underutilised or even unutilised, while the hospital beds have very high occupancy rates of 90 per cent or more. At Monze and Choma hospitals in Southern Province, 43 and 47 per cent of bed days respectively were taken up by patients with HIV disease (Foster 1995). Of the patients in a bed census conducted in Monze and Choma hospitals, 87 per cent had one or more clinical reasons for being in hospital that day, and 12 per cent non-clinical reasons; 24 per cent could have been treated at a lower-level facility.

In a separate study, Hira *et al.* (1993) attempted to estimate the direct costs of AIDS and HIV diseases to the health system. The cost of each case managed was estimated for UTH and was categorised under the following items: professional staff, diagnostic tests/procedures, drugs, in-patients, out-patients, and home-based care. They concluded through extrapolation that the annual cost of clinical care of AIDS patients was $27.1 million and for HIV-related disease $27.3 million. This represents an unprecedented burden on the health services in Zambia. Two points are important here. First, the saving of costs within the health sector with regard to the decentralisation of health care for chronically ill patients to the community and household levels, through the saving on hospital costs and, second, transport of home-based care staff costs, represent a direct transfer of costs to the household level in terms of labour, time and material resources, with the additional loss in the quality of care provided. There are no real savings in that sense. Secondly, the proportion of patients in direct contact with home care is small, and is estimated to comprise between 5 and 20 per cent of the total. While it is estimated that 6.5 per cent of households in Zambia contain a chronically ill patient (Sichone *et al.* 1996), it must be realised that only a fraction of the real costs of HIV/AIDS are being borne by the formal health sector, and it has to be concluded that households are bearing, and will continue to bear, the largest burden of AIDS-related costs.

The Impact of AIDS and the Implications for the SADC

The example of Zambia provides several pertinent lessons which can be applied to the other high prevalence countries in the region, most notably Malawi, Zimbabwe, Botswana and to an increasing extent also South Africa and Namibia.

(i)   In the commercial sectors, the abundance of cheap labour has meant that companies are not facing huge direct costs related to recruitment and training, but reaction is being noted in relation to the increasing loss of skilled labour.

(ii) Company decision-making processes in the face of rising costs need to be monitored to understand the nature of the planning horizon, especially in the newly liberalised economic environment. In relation to mortality-related costs, planning horizons remain close.

(iii) In the agricultural sector, currently AIDS is not seen to be a determining factor of production as compared with market conditions and environmental factors. Even in agricultural households, AIDS is not perceived as a priority and changes in labour composition and production activity are the norm, even under normal conditions. AIDS is perceived as only exacerbating pre-existing stresses rather than creating new ones.

(iv) The public sector is being affected by rising costs but there has been no discernible policy response in terms of mitigation.

(v)   In the health sector, the potentially enormous costs are being transferred to the household and community level, both by the current process of health reforms and by the development of home care structures.

(vi) At household level, the demographic changes are in the context of extreme poverty, making the specific impacts difficult to ascertain.

The factor of increasing costs in the private sector is crucial. With the economic focus in southern Africa closely linked to liberalisation and increased intra-regional (primarily northward) flows of investment capital, companies will increasingly be drawn into the international competitive environment. This integration is occurring without the buffering effect of the previously protectionist macroeconomic policies. Cost-cutting in relation to production costs is thus a central theme of the recent wave of privatisations. Within the Zambian context, for example, the projected impact of AIDS on sectoral activity will place added pressure on companies to keep costs down, specifically in the light of increasing training costs, absenteeism, growing morbidity and mortality rates and record levels of ex-gratia payments.

The reconciliation of these combined economic effects with higher levels of competition faces an additional problem, namely the trend towards the 'regionalisation' of policies relating to workplace practices pertaining to chronic illness. Such legislation attempts to uphold the rights of seropositive workers, by removing any form of discrimination based on HIV status. With increasing levels of adult mortality within companies, such legislation would arguably negate current economic acumen (i.e. pure profit motive) and result in conflict between the policy-makers within governments and the SADC, and the private sector itself. Large-scale industries in the region tend to deny any debilitating impacts of AIDS so far (Amanor-Wilks 1995) but with the South African mines expected to experience an estimated 12,000–40,000 deaths per annum in the coming years, for example, (Heywood 1996), the potential for conflict between human rights and economic interests is very real.

Slow realisation at managerial level of the full implications of AIDS has inhibited widespread progressive policies, namely, in-house education programmes, improved health services and condom provision, being introduced in the workplace. A widely accepted, if clandestine, policy of pre-employment and pre-training HIV screening in the larger Zambian companies has been the most common response to the epidemic so far in terms of mitigating its impact. This practice, which is discouraged by both the World Health Organization (WHO) and the International Labour Organization (ILO), is increasingly facing regulatory sanctions in the region. In South Africa a reported 18 per cent of companies test prospective employees, but on closer analysis many anomalies within company policy become apparent, with evidence of workplace discrimination against HIV-positive employees (Wilkins 1995). The pre-employment testing of employees in the South African mines has been commonplace despite an agreement between the Chamber of Mines and the National Union of Mineworkers which prohibits such practices (Heywood 1996).

Ambiguities in existing laws and directives have led to a region-wide development of codes of conduct which attempt to enforce relatively liberal policies on HIV testing, and recruitment and training procedures, as well as employee benefits (Loewenson 1995). Regional institutions such as the Southern African Trade Union Co-ordinating Council (SATUCC) and the Organisation of African Trade Union Unity (OATUU) as well as the ILO are integrally involved. The aim is to push for a regional code to be accepted by the SADC Labour and Employment Commission, a process started in late 1996 (Klouda 1997).

The central point will be the extent of the legislation regarding workplace policies in the region and the nature of subsequent enforcement. The Zambian Federation of Employers (ZFE) maintains that pre-employment testing is unacceptable while acknowledging that it is common practice amongst its members. Regionally mandated codes are given lip-service, as employers are unwilling to object to them openly, but they would not be adhered to in practice. The impression given by the ZFE is that few companies are regional in their outlook on these matters, and that the frame of reference remains national for most Zambian companies. The next question relates to the power of SADC member states to enforce such legislation. In Zambia, the influence of the labour force on government is relatively weak, and resistance from government to private sector practice is unlikely to be considerable. Given the poor economic position of the government in Zambia, any other attitude would be untenable in any case. In South Africa and Zimbabwe, however, the governments are far more involved with the welfare of employees and their influence on private sector practice is extremely strong. The nature of the enforcement of the recently drafted tripartite (i.e. employers, trade unions and government) AIDS and Employment Code in Botswana could give an advance indication of likely enforcement patterns across the region. Enforcement of national and/or regional codes, however, is likely to be inconsistent across the region, so bringing their validity into question. If widespread variations in enforcement and practice do indeed emerge, this could become a factor in some industrial (re)location, from relatively high-cost South Africa and Zimbabwe to other states within the region. It is likely that South Africa will lead the way within the SADC on these issues, because of both relatively strong government and NGO commitment to human rights, and will be the source of legal test cases which could heavily influence the direction of SADC policy.

The enormous costs of the epidemic are likely to become a political issue over the coming decade. The probable reliance on South Africa as the regional welfare provider will reflect both its economic dominance and its lingering obligations to other countries in the region in acknowledgement of support for the freedom movement during the apartheid years and the large numbers of migrants from across the region working in South Africa during the last century. For example, President Mandela's desire to postpone the November 1996 elections in Zambia reflected a certain degree of allegiance to the former president, Kenneth Kaunda, a keen host of ANC exiles in the decades preceding the 1994 South African elections. Mandela has subsequently made further public gestures of support for Kaunda, who has faced harassment from the Zambian government. Clearly, the ANC government is conscious of its debt to neighbouring states and the SADC may be viewed as the most appropriate conduit of South African welfare support to the rest of the region. The limits of support appear to go no further north than the SADC boundary, as testified by South Africa's initial unwillingness to involve itself in the crisis in Eastern Zaire (now the Democratic Republic of Congo) in late 1996. If the SADC does not adopt this welfare role then a reactionary return to isolationism may be the result, and chronic economic problems across the region may force governments to rebuild economic and immigration boundaries which are being removed in the name of regionalism.

Conclusion: An Increase in Political and Social Instability?

In the medium and long term, the impact of AIDS in the region will severely test the resilience of regional and national structures. The enormous welfare implications of the epidemic are self-evident, but other effects of demographic restructuring are more subtle, yet pervasive. The growing number of destitute children and adolescents in the region will have a severe impact on the human resource base. Increasing costs in the public sector, in education especially, result in rationalised services and, in the Zambian context, a likely overall contraction of the educational sector itself. In South Africa, an estimated 52 per cent of the 11 million people aged 16–30 are unemployed; 27 per cent of this age group are classified as marginalised (i.e. unemployed, poorly educated, with few prospects of formal sector employment), with another 43 per cent at risk of being marginalised (Barnard 1996). These marginalised young people are themselves at risk of contracting HIV (Webb 1996a), and overall the at-risk population is steadily increasing rather than decreasing. The effects of this growing number of marginalised young people, both in absolute and proportional terms, are unknown, and research must urgently focus on this aspect of demographic restructuring. The focus to date has been on the declining number of producers aged over 30, rather than on the increasing proportion of adolescents aged 15–25 (Rowley et al. 1990; Fleming 1993). The need for this group to become producers earlier than the same-aged counterparts in previous decades to compensate for the loss of older producers could have severe consequences, such as increasing the incidence of child (informal) labour and raising the numbers of street children, both of which would have concomitant implications for levels of delinquency and disempowerment in young people. If current orphan estimates in

Zambia are anywhere near correct, there are approximately 2 million Zambian children who had lost one or both parents by late 1996, out of a total population of around 9 million. This situation is potentially very serious and certainly unprecedented.

Other signs of instability relate to the impact of AIDS on the military in the region (Jackson 1996; Yeager 1995; Webb 1994b), with very high expected mortality rates amongst uniformed personnel. HIV prevalence rates in the region's military are likely to be far higher than those in the corresponding civilian populations. Political instability in central Africa has been linked to high AIDS mortality rates, and in southern Africa political unrest in the future could be in the context of inefficient and depleted military resources, combined with large numbers of disenfranchised adolescents. How the SADC copes with this realisation is still an open question.

Overall the HIV/AIDS pandemic has come at the wrong time in the region. Existing stresses, now being addressed at a regional level, will be exacerbated to unmanageable levels by the cumulative impact of AIDS-related mortality. Both the full economic and human consequences of AIDS are still to be seen and the reintegration process itself may not survive such a shock, even if it is over the long term and is continually denied by many of the key actors. Reliance on donor aid is becoming endemic in many parts of sub-Saharan Africa, including most SADC states, and no end to the trend is in sight. AIDS may well increase this reliance. Future historians of Africa may trace the resurgence in neo-colonial activity back to the time when the strains placed upon the region by AIDS became simply too great.

Notes

1. Figures released by the Department of Health, Government of South Africa, 1996.
2. Figures from the Ministry of Health, Gaborone, reported in *AIDS Analysis Africa* 6 (3), June 1996.
3. Figures from the NACP, presented to the SANASO Conference in Maputo in July 1994, reported in *AIDSLink*, No. 20, September 1995.
4. 'Sex-for-release at border post', *The Namibian*, 4 February 1994.

References

AIDSCAP (1996) Family Health International, Harvard School of Public Health and UNAIDS (1996) *The Status and Trends of the Global HIV/AIDS Pandemic Symposium Final Report.* Vancouver, July.

Amanor-Wilks, D. (1995) 'Business Confidence Still High in Zimbabwe', *AIDS Analysis Africa*, 5(6): 2.

Baggaley, R. (1996) 'Pilot Anti-AIDS Campaign for Farm Workers, Mazabuka District'. Zambia National Farmers Union/ UNICEF, Mano Consultancy Services, Lusaka.

Baggaley, R., Godfrey-Faussett, P., Msiska, R. *et al.* (1994) 'Impact of HIV on Zambian Businesses', *British Medical Journal* 309: 1549–50.

Barnard, D. (1996) 'The Challenge of the New Generation', *PRODDER Newsletter* 7(4): 1–3. Data produced by the Community Agency for Social Enquiry (CASE).

Barnett, T. (1994) *The Effects of HIV/AIDS on Farming Systems and Rural Livelihoods in Uganda, Tanzania and Zambia.* FAO, Lusaka.

Baylies, C. (1996) 'Fertility Choices in the Context of AIDS-Induced Burdens on Households and the Environment', University of Leeds, unpublished manuscript.

Buve, A., Foster, S., Mbwili, C., Mungo, E., Tollenare, N. *et al.* (1994) 'Mortality among Female Nurses in the Face of the AIDS Epidemic: a Pilot Study in Zambia', *AIDS* 8(3): 396.

Caldwell, J.C. and Caldwell, P. (1996) 'The African AIDS Epidemic', *Scientific American*, March: 62–8.

Chalowandya, M.C., Nkunika, M.D., Chitomfwa, P.B. (1996) 'Drought as a Deterrent to Safer Sexual Behaviour among the Youths in rural Zambia', unpublished report, Family Health Trust, Lusaka.

Ching'ambo, L.J. (1993) *Zambia: The Impact of HIV/AIDS on the Productive Labour Force.* ILO, Lusaka.

Ching'ambo, L.J., Mwanza, K. M., Kalyalya, D.H., Phiri, M.F., Kunkhuli, S.W.M. (1995) *The Socio-economic Impact of HIV/AIDS on Selected industries in Zambia*. SIDA/WHO, Lusaka.

Cross, S. and Whiteside, A. (eds.) (1993) *Facing up to AIDS; the Socio-economic Impact in Southern Africa*. Macmillan, London.

Cuddington, J. T. and Hancock, J. D. (1995) 'The Macroeconomic Impact of AIDS in Malawi: a Dualistic, Labour Surplus Economy', *Journal of African Economies* 4(1): 1–28.

Department of Health (1995), *Epidemiological Comments*, 22(5), Department of Health, August 1996, Johannesburg.

Doyle, P. (1993) 'The Demographic Impact of AIDS on the South African Population' in Cross and Whiteside.

Drinkwater, M. (1993) *The Effects of HIV/AIDS on Agricultural Production Systems in Zambia; An Analysis and Field Reports of Case Studies Carried out in Mpongwe, Ndola Rural District and Teta, Serenje District*. FAO, Lusaka.

Fleming, A. (1993) 'Lessons from Tropical Africa for Addressing the HIV/AIDS Epidemic in South Africa' in Cross and Whiteside.

Forgy, L. and Mwanza, K. (1994) *The Economic Impact of AIDS in Zambia*. USAID, Lusaka.

Foster, S. (1993) *Cost and Burden of AIDS on the Zambian Health Care System: Policies to Mitigate the Impact on Health Services*. USAID, Lusaka.

Foster, S. (1995) *Study of Adult Disease in Zambia (Final Report – Preliminary Version)*. Overseas Development Administration, Lusaka.

Foster, G. (1996) 'AIDS and the Orphan Crisis in Zimbabwe', *AIDS Analysis Africa* 6(3): 12–13.

Frontlines (1995) 'Zambian children speak out on AIDS', 3, Lusaka.

Fylkesnes, K. (1995) 'An Update on the Current HIV/AIDS Situation and Future Demographic Impact', Paper presented at a conference on the socio-economic impact of HIV/AIDS in Zambia, Lusaka, May.

Fylkesnes, K., Brunborg, H., Msiska, R. (1994) *The Socio-Economic Impact of AIDS: Zambia: The Current HIV/AIDS Situation and Future Demographic Impact*. National AIDS/STD/TB/Leprosy Programme, Ministry of Health, Lusaka.

Government of the Republic of Zambia/United Nations (1996) *Prospects for Sustainable Human Development in Zambia; More Prospects for Our People*. United Nations, Lusaka.

Haslwimmer, M. (1994) *The Social and Economic Impact of HIV/AIDS on Nakambala Sugar Estate*. FAO, Lusaka.

Heywood, M. (1996) 'Mining Industry Enters a New Era of AIDS prevention', *AIDS Analysis Africa* 6(3): 16.

Hira, S., Sunkutu, R., Wadhawan, D., Mamtani, H., (1993) 'Direct Cost of AIDS Case Management in Zambia', Paper presented to the IXth International Conference on AIDS, Berlin.

Hu, D.J., Dondero, T.J., Rayfield, M.A. *et al.* (1996) 'The Emerging Genetic Diversity of HIV', *Journal of the American Medical Association* 275(3): 210–16.

Jackson, H. (1996) 'AIDS and the Military; the Quintessential AIDS in the Workplace Issue', *SAFAIDS News* 4(2): 2-6.

Keembe, A.L. (1993), 'The Employer's Response to HIV/AIDS and the Workplace', unpublished, Lusaka.

Klouda, A. (1997) 'SADC Establishes a Regional Action Plan', *AIDS Analysis Africa*, 7(1): 4-7.

Loewenson, R. (1995) 'SATUCC Drafts Regional Code on AIDS and Employment', *SAFAIDS News* 3(3): 6-7.

McKerrow, N. (1996) *Responses to Orphaned Children*. UNICEF, Lusaka.

Mulenga, C. (1993) *Orphans, Widows and Widowers in Zambia: a Situation Analysis and Options for HIV/AIDS Survival Assistance*. Social Policy Research Group, UNZA/MOH.

Mwanza, K.M. (1995) 'The Impact of HIV/AIDS on Agriculture' in Ching'ambo et al.

NASTLP (1994) *Report of the Workshop on the Effects of HIV/AIDS on Agricultural Production Systems*. Ministry of Health, Lusaka.

Nyirenda, B.N. (1993) 'Experiences at Barclays Bank', Paper presented at the national workshop for AIDS and the workplace, Siavonga, July 1993.

Poulter, C. (1996) 'Review of Demographic Characteristics of Patients of a Home Based Care Team', Paper presented to the XIth International Conference on AIDS, Vancouver, July.

Preston, R. (1993) *The Integration of Returned Exiles, Former Combatants and Other War-affected Namibians: Final Report*. Namibian Institute for Social and Economic Research, Windhoek.

Rowley, J.T., Anderson, R.M., Ng, T.W. (1990) 'Reproducing the Spread of HIV infection in Sub-Saharan Africa: Some Demographic and Economic Implications', *AIDS* 4: 47–56.

Shinkanga, M. (1996) *Child Sexual Abuse in Zambia*. YWCA, Lusaka.

Sichone, M., Mulenga, D., Msiska, R., Fylkesnses, K. (1996) *Care of Chronically ill/HIV Diseased at Home: Adequacy, Coping Capacities and Support Needs in some Zambian Communities*. NASTLP, Lusaka.

Simon, D. and Preston, R. (1993) 'Return to the Promised Land: Repatriation and Resettlement of Namibian Refugees, 1989–1990', in Black, R. and Robinson, V. (eds) *Geography and Refugees: Patterns and Processes of Change*. Belhaven, London.

United Nations (1994) *AIDS and the Demography of Africa*. Department for Economic and Social Information and Policy Analysis, New York.

Webb, D. (1994a) 'Modelling the Emerging Geography of HIV', *AIDS Analysis Africa* 4(4): 8.

Webb, D. (1994b) 'AIDS and the Military: the Case of Namibia', *AIDS Analysis Africa*, 4(2): 6.

Webb, D. (1996a) 'A Situation Analysis of Children in Especially Difficult Circumstances in Zambia', *SAFAIDS News*, 4(1): 2–6.

Webb, D. (1996b) 'The Socio-economic Impact of AIDS in Zambia', *SAFAIDS News* 4(4): 2–10

Webb, D. (1997) *HIV and AIDS in Africa*. Pluto Press, London.

Webb, D. and Simon, D. (1993) *Migrants, Money and the Military; the social epidemiology of HIV in northern Namibia*. CEDAR Research Paper No. 8, Department of Geography, Royal Holloway, University of London, Egham, Surrey; and copublished (1995) as Occasional Paper No. 4, Namibian Economic Policy Research Unit (NEPRU), Windhoek.

Whiteside, A. (1995) 'Planning for AIDS Beyond the Health Sector', Paper Presented to the IXth International Conference on AIDS in Africa, Kampala.

Wilkins, N. (1995) 'The Response of South African Companies to HIV/AIDS', *AIDS Analysis Africa* (Southern African Edition) 6(3): 8.

World Bank (1996) *AIDS Prevention and Mitigation in Sub-Saharan Africa; an Updated World Bank Strategy*. Washington, DC.

Yeager, R. (1995) 'Armies of East and Southern Africa Fighting a Guerilla War with AIDS', *AIDS Analysis Africa* 5(6): 10–12.

Conclusion

14 Reflections:
Writing (on) the Region
DAVID SIMON

On Writing (on) the Region

It became fashionable at the beginning of the 1990s to talk about South, and indeed southern, Africa being 'at the crossroads', by which it was meant that the choice of overall direction then to be made would be critical in determining the future. In one sense this was no doubt true, in as much as any one historic moment – the ceremonial act of conferring independence on Namibia, the Rome Peace Accords on Mozambique, Kamuzu Banda's electoral defeat in Malawi, or Nelson Mandela's inauguration as South Africa's first black President, for example – can be said to represent such a juncture.

This is certainly a widespread conception in the popular and scholarly mind alike. The attraction of such a construct – for simplicity, as a form of shorthand, because of romantic attachment or its symbolic potency – is clear and perfectly legitimate. Analytically, however, it is generally more accurate and insightful to focus on the *processes* in which these specific events are entrained. This is not to suggest that, apart from unheralded cataclysms, one-off events inevitably lack catalytic or cathartic effect or cannot represent fundamental ruptures. Nor am I implying that we should not be concerned with them. After all, any attempt at periodisation, no matter how contemporary or historical, relies on particular events or dates to discern the various periods in terms of distinguishing features or processes. Rather I am reasserting the importance of that broader dynamic, the process through which pressures and contradictions build up and momentum is generated towards a landmark event, and what happens thereafter. Social and political earthquakes generally arise no more instantly in peaceful, frictionless contexts than do their tectonic equivalents. Whether perceived or not, there is a build-up and, following a transitional period of instability or uncertainty, a new state of 'normality' evolves. This may or may not resemble its predecessor but 'normality' should in any case not be conceived of as being static. In other words, southern Africa is currently undergoing a period of marked and often dramatic transitions at different scales, rates and of varying significance. In most cases, the signal events have – as far as one can tell – already occurred but the processes of accommodating and addressing their implications are at very different stages.

This book has sought to capture the mood and import of this exciting time by charting and analysing selected themes and processes which transcend individual localities, provinces and countries, thereby highlighting broader regional dynamics. In so doing, the objectives have been to offer the insights of a leading group of scholars and writers with first-hand experience in and of southern Africa; to fill a gap in the existing literature on transitions within the region, which focuses overwhelmingly on individual countries and localities, sectors or communities within them; and to make connections between current southern African processes and wider post-Cold War geopolitical and social transitions and the intellectual debates surrounding them.

Inevitably, despite a clear brief and an active editorial role, the extent to which each chapter addresses all these objectives varies. This reflects the nature of the individual subject areas as well as the predispositions of the respective contributors. There is no shared theoretical or analytical position, and (by design) certainly no attempt to convey a single, hegemonic perspective. This would be intellectually of questionable value, very difficult to achieve and arguably also un-postmodern. Moreover, for some of us, one or more parts of southern Africa are 'home', past and/or present, literal and/or imagined, with all that this entails, given the starkness of contrasts between wealth and poverty, social and political inclusion versus oppression, natural beauty and widespread human misery, serene peace and unspeakable violence, and our individual positionalities in respect of the resultant dilemmas. I, for one, had never desired to live anywhere else and never imagined in any sense that I would become a long-term resident of the UK, acquiring such multiple and overlapping identities – when it became necessary as well as academically attractive to leave Cape Town in late 1977 to study at Reading University. For others of us, southern Africa is an 'other' region, albeit one which has come to occupy a significant part of our lives, often invested with vivid and complex meanings well beyond mere professional interest.

Frankly, I feel the collection to be far better balanced on account of an element of diversity on all these counts, especially in view of the range of subjects and issues addressed. The latter is important in order to highlight the interrelationships between superficially distinct issues and arenas of contestation and action in the search for more equitable and sustainable regional futures. This thematic breadth also underpinned my decision to produce a carefully edited volume, so as to draw directly on expertise in the specific fields, rather than attempt to synthesise largely secondary material into a single-authored book. I hope that readers will share my pleasure in the result.

In this reflexive context, it is appropriate to problematise 'southern Africa' briefly. It will have become clear through the foregoing chapters that we do not attribute to the concept of southern Africa as a region any inherent organic meaning or qualities. There is, and can be, no unique definition of the region in the sense either of an uncontested boundary or a set of one or more meanings with which it might be invested and which would set it apart from others which lie immediately across that boundary or further afield. As pointed out in Chapter 1, the definition of southern Africa adopted is essentially instrumental, i.e. one of convenience and common usage. It is not meant to be watertight or immutable. The ten countries of Angola, Botswana, Lesotho, Malawi, Mozambique, Namibia, South Africa, Swaziland, Zambia and Zimbabwe are those most widely considered to make up the region, by virtue of contiguity, important elements of shared environment and history, and many common interests. However, other countries may be included for specific purposes or in certain institutional contexts. We could not meaningfully have discussed the Southern African Power Pool by excluding its two other members, Tanzania and especially the Democratic Republic of Congo with its extensive hydro-electric generating capacity and even greater potential. Similarly, Tanzania was a founder member of the Frontline states grouping and of the SADCC and SADC, while Mauritius became the twelfth member in August 1995, followed by the DRC and Seychelles in 1997.

Conversely, some continental and global institutions, such as the UN Economic Commission for Africa and the Commonwealth Development Corporation, include one or more of the ten countries listed above within their East or Central African regions for operational or data collection purposes. Occasionally, Angola has even been referred to as part of West Africa. The rationales for so doing are unclear but may have no lesser historical contingency, convenience or validity. Angola's ties to the north pre-date Portuguese colonial rule, encompass the slave trade experience and reflect long-standing indigenous political, economic and cultural relations which both were and still are at least as important as those in central and southern Angola which connect with parts of Namibia, Botswana, Zambia and southern regions of the Democratic Republic of Congo, for example. However, for political and historical reasons, the government has decided to identify primarily with southern Africa. Yet even after 20-odd years of publicity, propaganda and institutional involvement reflecting that decision, perceptions among Angolans as to their own primary orientations are likely to be diverse and dependent upon where within the country they live, their familial, ethnic and other loyalties, and – for many – their experiences of oppression, displacement and war. By now it is likely that virtually everyone within that country's boundaries is at least vaguely aware of living in a state called Angola, but far fewer will be conscious of any real or imagined construct of 'southern Africa'.

One response might be that we should redouble our efforts to build or strengthen such regional affiliations and the institutions which give concrete expression to them. In other words, some people will be concerned that southern Africa is a 'weak' region and that the links among its constituent countries and peoples remain tenuous. They might perceive that part of the reason for this situation is that there are diverse and conflicting interests and loyalties, drawing attention and involvement towards other countries, regions and organisations, and that the strengthening of southern Africa requires undivided loyalty. However, the prospects for achieving such a singular focus seem slim and any attempt to enforce it doomed to failure. After all, even within the region, several countries have maintained simultaneous membership of SACU and SADC(C), despite these bodies' diametrically contradictory rationales and objectives until at least 1992. This could be interpreted variously as official schizophrenia, as indecisiveness or as intelligent self-interest. Multiple, overlapping and even apparently conflicting individual as well as collective affiliations and loyalties are nothing new; indeed they characterised dilemmas and conflicts of tradition versus modernity, indigenous versus Western during the colonial and 'modern' periods, and contested claims to territory and sovereignty right up to the present. They were certainly not 'invented' by postmodernists and are not constitutive of postmodernity. What is now different, it is to be hoped, in the sense of the postmodern as a problematic, is that the ideological and practical necessity of making a categorical and irrevocable choice is giving way to a more open, tolerant context for their co-existence.

Individuals as well as governments now perceive it to be in their interests to join increasing numbers of organisations, to diversify their involvements and maximise their opportunities. Institutional and ideological monogamy are unfashionable, and efforts to promote them unrealistic. Perhaps paradoxically, the world today is increasingly competitive in economic terms, a trend accelerated by the agendas of privatisation, liberalisation and 'free' trade under the auspices of the WTO. Nevertheless, the pressures to comply – and the resultant vulnerability of individual poor national economies – have recently been providing one of the leading impulses towards trading bloc formation and other forms of transboundary co-operation and integration by countries within specific continental (sub)regions.

Regional Dynamics in Southern Africa

In southern Africa, the historically entrenched politico-military obstacles to such efforts have now been largely swept away, and this book has demonstrated some of the many ways in which political boundaries are being transcended in efforts to promote safer and more equitable and sustainable regional futures. Some of these centre on cleaning up the post-conflict aftermath, such as reducing the size of armed forces and reorienting them for rather more productive future tasks, and the imperative of combating the proliferation of small arms, as discussed by Susan Willett and Alex Vines respectively. Angola and South Africa have undertaken the largest real cutbacks, and military expenditure in both dollar terms and as a percentage of GDP has fallen almost everywhere. However, Botswana, Namibia and Zimbabwe, for different reasons, are currently moving against the trend. Retraining and reorientation of armed forces for different roles in peacekeeping, disaster relief and more active development operations are under way. Small arms have found their way in vast numbers from former conflict zones via ex-combatants and black market trade into everyday use in criminal activities, and the few programmes designed to encourage their surrender have proved disappointing. Urgent action is vital, especially in a situation where the incentive among unemployed and poor people to obtain with menaces what they cannot get through other channels remains strong.

Similarly, some colonial, historical and economic anachronisms have been rectified as part of the efforts to resolve conflicts and to promote further integration. This is well exemplified by my account of Namibia's peaceable reclaiming of the port and enclave of Walvis Bay, now able to be developed to its full potential as a national and perhaps even a modest subregional lifeline rather than serving as a potential noose by which South Africa could 'hang' Namibia. However, the evidence strongly suggested that Namibian aspirations to develop another major transport corridor serving the interior of the subcontinent from Gauteng to the Democratic Republic of Congo were unrealistic in a context where competition among existing harbours and bulk transport routes – many of which have far greater capacities than Walvis Bay could ever aspire to – is increasingly keen and some are already losing out.

Modern political boundaries have as much to do with keeping 'foreigners' (i.e. non-members of the state or other entity) out as with keeping members in. If the boundaries can be adequately policed, the terms of human movement and trade across them can then be regulated by the states concerned and their agents. Of course, no normal border can be hermetically sealed and, especially in the South, many borders or segments of them remain highly permeable. Where wide disparities of opportunity and income exist or are perceived to exist, as within southern Africa, people seek access to the better ones by whatever means they can. If formal, legal routes (both literal and figurative) are kept closed or are inaccessible in terms of affordability or qualifying criteria, many people try to circumvent them, even at the risk of fines, imprisonment or deportation. In relation to Batswana women, Kavita Datta's chapter showed the historical depth of imperatives to migrate, the gendered social constraints and pressures associated with changing indigenous institutions and values through the colonial and postcolonial periods, and the way in which the women concerned articulate internal and international migration according to circumstances and relative opportunities. This illustrated often stark choices between personal and material independence, on the one hand, and potential ostracisation or at least marginalisation through breaking social sanctions, on the other.

Sally Peberdy has shown that ethnically and religiously discriminatory immigration restrictions have a long pedigree in South Africa and that, notwithstanding the nature of political transition and the admission of larger numbers of Africans from various parts of the continent since the early 1990s, the relevant legislation – and the attitudes which lie behind it – have yet to change substantively. The South African case also illustrates clearly how definitions of legal and illegal migration are socially contingent, and can be manipulated or exploited in ways which bear little relation to the actual situation. Hence a new xenophobia is rising among black and white South Africans alike, fanned by wild estimates of the numbers of foreign migrants (especially illegal ones) coupled with some high-profile criminal activities involving foreigners. These issues have been linked by the media and some politicians in ways which suggest that most migrants – certainly black migrants – are illegal (which may be technically accurate for historically discriminatory reasons) and are also likely to be criminals and/or guilty of taking jobs away from un- and semi-skilled South Africans.

Greater mobility, social dislocation and hardship of the sort associated with war, displacement, large-scale migration, drought/famine and structural adjustment provide a ready context for the rapid spread of invisible pandemics such as HIV/AIDS, for which there is still no effective cure. Douglas Webb has charted the magnitude of the problem, which has crossed national frontiers and social categories without impediment, especially along migration and major transport routes. Efforts to raise consciousness and to translate that into behavioural change lie at the heart of national AIDS control programmes. Issues of appropriateness and coverage were not adequately thought through initially, and seropositivity rates are continuing to rise alarmingly in most of the region, but recent evidence is beginning to show at least a glimmer of hope in specific localities. While locally appropriate campaigns and support systems are vital, international epidemics and other such phenomena cannot be tackled by any single government or agency. Co-operation is vital.

This is perhaps more readily demonstrated in relation to environmental conservation and physical infrastructure. Transboundary superparks are now widely believed to hold the key to effective but sustainable utilisation of wildlife and other environmental resources which are increasingly threatened outside formal conservation areas but which require larger ecosystems and biomes for long-term viability than can be enclosed within any single reserve. Eddie Koch has provided a detailed and at times critical account of the evolving proposals, the interests behind them, and the obstacles to be overcome. Much of his analysis focused on the border zone linking Zimbabwe, Mozambique and South Africa. Overall, his prognosis is optimistic under the right conditions, although the likely impact of James Blanchard's surreal and possibly postmodern themepark may change the equation.

Similarly, the notion of an integrated electricity grid covering much of southern and central Africa has existed for a considerable time but was unviable until the resolution of the conflicts and great apartheid divide which plagued the subcontinent. Since parastatal corporations rather than political leaders are responsible for this sector, progress has been swift and relatively unproblematic, far outstripping the formal political agreements and regional institutional evolution within organisations like SACU and SADC. Tore Horvei's chapter shows how important this 'lead' sector has become and how it is beginning to make a real difference in facilitating industrial restructuring and recovery, promoting the electrification of low-income households in different countries, and moving towards more integrated energy/power strategies designed to optimise regional resources and complementarities. Of course, such processes are highly modern(ist) and in line with the development aspirations of many poor people and governments. Importantly, however, the deregulation and far greater flexibility which new arrangements are ushering in, enable such basic needs to be met via a wider range of processes. Official hegemony is therefore much reduced.

The private sector has also moved rapidly to exploit new post-apartheid opportunities and to position itself to compete effectively in an increasingly aggressive international marketplace. Alan Terry and Steve Atkins demonstrated this clearly in relation to the sugar industry, where privatisation, commercialisation, restructuring and a marked shift in the organisation of production from large commercial plantations in South Africa to the use of outgrowers in KwaZulu-Natal and other countries in the region have all been occurring simultaneously. The industry is in many respects unrecognisable from that of a decade or so ago.

Industrial restructuring and the impact of liberalised international trade have also had their downsides, in southern Africa as elsewhere. Colin Stoneman has indicated how Zimbabwe and South Africa have been brought into conflict over renewal of their long-standing bilateral preferential trade agreement by changes in the textile market in particular. The great imbalance in population and economic muscle between the two countries actually meant that South Africa could have made more concessions without undermining its own domestic manufacturing base, although Far Eastern competition was also a major factor. More generally, he argued that Zimbabwe initially pursued some remarkably successful policies after independence but that some of the gains have been undermined by ill-advised policies and especially the Economic Structural Adjustment Programme (ESAP), exacerbated by the severe recent drought. The country might have learnt rather more from relevant experiences of previously decolonised countries, especially in relation to land policy and practice, and South Africa in turn has much to learn from Zimbabwe.

Such dualities, of individual self-interest versus collective benefit, of the burden of history and accumulated wisdom among serving civil servants versus the imperatives of a new era and the priorities of new senior officials with experience in exile or underground, underlie efforts to reformulate South Africa's post-apartheid foreign policy. As Greg Mills has shown, there are strong elements of continuity in personnel and policy, compounded by a minister whose public image is among the lowest in the cabinet. An elaborate parliamentary process to formulate a new foreign policy seems so far to have had little impact on day-to-day activities. Trading on the Mandela factor, the principal objective has been to make and try to keep friends everywhere, although experience in relation to Nigeria and Taiwan/China has shown this not to be possible. It is perhaps in relation to sub-Saharan Africa that the rethinking is most urgent and the priorities most in need of change. President Mandela's efforts in May 1997 to broker a settlement of the Zairean crisis in a manner rather more sustained and subtle than his engagement with presidents Masire and Mugabe over Lesotho in 1995, suggest that this may now be occurring.

If bilateral relations are complex and slow to evolve, it is little wonder that it is taking far longer than initially hoped to change the course and complexion of regional institutions for economic and political co-operation. Summits and declarations are essential but inadequate in themselves to maintain momentum. Experience to date with SACU, SADC and COMESA shows how individual institutional interests and rivalries can be resistant to change if and when this threatens their own positions and prestige. Everyone agrees that a streamlining and rationalisation is essential, now that their memberships, as well as their stated goals and objectives, are increasingly overlapping. Yet, as James Sidaway and Richard Gibb have demonstrated, each institution is engaged principally in 'internal' restructuring negotiations with little regard to parallel developments in the others. By April/May 1997, the first signs were beginning to emerge of individual southern African countries opting out of COMESA in favour of SADC. If this process gathers pace, it may resolve some of the issues via the back door, but this seems a poor alternative to a merger or formal division of labour among the respective institutions.

Concluding Thoughts

Against the background of such complex and on-going processes of transition and reorientation, it seems churlish to attempt to formulate any firm or definitive conclusion. The one fundamental difference is that South Africa is now unequivocally at the heart of the region in every sense. The previous schizophrenia, of an economic giant subject to international sanctions and isolation while still trading and investing in neighbouring states and hosting large numbers of migrant workers, has given way to more 'normal' circumstances. As we have demonstrated, this has already helped to resolve some major problems and legacies and to open all manner of new challenges and opportunities for bilateral and multilateral co-operation within the region. However, it has certainly not heralded in South Africa, more than perhaps very fleetingly, an organic sense of belonging and openness to the region, or a desire to bend over backwards to proffer reparations for destabilisation, as some had hoped. Migration policy is a case in point. Certainly, there have been some signal gestures, such as Mandela's commitment not to demand that Namibia repay the accumulated public debt from its pre-independence period, although this has yet to be formally written off.

South Africa is taking time to formulate and activate detailed external policies, not least because of the rapid pace of international change as well as change within the country. The other countries in southern Africa all have high expectations of improved relations with, and especially of investment, technical assistance and other forms of aid from, South Africa. Many of these are also exaggerated, given the extent of internal reconstruction and development required after apartheid. However, we have shown that there are many spheres in which important transborder initiatives are moving forward, both under the auspices of official governmental bodies and beyond their immediate control. Perhaps the dominant characteristic of this still young post-apartheid era is that there is now likely to be a greater overlap between the self-interest of individual states and collective benefit in many respects. The same is true in the NGO and private sectors, and in civil society more generally. Equally, however, the wide disparities on almost every variable which have come to undergird the inherited political economy and social economy of southern Africa, cannot and will not be wished away in the short term.

Moreover, it is entirely possible that some disparities, and certainly the degree of economic polarisation within and between countries, will actually increase rather than decrease. Several reasons for this can be distinguished. Barriers to trade will gradually be reduced and borders become less 'sticky' for commodity and financial flows, if not for people. This will tend to favour production in a smaller number of locations (particularly those attractive to managers), and geared increasingly to regional rather than national markets. Reinforcing this tendency will be the increasingly competitive struggle to attract foreign direct investment from South Africa into the region and from abroad into South Africa as well as the rest of the region. In this respect, there is at least some indication in the most recent financial reports that foreign investors are beginning to perceive southern Africa in a more favourable light as rates of return and the general economic environment have improved. These trends also suggest that the region may have more to gain through collective action in the form of a coherent trading bloc than through individual rivalries. The existing regional institutions will need to be marshalled into structures with mechanisms more appropriate to these changing circumstances, global as well as intra-regional, and able to utilise both official institutions and resources as well as those of the NGO and private sectors.

South Africa is taking its regional position and role increasingly seriously, and as President Nelson Mandela made explicit in his opening address to the fourth session of Parliament on 7 February 1997, this is bound up with aspects of South Africa's self-rediscovery:

> Our young democracy is still grappling with the challenge of its positioning in the international milieu.

> It is understandable that at times this debate will be heated and acrimonious; because it is a debate more than just about how we relate to the world. It is part of the process of defining who we are. It is part of the resolution of past divisions within South African society – divisions which informed our divergent views of the world.

> Within the Southern African Development Community, the first steps have been taken towards a free trade area within 8 years. Historic initiatives exemplified by the Maputo Development Corridor are gradually going to become the norm, as we bring our collective strength to bear to meet common challenges. It is a measure of our collective destiny that even bilateral negotiations between ourselves and the European Community had to be underpinned by regional realities.

Whatever the eventual outcome, there can be little doubt that southern Africa as a region will be invested with new meanings – multiple, flexible and contingent – by its people and governments. Such reconfigurations will ensure that the region remains far more than a mere geographical expression, however it may be bounded for specific purposes. To coin a phrase, it will become *terra recognita*; the salient questions relate to how that re-cognition occurs and what forms it takes.

About the Contributors

Stephen Atkins has been employed as Senior Planning Officer at the European Union Delegation in Swaziland since November 1996. He studied Agricultural Economics at University College of Wales, Aberystwyth and has a wide range of field experience in 25 countries, mainly within sub-Saharan Africa and the West Indies. From 1986 to 1996, he worked for the Commonwealth Development Corporation as an agricultural economist, financial analyst, and manager of Mananga Consultancy Services, Swaziland. Stephen has written numerous studies and reports on a variety of development issues. Recent interests include setting up a Monitoring and Evaluation System for the Small Growers Development Trust, South Africa, with similar work having been completed in Swaziland and Mozambique. In recent years he has also carried out similar assignments in Tanzania and Namibia. He is currently in charge of EU rural policy within Swaziland, with particular responsibility for agricultural development.

Kavita Datta hails from Botswana, where she gained her first degree. She also holds a PhD in Geography from Cambridge and is Lecturer in Geography, University of Wales, Swansea. Her research interests focus particularly on urban and gender issues in Botswana and South Africa, where she has worked on the functioning of urban property markets; the organisation and performance of rental and sharing markets and relations between landlords and tenants; gender-specific migration patterns; rural-urban interactions and the imagination of home. Most recently, she has investigated housing finance and gender issues; the role of NGOs in mediating between formal finance institutions and households; and household saving regimes. Kavita is co-editor of *Housing, Finance and Gender in Developing Countries* (with G.A. Jones, Routledge, London, 1997), and has published papers in *Habitat International, Cities*, and *International Journal of Population Studies*.

Richard Gibb is Reader in Human Geography at the University of Plymouth, UK. His research interests focus on regional integration, with a particular emphasis on the European Union and southern Africa. His current research includes work on the establishment of a South Africa-European Union free trade area. He is the author and co-editor of numerous publications in these fields, including (as co-editor) *Continental Trading Blocs: the Growth of Regionalism in the World Economy* (Wiley, Chichester, 1994).

Tore Horvei is an energy economist with an MBA from the Norwegian School of Economics and Business Administration. He is a Norwegian citizen and has more than 12 years of professional experience in the management of development organisations, consulting and applied research, the last 8 years mainly in southern Africa. Since 1995 he has been the Chief Executive of SAD-ELEC (Southern African Development through Electricity), an independent non-profit regional development organisation, working specifically with the southern African electricity sector.

Eddie Koch is Environmental Editor at the *Mail and Guardian* newspaper in South Africa. He has co-edited two books on politics and the environment, *Going Green:*

People, Politics and the Environment in South Africa (Oxford University Press, 1994, with Jacky Cock) and *Water, Waste and Wildlife: the Politics of Ecology in South Africa* (Penguin, 1992, with David Cooper and Henk Coetsee). He has completed studies for the United Nations Research Institute for Social Development on ecotourism and transfrontier parks in southern Africa.

Greg Mills was born in Cape Town and holds an Honours degree in African Studies from the University of Cape Town, and an MA and PhD in International Relations from Lancaster University in the UK. Since July 1996 he has been National Director of the South African Institute of International Affairs (SAIIA) at Jan Smuts House in Johannesburg, where he had been Director of Studies since January 1994. Before this, he taught at the Universities of the Western Cape (1990-94) and Cape Town (1991-93). He specialises in security-related and regional foreign policy analysis, and has published widely. His eight books with SAIIA are entitled: *From Pariah to Participant: South Africa's Evolving Relations 1990-1994; South Africa in the Global Economy, Maritime Policy for Developing Nations; Peacekeeping in Africa; South Africa and the Two Chinas Dilemma; Unchartered Waters: A Review of South Africa's Naval Options;* the first ever *South African Yearbook of International Affairs;* and most recently *From Isolation to Integration? The South African Economy in the 1990s.*

Sally Ann Peberdy is a mature student, currently writing up her PhD thesis for Queen's University, Canada, while working as a research fellow for the Southern African Migration Project, based in Johannesburg. Her thesis is entitled 'Tainting the Blood, Tainting the Nation: Immigration, Race and Disease in South Africa'. She has held several prestigious awards and completed her Master's thesis on HIV/AIDS and Aboriginal Communities in Canada at Carleton University. She has recently prepared several papers for the South African Green Paper Task Group on International Migration.

James D. Sidaway is a Lecturer at the School of Geography at the University of Birmingham, UK. His main research interests focus on geopolitics, particularly of the South, post-colonial theory and the sociology of knowledge. He is currently working on integration in southern Africa in comparative terms, funded by a Research Fellowship from the Economic & Social Research Council. He has published widely on Mozambique's post-socialist transition and on aspects of geopolitics in journals including the *International Journal of Urban and Regional Research, Journal of Southern African Studies, Environment and Planning A, Society and Space* and *Geojournal.*

David Simon is Reader in Development Geography and Director of the Centre for Developing Areas Research (CEDAR) at Royal Holloway, University of London. He holds degrees from the Universities of Cape Town, Reading and Oxford, and has published widely on development theory and development issues relating particularly to Africa, and especially southern Africa. He is also a leading specialist on Namibia. His most recent books are: *Cities, Capital and Development: African Cities in the World Economy* (London: Belhaven, 1992); (as first editor) *Structurally Adjusted Africa: Poverty, Debt and Basic Needs* (London: Pluto, 1995); and *Transport and Development in the Third World* (London and New York: Routledge, 1996).

Colin Stoneman is a development economist. He taught for many years in the Centre for Southern African Studies at the University of York, where he is still based.

He now teaches mainly in the Universities of Leeds and Bradford. He has written the quarterly reports and annual profiles on Zimbabwe for the Economist Intelligence Unit for the last eleven years, visiting southern Africa about twice a year on average, often for the Commonwealth Secretariat. He is on the editorial board of the *Journal of Southern African Studies* and was editor from 1988 to 1994.

Alan Terry has been Senior Lecturer in Geography at the University of the West of England, Bristol since 1994. Previously he was Senior Lecturer in Geography, Gwent College of Higher Education, and gained his PhD from University College of Wales, Aberystwyth in 1993. His recent research has concentrated on the economic and social impact of the sugar industry in Swaziland and South Africa. Particular interests include the expansion of small grower sugar cane in both countries and the problems associated with water management within the sugar producing areas, especially the development of the Maguga Dam on the Komati River. Alan has been employed by Mananga Management Centre, Swaziland as a visiting lecturer on Project and Environmental Management courses.

Alex Vines is a MacArthur NGO Fellow at the Department of War Studies, King's College London. He is also on the staff of Human Rights Watch Africa, specialising in political and associated military issues in southern Africa. His most recent books are: *Renamo: from Terrorism to Democracy in Mozambique* (James Currey, London,1996, second edition); and *Still Killing: Landmines in Southern Africa* (Human Rights Watch, New York, 1997).

Douglas Webb received his PhD from the Department of Geography, Royal Holloway, University of London in 1995. His thesis explored the social epidemiology of HIV in southern Africa. Since then he has been working in Lusaka, Zambia with UNICEF and UNAIDS on a wide range of programmes covering aspects of HIV prevention and AIDS impact mitigation. Research work includes the impact of AIDS on children and programme development in relation to education initiatives and UNAIDS support to the Zambian National AIDS Programme. He has published widely and his book *HIV and AIDS in Africa* was published in August 1997 by Pluto Press, London.

Susan Willett is Senior Research Project Fellow at the Copenhagen Peace Research Institute (COPRI), working on a project addressing military restructuring. Until autumn 1997, she was Senior Research Fellow and Director of the Comparative International Security Programme, King's College London. As a defence economist, her areas of specialisation include defence expenditure trends and defence industrial and arms trade issues. She has worked on southern African security for a number of years and has published widely on the subject in journals including the *Review of African Political Economy* and *International Peacekeeping*. In January 1997, she completed a report for the OECD on *Military Spending Trends and Development Cooperation in Southern Africa: South Africa, Angola, Zimbabwe and Mozambique*, and has just completed a book with Peter Batchelor entitled *Disarmament and Defence Industrial Adjustment in South Africa*, to be published by the Stockholm International Peace Research Institute (SIPRI).

Index